1

SAYONARA, FOOTBALL

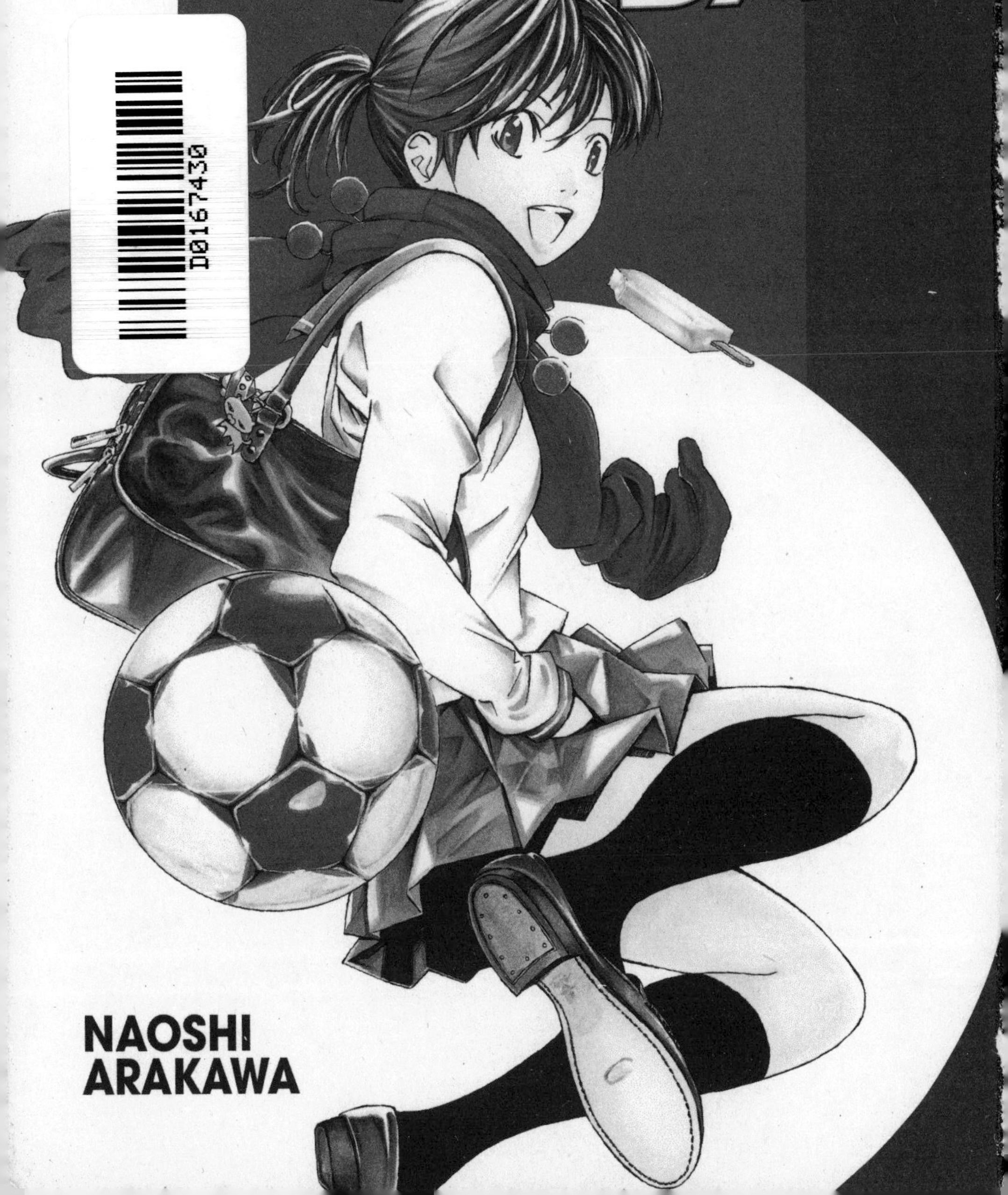

NAOSHI
ARAKAWA

1

SAYONARA. FOOTBALL

CONTENTS

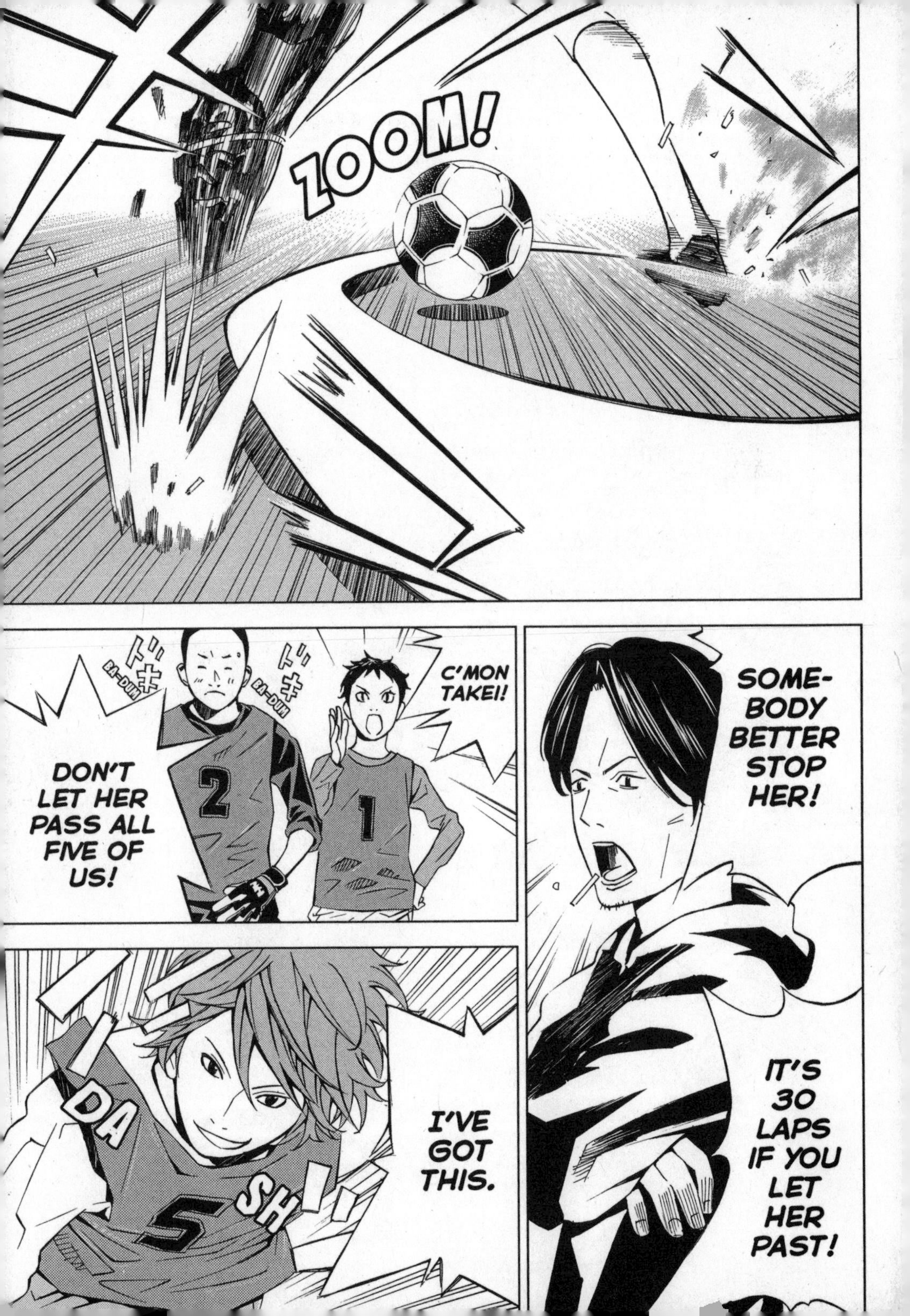
ZOOM!
SOME-BODY BETTER STOP HER!
IT'S 30 LAPS IF YOU LET HER PAST!
C'MON TAKEI!
ドキ BA-DUM
ドキ BA-DUM
DON'T LET HER PASS ALL FIVE OF US!
I'VE GOT THIS.
DASH

Chapter 1
Enter the Wild One

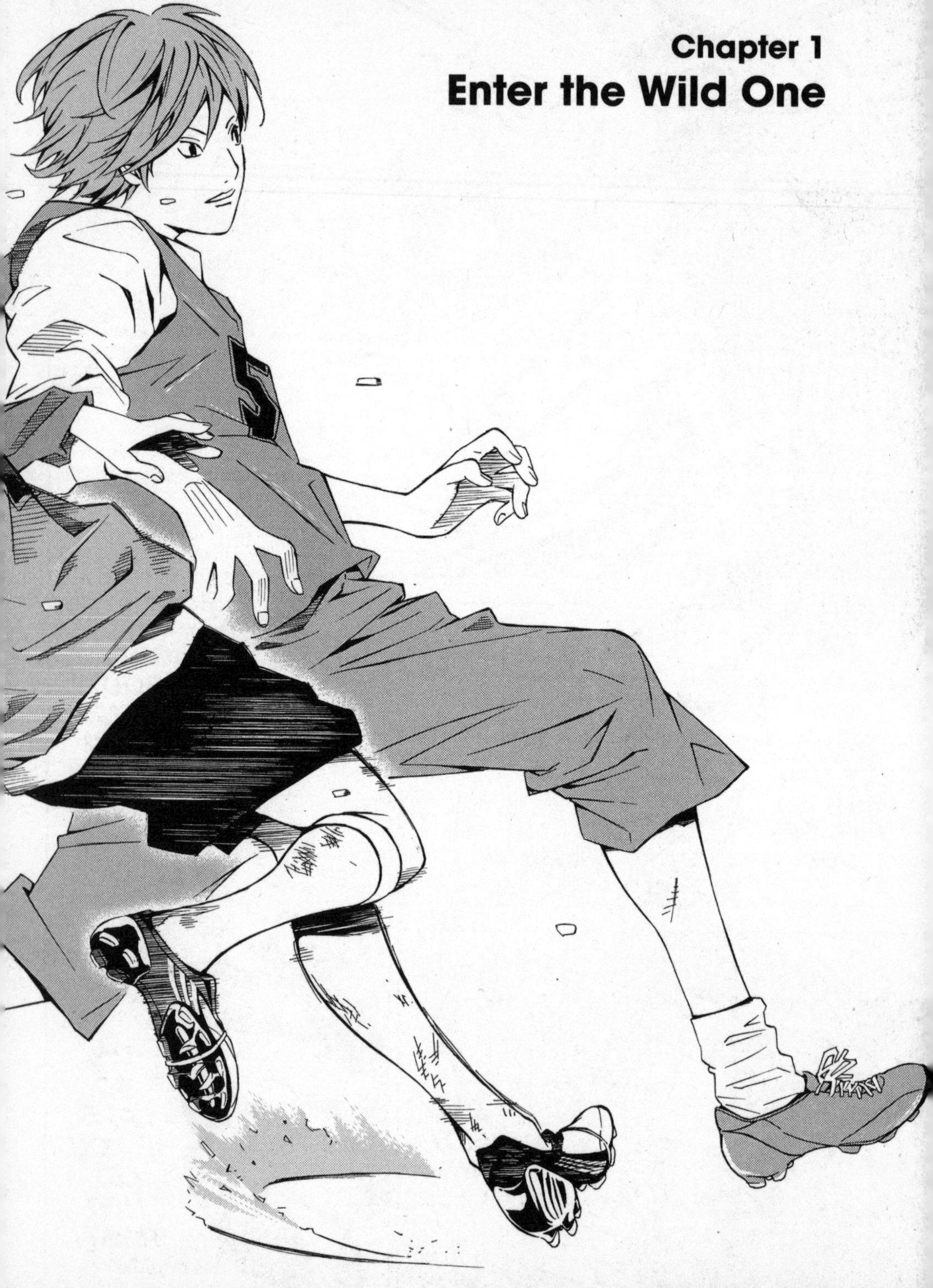

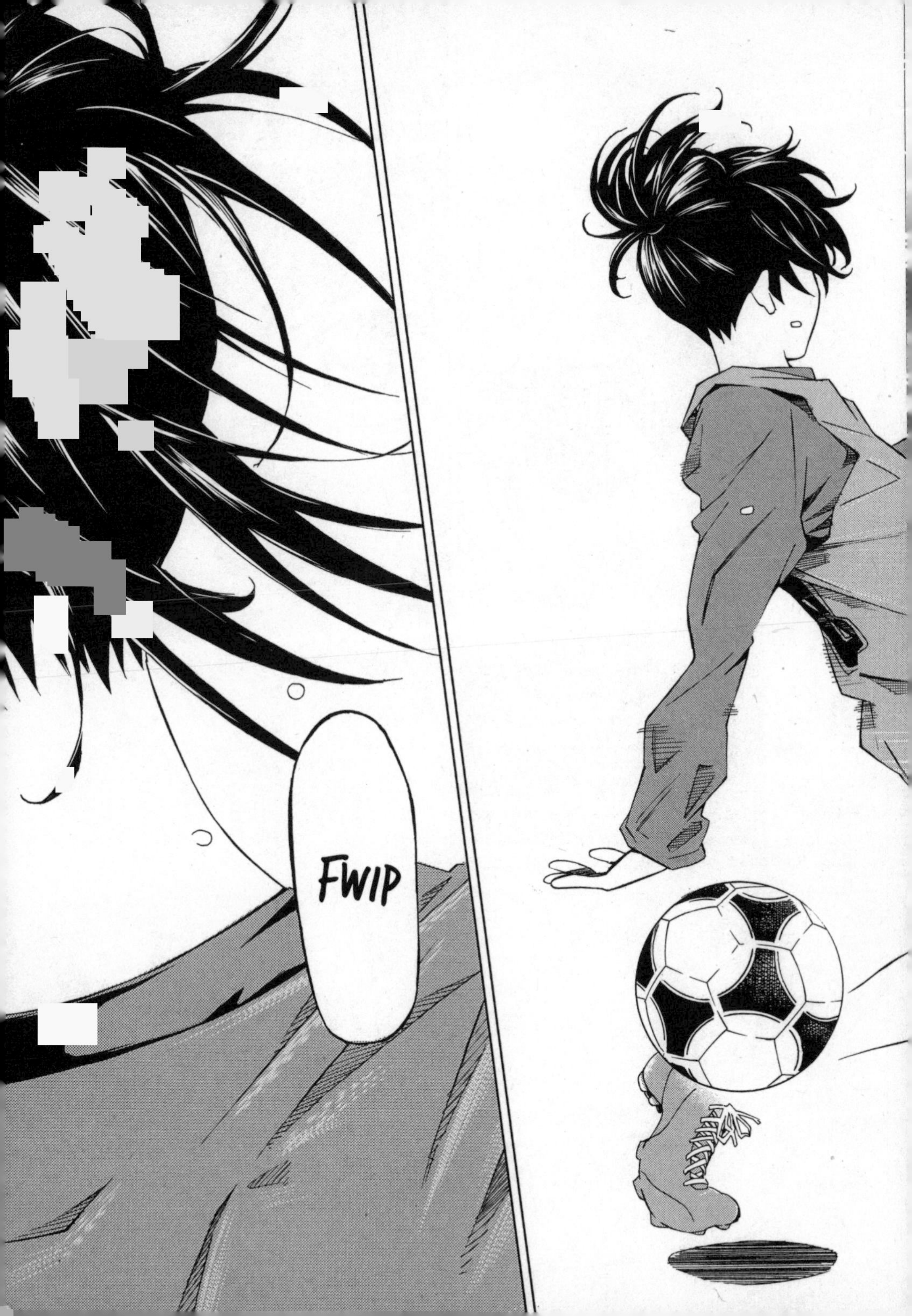
FWIP

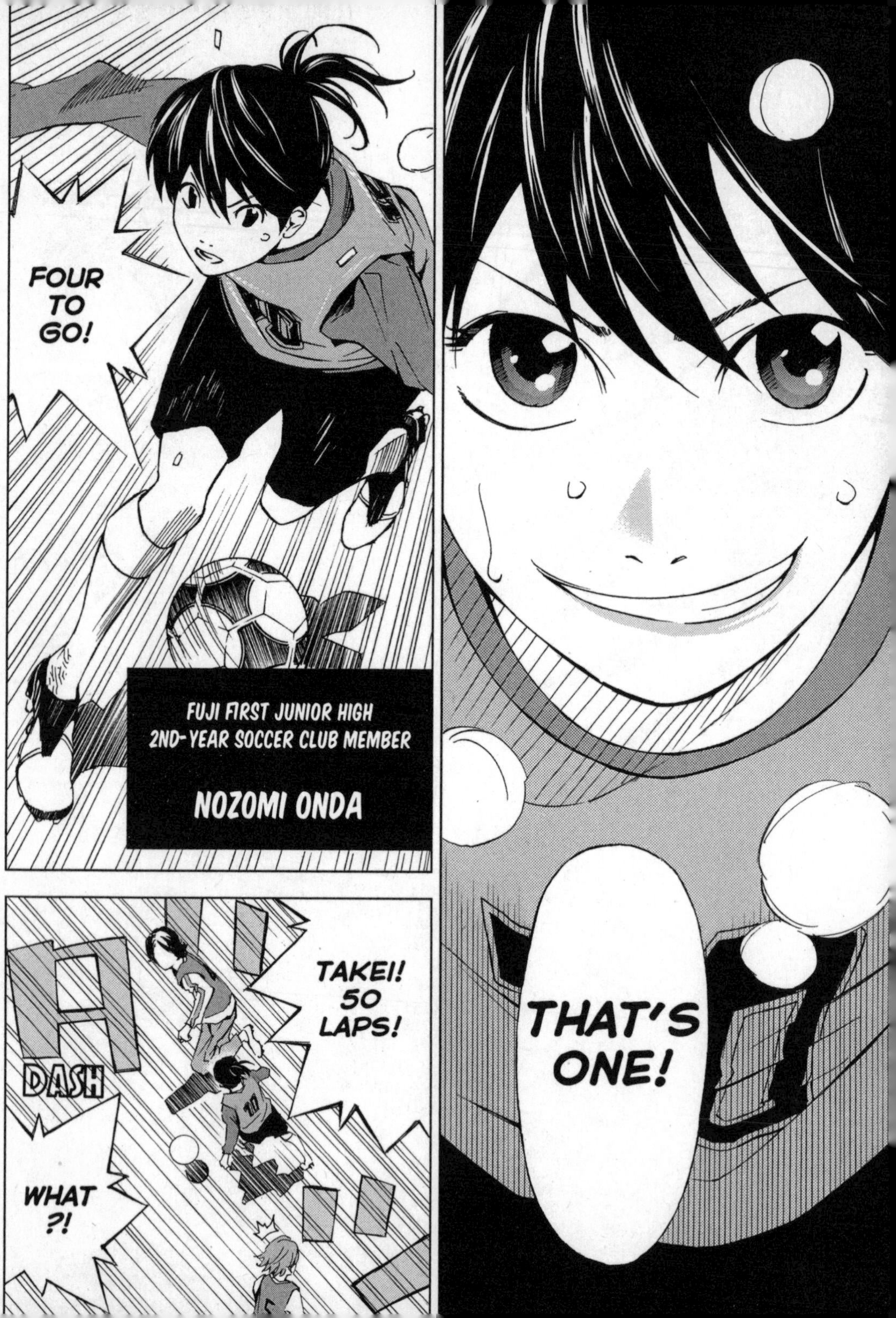
THAT'S ONE!
FOUR TO GO!
FUJI FIRST JUNIOR HIGH
2ND-YEAR SOCCER CLUB MEMBER
NOZOMI ONDA
TAKEI! 50 LAPS!
DASH
WHAT ?!

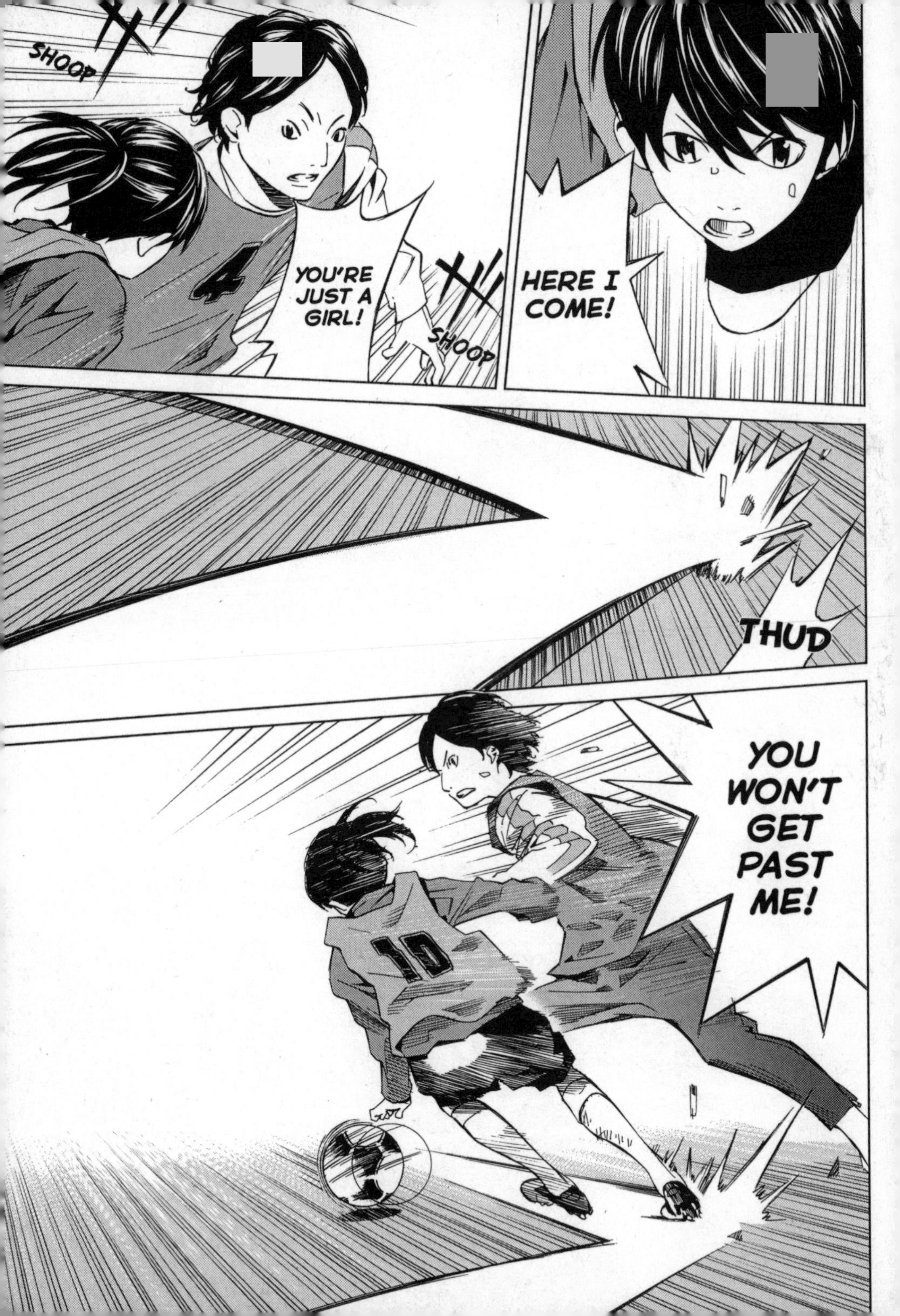
HERE I COME!
SHOOP
YOU'RE JUST A GIRL!
SHOOP
THUD
YOU WON'T GET PAST ME!

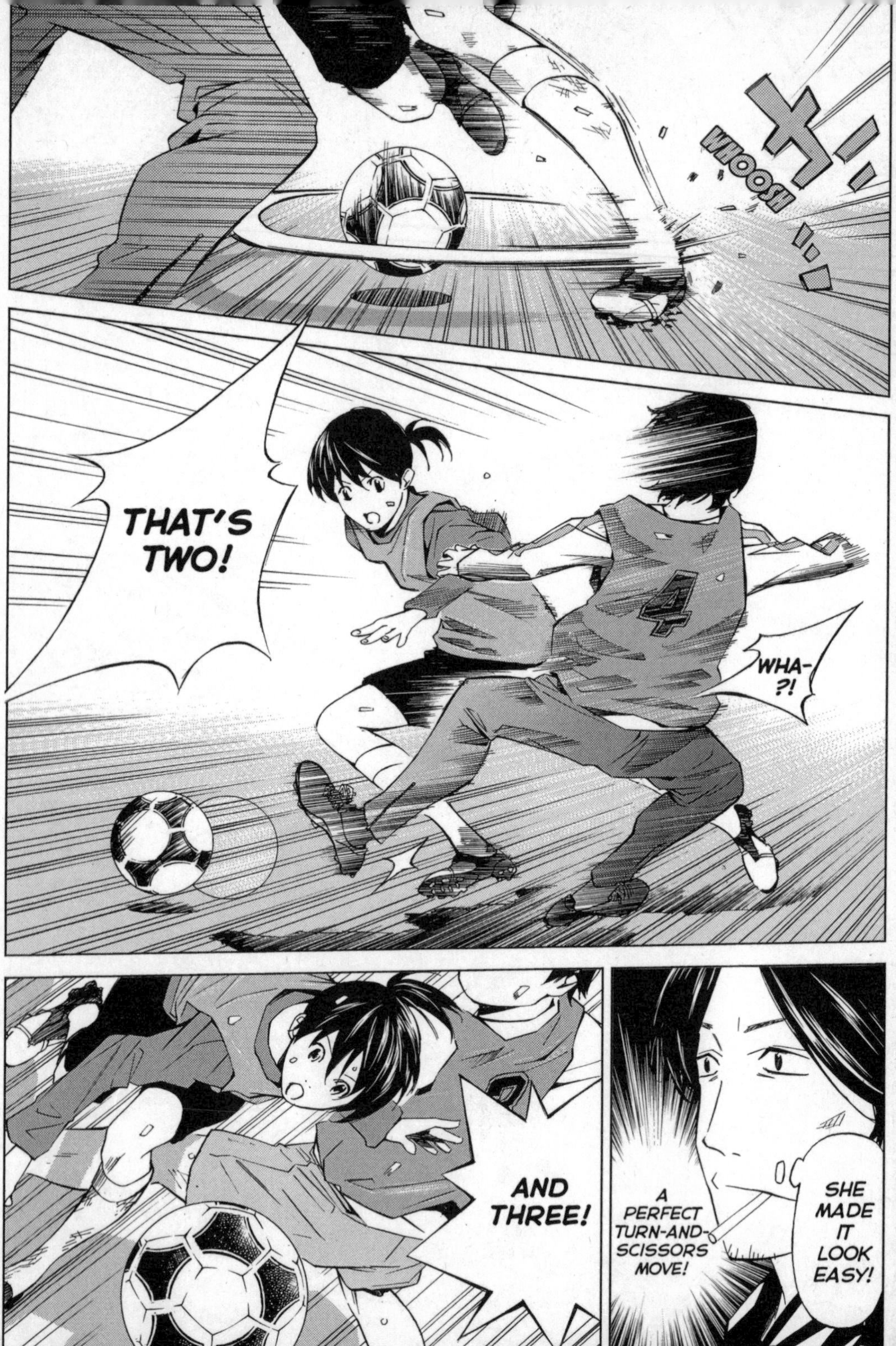
WHOOSH
WHA-?!
THAT'S TWO!
SHE MADE IT LOOK EASY!
A PERFECT TURN-AND-SCISSORS MOVE!
AND THREE!

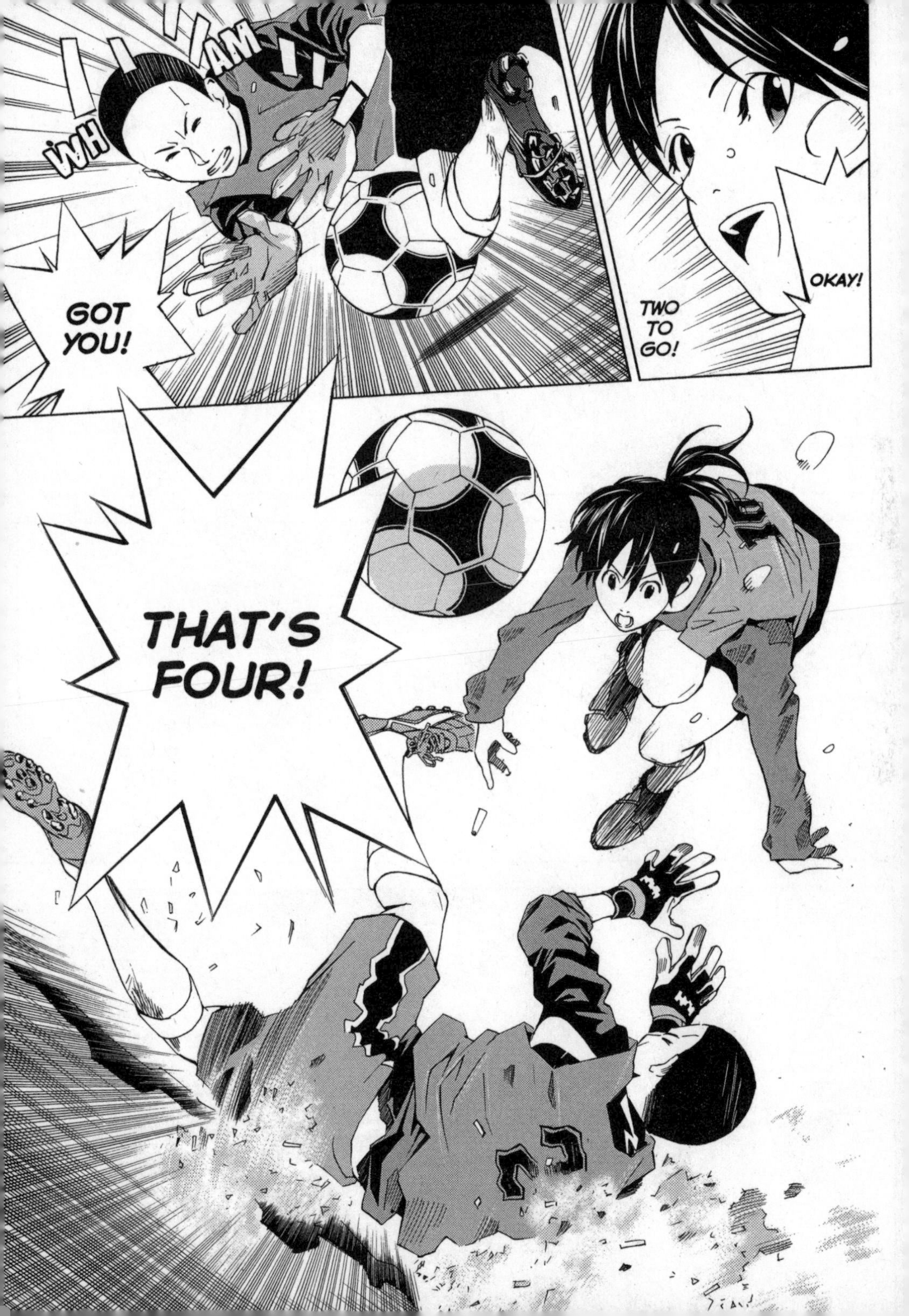
OKAY!
TWO TO GO!
WHAM!!
GOT YOU!
THAT'S FOUR!

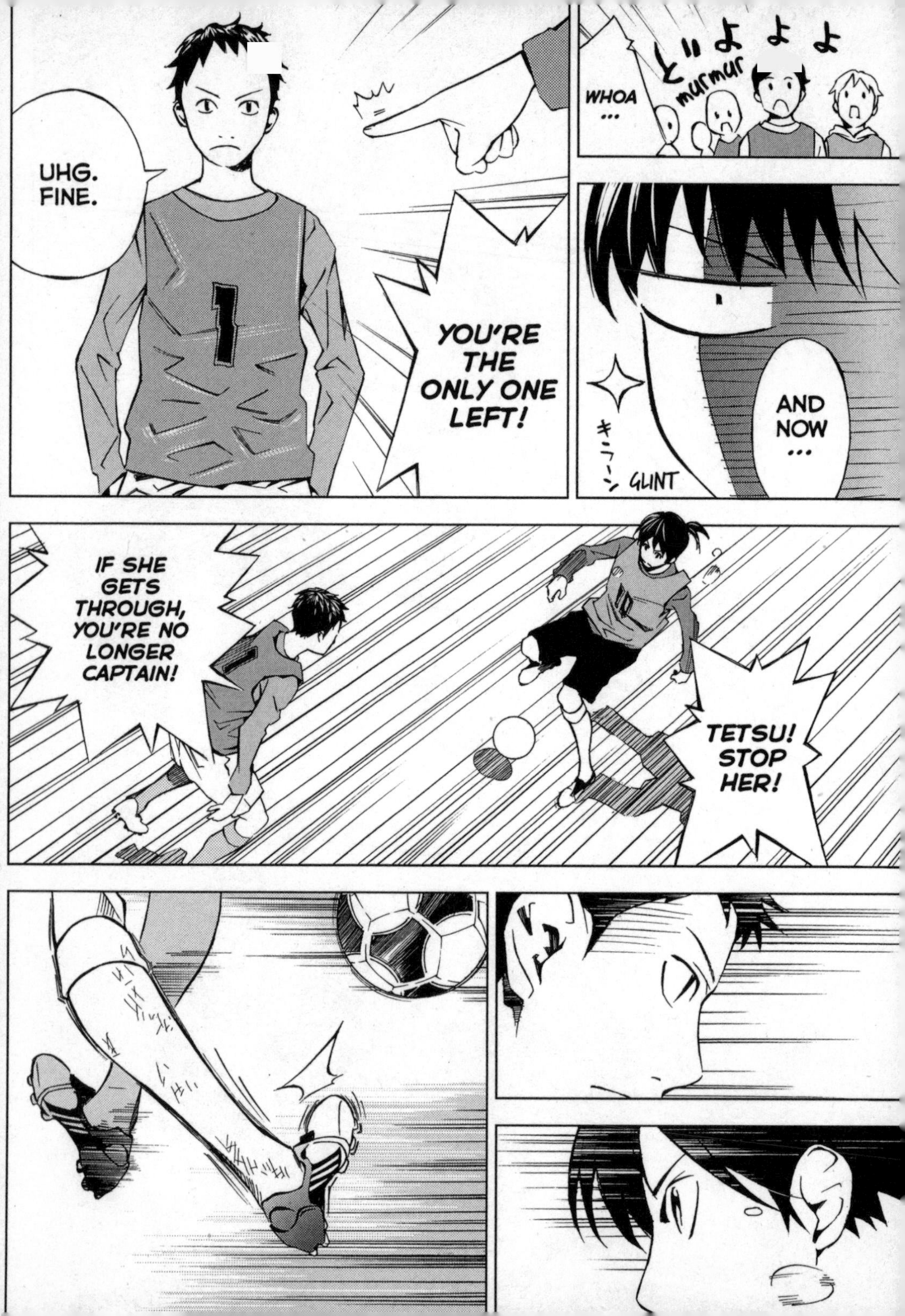
WHOA ...
murmur
AND NOW ...
キラーン
GLINT
YOU'RE THE ONLY ONE LEFT!
UHG. FINE.
TETSU! STOP HER!
IF SHE GETS THROUGH, YOU'RE NO LONGER CAPTAIN!

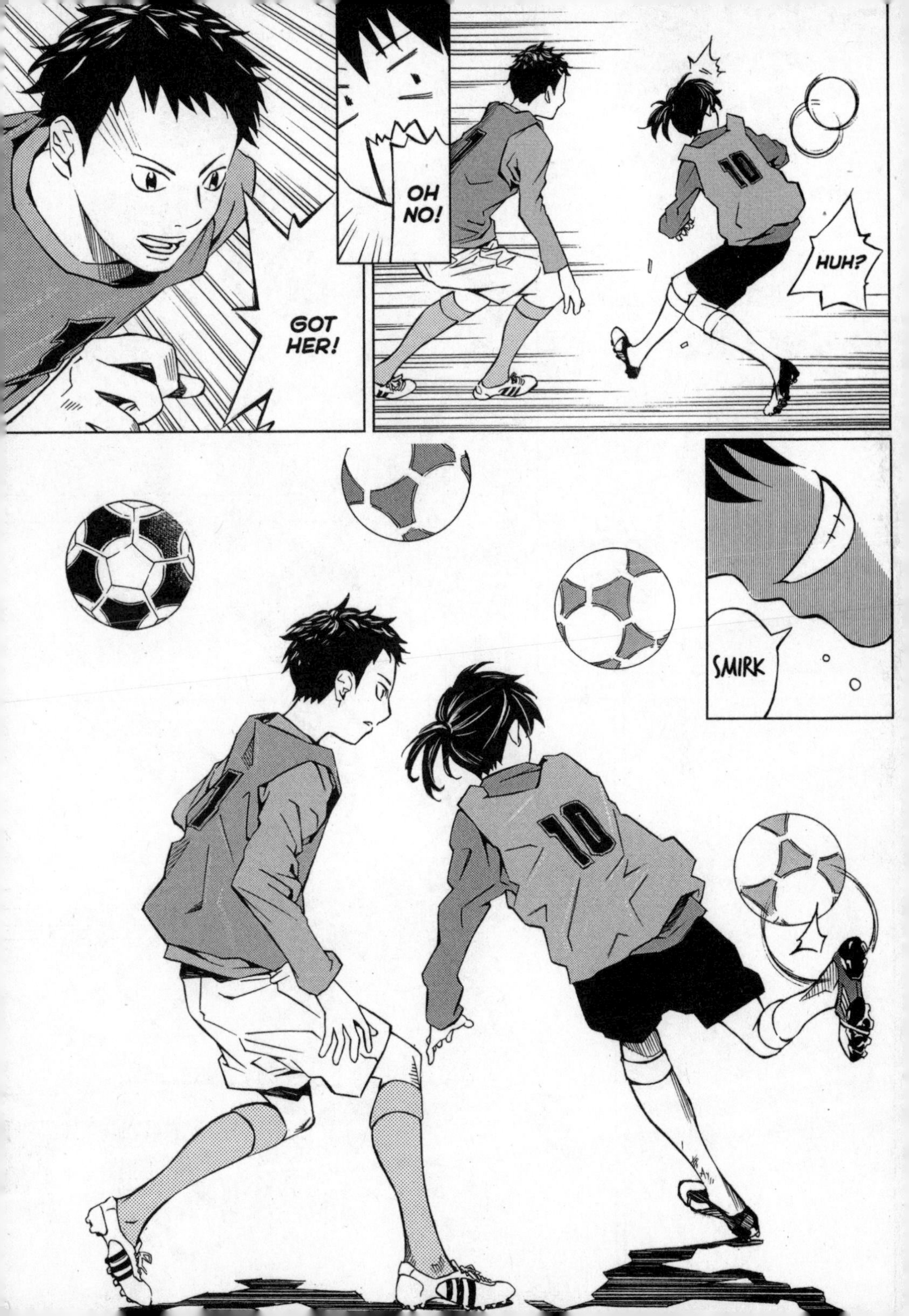
HUH?
OH NO!
GOT HER!
SMIRK

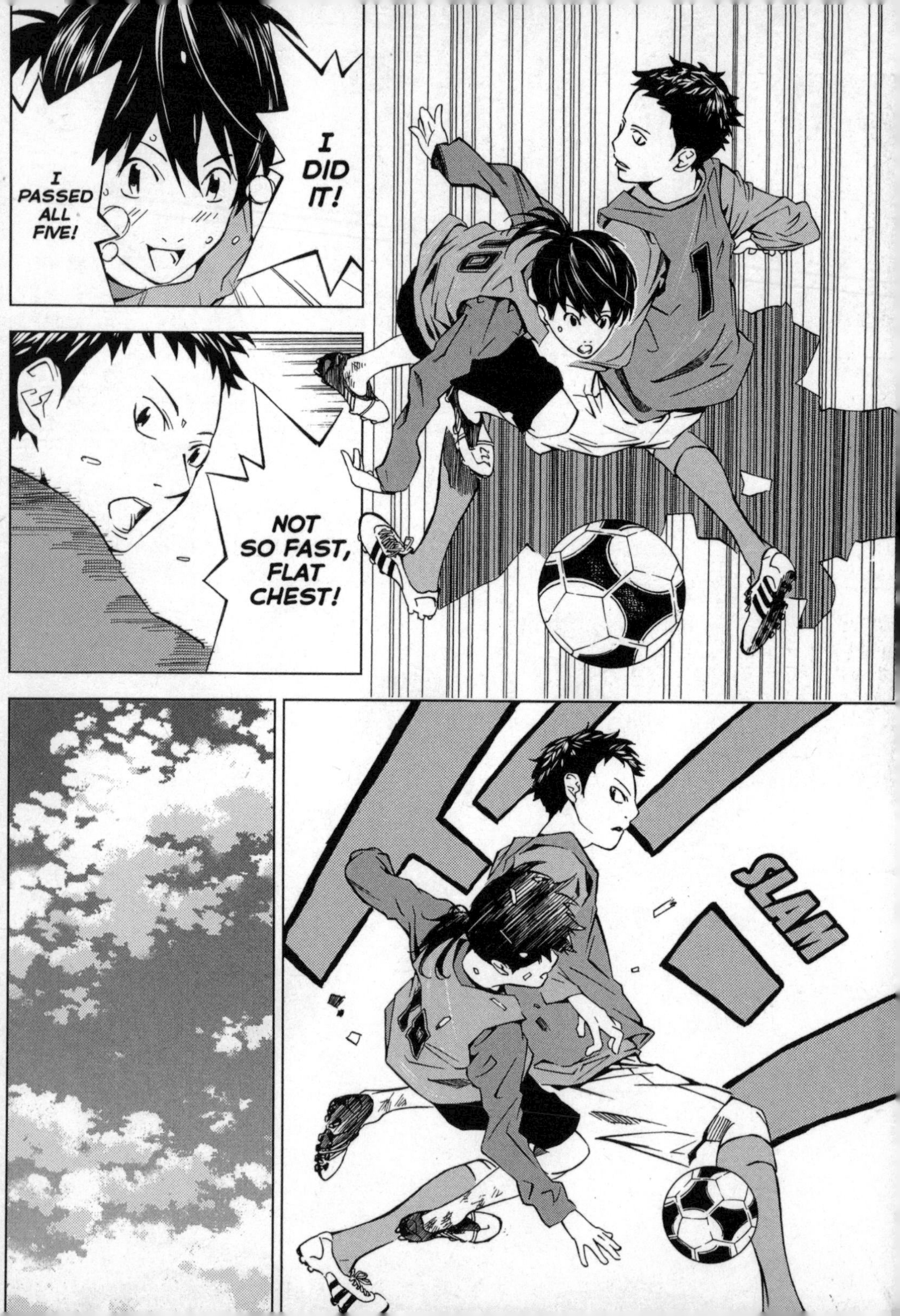
I DID IT!
I PASSED ALL FIVE!
NOT SO FAST, FLAT CHEST!
SLAM

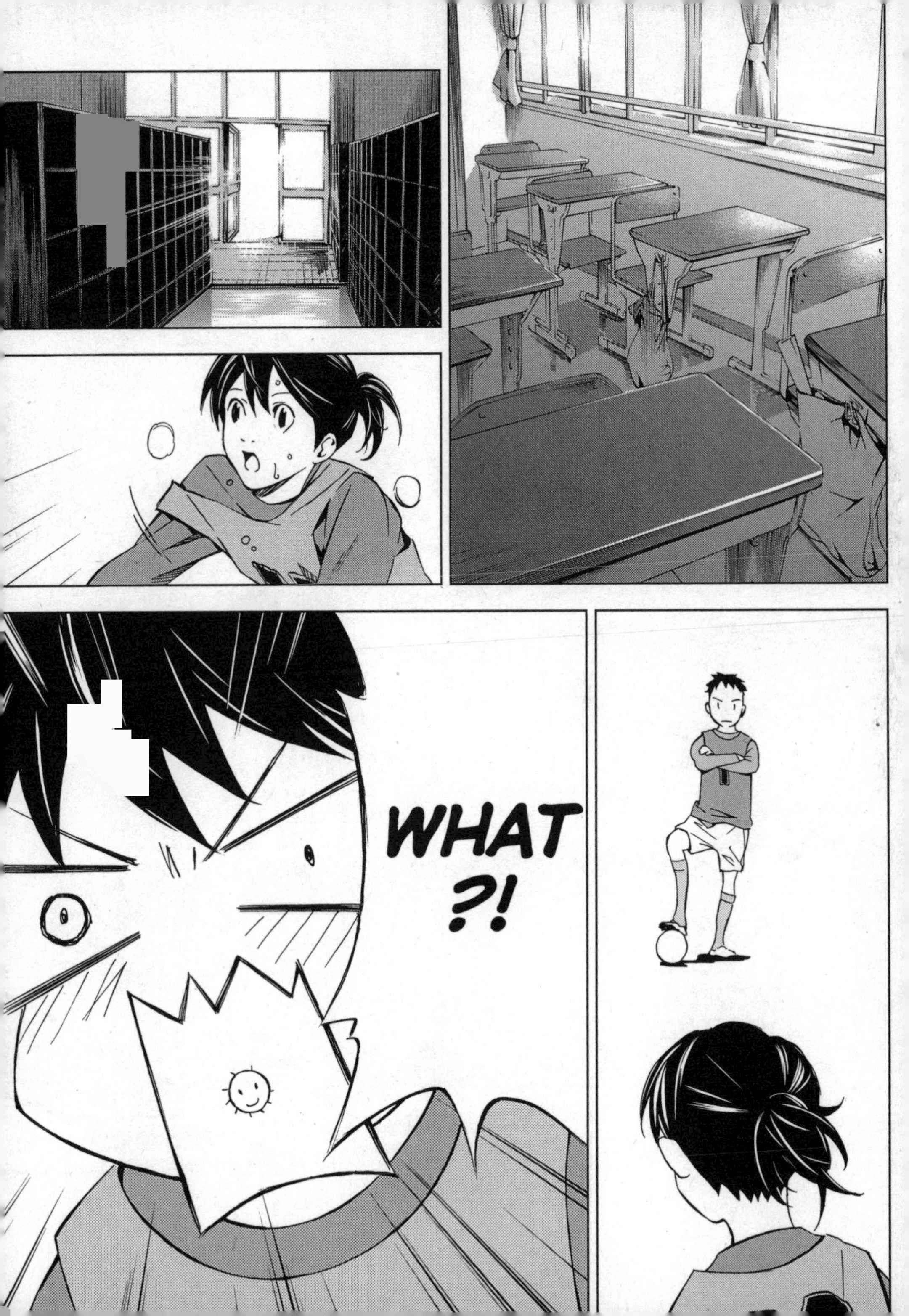
WHAT ?!

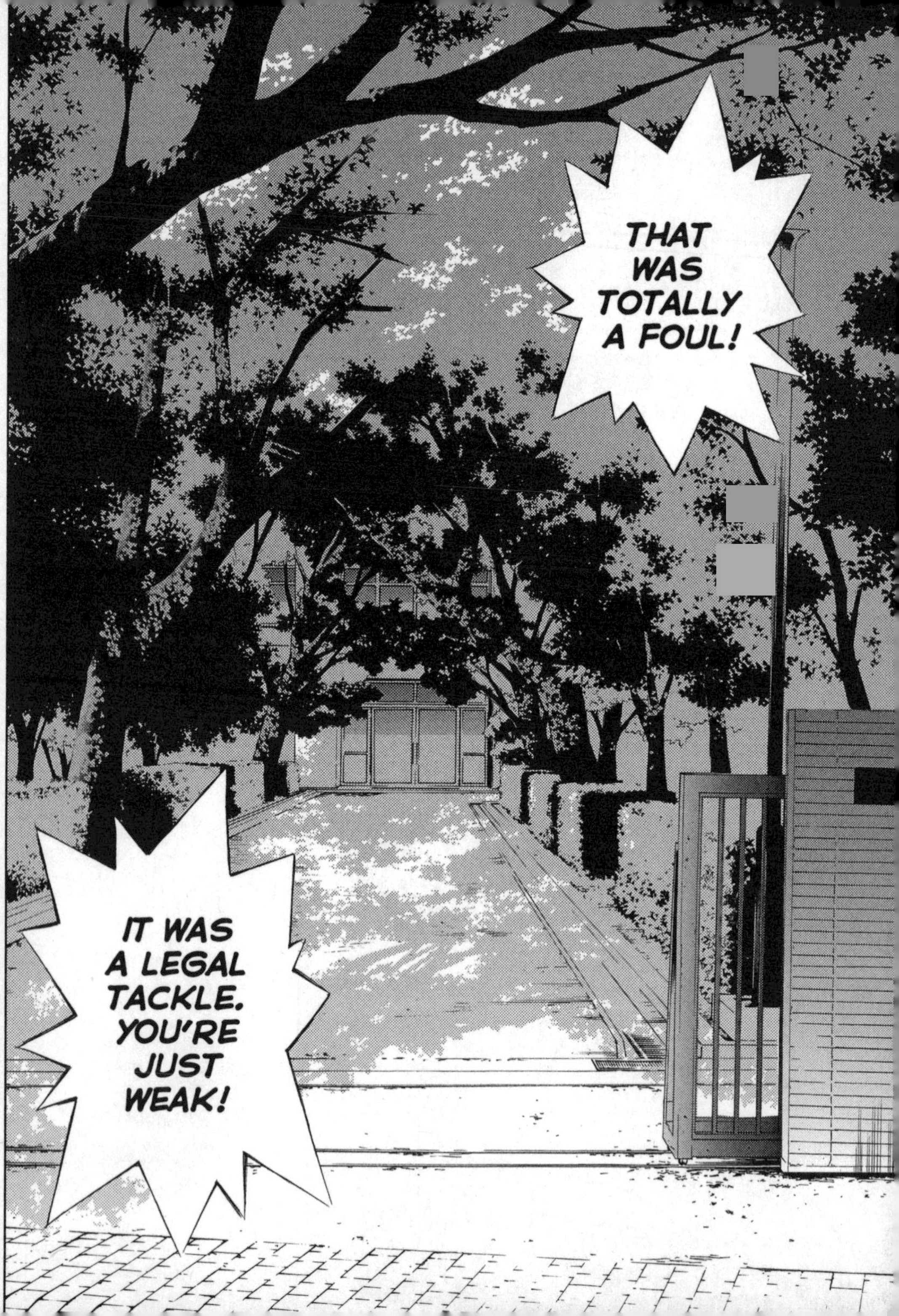
THAT WAS TOTALLY A FOUL!
IT WAS A LEGAL TACKLE. YOU'RE JUST WEAK!

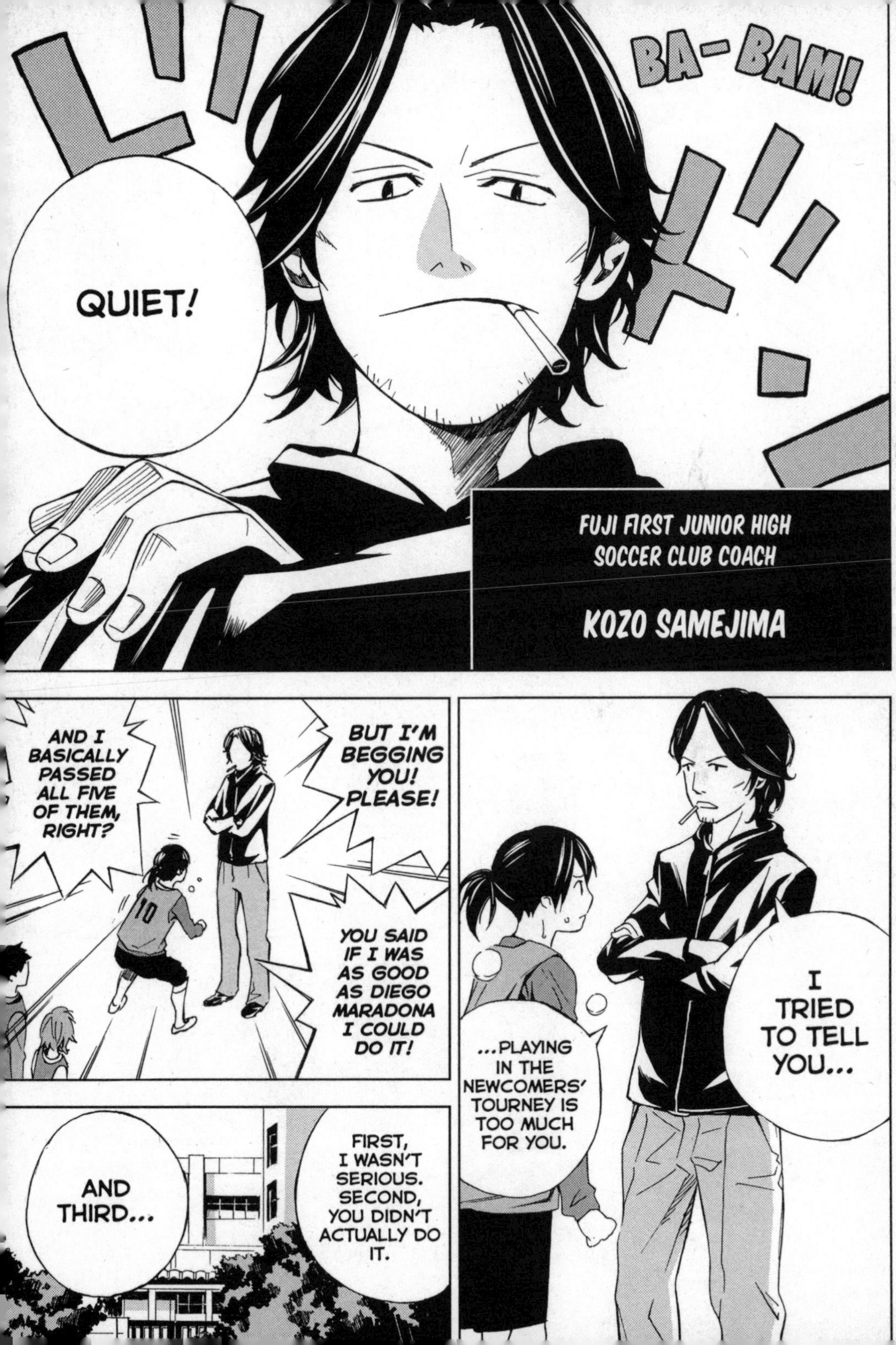
BA-BAM!
QUIET!
FUJI FIRST JUNIOR HIGH SOCCER CLUB COACH
KOZO SAMEJIMA
I TRIED TO TELL YOU...
...PLAYING IN THE NEWCOMERS' TOURNEY IS TOO MUCH FOR YOU.
BUT I'M BEGGING YOU! PLEASE!
AND I BASICALLY PASSED ALL FIVE OF THEM, RIGHT?
YOU SAID IF I WAS AS GOOD AS DIEGO MARADONA I COULD DO IT!
FIRST, I WASN'T SERIOUS. SECOND, YOU DIDN'T ACTUALLY DO IT.
AND THIRD...

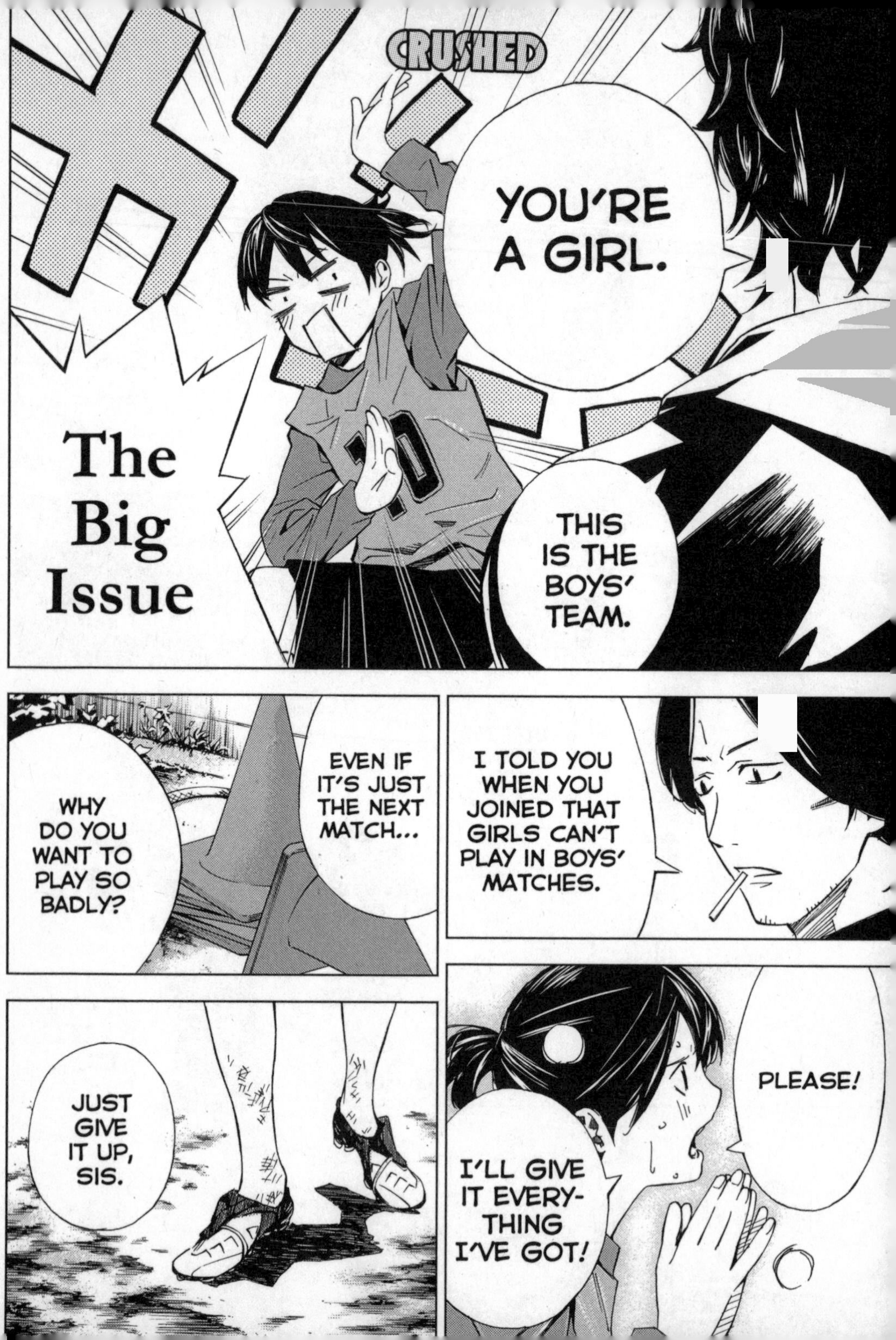
CRUSHED
YOU'RE A GIRL.
THIS IS THE BOYS' TEAM.
The Big Issue
I TOLD YOU WHEN YOU JOINED THAT GIRLS CAN'T PLAY IN BOYS' MATCHES.
EVEN IF IT'S JUST THE NEXT MATCH...
WHY DO YOU WANT TO PLAY SO BADLY?
PLEASE!
I'LL GIVE IT EVERY-THING I'VE GOT!
JUST GIVE IT UP, SIS.

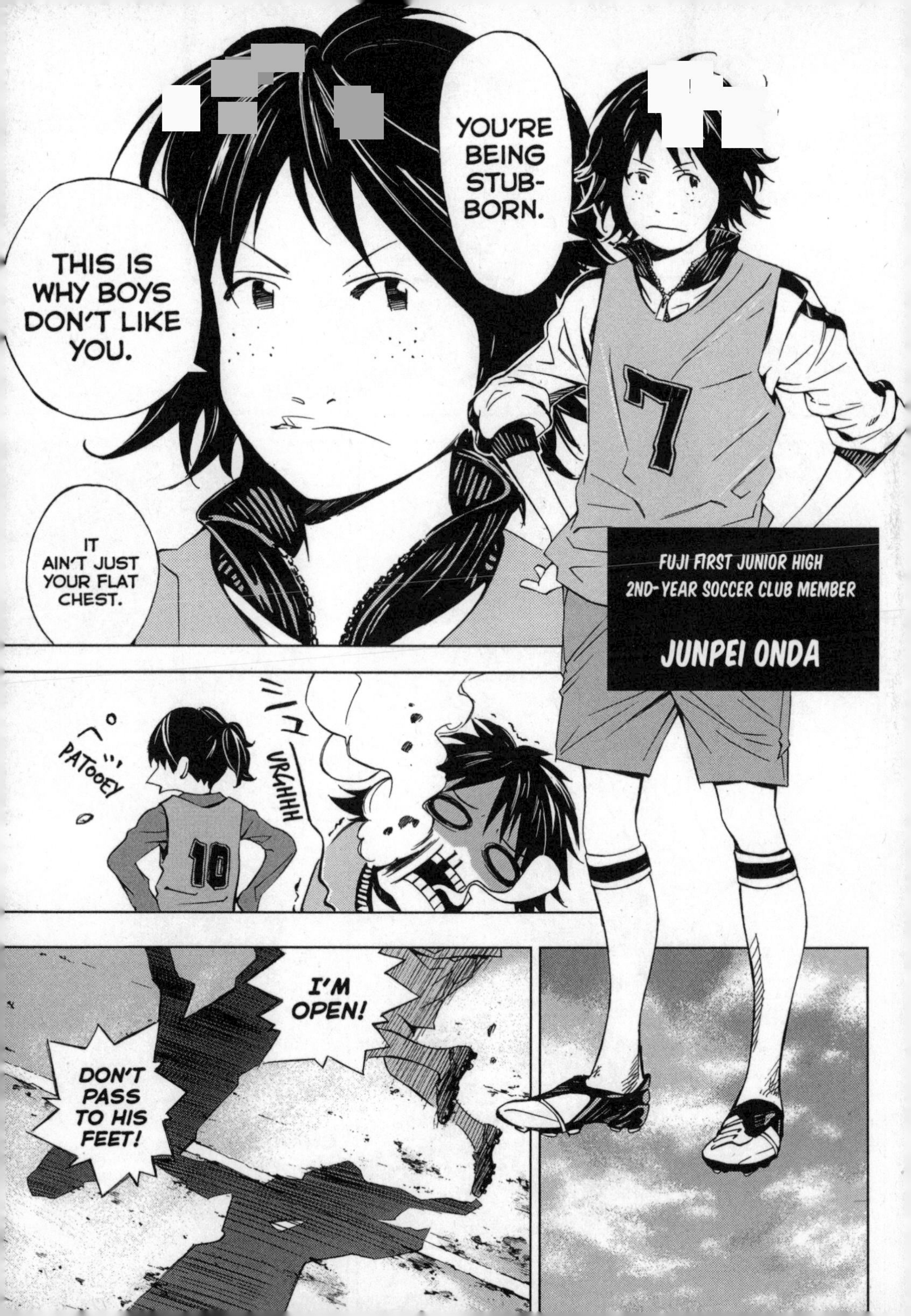
YOU'RE BEING STUB-BORN.
THIS IS WHY BOYS DON'T LIKE YOU.
IT AIN'T JUST YOUR FLAT CHEST.
FUJI FIRST JUNIOR HIGH 2ND-YEAR SOCCER CLUB MEMBER
JUNPEI ONDA
URGHHH
PATOOEY
I'M OPEN!
DON'T PASS TO HIS FEET!

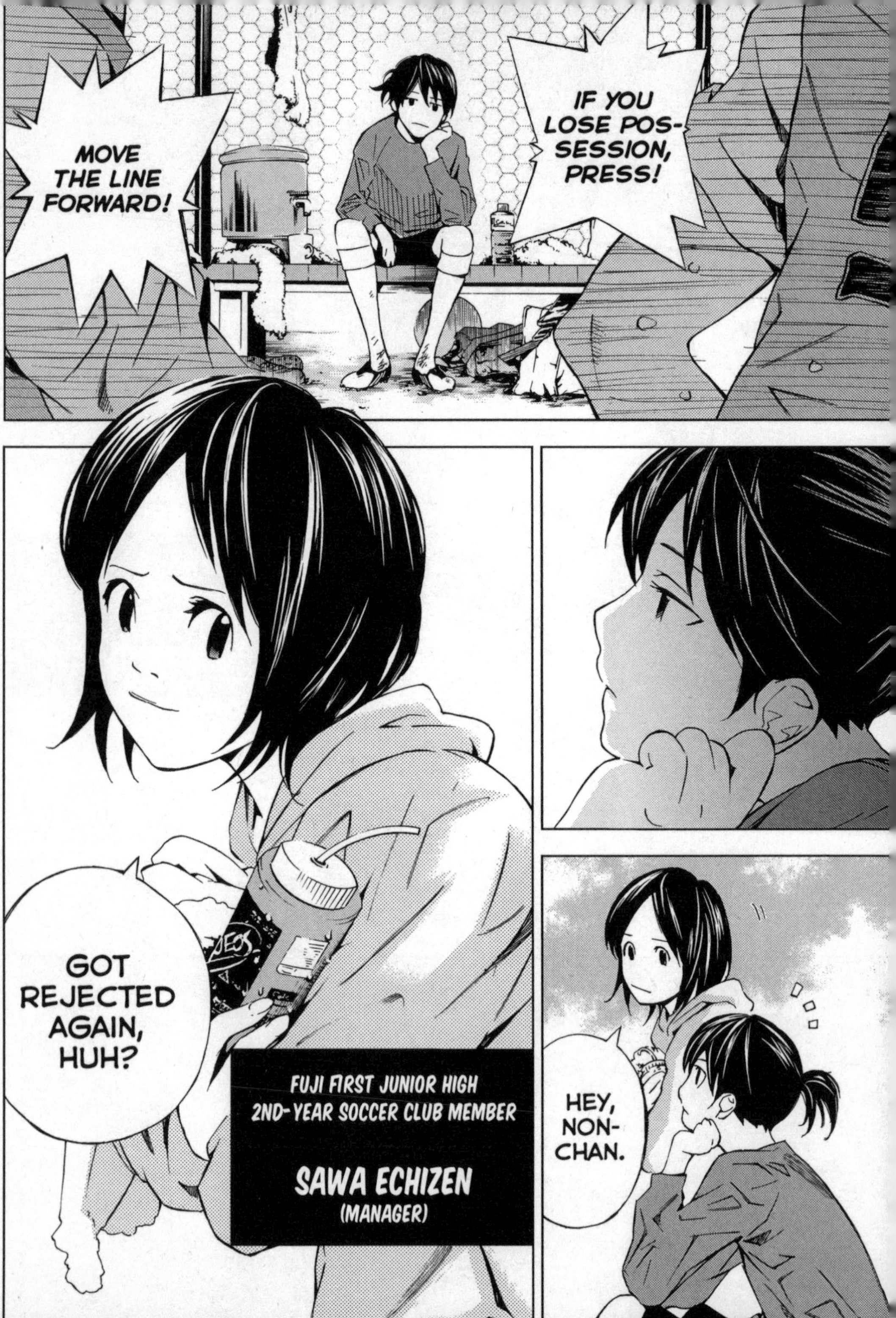
IF YOU LOSE POS-SESSION, PRESS!
MOVE THE LINE FORWARD!
HEY, NON-CHAN.
FUJI FIRST JUNIOR HIGH
2ND-YEAR SOCCER CLUB MEMBER
SAWA ECHIZEN
(MANAGER)
GOT REJECTED AGAIN, HUH?

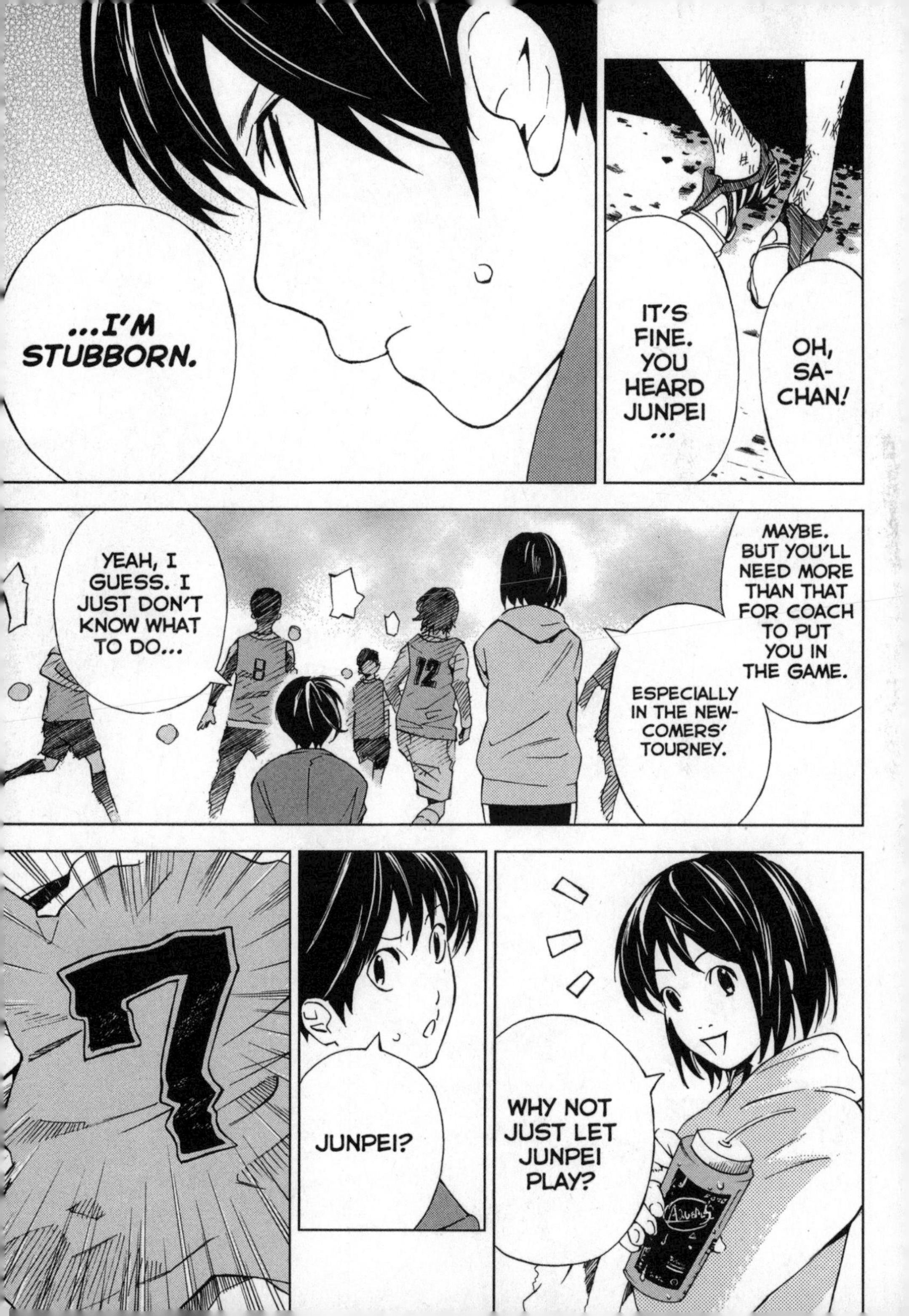
OH, SA-CHAN!
IT'S FINE. YOU HEARD JUNPEI ...
...I'M STUBBORN.
MAYBE. BUT YOU'LL NEED MORE THAN THAT FOR COACH TO PUT YOU IN THE GAME.
ESPECIALLY IN THE NEW-COMERS' TOURNEY.
YEAH, I GUESS. I JUST DON'T KNOW WHAT TO DO...
WHY NOT JUST LET JUNPEI PLAY?
JUNPEI?

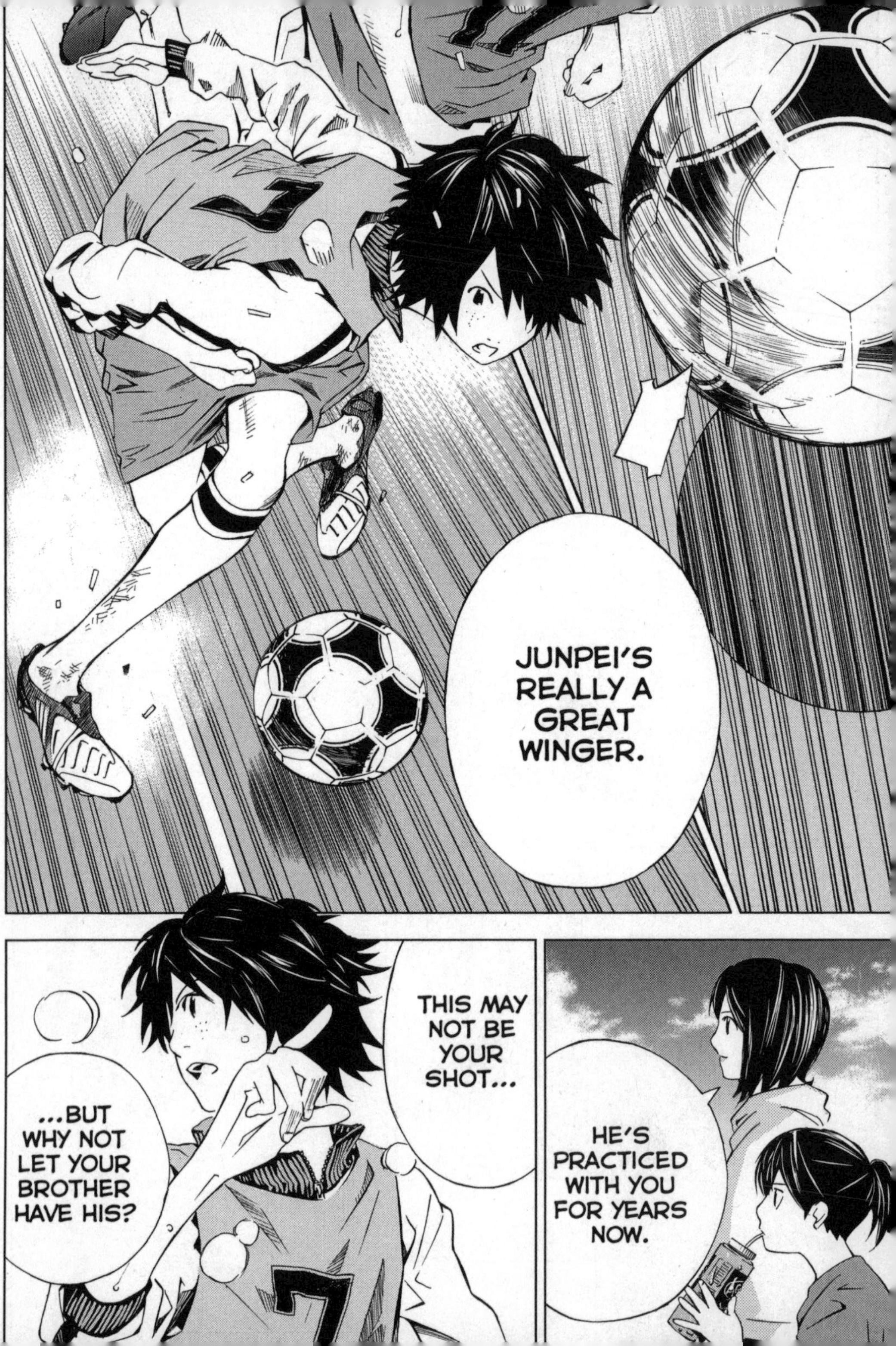
JUNPEI'S REALLY A GREAT WINGER.
HE'S PRACTICED WITH YOU FOR YEARS NOW.
THIS MAY NOT BE YOUR SHOT...
...BUT WHY NOT LET YOUR BROTHER HAVE HIS?

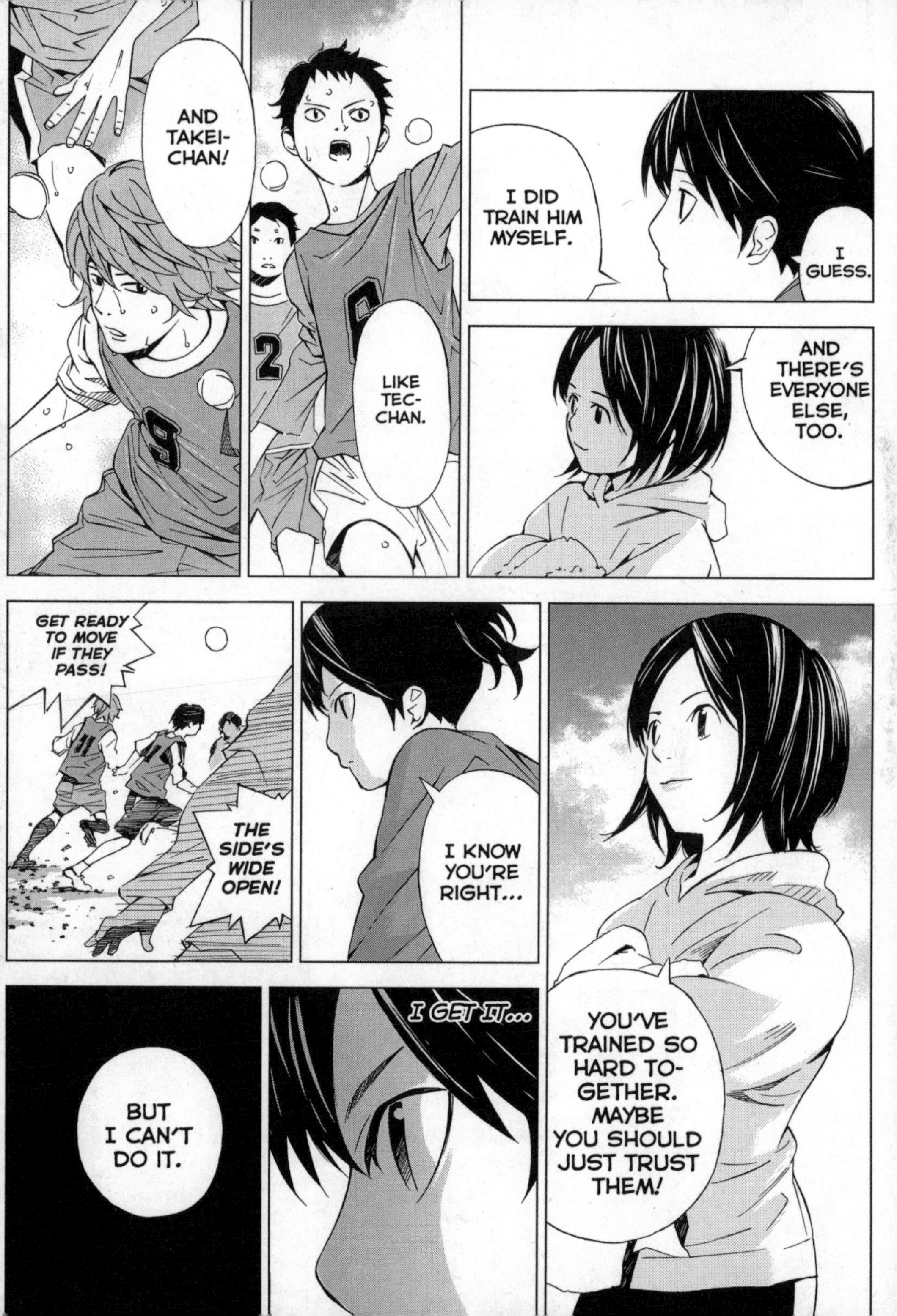
I DID TRAIN HIM MYSELF.
I GUESS.
AND THERE'S EVERYONE ELSE, TOO.
LIKE TEC-CHAN.
AND TAKEI-CHAN!
YOU'VE TRAINED SO HARD TO-GETHER. MAYBE YOU SHOULD JUST TRUST THEM!
I KNOW YOU'RE RIGHT...
GET READY TO MOVE IF THEY PASS!
THE SIDE'S WIDE OPEN!
I GET IT...
BUT I CAN'T DO IT.

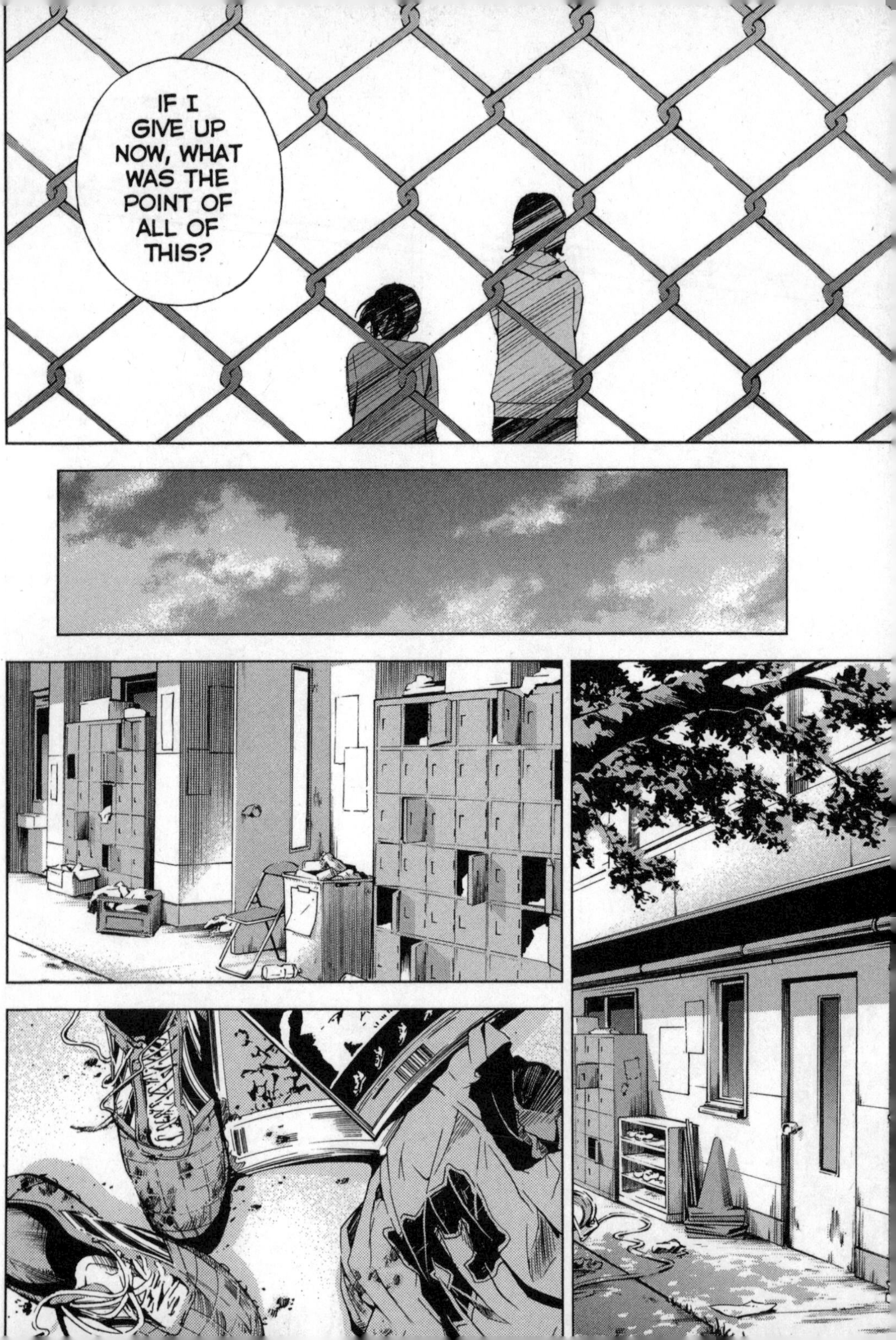
IF I GIVE UP NOW, WHAT WAS THE POINT OF ALL OF THIS?

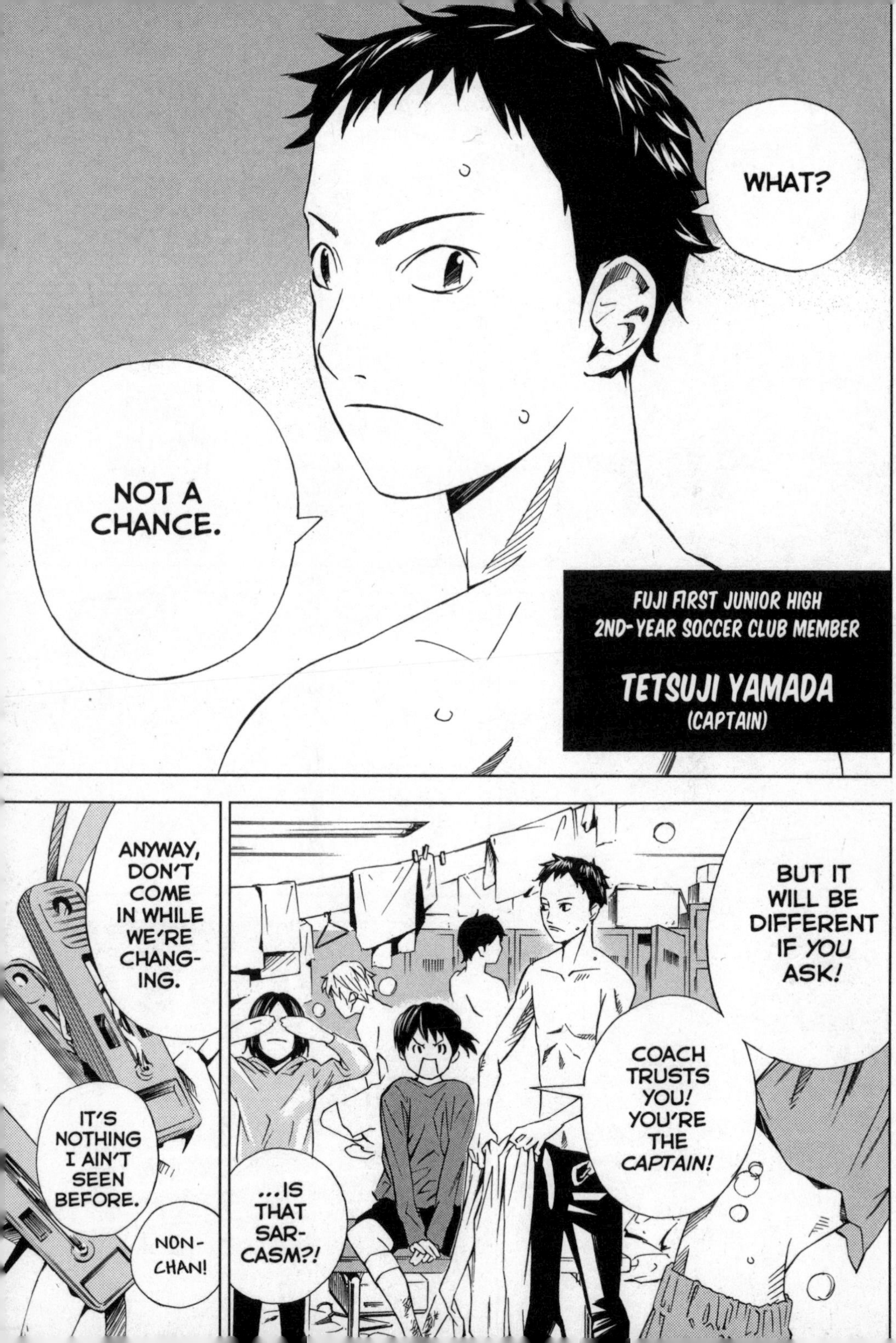
WHAT?
NOT A CHANCE.
FUJI FIRST JUNIOR HIGH 2ND-YEAR SOCCER CLUB MEMBER
TETSUJI YAMADA (CAPTAIN)
BUT IT WILL BE DIFFERENT IF *YOU* ASK!
COACH TRUSTS YOU! YOU'RE THE *CAPTAIN!*
...IS THAT SARCASM?!
ANYWAY, DON'T COME IN WHILE WE'RE CHANGING.
IT'S NOTHING I AIN'T SEEN BEFORE.
NON-CHAN!

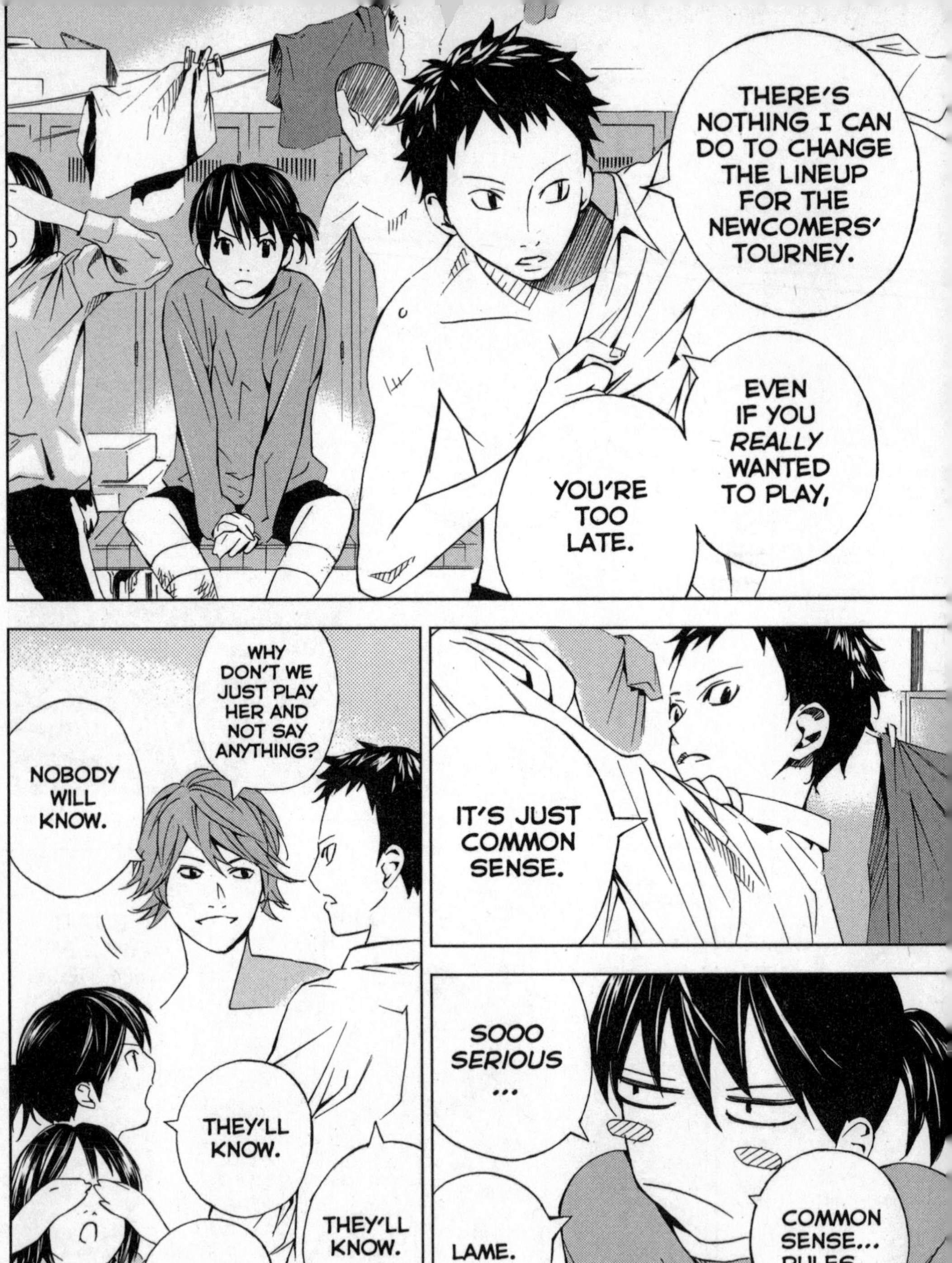
THERE'S NOTHING I CAN DO TO CHANGE THE LINEUP FOR THE NEWCOMERS' TOURNEY.
EVEN IF YOU *REALLY* WANTED TO PLAY,
YOU'RE TOO LATE.
IT'S JUST COMMON SENSE.
SOOO SERIOUS ...
COMMON SENSE... RULES...
LAME.
WHY DON'T WE JUST PLAY HER AND NOT SAY ANYTHING?
NOBODY WILL KNOW.
THEY'LL KNOW.
THEY'LL KNOW.
THEY'LL KNOW.

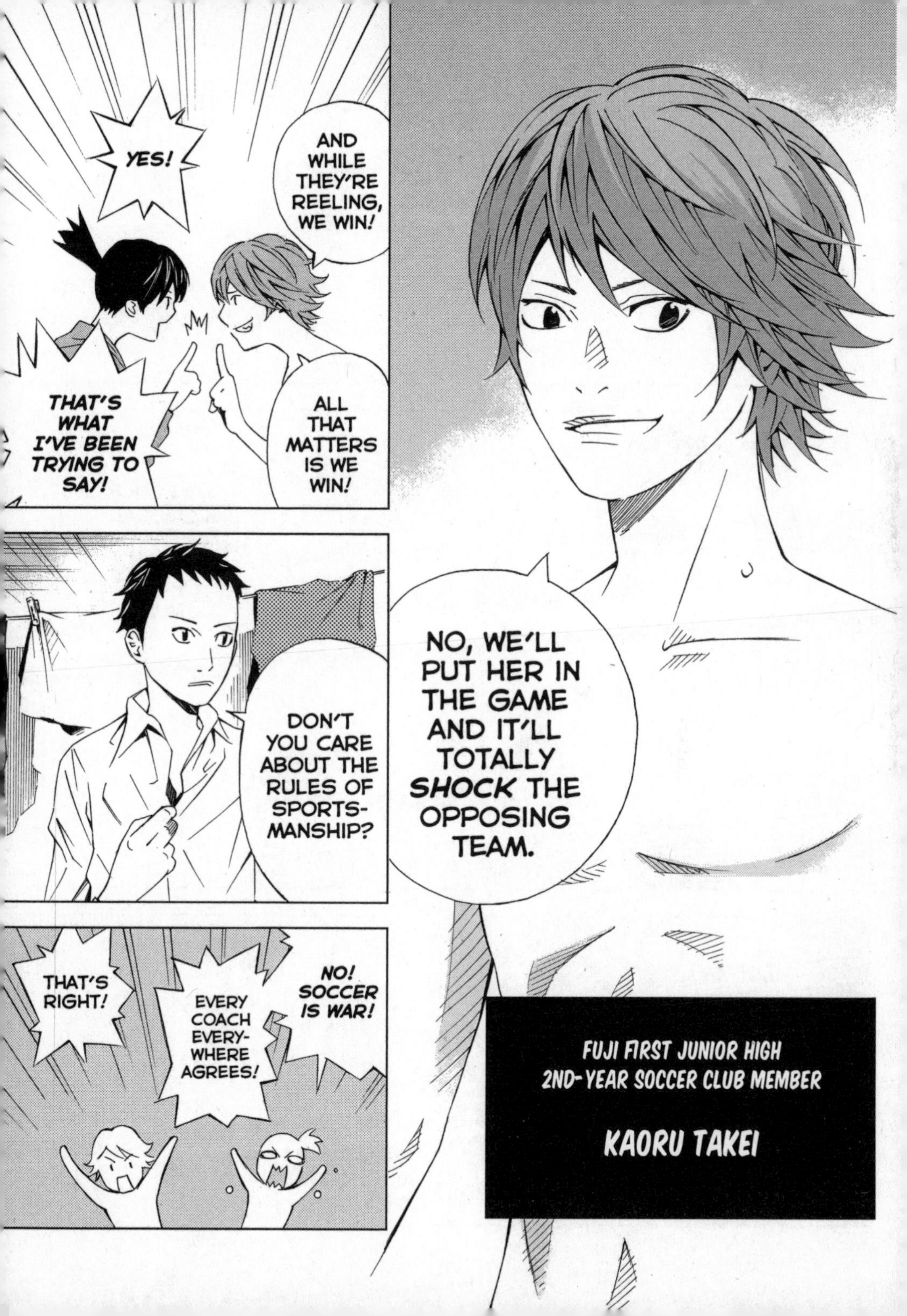
NO, WE'LL PUT HER IN THE GAME AND IT'LL TOTALLY *SHOCK* THE OPPOSING TEAM.
FUJI FIRST JUNIOR HIGH
2ND-YEAR SOCCER CLUB MEMBER
KAORU TAKEI
AND WHILE THEY'RE REELING, WE WIN!
YES!
ALL THAT MATTERS IS WE WIN!
THAT'S WHAT I'VE BEEN TRYING TO SAY!
DON'T YOU CARE ABOUT THE RULES OF SPORTS-MANSHIP?
NO! SOCCER IS WAR!
EVERY COACH EVERY-WHERE AGREES!
THAT'S RIGHT!

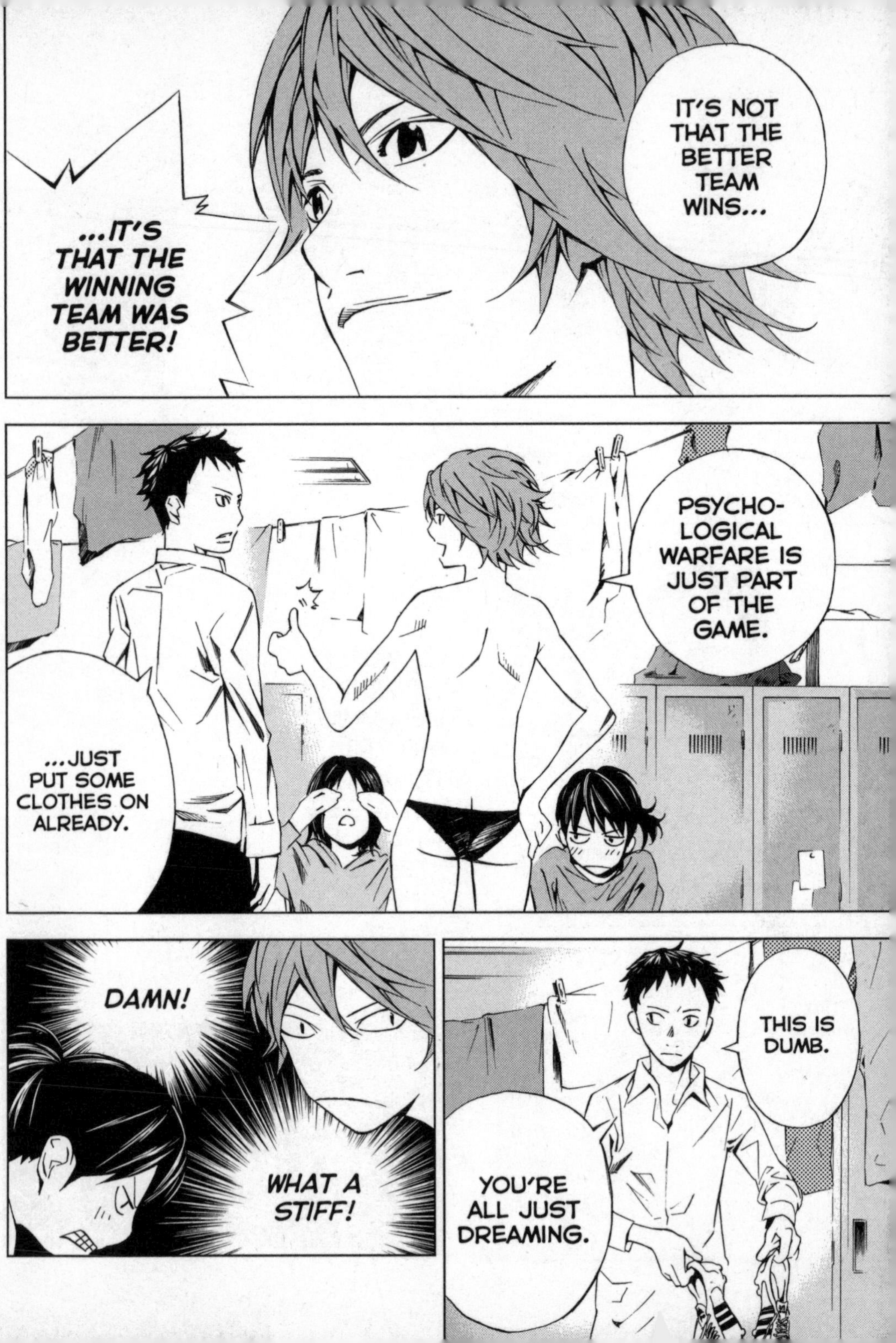
IT'S NOT THAT THE BETTER TEAM WINS...
...IT'S THAT THE WINNING TEAM WAS BETTER!
PSYCHOLOGICAL WARFARE IS JUST PART OF THE GAME.
...JUST PUT SOME CLOTHES ON ALREADY.
THIS IS DUMB.
YOU'RE ALL JUST DREAMING.
DAMN!
WHAT A STIFF!

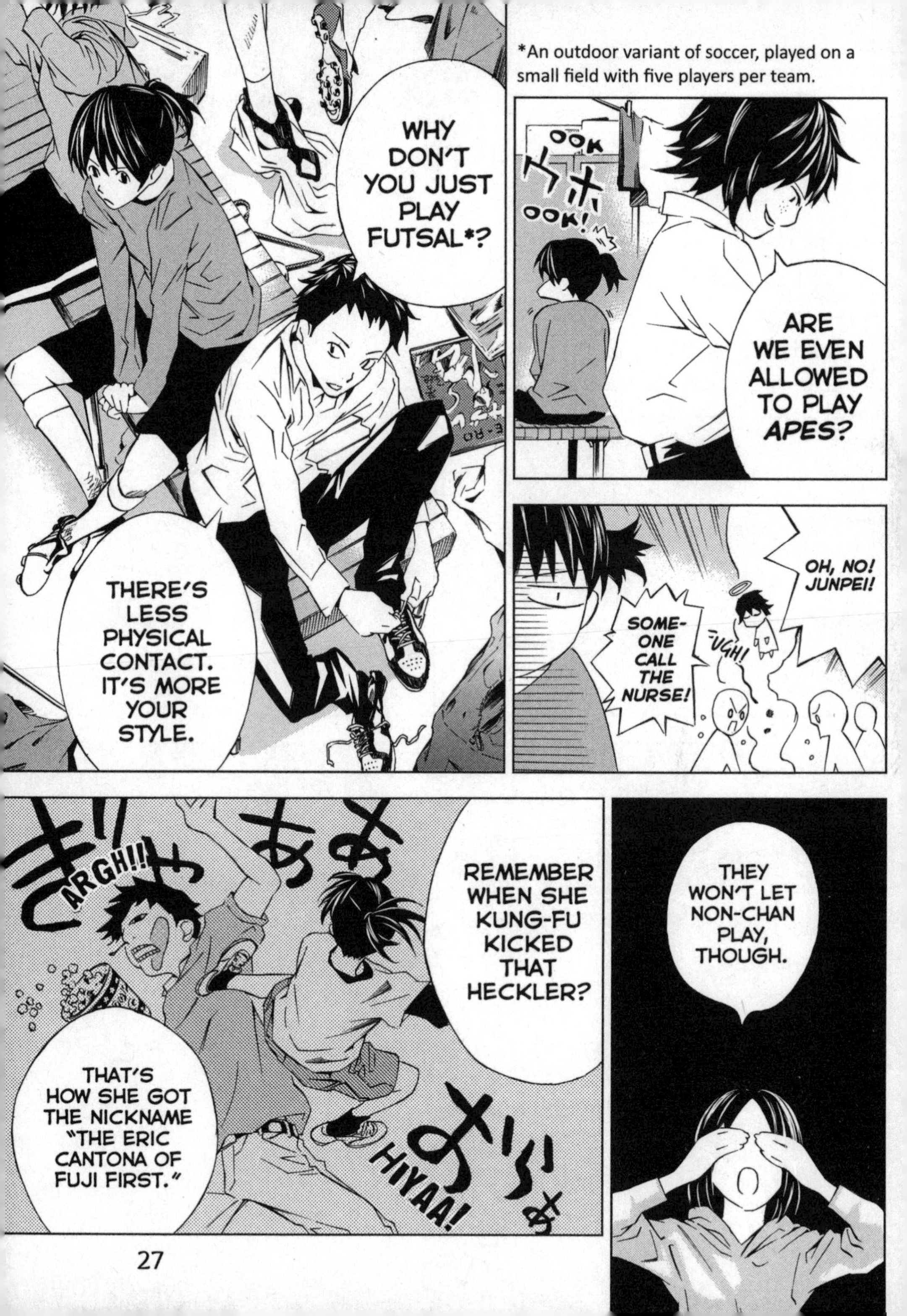
OOK
OOK!
ARE WE EVEN ALLOWED TO PLAY APES?
OH, NO! JUNPEI!
SOME-ONE CALL THE NURSE!
UGH!
WHY DON'T YOU JUST PLAY FUTSAL*?
THERE'S LESS PHYSICAL CONTACT. IT'S MORE YOUR STYLE.
THEY WON'T LET NON-CHAN PLAY, THOUGH.
REMEMBER WHEN SHE KUNG-FU KICKED THAT HECKLER?
ARGH!!
HIYAA!
THAT'S HOW SHE GOT THE NICKNAME "THE ERIC CANTONA OF FUJI FIRST."

*An outdoor variant of soccer, played on a small field with five players per team.

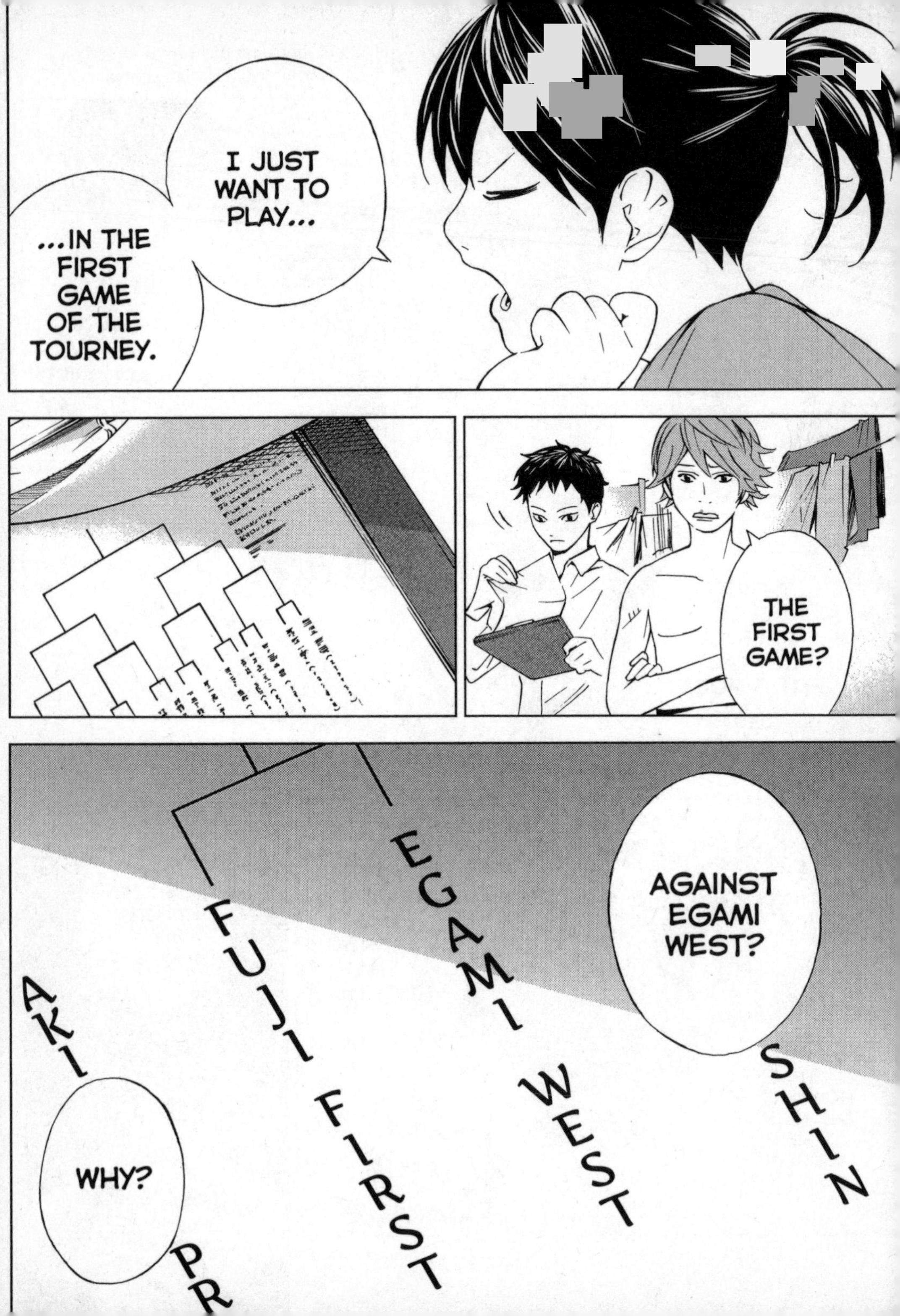
I JUST WANT TO PLAY...
...IN THE FIRST GAME OF THE TOURNEY.
THE FIRST GAME?
AGAINST EGAMI WEST?
SHIN
EGAMI WEST
FUJI FIRST
AKI
PR
WHY?

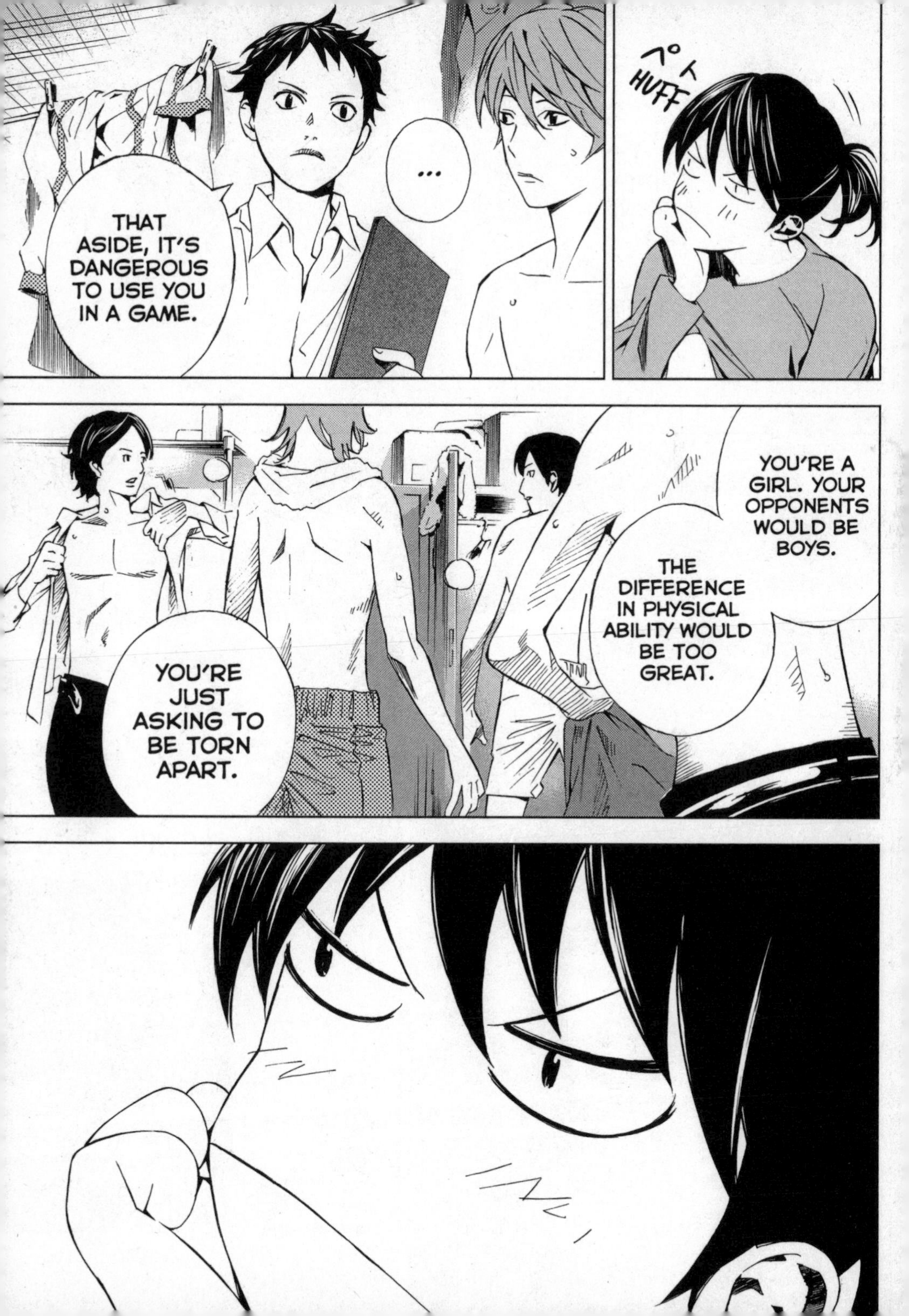
ペト
HUFF
...
THAT ASIDE, IT'S DANGEROUS TO USE YOU IN A GAME.
YOU'RE A GIRL. YOUR OPPONENTS WOULD BE BOYS.
THE DIFFERENCE IN PHYSICAL ABILITY WOULD BE TOO GREAT.
YOU'RE JUST ASKING TO BE TORN APART.

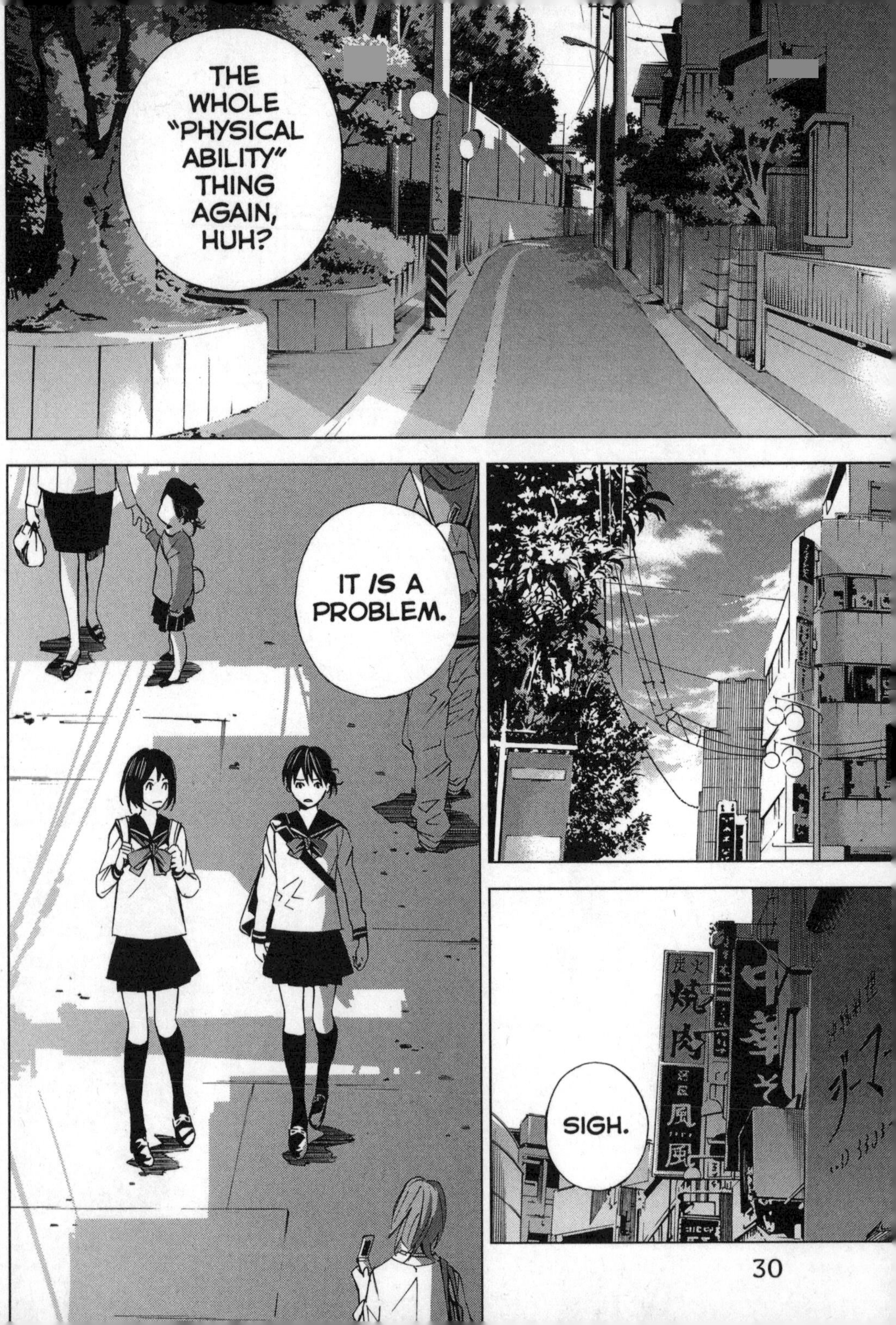
THE WHOLE "PHYSICAL ABILITY" THING AGAIN, HUH?
SIGH.
IT *IS* A PROBLEM.

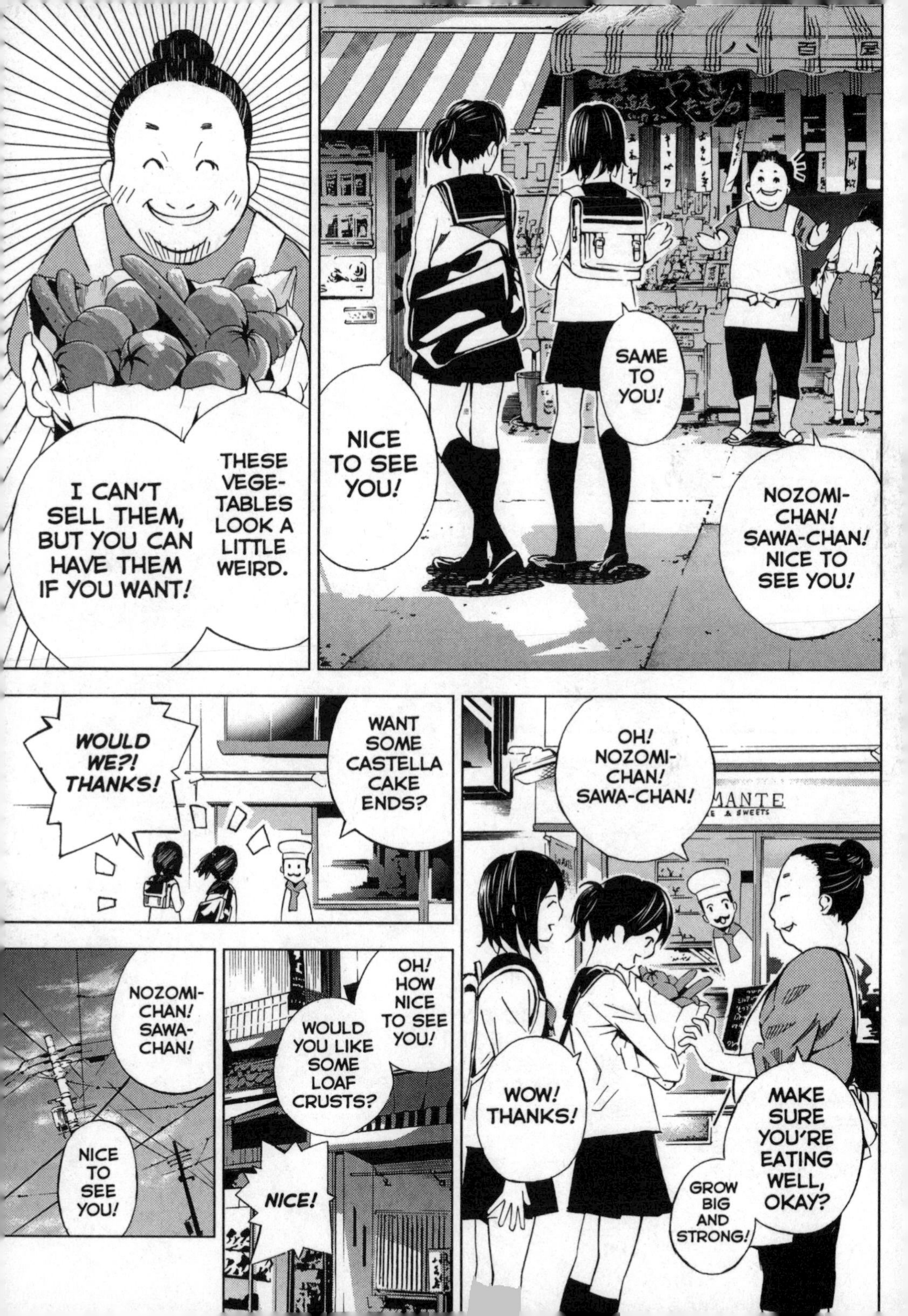
NOZOMI-CHAN! SAWA-CHAN! NICE TO SEE YOU!
NICE TO SEE YOU!
SAME TO YOU!
THESE VEGE-TABLES LOOK A LITTLE WEIRD.
I CAN'T SELL THEM, BUT YOU CAN HAVE THEM IF YOU WANT!
OH! NOZOMI-CHAN! SAWA-CHAN!
WOW! THANKS!
MAKE SURE YOU'RE EATING WELL, OKAY?
GROW BIG AND STRONG!
WANT SOME CASTELLA CAKE ENDS?
WOULD WE?! THANKS!
OH! HOW NICE TO SEE YOU!
WOULD YOU LIKE SOME LOAF CRUSTS?
NICE!
NOZOMI-CHAN! SAWA-CHAN!
NICE TO SEE YOU!

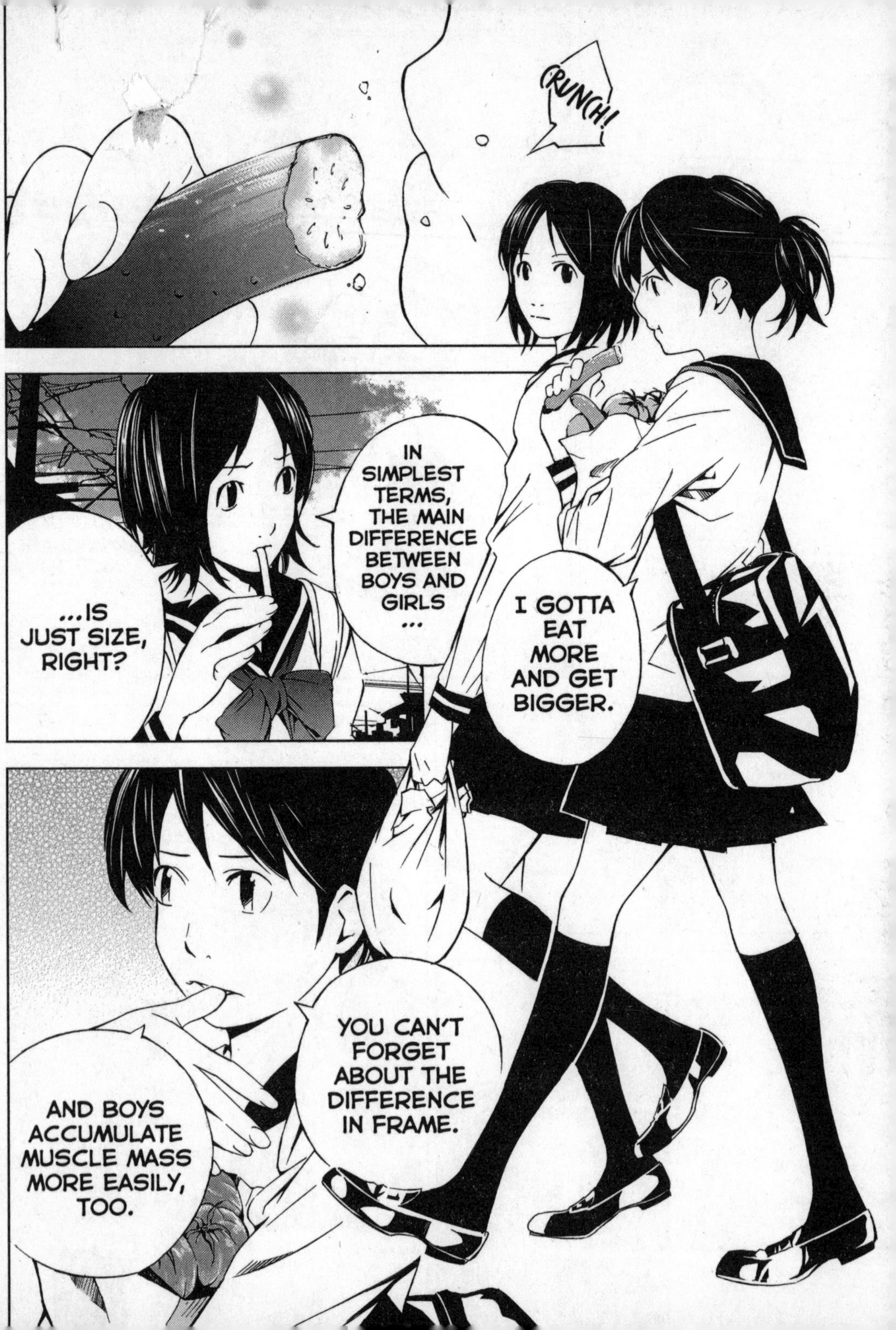
CRUNCH!
I GOTTA EAT MORE AND GET BIGGER.
IN SIMPLEST TERMS, THE MAIN DIFFERENCE BETWEEN BOYS AND GIRLS ...
...IS JUST SIZE, RIGHT?
YOU CAN'T FORGET ABOUT THE DIFFERENCE IN FRAME.
AND BOYS ACCUMULATE MUSCLE MASS MORE EASILY, TOO.

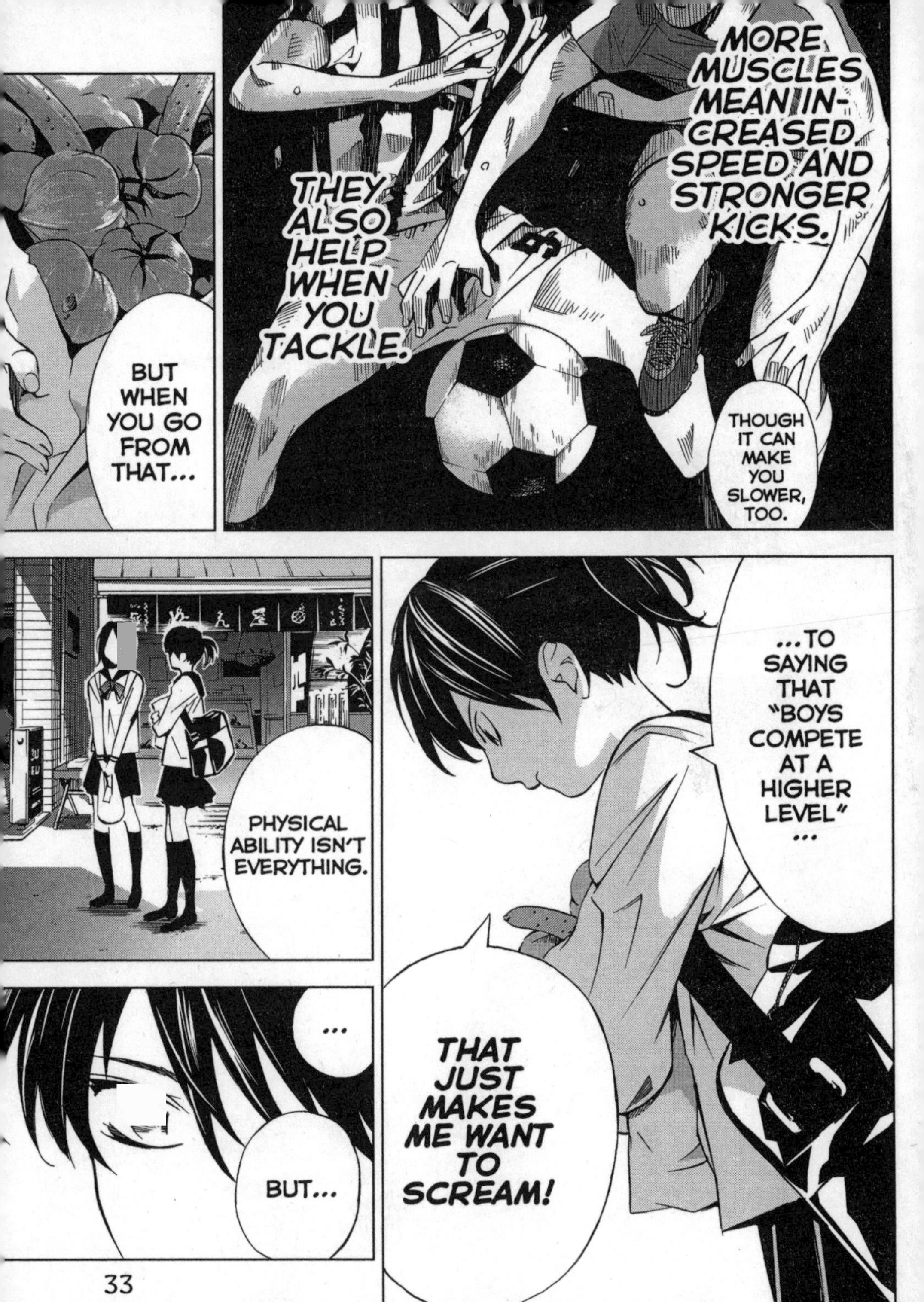
MORE MUSCLES MEAN IN-CREASED SPEED AND STRONGER KICKS.
THEY ALSO HELP WHEN YOU TACKLE.
THOUGH IT CAN MAKE YOU SLOWER, TOO.
BUT WHEN YOU GO FROM THAT...
...TO SAYING THAT "BOYS COMPETE AT A HIGHER LEVEL"...
THAT JUST MAKES ME WANT TO SCREAM!
PHYSICAL ABILITY ISN'T EVERYTHING.
...
BUT...

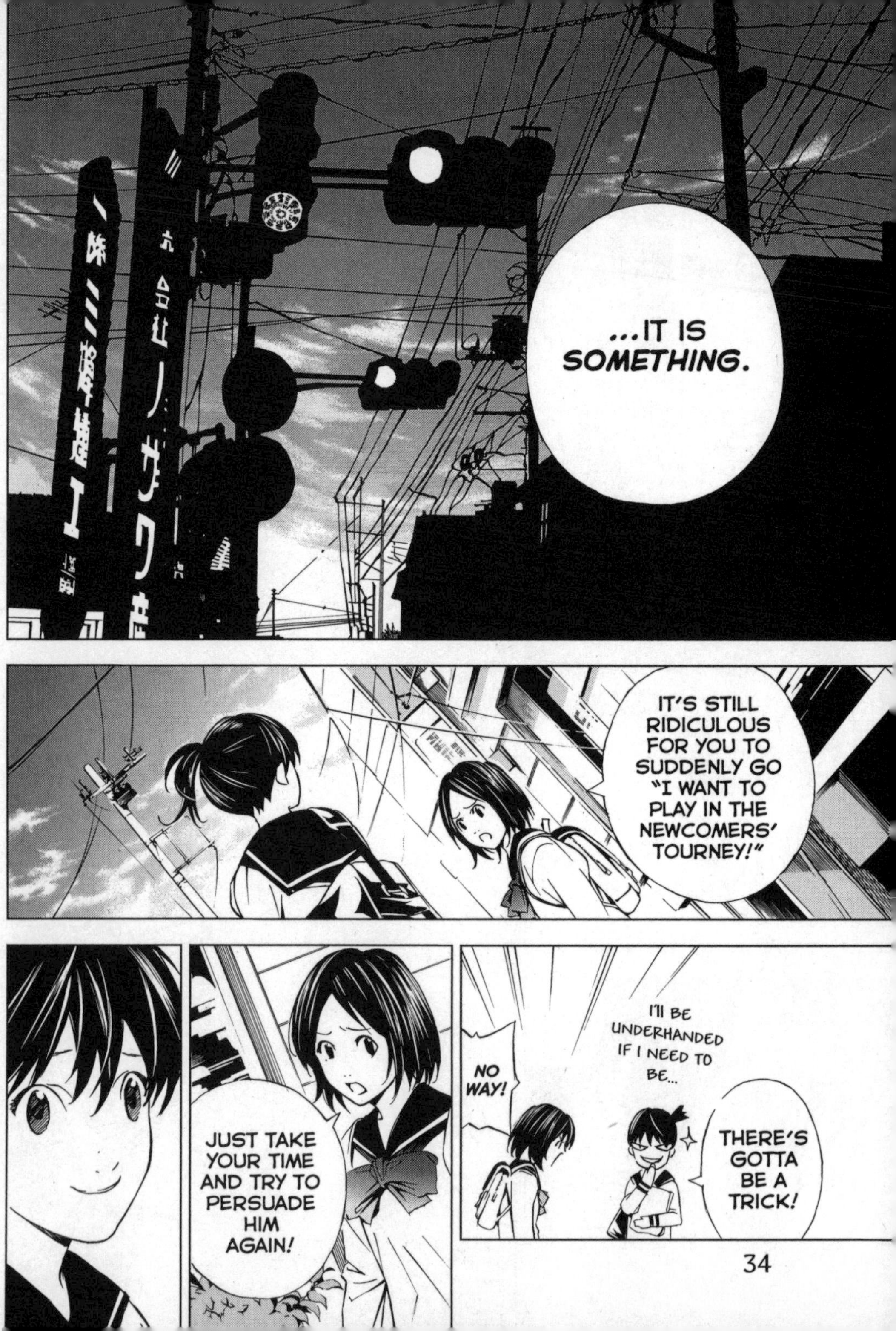
...IT IS SOMETHING.
IT'S STILL RIDICULOUS FOR YOU TO SUDDENLY GO "I WANT TO PLAY IN THE NEWCOMERS' TOURNEY!"
THERE'S GOTTA BE A TRICK!
I'll BE UNDERHANDED IF I NEED TO BE...
NO WAY!
JUST TAKE YOUR TIME AND TRY TO PERSUADE HIM AGAIN!

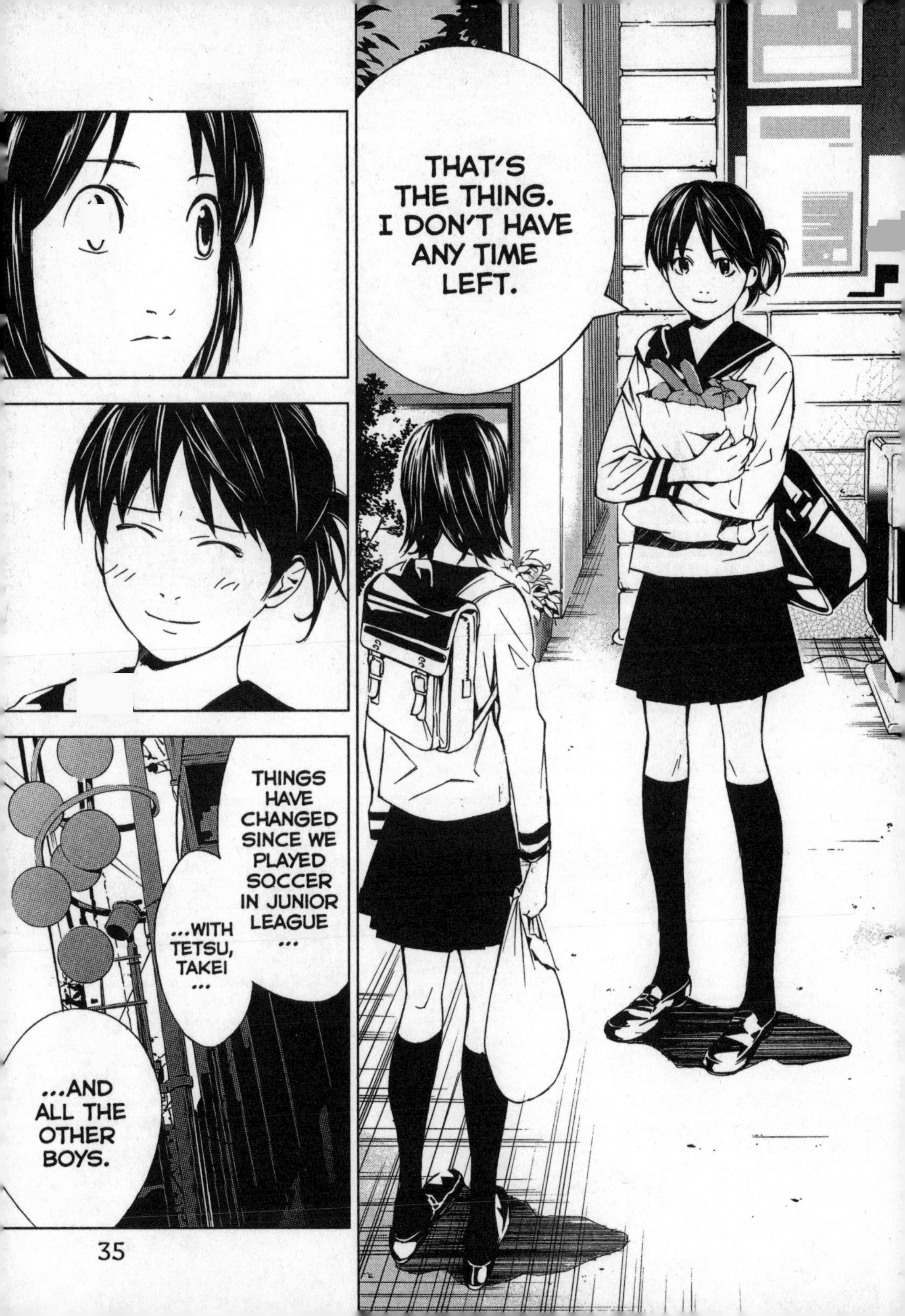
THAT'S THE THING. I DON'T HAVE ANY TIME LEFT.
THINGS HAVE CHANGED SINCE WE PLAYED SOCCER IN JUNIOR LEAGUE ...
...WITH TETSU, TAKEI ...
...AND ALL THE OTHER BOYS.

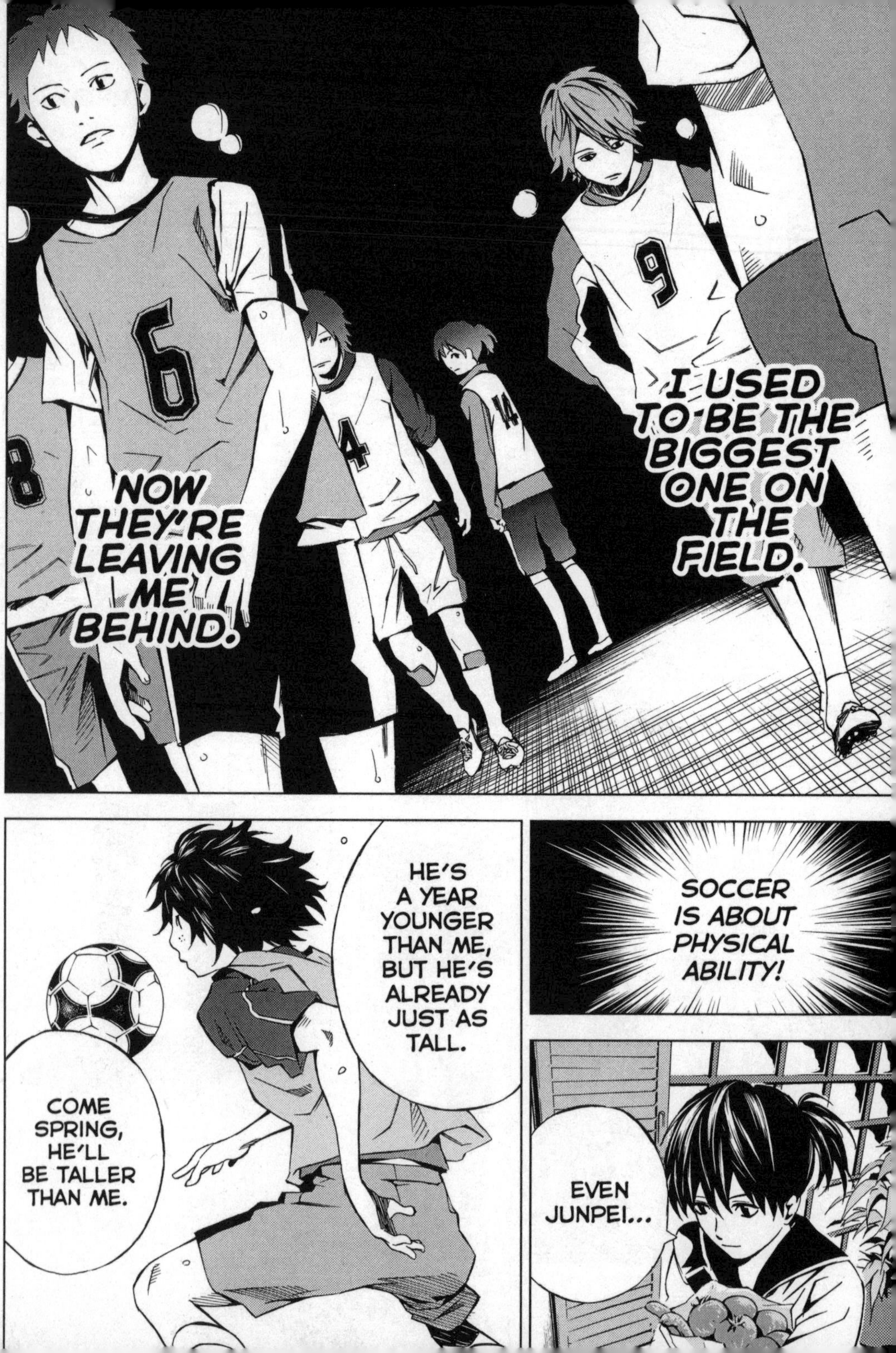
I USED TO BE THE BIGGEST ONE ON THE FIELD.
NOW THEY'RE LEAVING ME BEHIND.
SOCCER IS ABOUT PHYSICAL ABILITY!
EVEN JUNPEI...
HE'S A YEAR YOUNGER THAN ME, BUT HE'S ALREADY JUST AS TALL.
COME SPRING, HE'LL BE TALLER THAN ME.

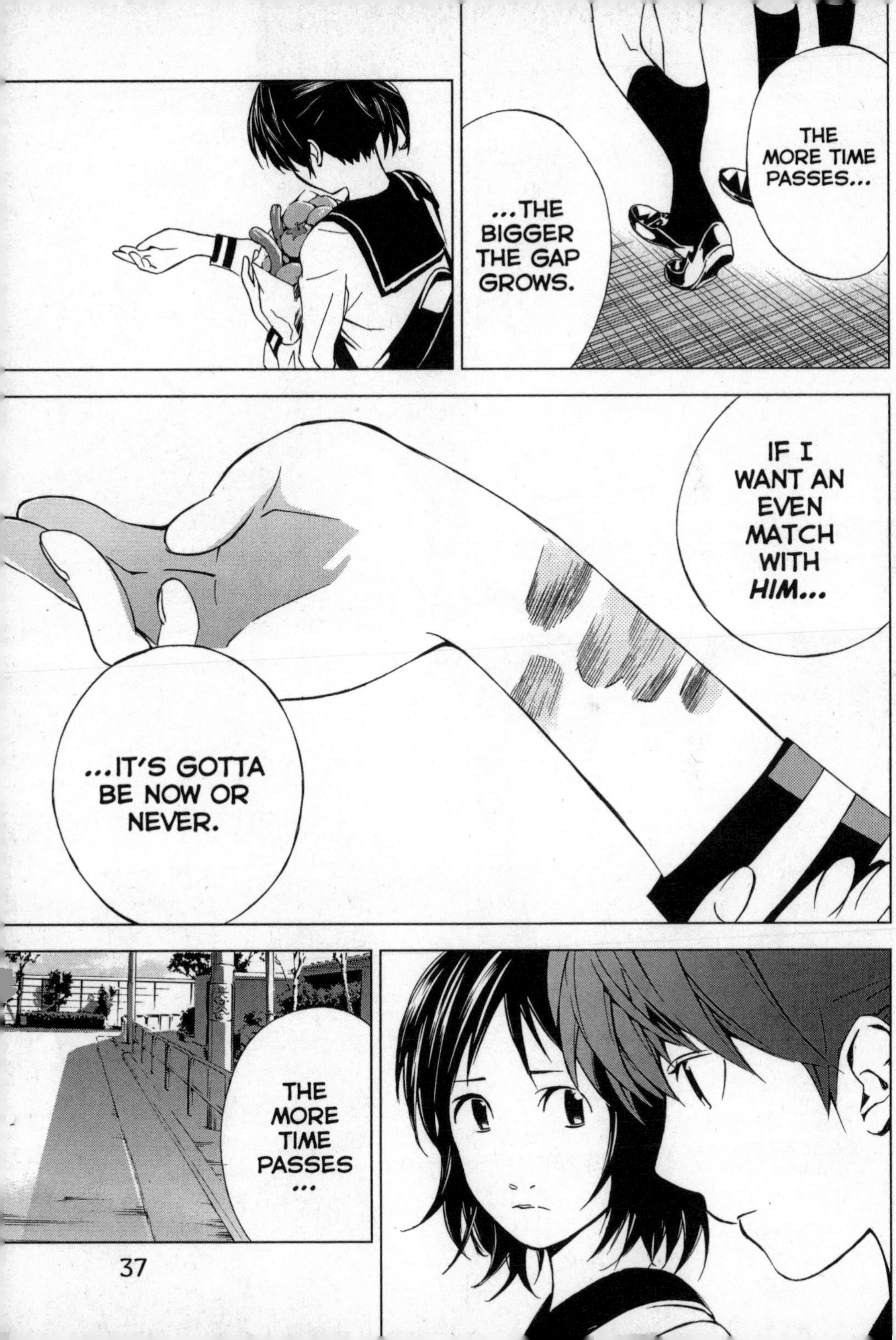
THE MORE TIME PASSES...
...THE BIGGER THE GAP GROWS.
IF I WANT AN EVEN MATCH WITH *HIM*...
...IT'S GOTTA BE NOW OR NEVER.
THE MORE TIME PASSES ...

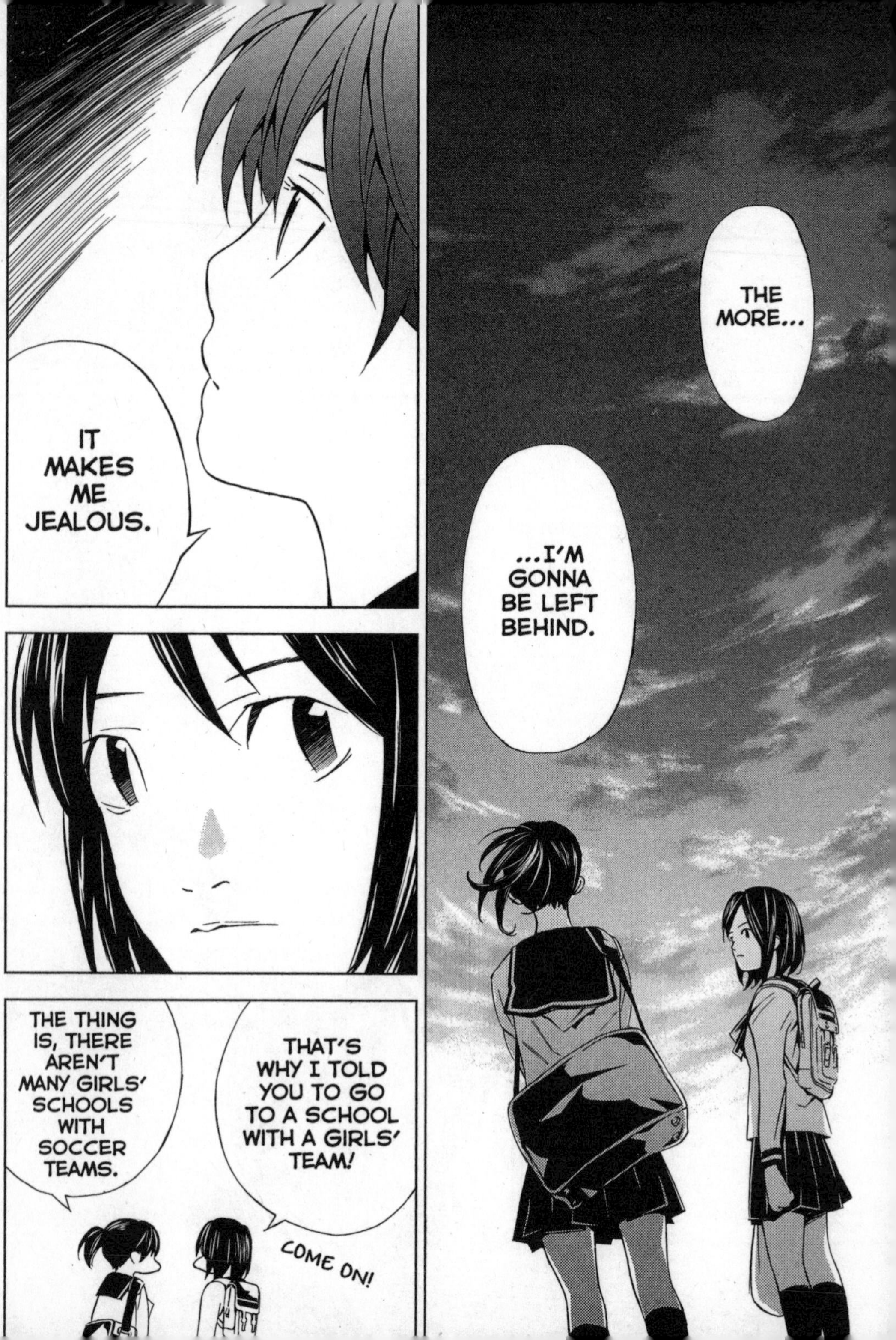
THE MORE...
...I'M GONNA BE LEFT BEHIND.
IT MAKES ME JEALOUS.
THAT'S WHY I TOLD YOU TO GO TO A SCHOOL WITH A GIRLS' TEAM!
THE THING IS, THERE AREN'T MANY GIRLS' SCHOOLS WITH SOCCER TEAMS.
COME ON!

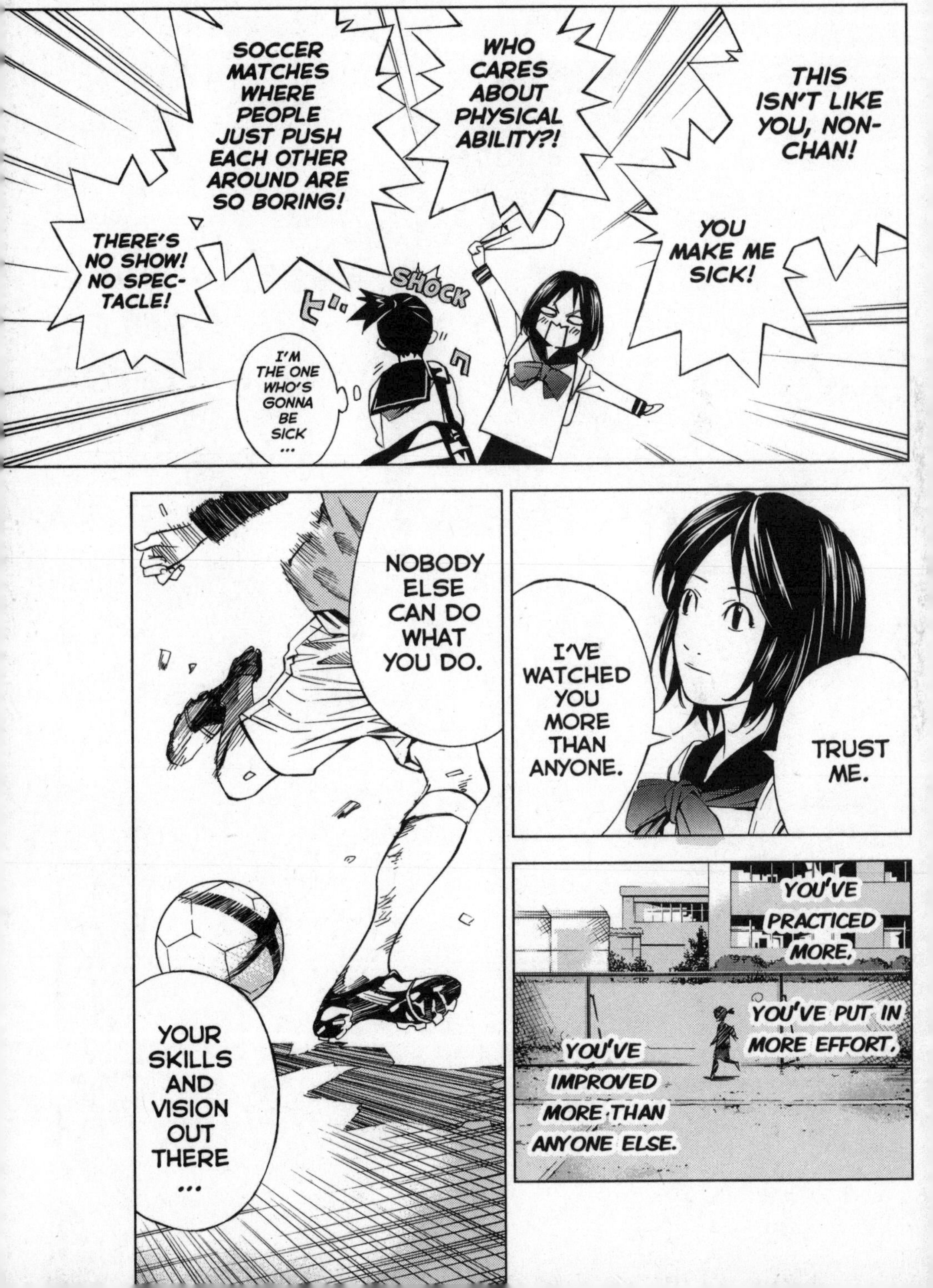
THIS ISN'T LIKE YOU, NON-CHAN!
WHO CARES ABOUT PHYSICAL ABILITY?!
SOCCER MATCHES WHERE PEOPLE JUST PUSH EACH OTHER AROUND ARE SO BORING!
YOU MAKE ME SICK!
THERE'S NO SHOW! NO SPEC-TACLE!
SHOCK
I'M THE ONE WHO'S GONNA BE SICK...
TRUST ME.
I'VE WATCHED YOU MORE THAN ANYONE.
YOU'VE PRACTICED MORE.
YOU'VE PUT IN MORE EFFORT.
YOU'VE IMPROVED MORE THAN ANYONE ELSE.
NOBODY ELSE CAN DO WHAT YOU DO.
YOUR SKILLS AND VISION OUT THERE...

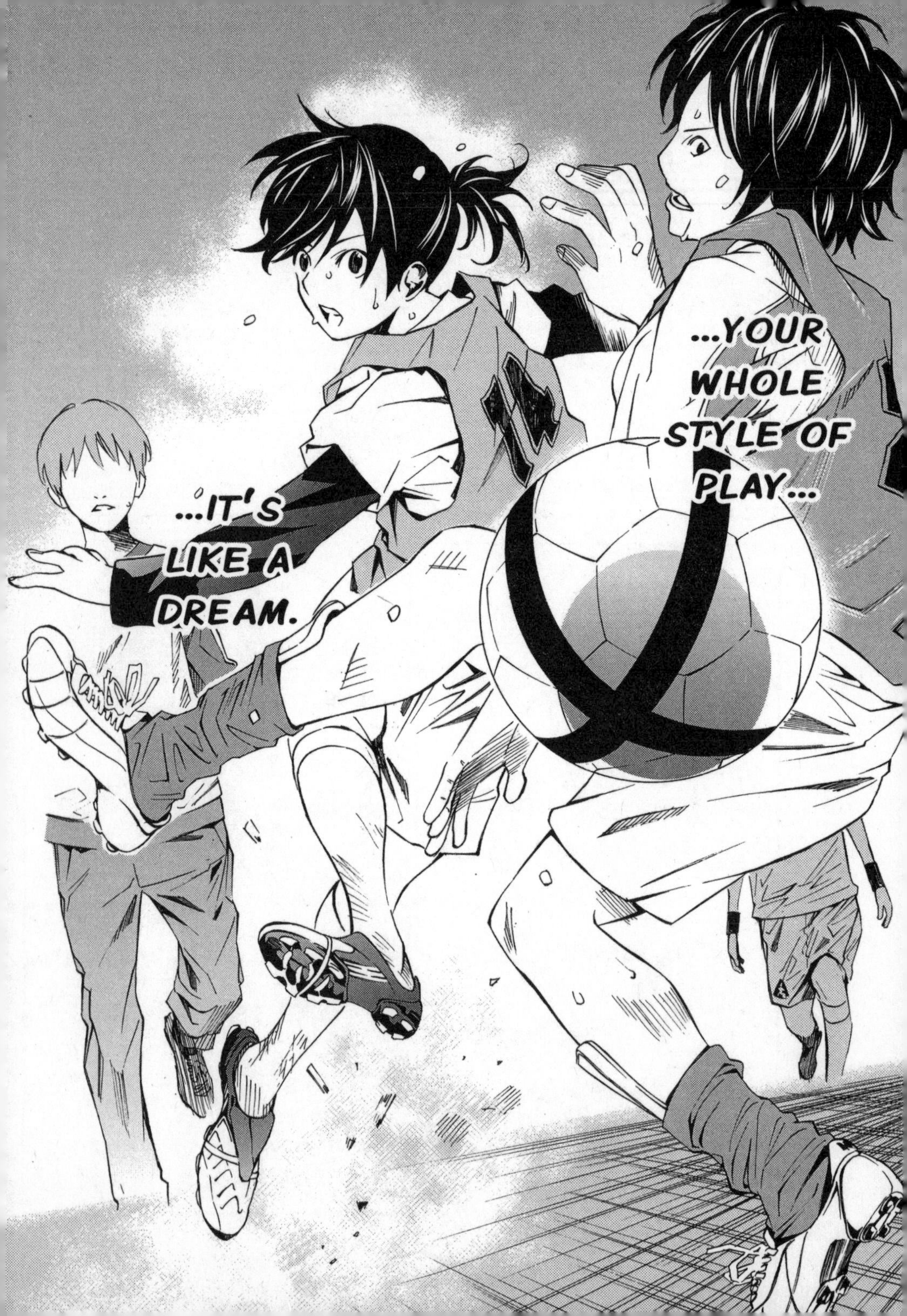
...YOUR WHOLE STYLE OF PLAY...
...IT'S LIKE A DREAM.

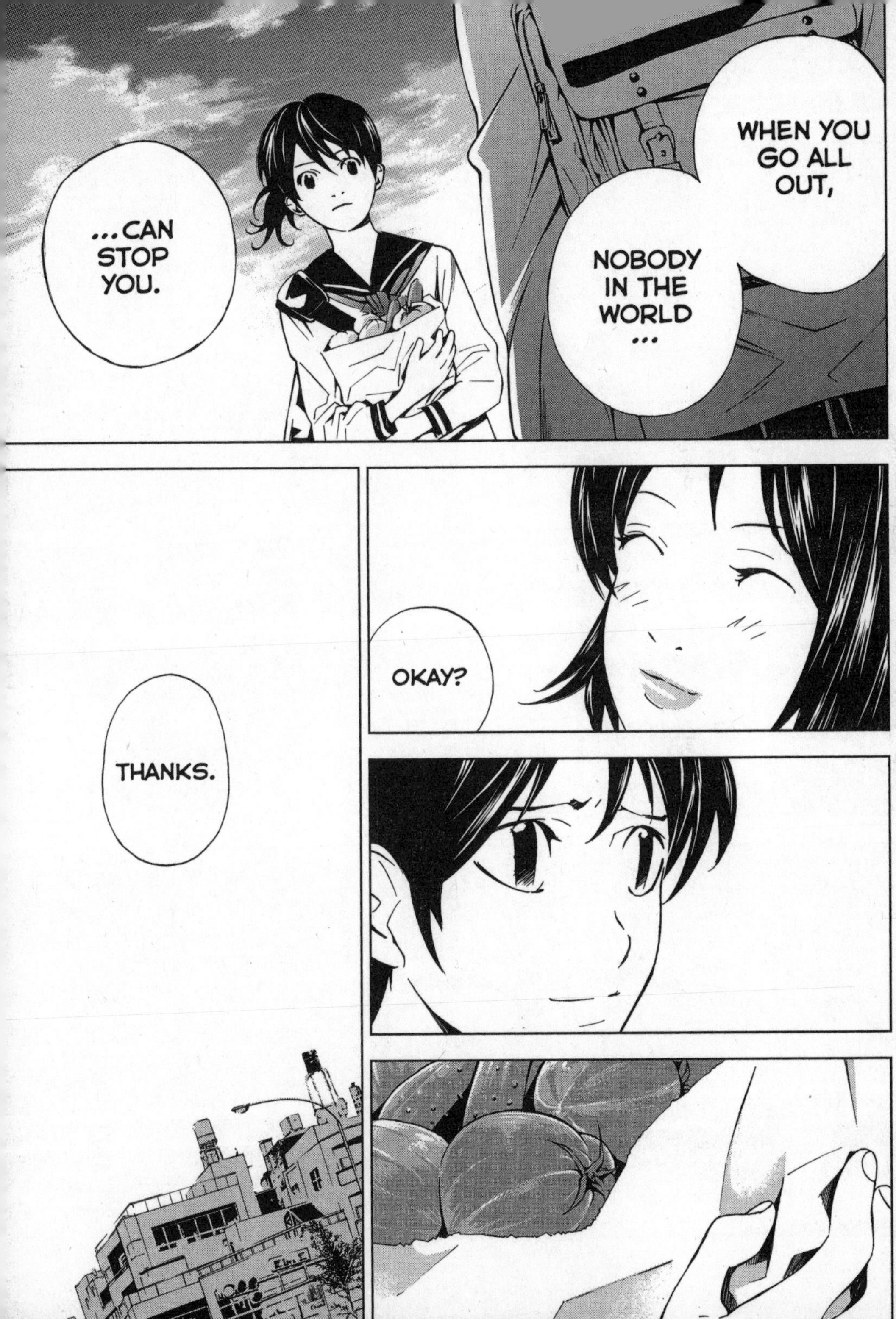
WHEN YOU GO ALL OUT,
NOBODY IN THE WORLD ...
...CAN STOP YOU.
OKAY?
THANKS.

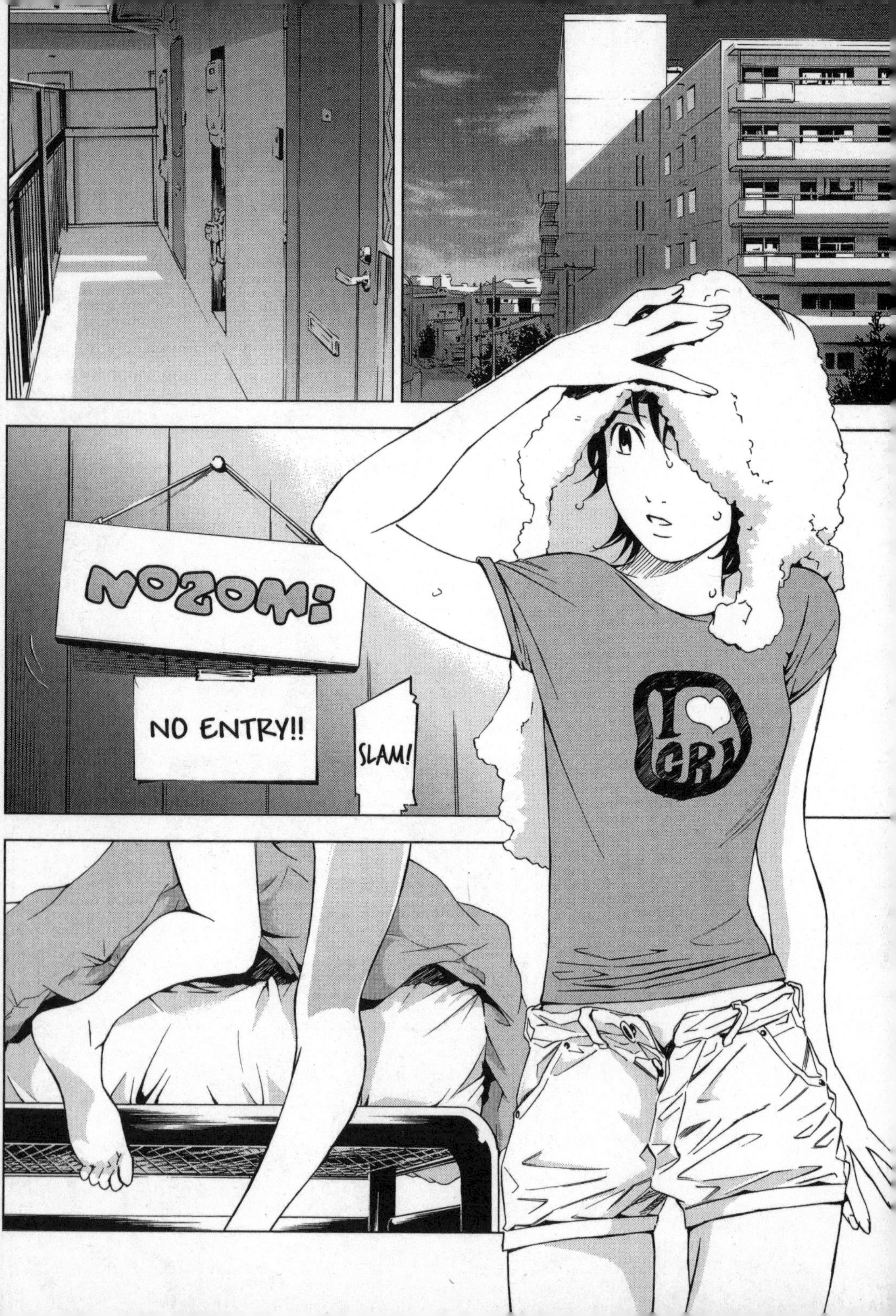

NOZOMI
NO ENTRY!!
SLAM!

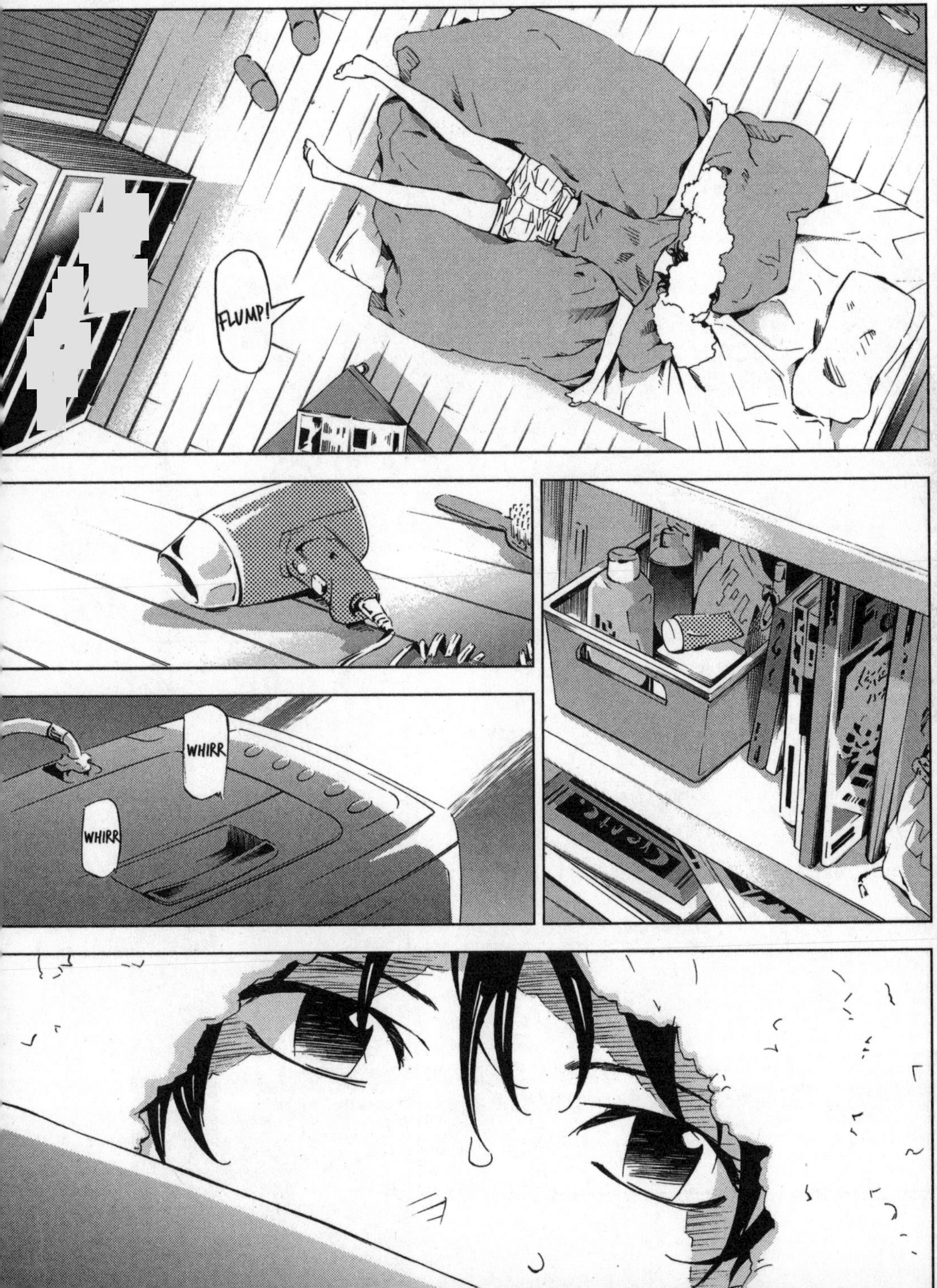
FLUMP!
WHIRR
WHIRR

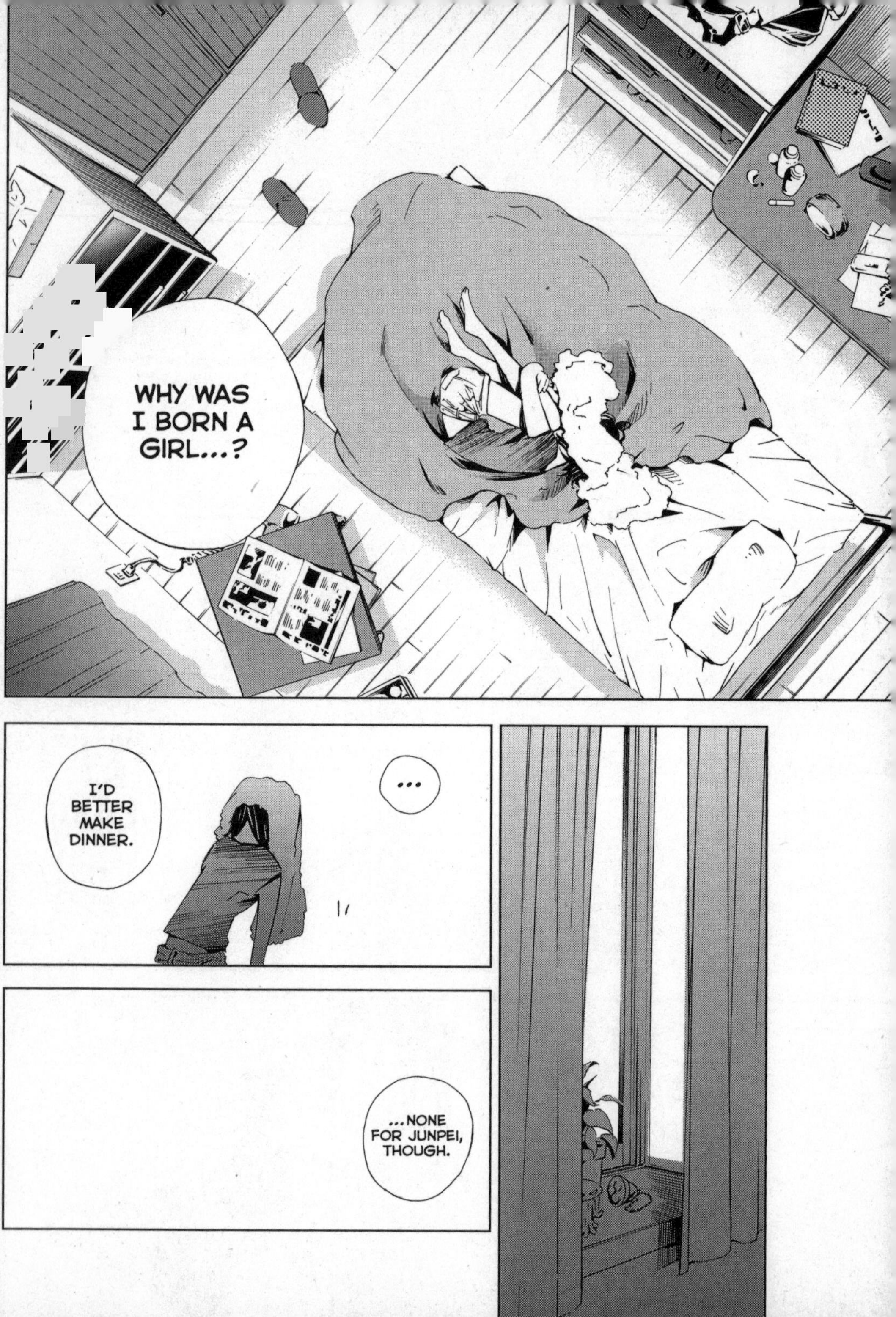
WHY WAS I BORN A GIRL...?
...
I'D BETTER MAKE DINNER.
...NONE FOR JUNPEI, THOUGH.

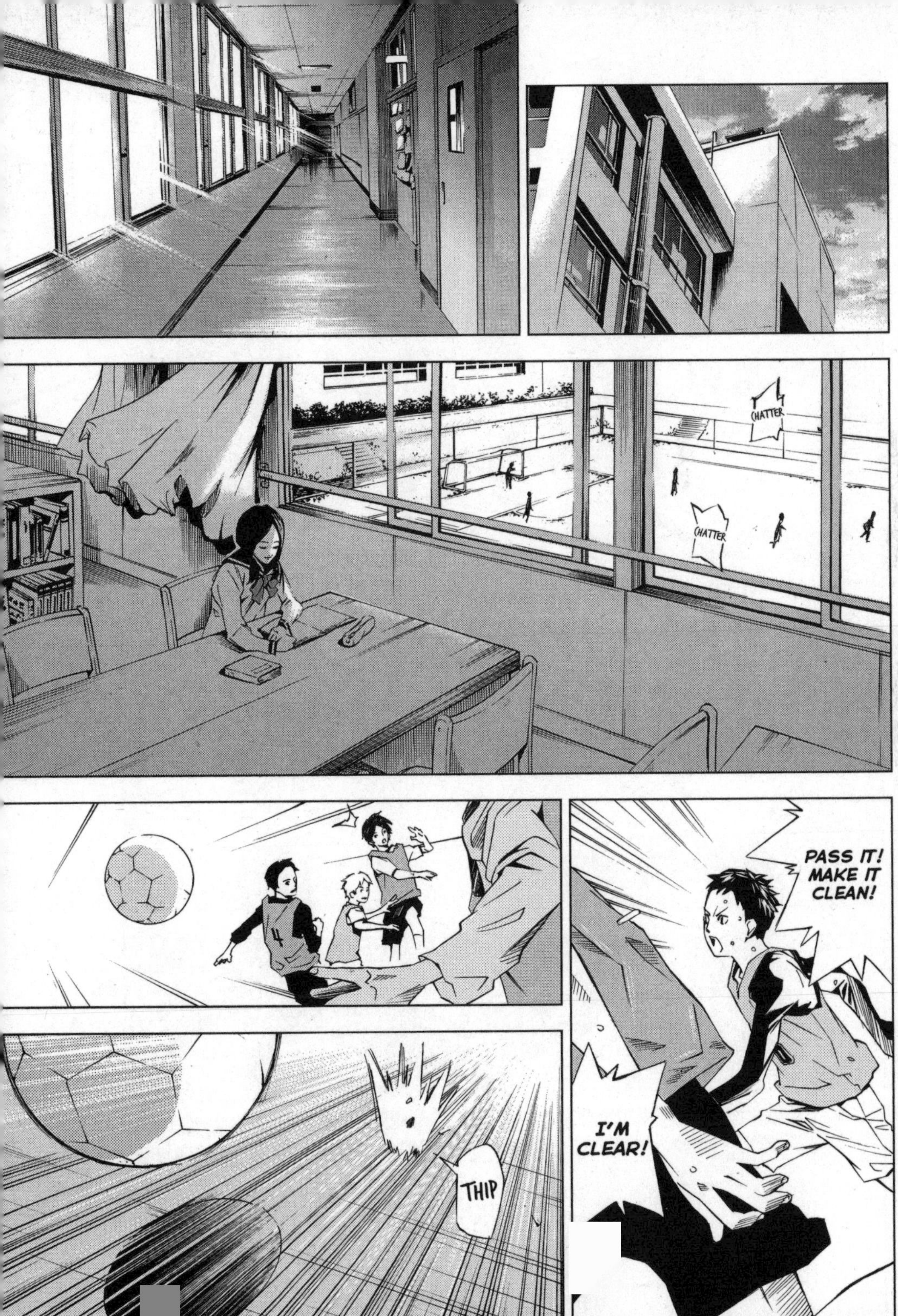
CHATTER
CHATTER
PASS IT! MAKE IT CLEAN!
I'M CLEAR!
THIP

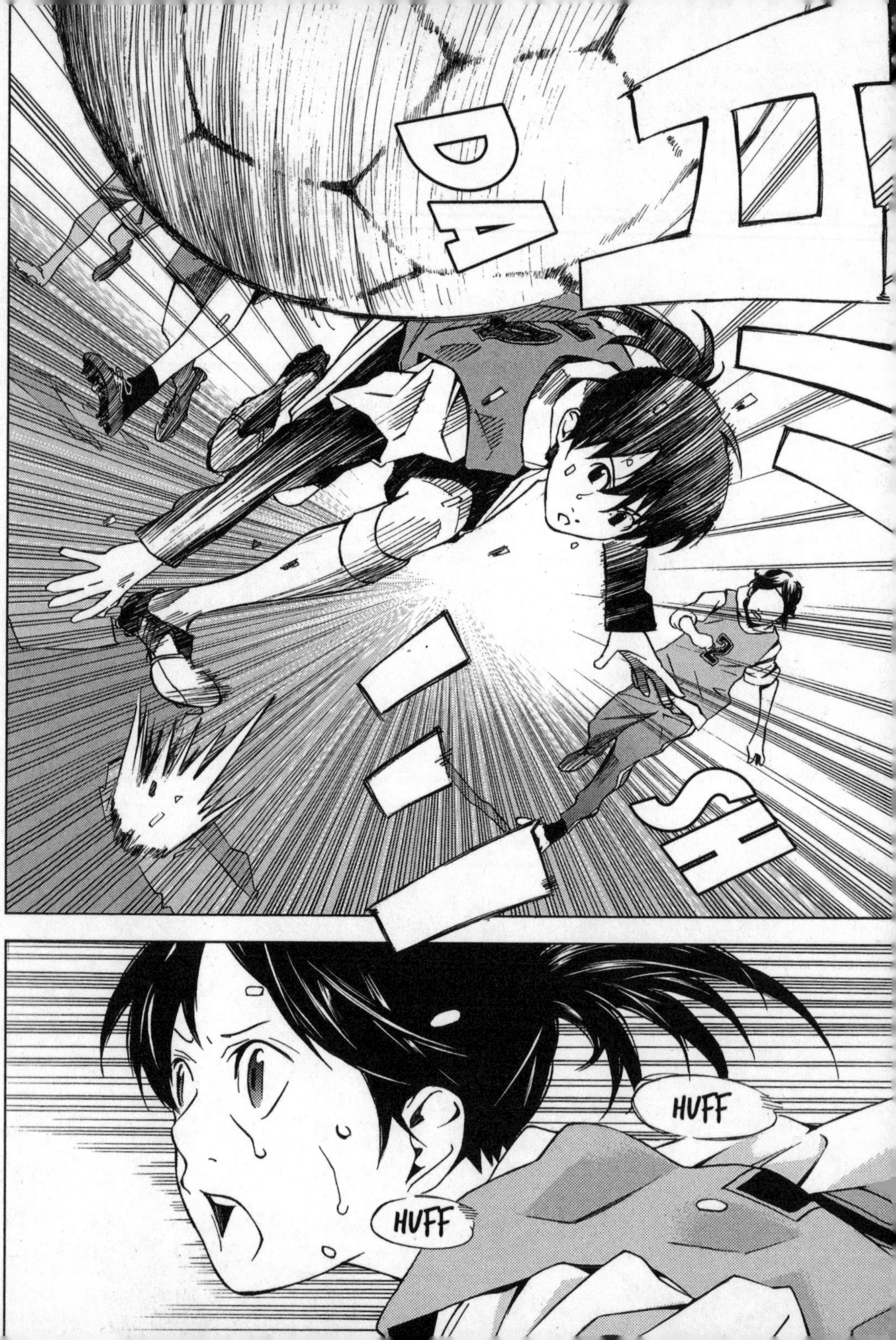
DASH
HUFF
HUFF

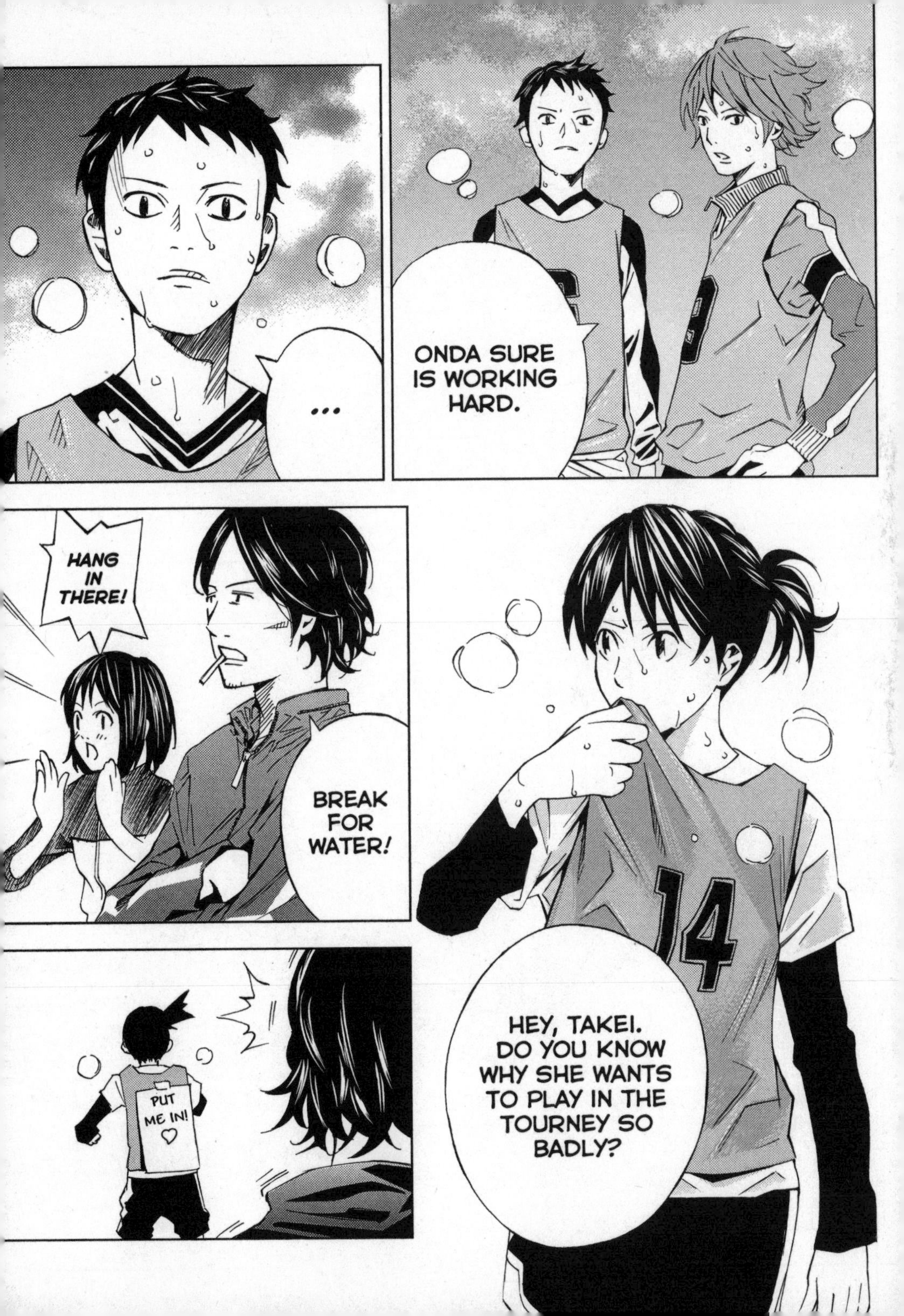
ONDA SURE IS WORKING HARD.
...
HEY, TAKEI. DO YOU KNOW WHY SHE WANTS TO PLAY IN THE TOURNEY SO BADLY?
BREAK FOR WATER!
HANG IN THERE!
PUT ME IN! ♡

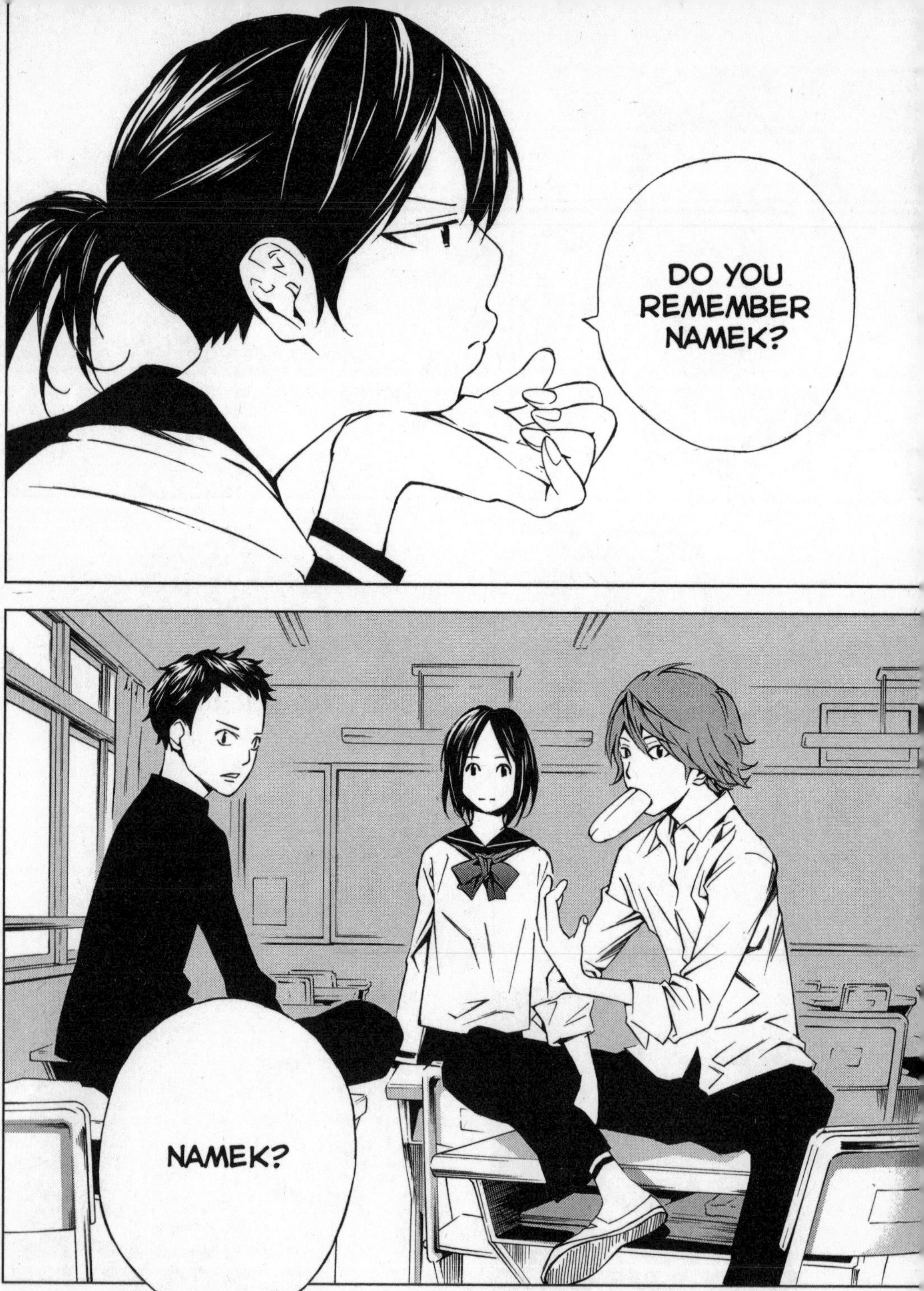
DO YOU REMEMBER NAMEK?
NAMEK?

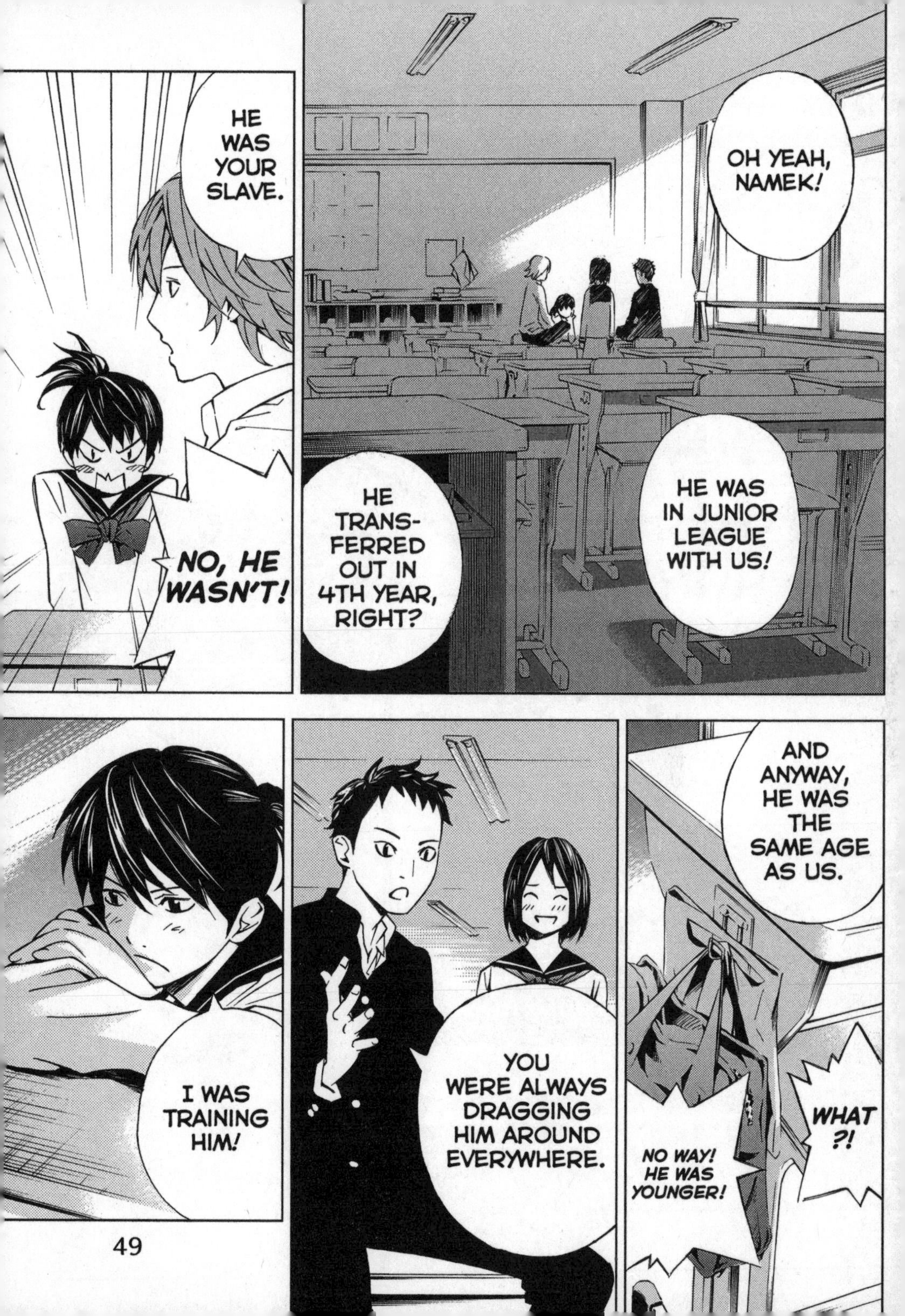
OH YEAH, NAMEK!
HE WAS IN JUNIOR LEAGUE WITH US!
HE TRANSFERRED OUT IN 4TH YEAR, RIGHT?
HE WAS YOUR SLAVE.
NO, HE WASN'T!
AND ANYWAY, HE WAS THE SAME AGE AS US.
WHAT?!
NO WAY! HE WAS YOUNGER!
YOU WERE ALWAYS DRAGGING HIM AROUND EVERYWHERE.
I WAS TRAINING HIM!

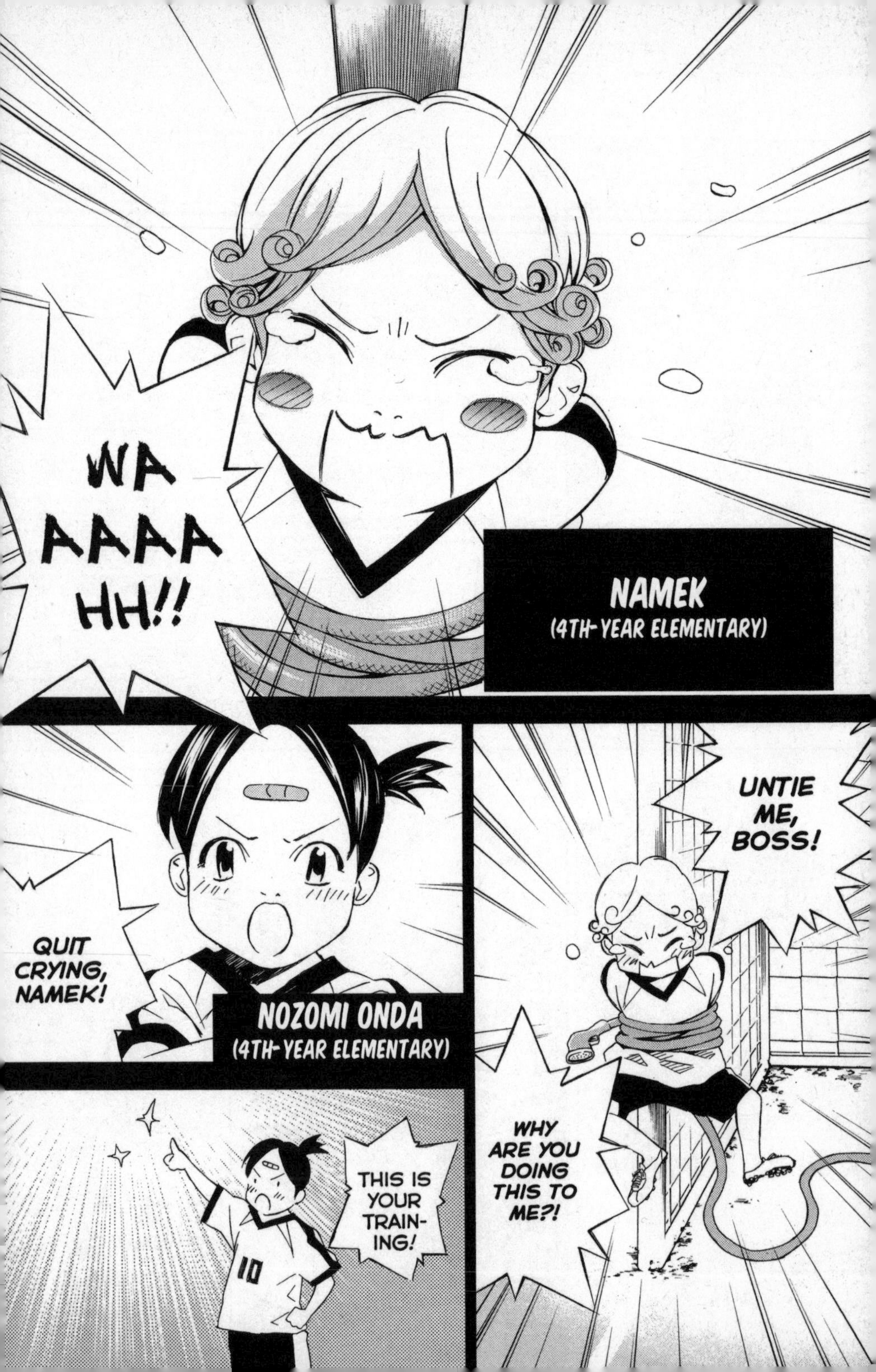
WA AAAA HH!!
NAMEK (4TH-YEAR ELEMENTARY)
UNTIE ME, BOSS!
WHY ARE YOU DOING THIS TO ME?!
QUIT CRYING, NAMEK!
NOZOMI ONDA (4TH-YEAR ELEMENTARY)
THIS IS YOUR TRAINING!

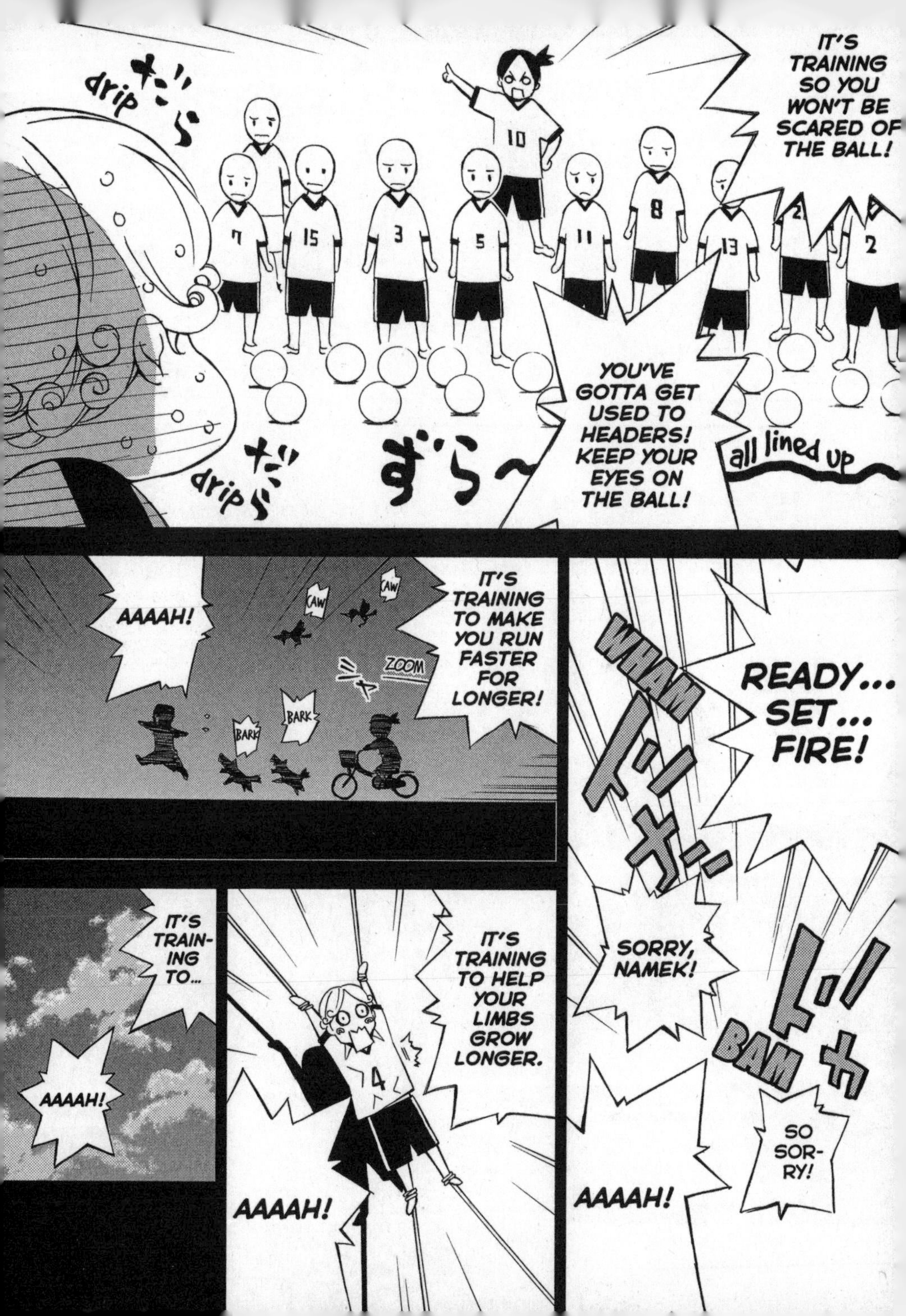
IT'S TRAINING SO YOU WON'T BE SCARED OF THE BALL!
YOU'VE GOTTA GET USED TO HEADERS! KEEP YOUR EYES ON THE BALL!
all lined up
ずら～
drip だら
drip だら
READY... SET... FIRE!
WHAM
SORRY, NAMEK!
BAM
SO SORRY!
AAAAH!
IT'S TRAINING TO MAKE YOU RUN FASTER FOR LONGER!
CAW
CAW
ZOOM
BARK
BARK
AAAAH!
IT'S TRAINING TO HELP YOUR LIMBS GROW LONGER.
AAAAH!
IT'S TRAIN-ING TO...
AAAAH!

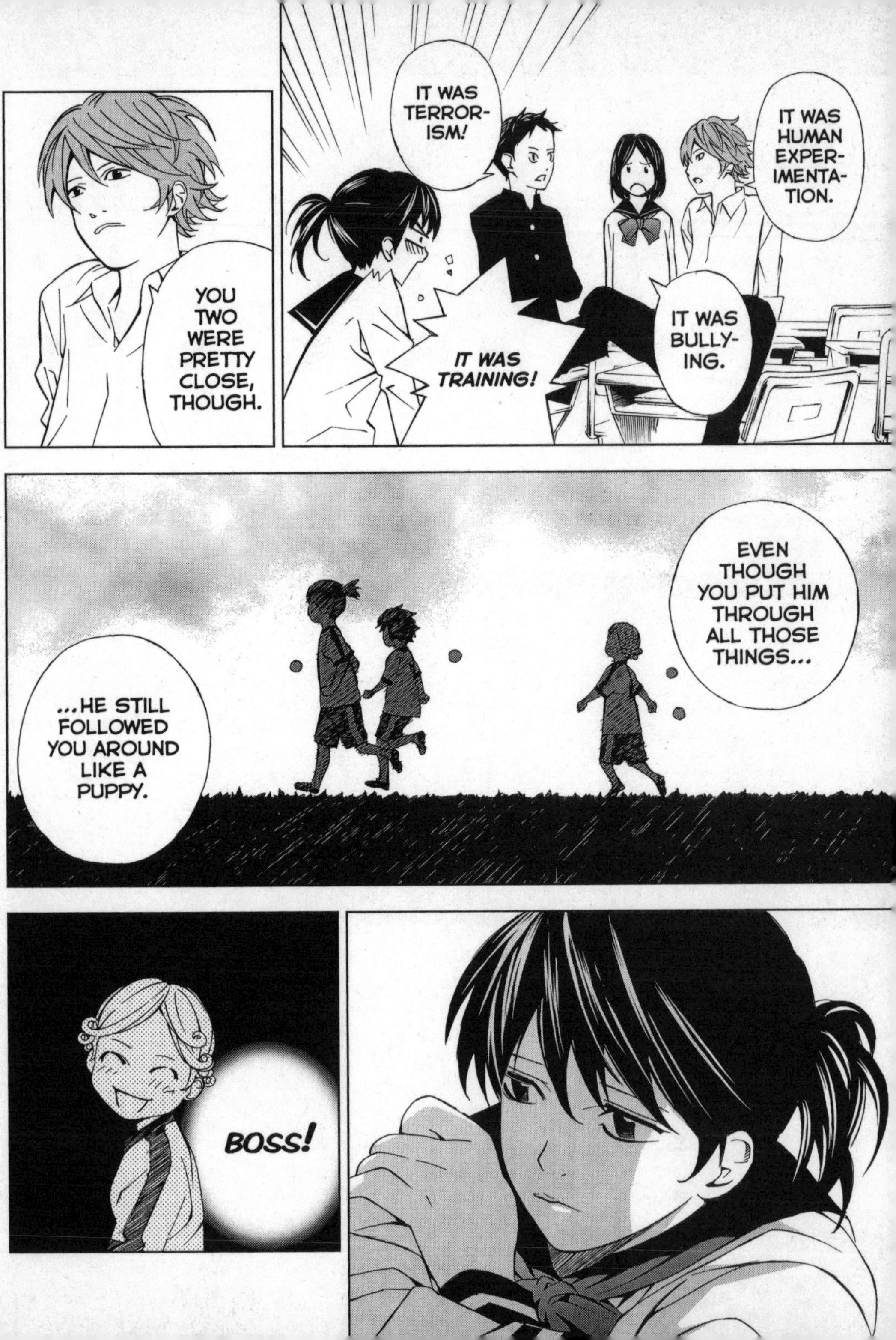
IT WAS HUMAN EXPERIMENTATION.
IT WAS TERRORISM!
IT WAS BULLYING.
IT WAS TRAINING!
YOU TWO WERE PRETTY CLOSE, THOUGH.
EVEN THOUGH YOU PUT HIM THROUGH ALL THOSE THINGS...
...HE STILL FOLLOWED YOU AROUND LIKE A PUPPY.
BOSS!

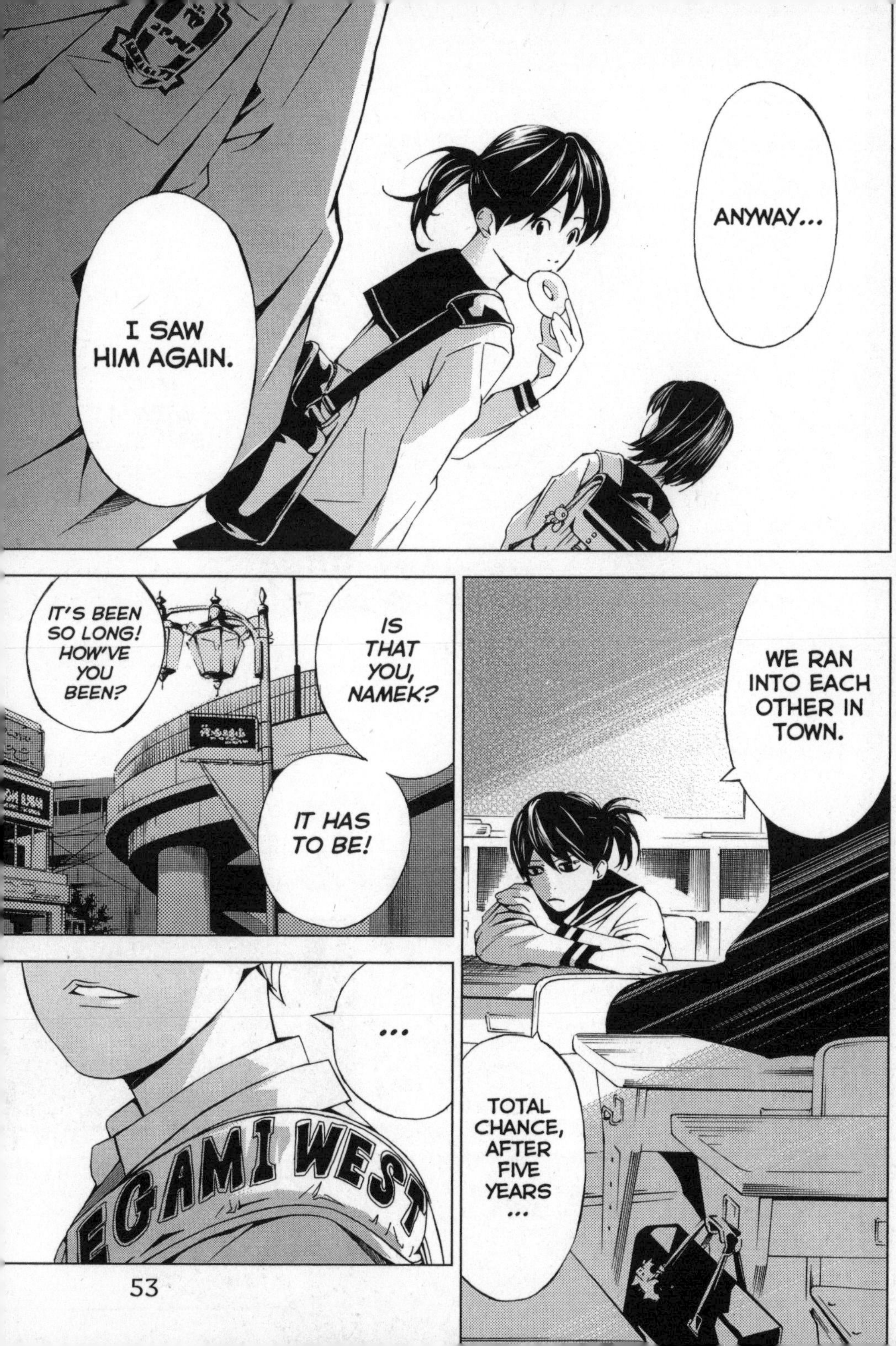
ANYWAY...
I SAW HIM AGAIN.
WE RAN INTO EACH OTHER IN TOWN.
TOTAL CHANCE, AFTER FIVE YEARS...
IS THAT YOU, NAMEK?
IT'S BEEN SO LONG! HOW'VE YOU BEEN?
IT HAS TO BE!
...
EGAMI WEST

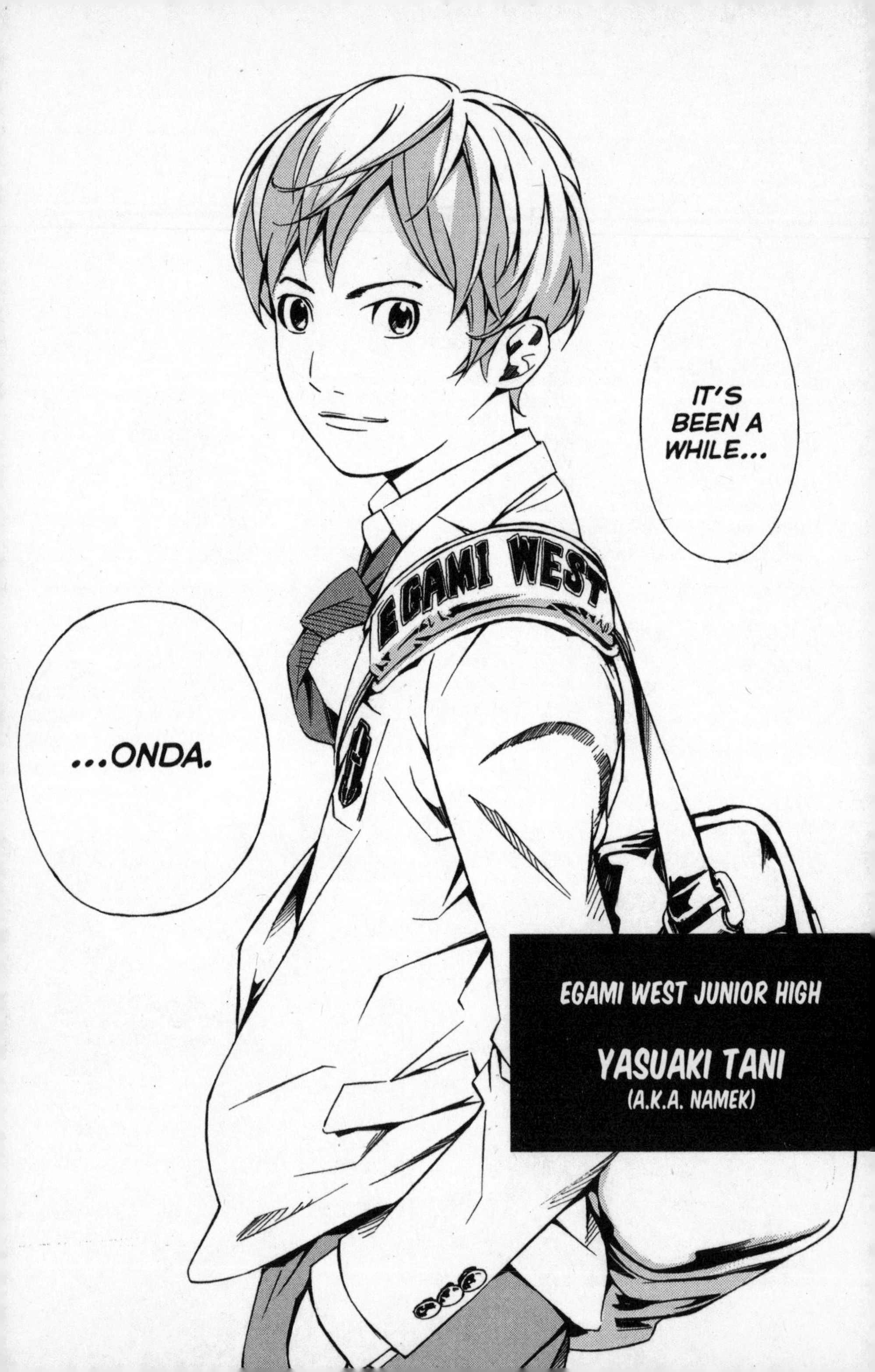
IT'S BEEN A WHILE...
...ONDA.
EGAMI WEST
EGAMI WEST JUNIOR HIGH
YASUAKI TANI
(A.K.A. NAMEK)

SAYONARA FOOTBALL

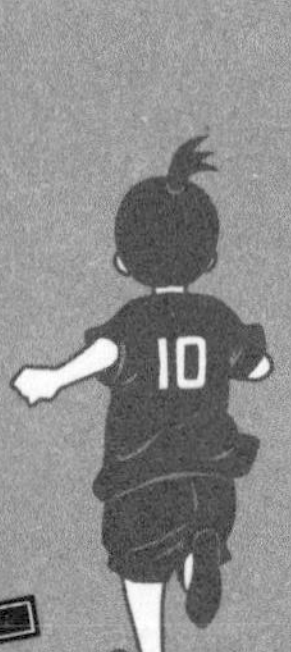
10

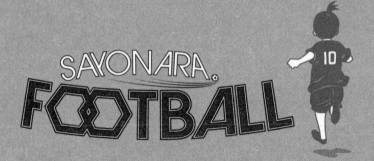

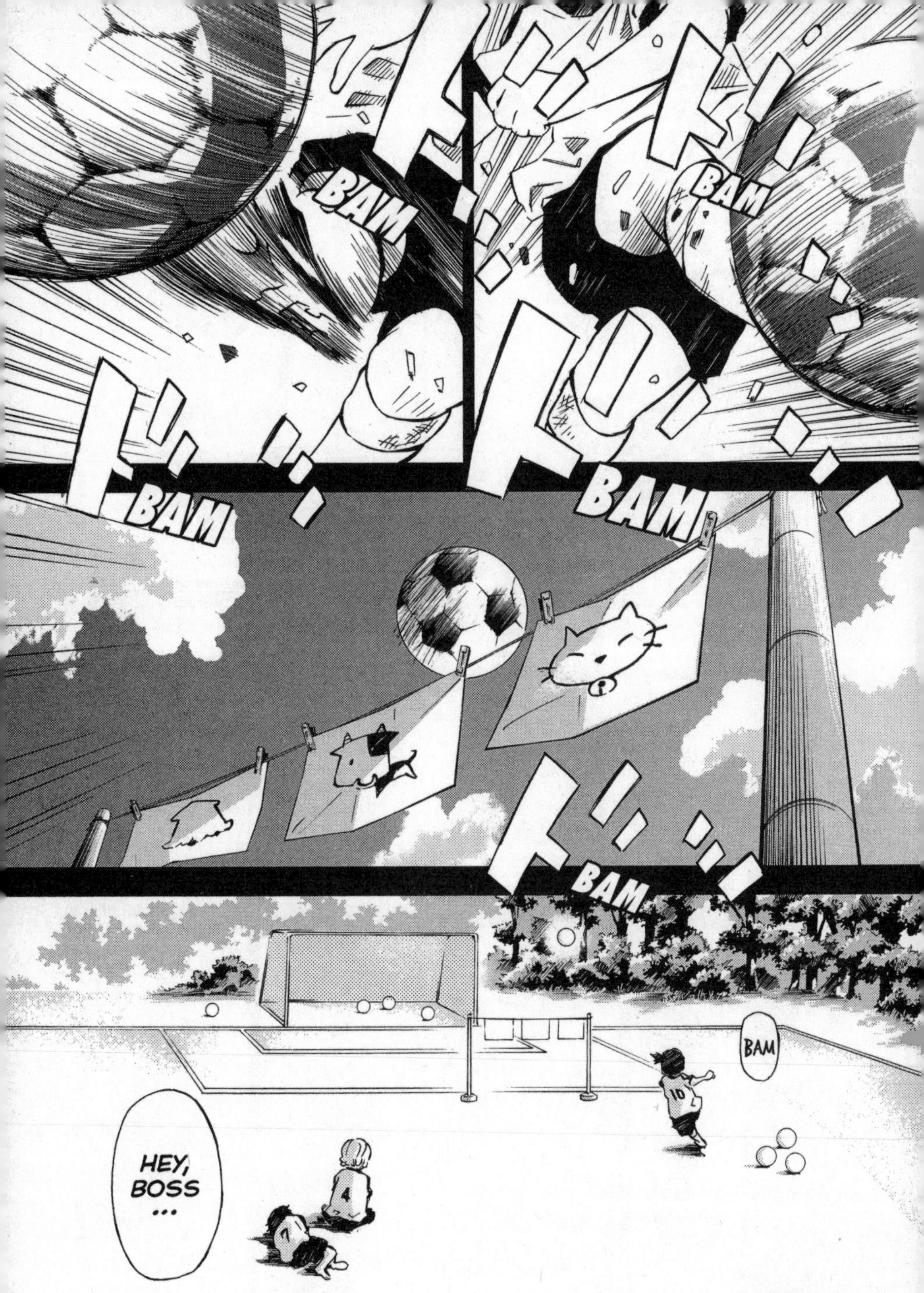
BAM
BAM
BAM
BAM
BAM
BAM
HEY, BOSS ...

Chapter 2
Then and Now

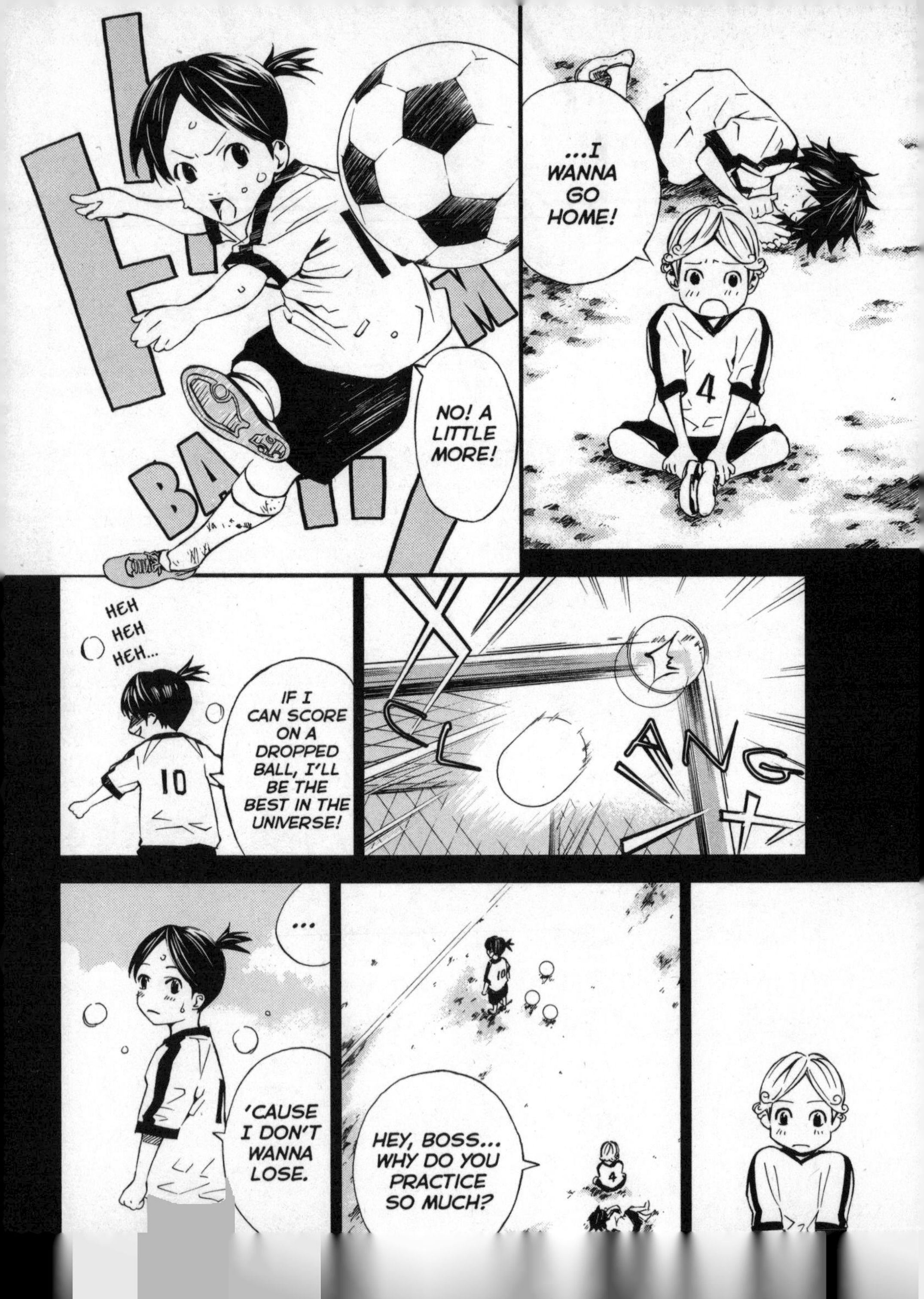
...I WANNA GO HOME!
NO! A LITTLE MORE!
CLANG
HEH HEH HEH...
IF I CAN SCORE ON A DROPPED BALL, I'LL BE THE BEST IN THE UNIVERSE!
HEY, BOSS... WHY DO YOU PRACTICE SO MUCH?
...
'CAUSE I DON'T WANNA LOSE.

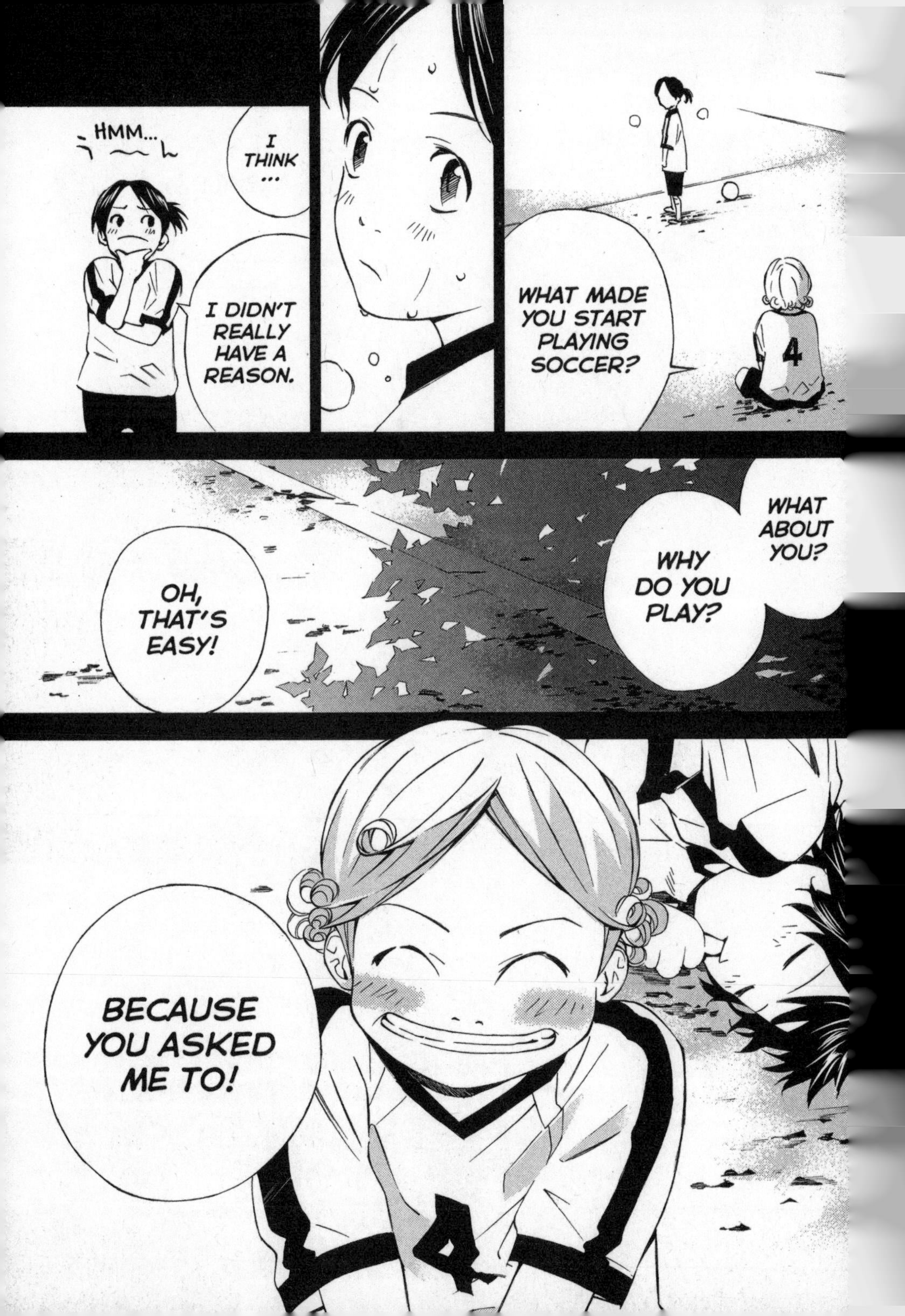
WHAT MADE YOU START PLAYING SOCCER?
HMM...
I THINK ...
I DIDN'T REALLY HAVE A REASON.
WHAT ABOUT YOU?
WHY DO YOU PLAY?
OH, THAT'S EASY!
BECAUSE YOU ASKED ME TO!

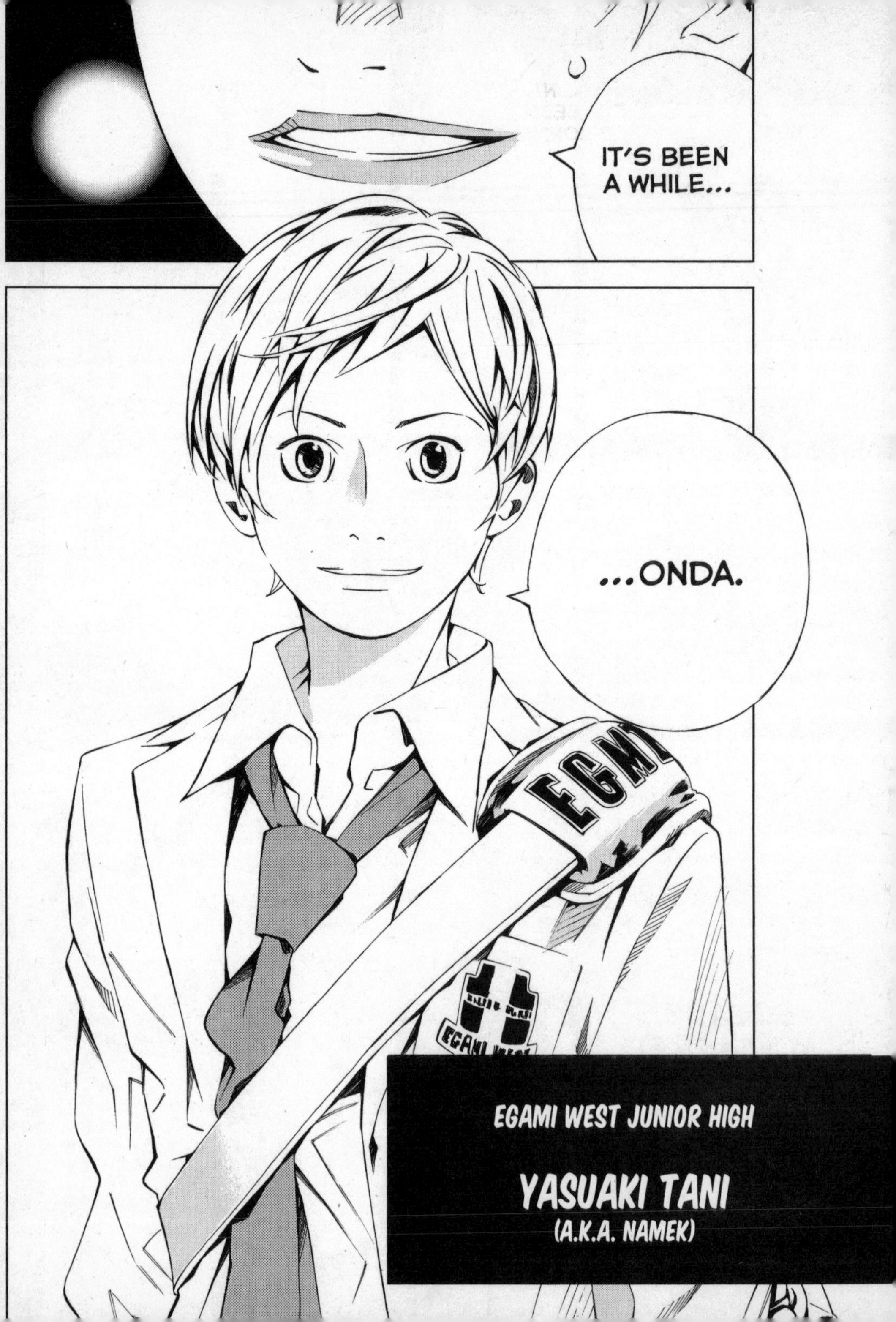
IT'S BEEN A WHILE...
...ONDA.
EGAMI WEST JUNIOR HIGH
YASUAKI TANI
(A.K.A. NAMEK)

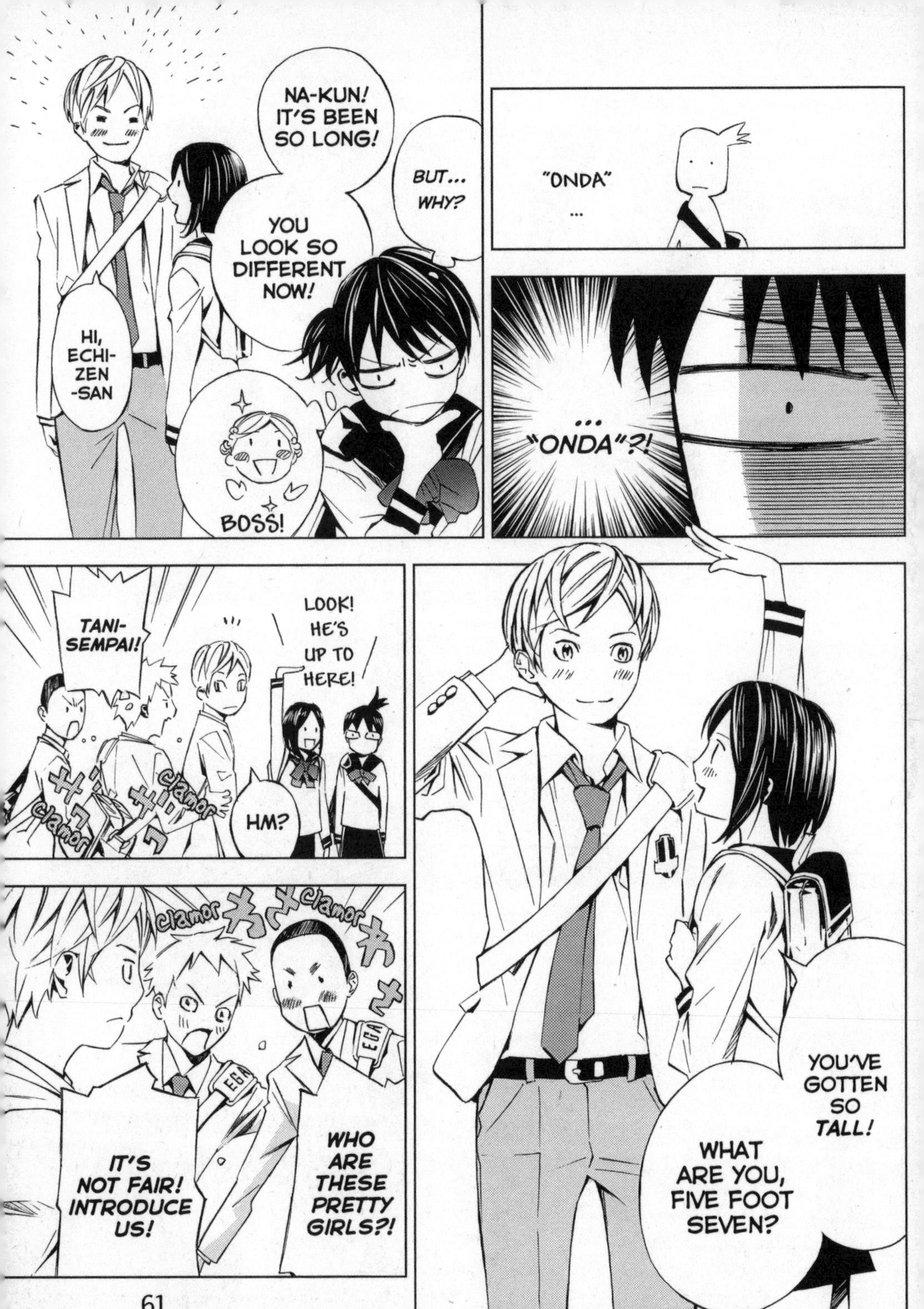
"ONDA"
...
... "ONDA"?!
BUT... WHY?
NA-KUN! IT'S BEEN SO LONG!
YOU LOOK SO DIFFERENT NOW!
HI, ECHI-ZEN -SAN
BOSS!
YOU'VE GOTTEN SO TALL!
WHAT ARE YOU, FIVE FOOT SEVEN?
LOOK! HE'S UP TO HERE!
TANI-SEMPAI!
HM?
clamor
clamor
clamor
clamor
WHO ARE THESE PRETTY GIRLS?!
IT'S NOT FAIR! INTRODUCE US!

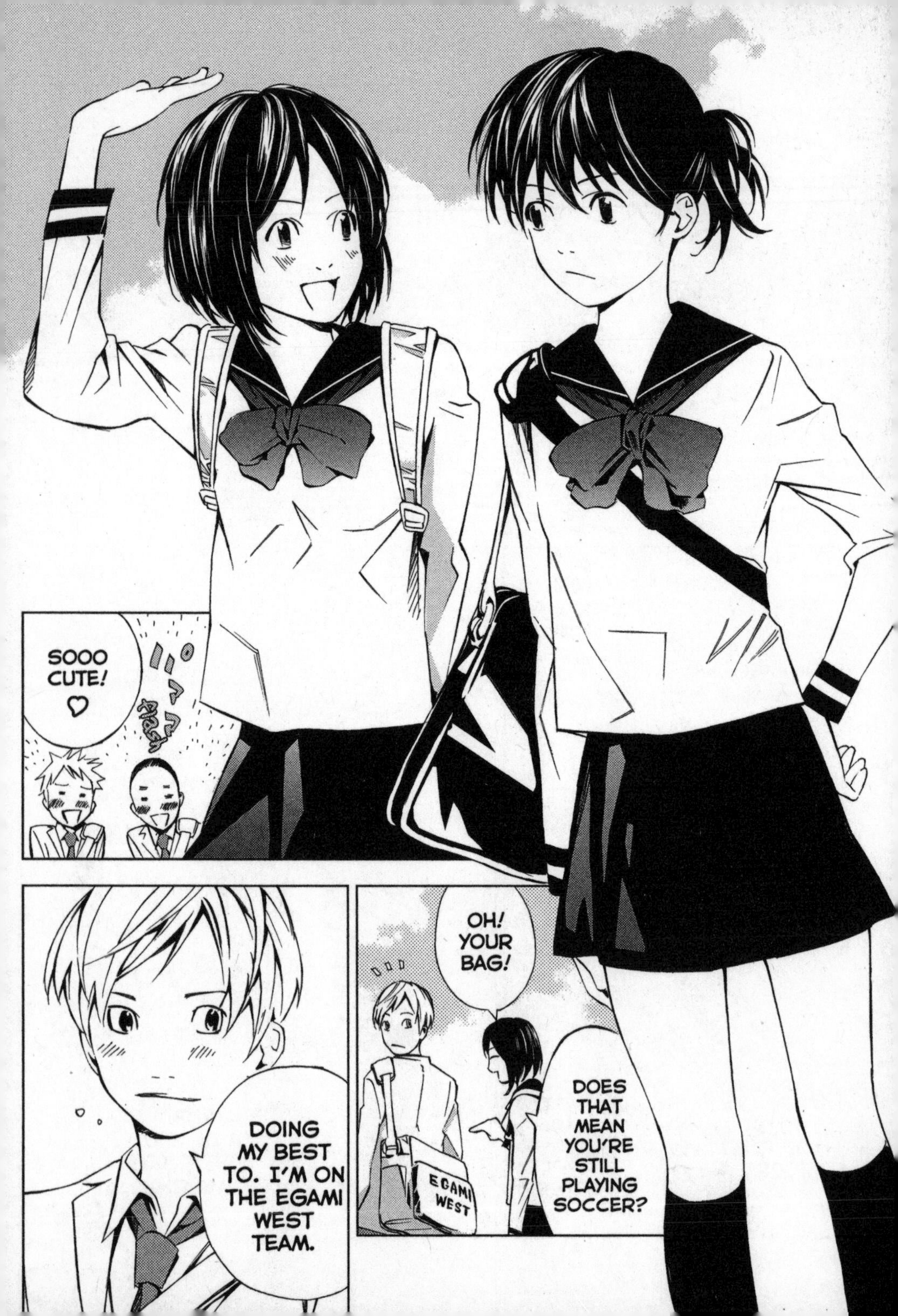
SOOO CUTE! ♡
OH! YOUR BAG!
DOES THAT MEAN YOU'RE STILL PLAYING SOCCER?
EGAMI WEST
DOING MY BEST TO. I'M ON THE EGAMI WEST TEAM.

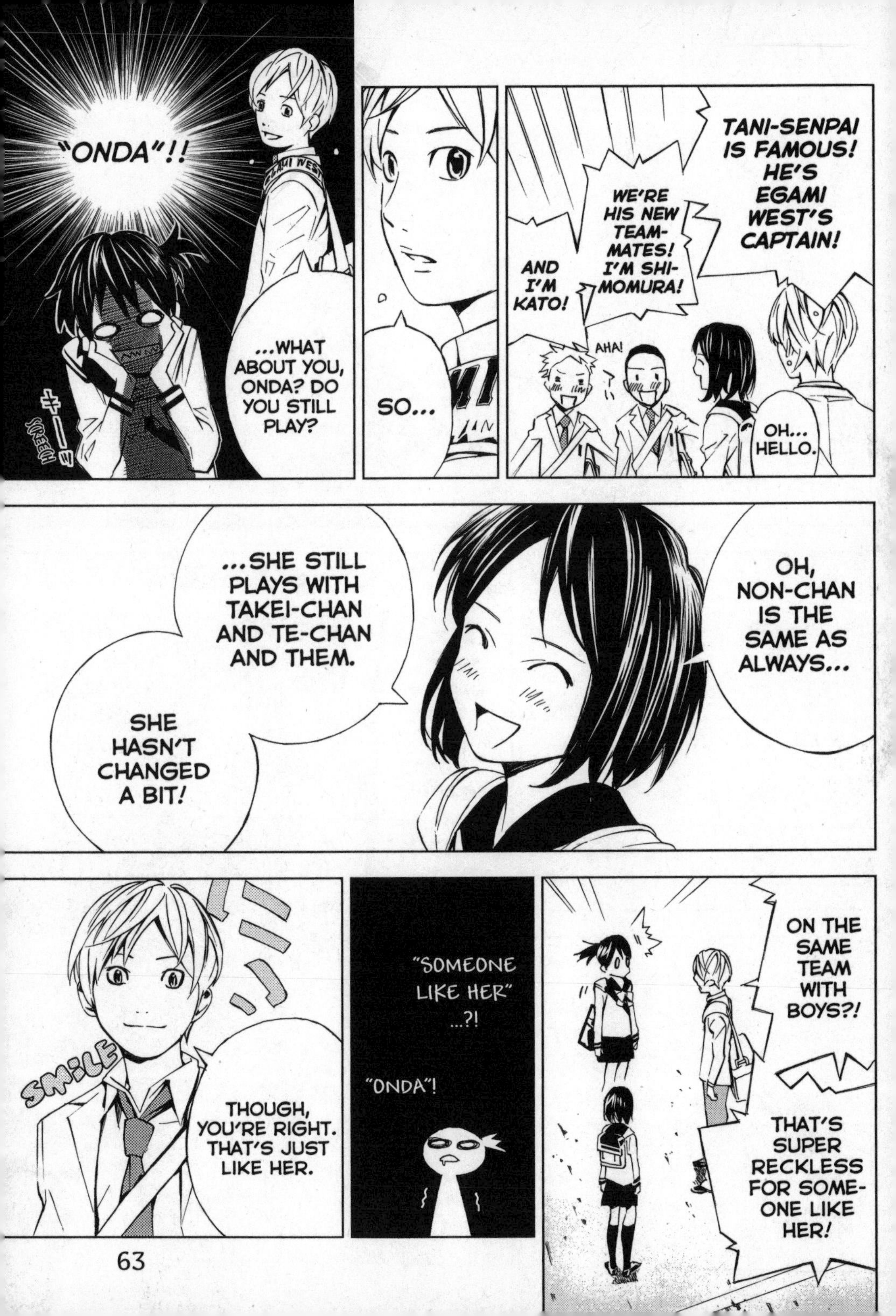
TANI-SENPAI IS FAMOUS! HE'S EGAMI WEST'S CAPTAIN!
WE'RE HIS NEW TEAM-MATES! I'M SHI-MOMURA!
AND I'M KATO!
AHA!
OH... HELLO.
SO...
...WHAT ABOUT YOU, ONDA? DO YOU STILL PLAY?
"ONDA"!!
SCREECH
OH, NON-CHAN IS THE SAME AS ALWAYS...
...SHE STILL PLAYS WITH TAKEI-CHAN AND TE-CHAN AND THEM.
SHE HASN'T CHANGED A BIT!
ON THE SAME TEAM WITH BOYS?!
THAT'S SUPER RECKLESS FOR SOME-ONE LIKE HER!
"SOMEONE LIKE HER" ...?!
"ONDA"!
SMILE
THOUGH, YOU'RE RIGHT. THAT'S JUST LIKE HER.

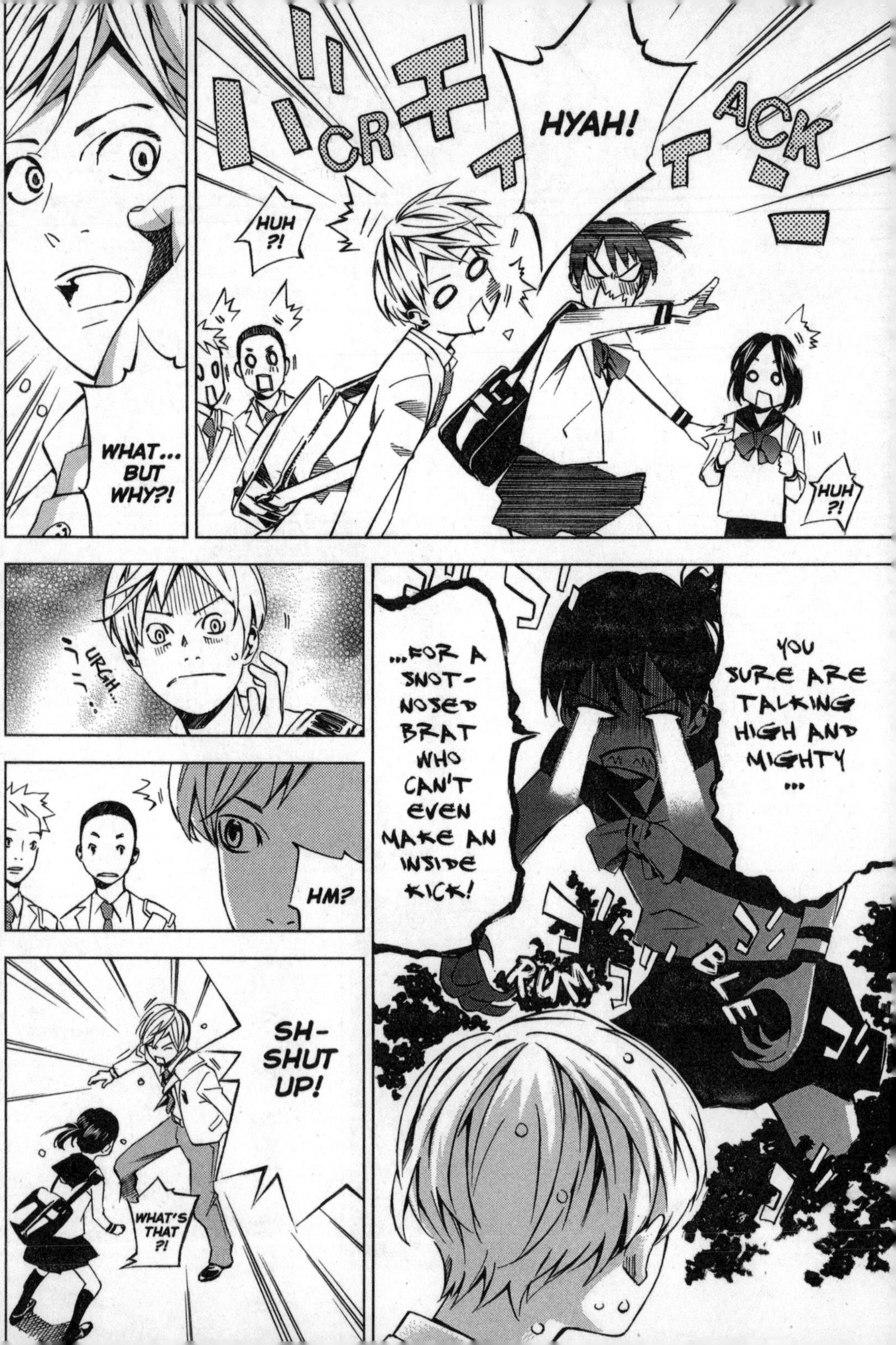

CR
ACK
HYAH!
HUH ?!
HUH ?!
WHAT... BUT WHY?!
YOU SURE ARE TALKING HIGH AND MIGHTY...
...FOR A SNOT-NOSED BRAT WHO CAN'T EVEN MAKE AN INSIDE KICK!
RUM
BLE
URGH...
HM?
SH-SHUT UP!
WHAT'S THAT ?!

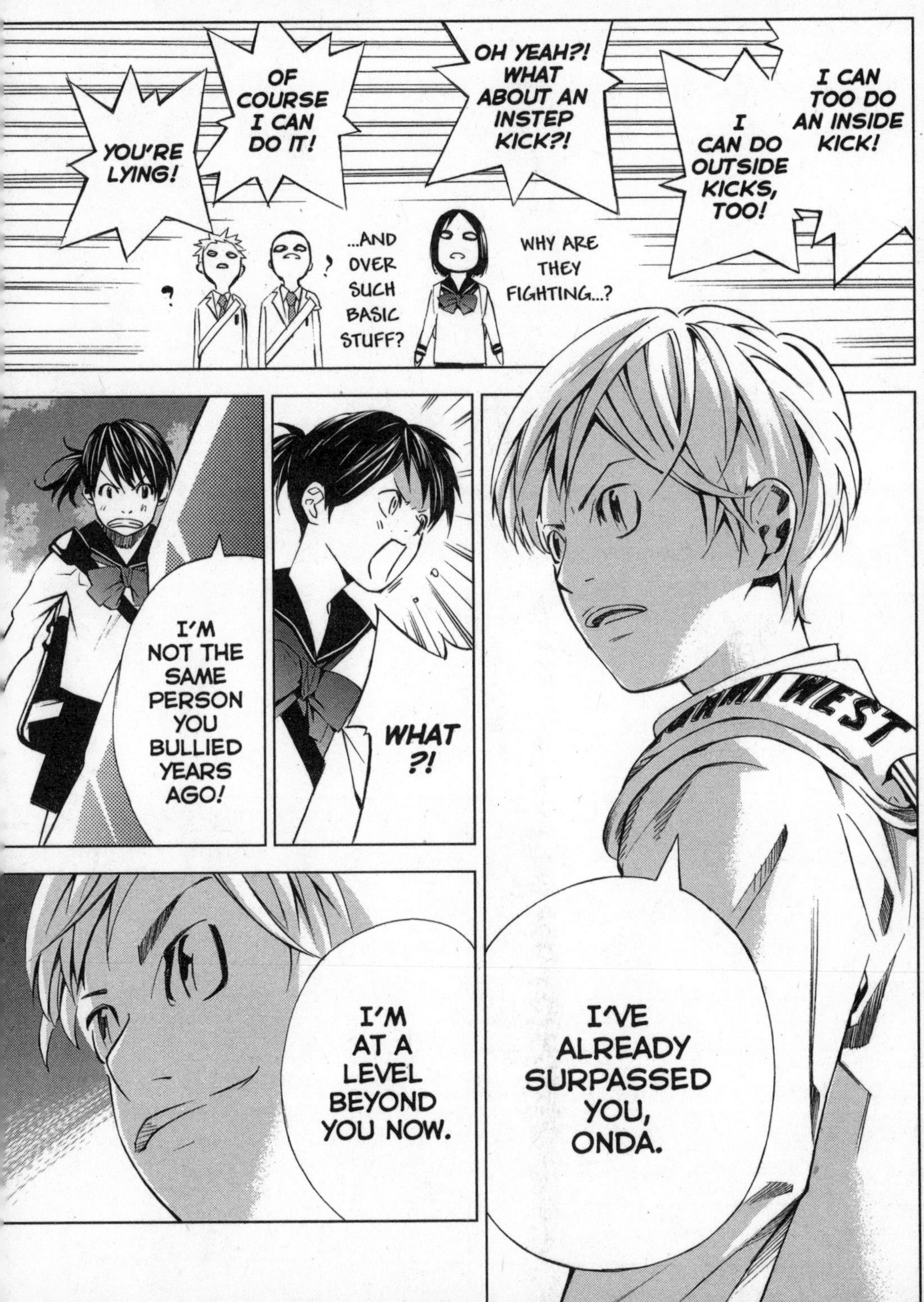
I CAN TOO DO AN INSIDE KICK!
I CAN DO OUTSIDE KICKS, TOO!
OH YEAH?! WHAT ABOUT AN INSTEP KICK?!
OF COURSE I CAN DO IT!
YOU'RE LYING!
WHY ARE THEY FIGHTING...?
...AND OVER SUCH BASIC STUFF?
I'VE ALREADY SURPASSED YOU, ONDA.
WHAT?!
I'M NOT THE SAME PERSON YOU BULLIED YEARS AGO!
I'M AT A LEVEL BEYOND YOU NOW.

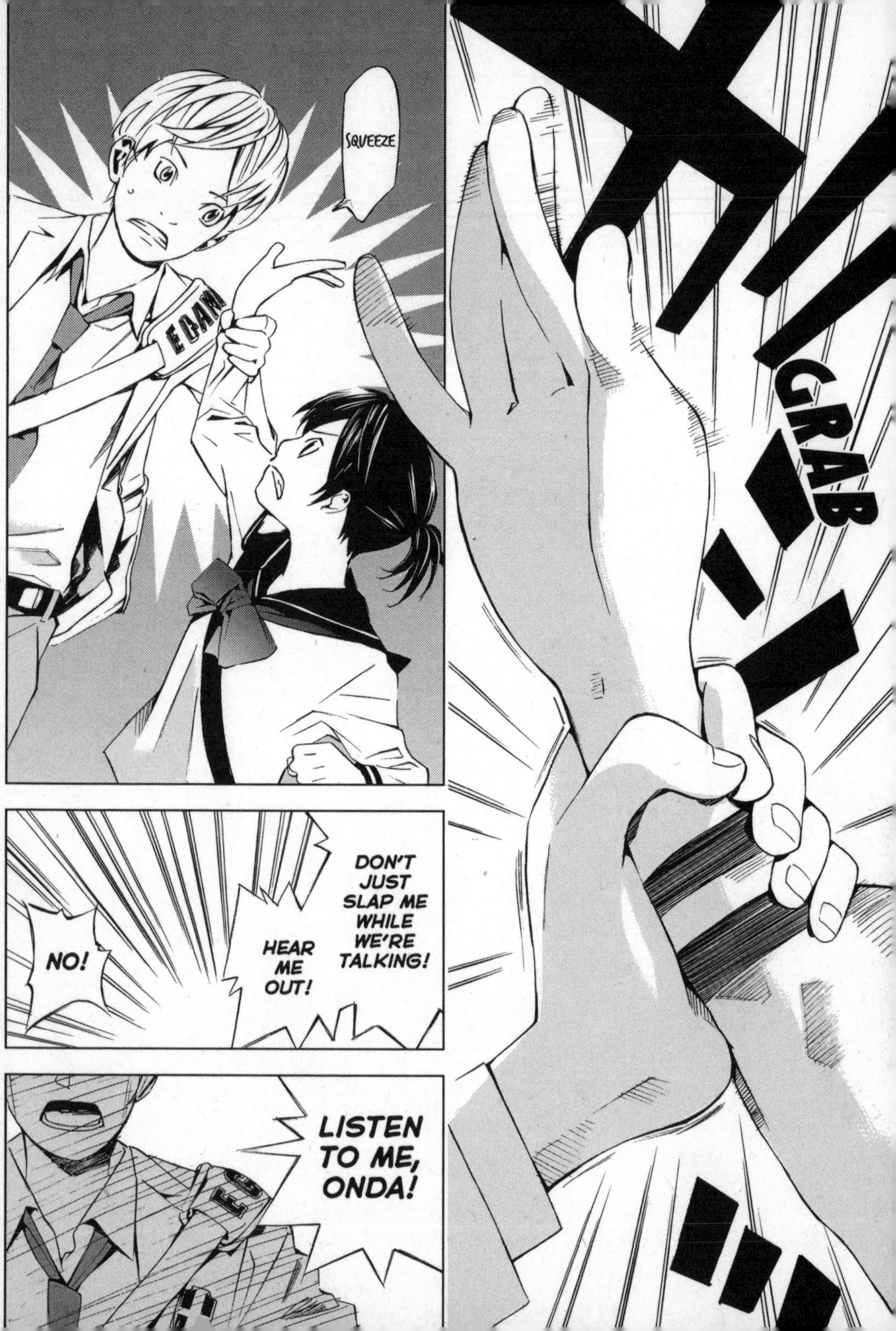
GRAB
SQUEEZE
DON'T JUST SLAP ME WHILE WE'RE TALKING!
HEAR ME OUT!
NO!
LISTEN TO ME, ONDA!

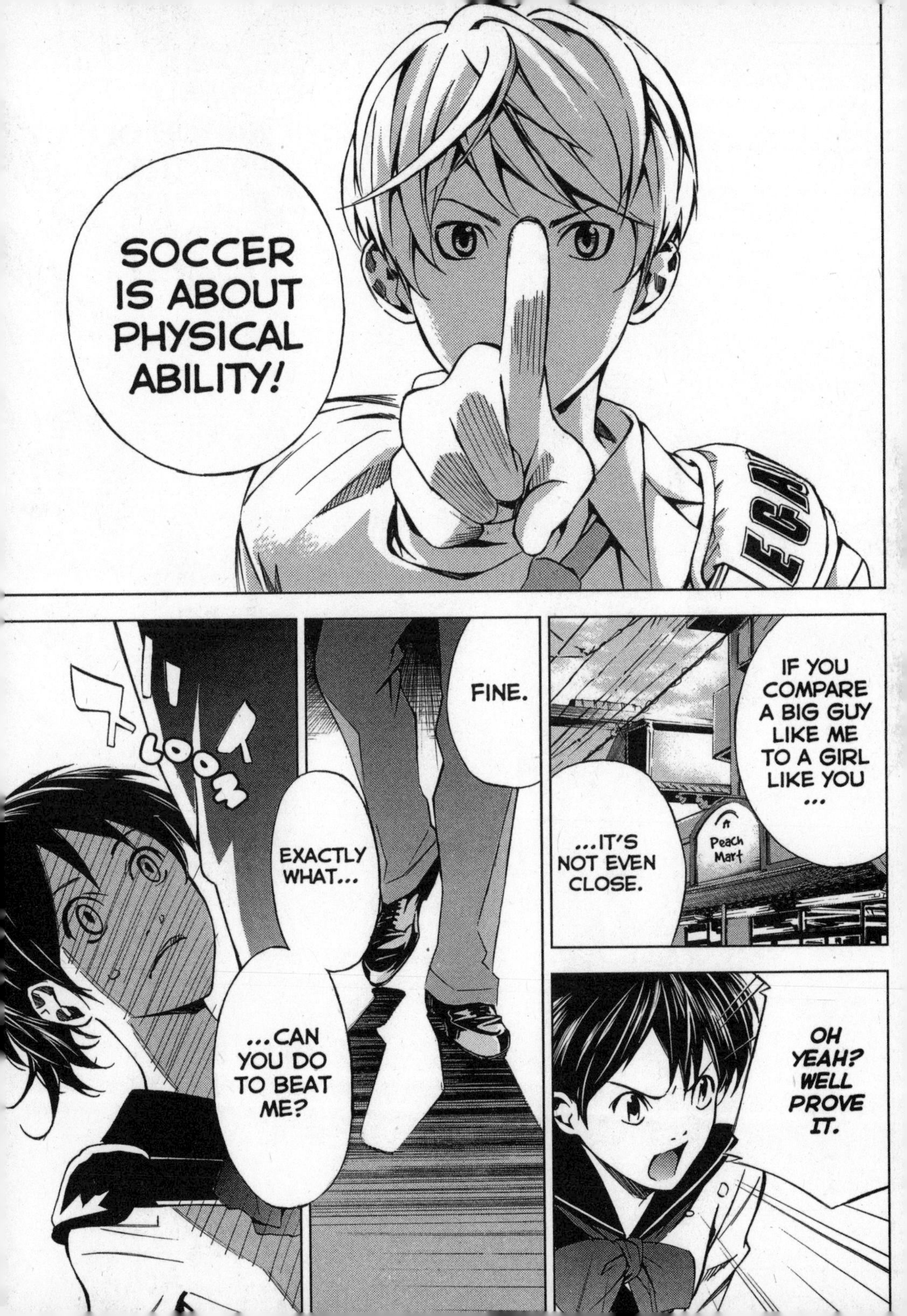
SOCCER IS ABOUT PHYSICAL ABILITY!
IF YOU COMPARE A BIG GUY LIKE ME TO A GIRL LIKE YOU ...
...IT'S NOT EVEN CLOSE.
Peach Mart
OH YEAH? WELL PROVE IT.
FINE.
EXACTLY WHAT...
...CAN YOU DO TO BEAT ME?
LOOM

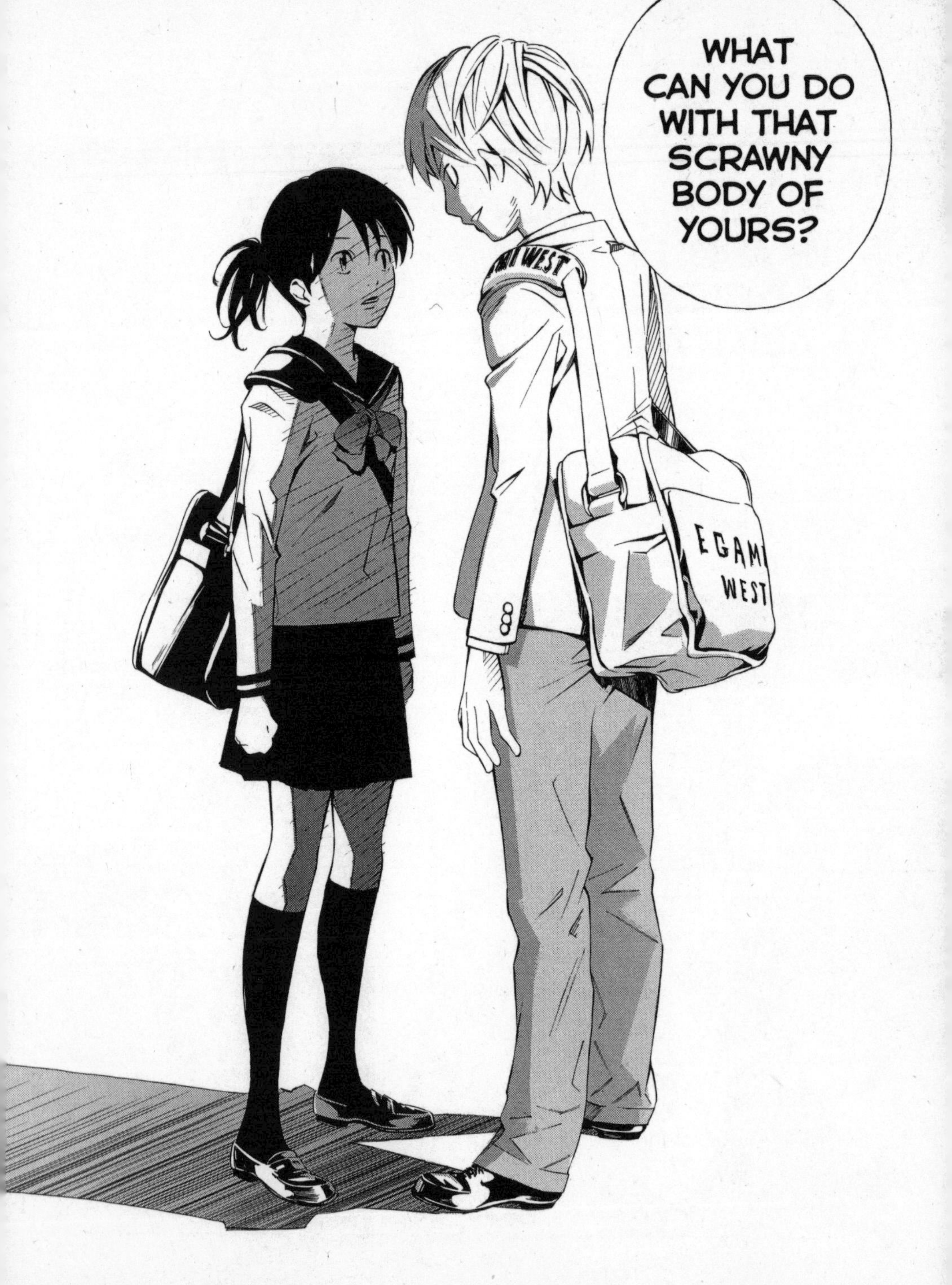
WHAT CAN YOU DO WITH THAT SCRAWNY BODY OF YOURS?
EGAMI WEST

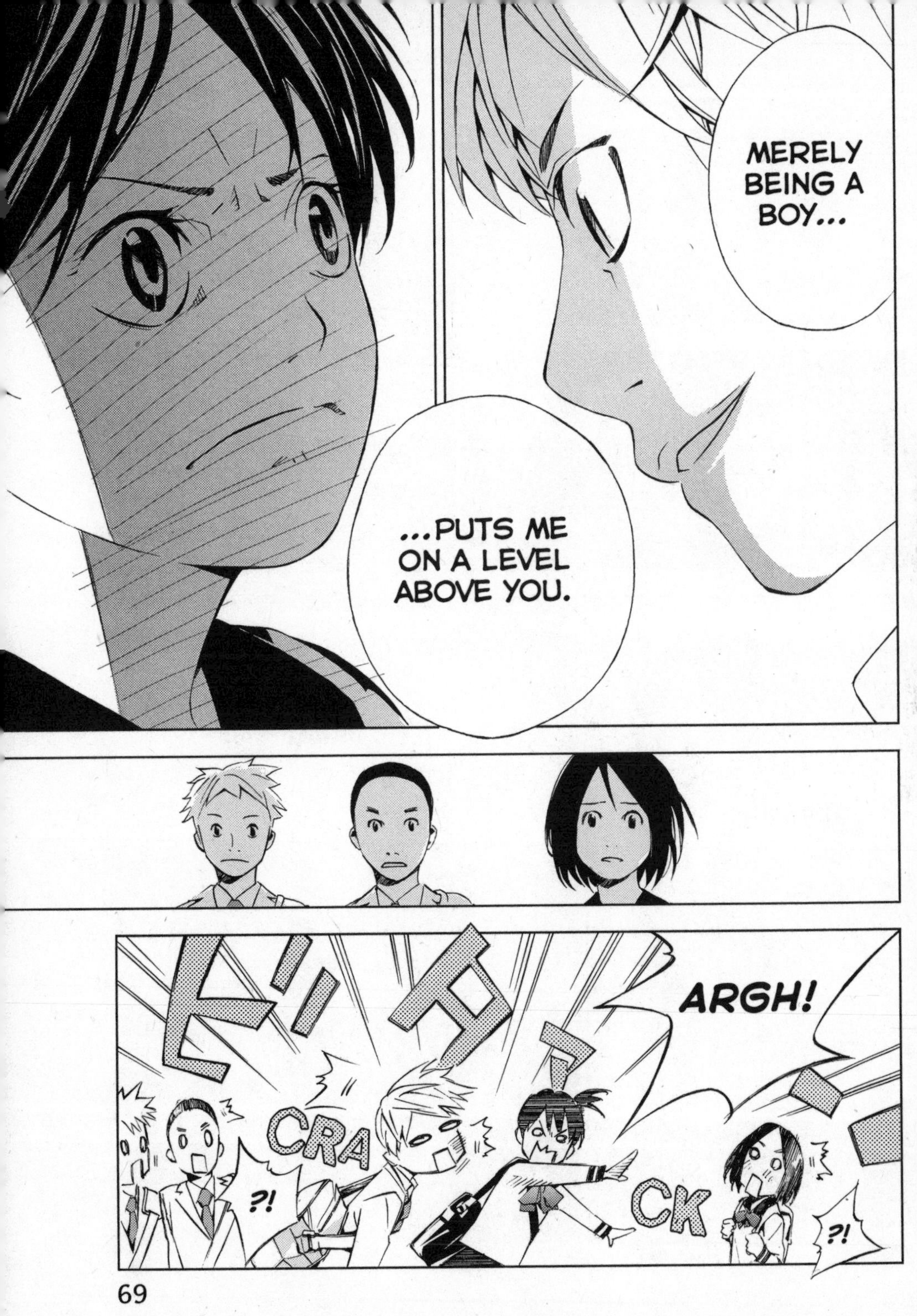
MERELY BEING A BOY...
...PUTS ME ON A LEVEL ABOVE YOU.
ARGH!
CRACK
?!
?!

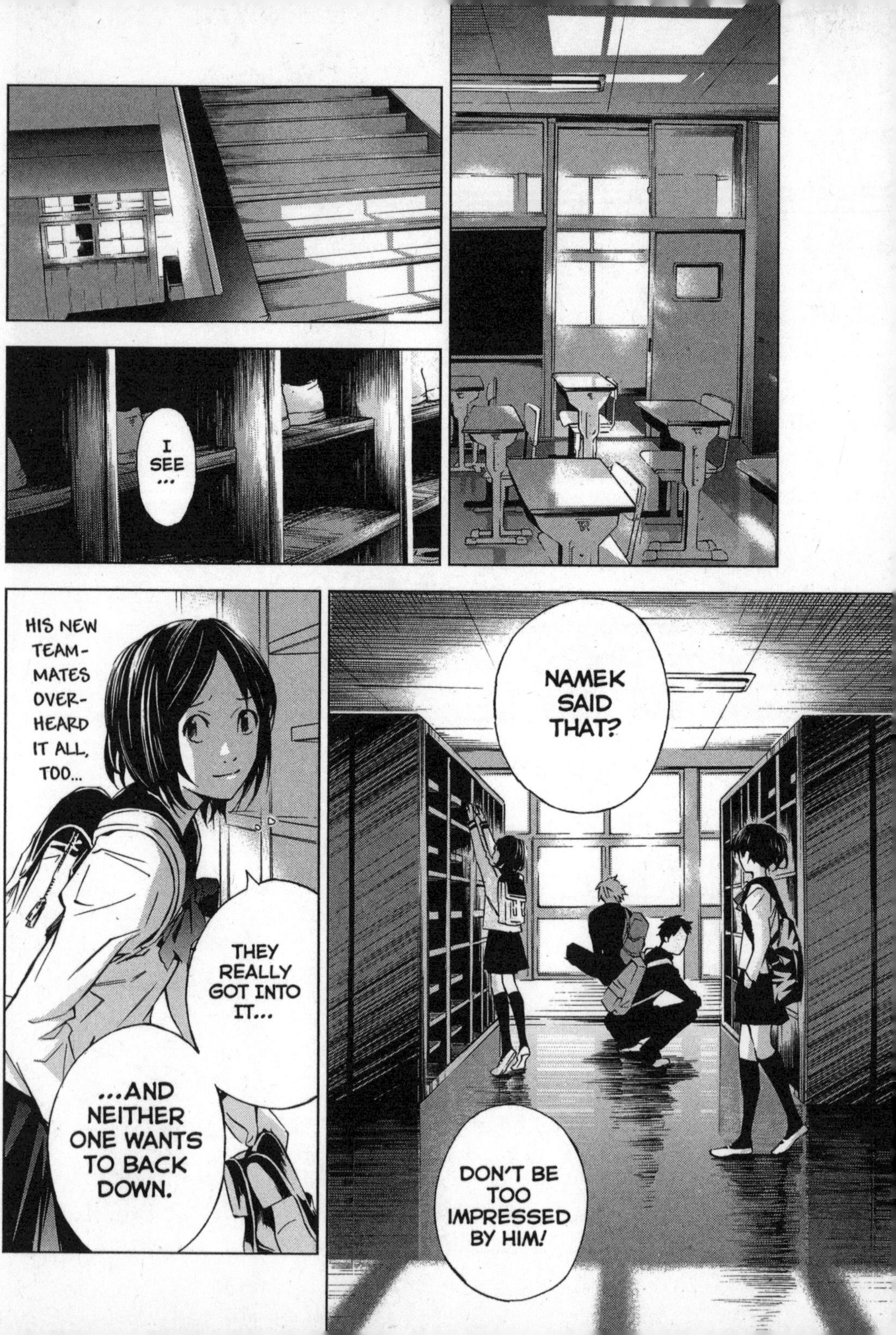
I SEE...
NAMEK SAID THAT?
DON'T BE TOO IMPRESSED BY HIM!
HIS NEW TEAM-MATES OVER-HEARD IT ALL, TOO...
THEY REALLY GOT INTO IT...
...AND NEITHER ONE WANTS TO BACK DOWN.

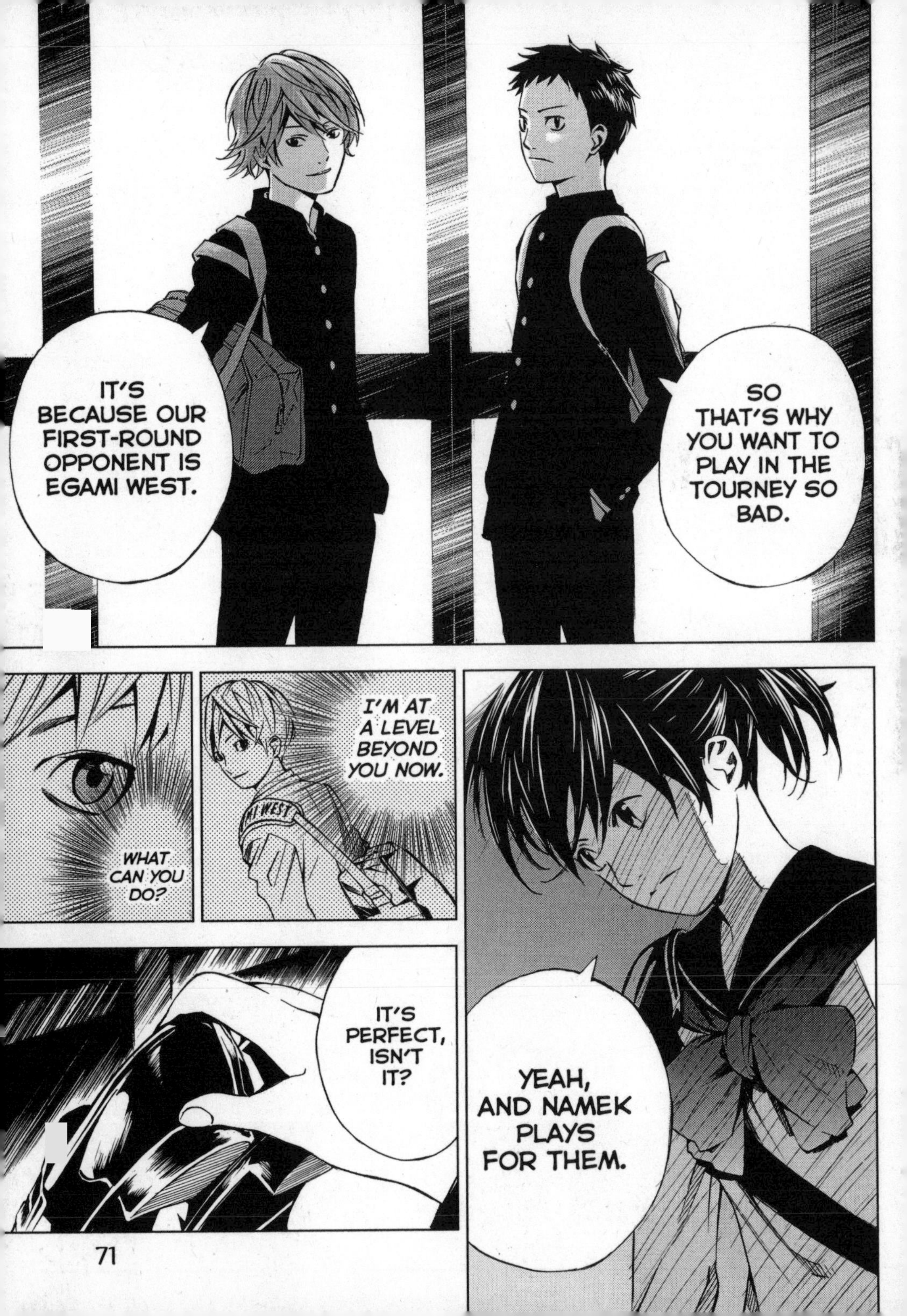
SO THAT'S WHY YOU WANT TO PLAY IN THE TOURNEY SO BAD.
IT'S BECAUSE OUR FIRST-ROUND OPPONENT IS EGAMI WEST.
YEAH, AND NAMEK PLAYS FOR THEM.
I'M AT A LEVEL BEYOND YOU NOW.
WHAT CAN YOU DO?
IT'S PERFECT, ISN'T IT?

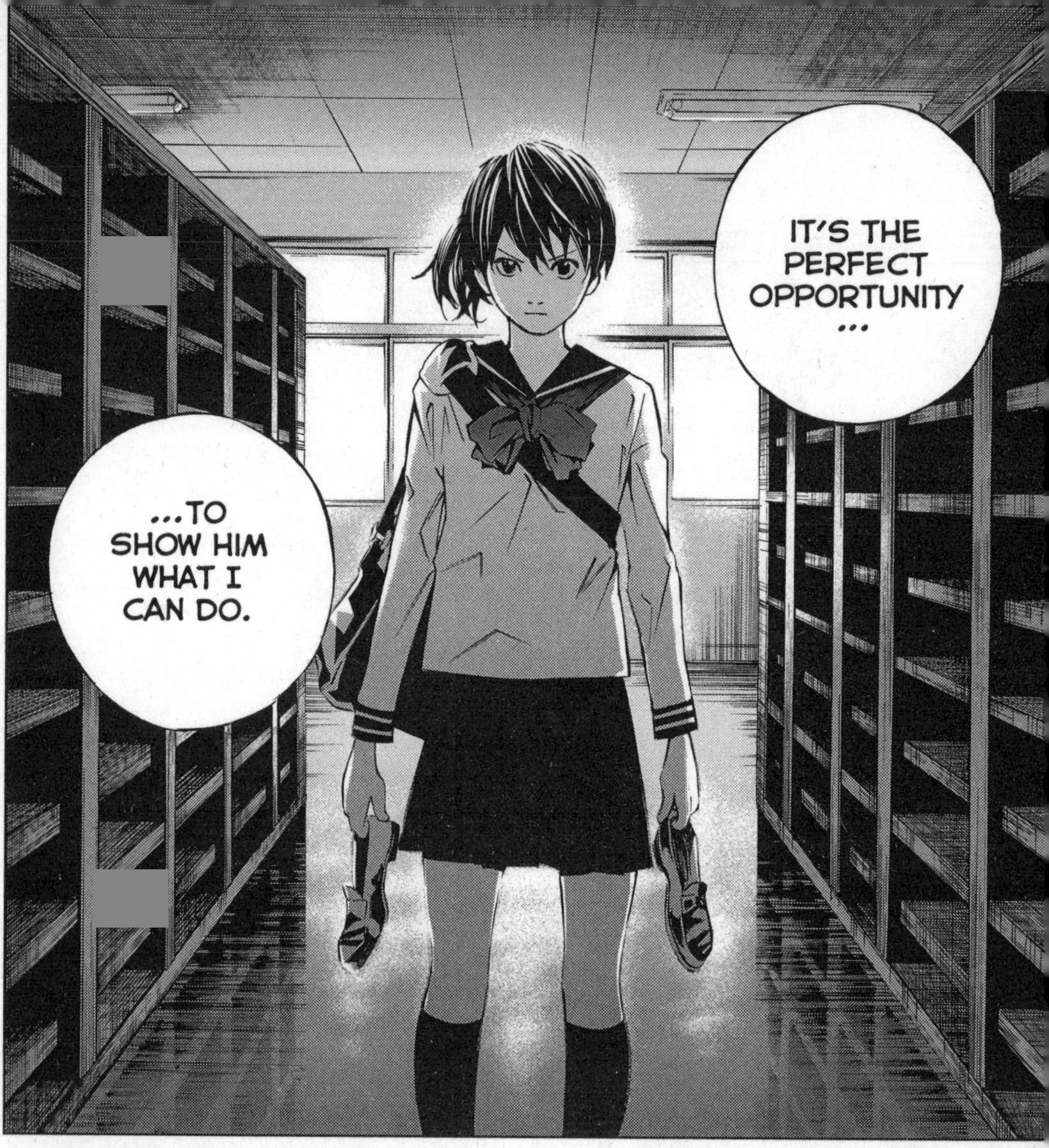
IT'S THE PERFECT OPPORTUNITY ...
...TO SHOW HIM WHAT I CAN DO.

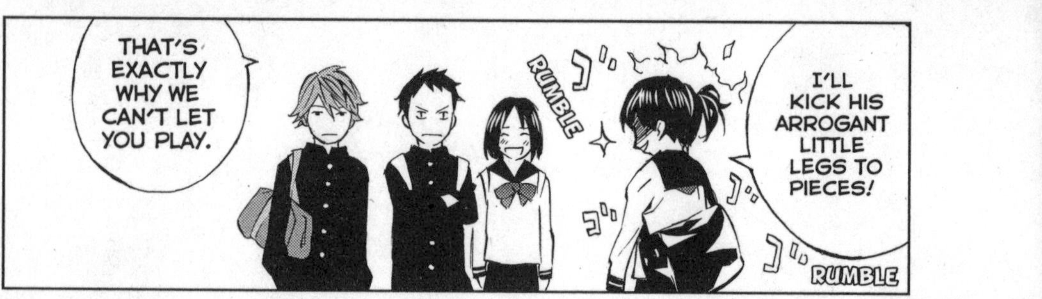
I'LL KICK HIS ARROGANT LITTLE LEGS TO PIECES!
RUMBLE
RUMBLE
THAT'S EXACTLY WHY WE CAN'T LET YOU PLAY.

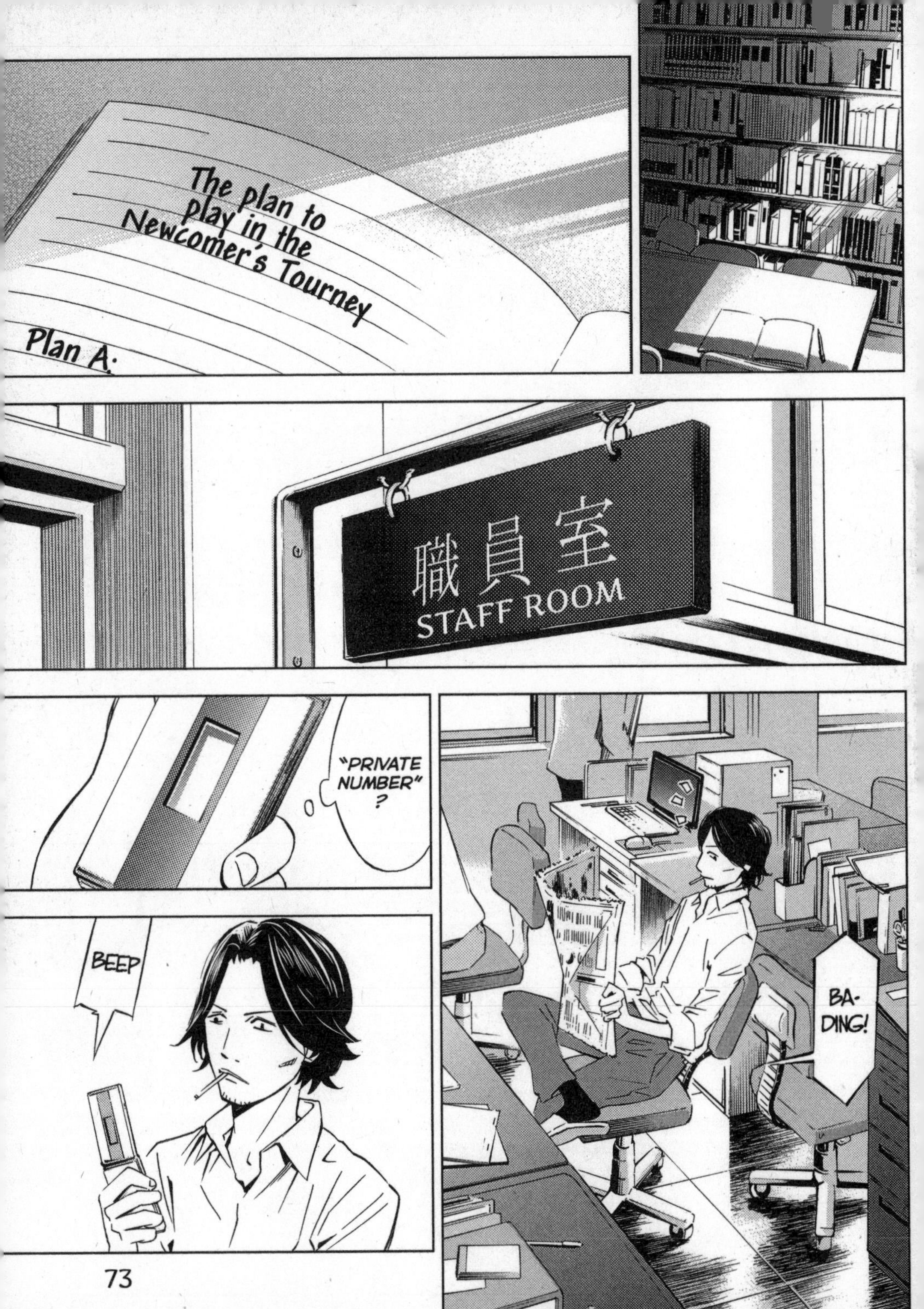
The plan to play in the Newcomer's Tourney
Plan A:
職員室
STAFF ROOM
BA-DING!
"PRIVATE NUMBER"?
BEEP

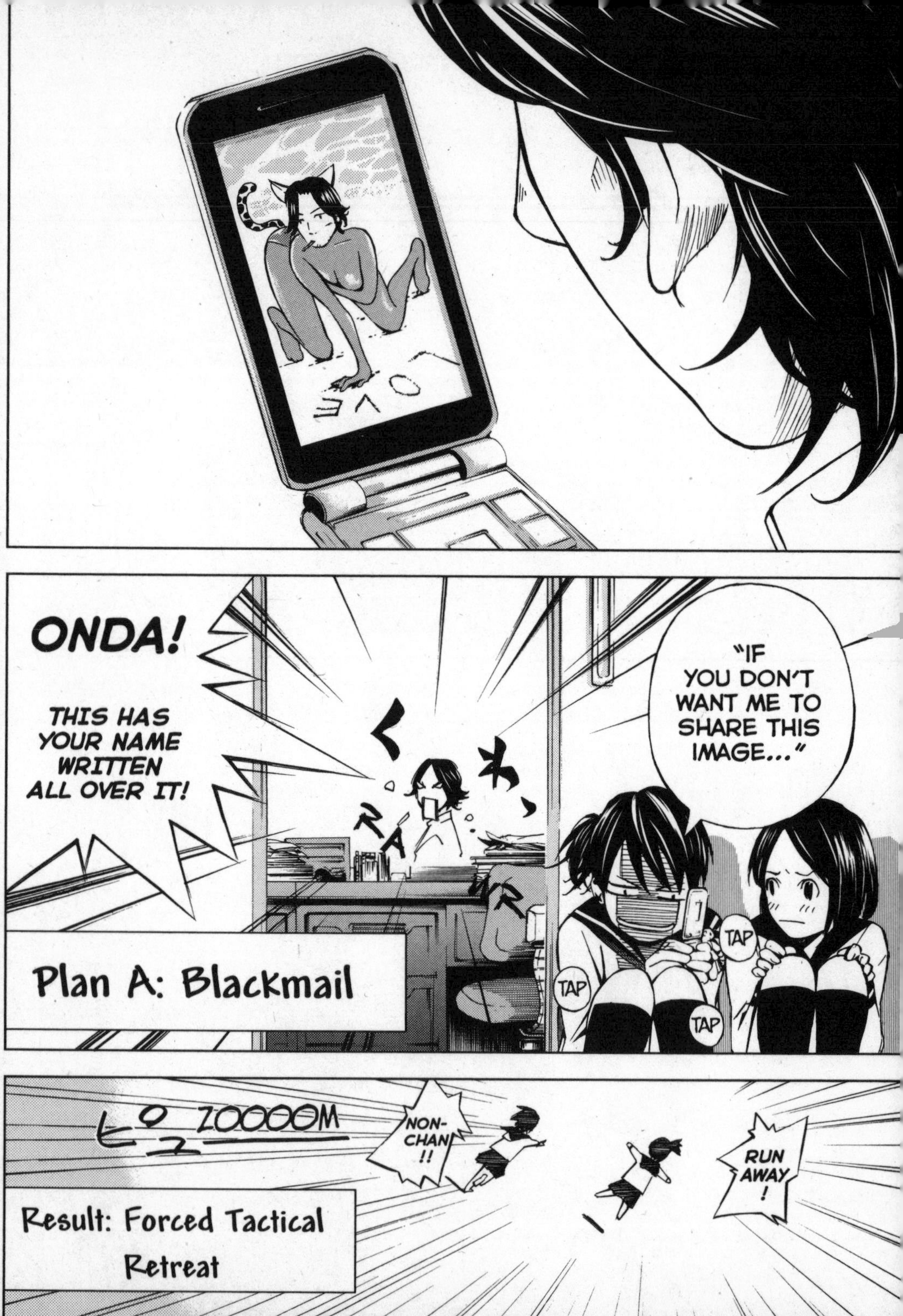
"IF YOU DON'T WANT ME TO SHARE THIS IMAGE..."
TAP
TAP
TAP
ONDA!
THIS HAS YOUR NAME WRITTEN ALL OVER IT!
Plan A: Blackmail
RUN AWAY!
NON-CHAN!!
ZOOOOOM
Result: Forced Tactical Retreat

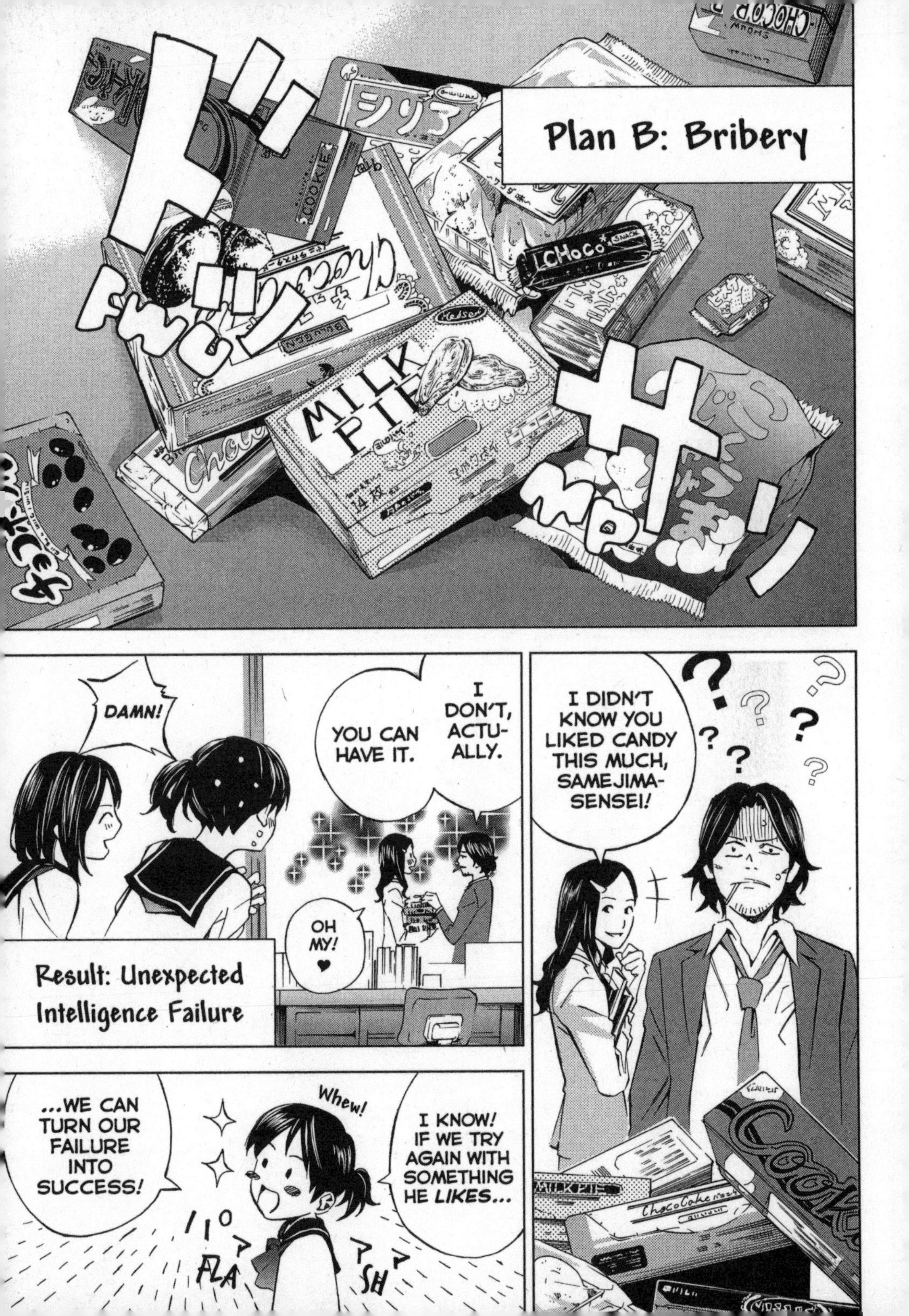
Plan B: Bribery
FWUMP
COOKIE
CHOCO SNACK
MILK PIE
I DIDN'T KNOW YOU LIKED CANDY THIS MUCH, SAMEJIMA-SENSEI!
I DON'T, ACTUALLY.
YOU CAN HAVE IT.
OH MY! ♥
DAMN!
Result: Unexpected Intelligence Failure
I KNOW! IF WE TRY AGAIN WITH SOMETHING HE *LIKES*...
Whew!
...WE CAN TURN OUR FAILURE INTO SUCCESS!
FLASH

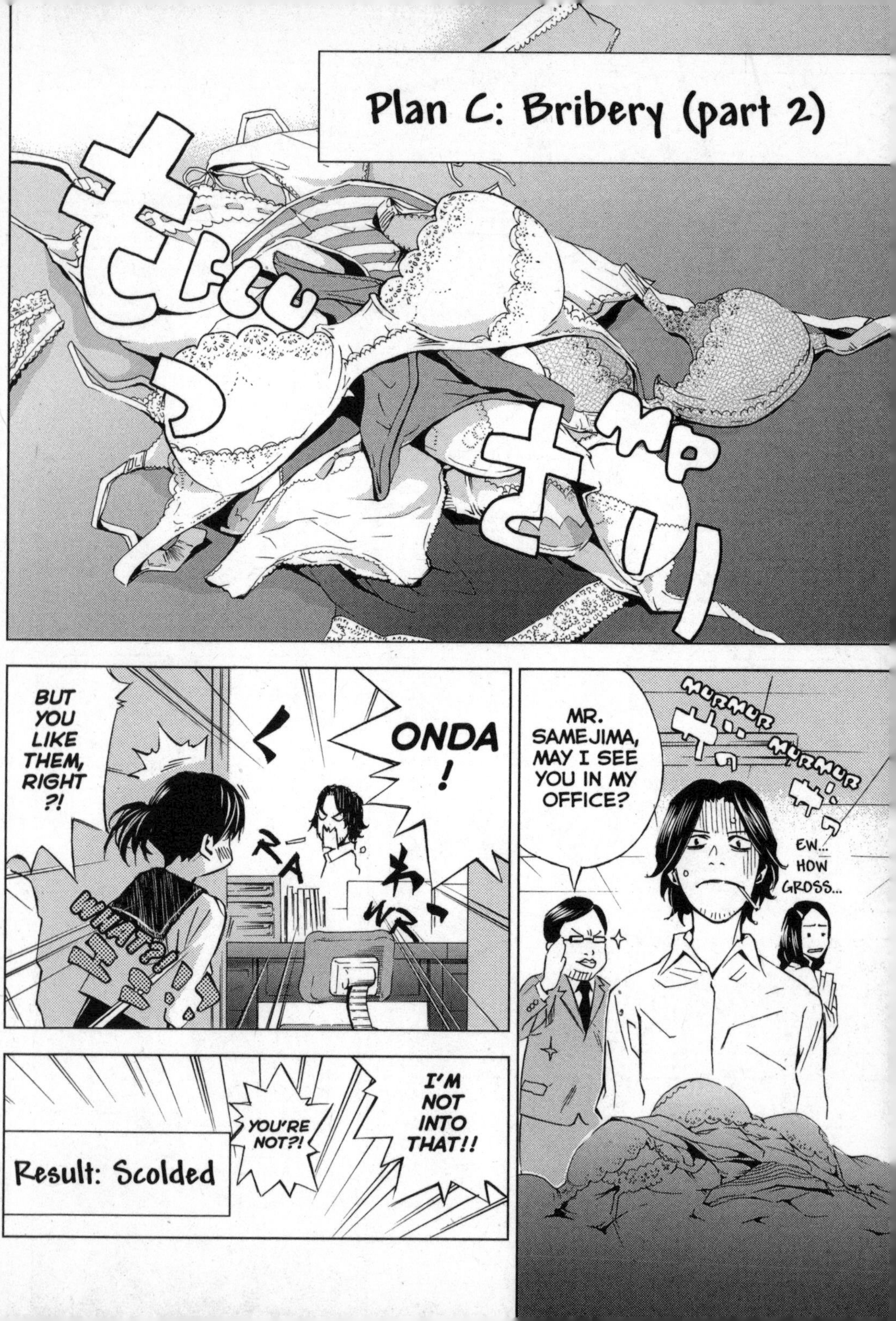
Plan C: Bribery (part 2)
MP
MR. SAMEJIMA, MAY I SEE YOU IN MY OFFICE?
MURMUR
MURMUR
EW... HOW GROSS...
ONDA!
BUT YOU LIKE THEM, RIGHT?!
WHAT?!
I'M NOT INTO THAT!!
YOU'RE NOT?!
Result: Scolded

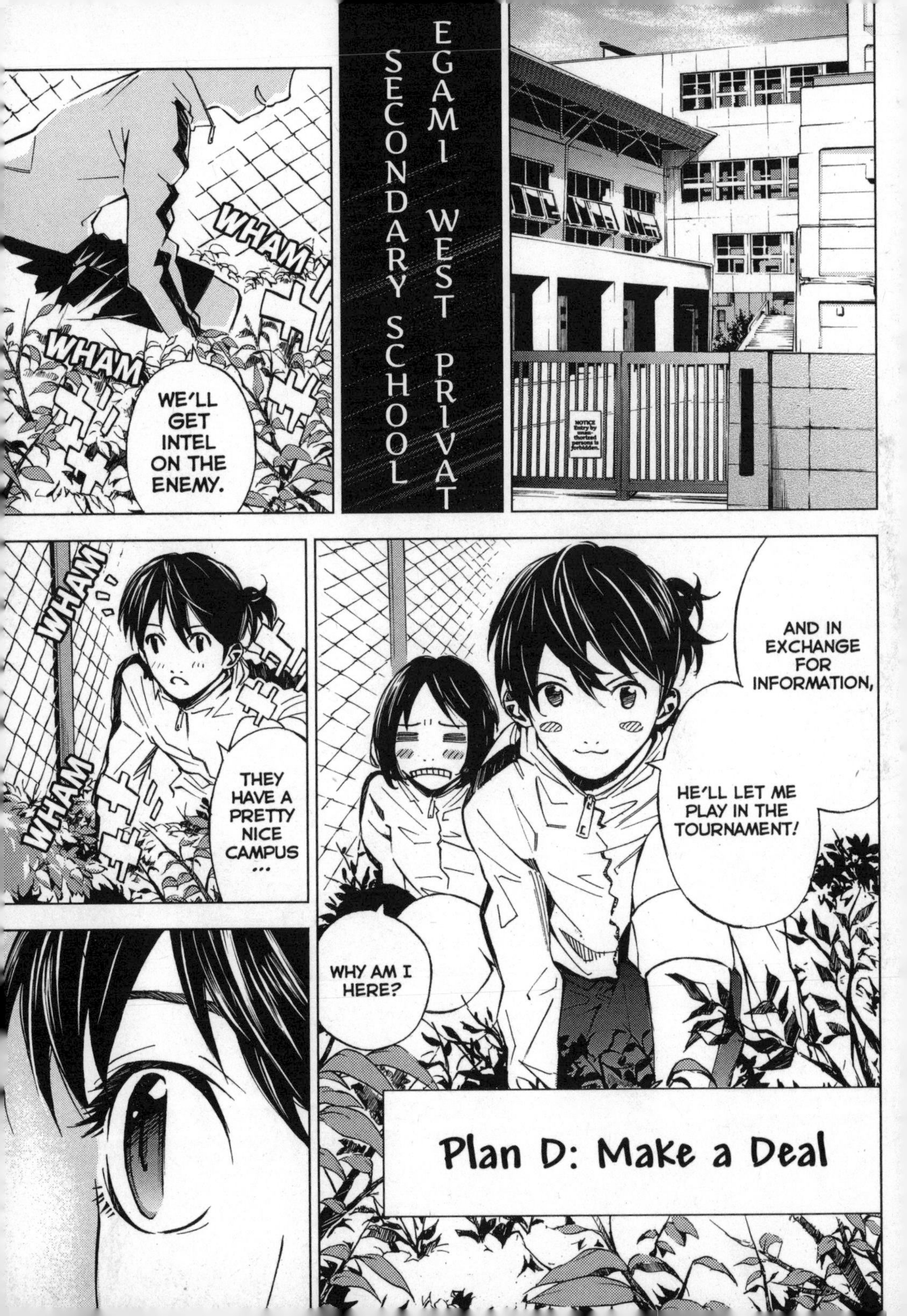
EGAMI WEST PRIVAT
SECONDARY SCHOOL
NOTICE Entry by unauthorized persons is forbidden.
WHAM
WHAM
WE'LL GET INTEL ON THE ENEMY.
AND IN EXCHANGE FOR INFORMATION,
HE'LL LET ME PLAY IN THE TOURNAMENT!
WHY AM I HERE?
Plan D: Make a Deal
WHAM
WHAM
THEY HAVE A PRETTY NICE CAMPUS ...

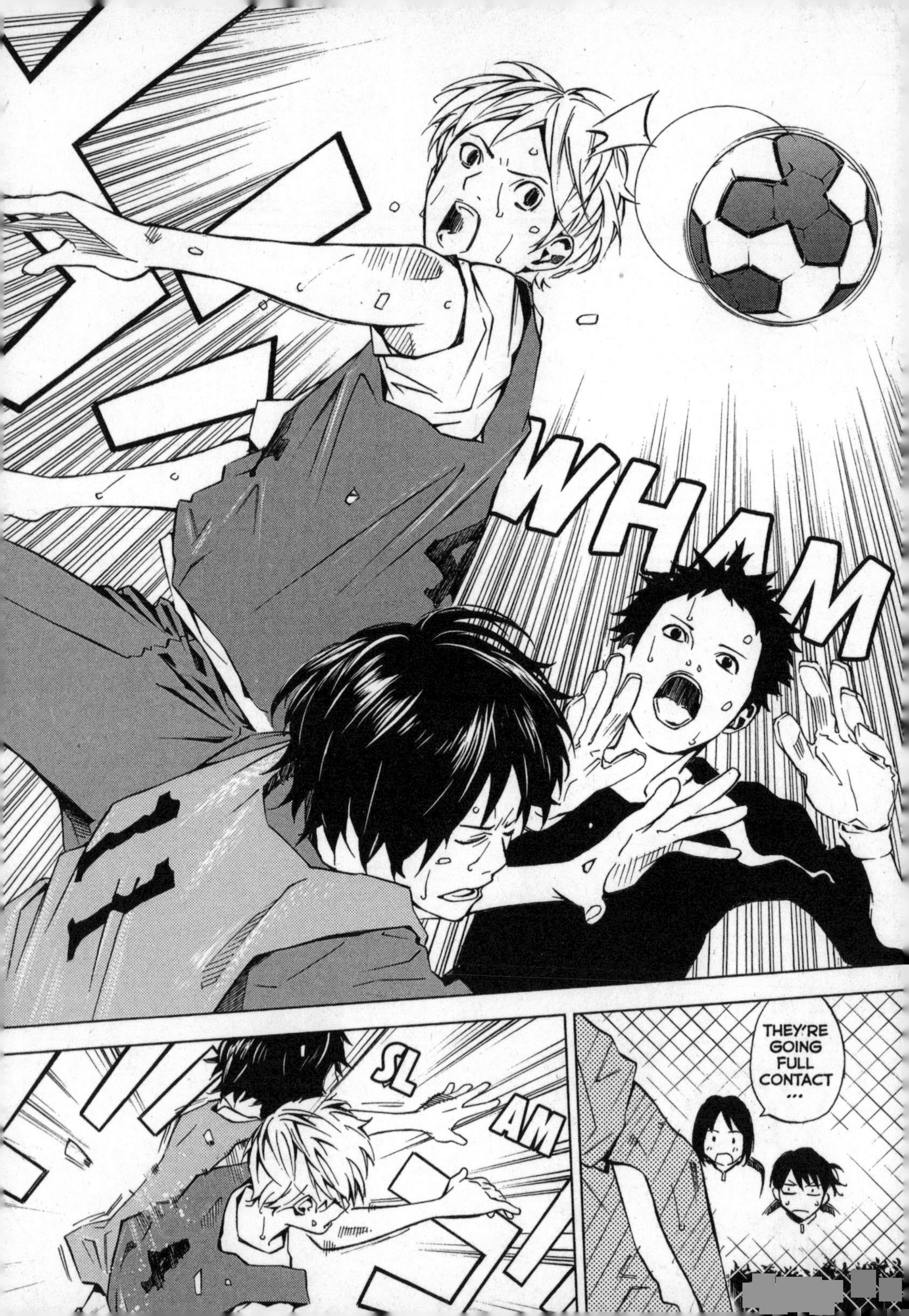
WHAM
THEY'RE GOING FULL CONTACT ...
SLAM

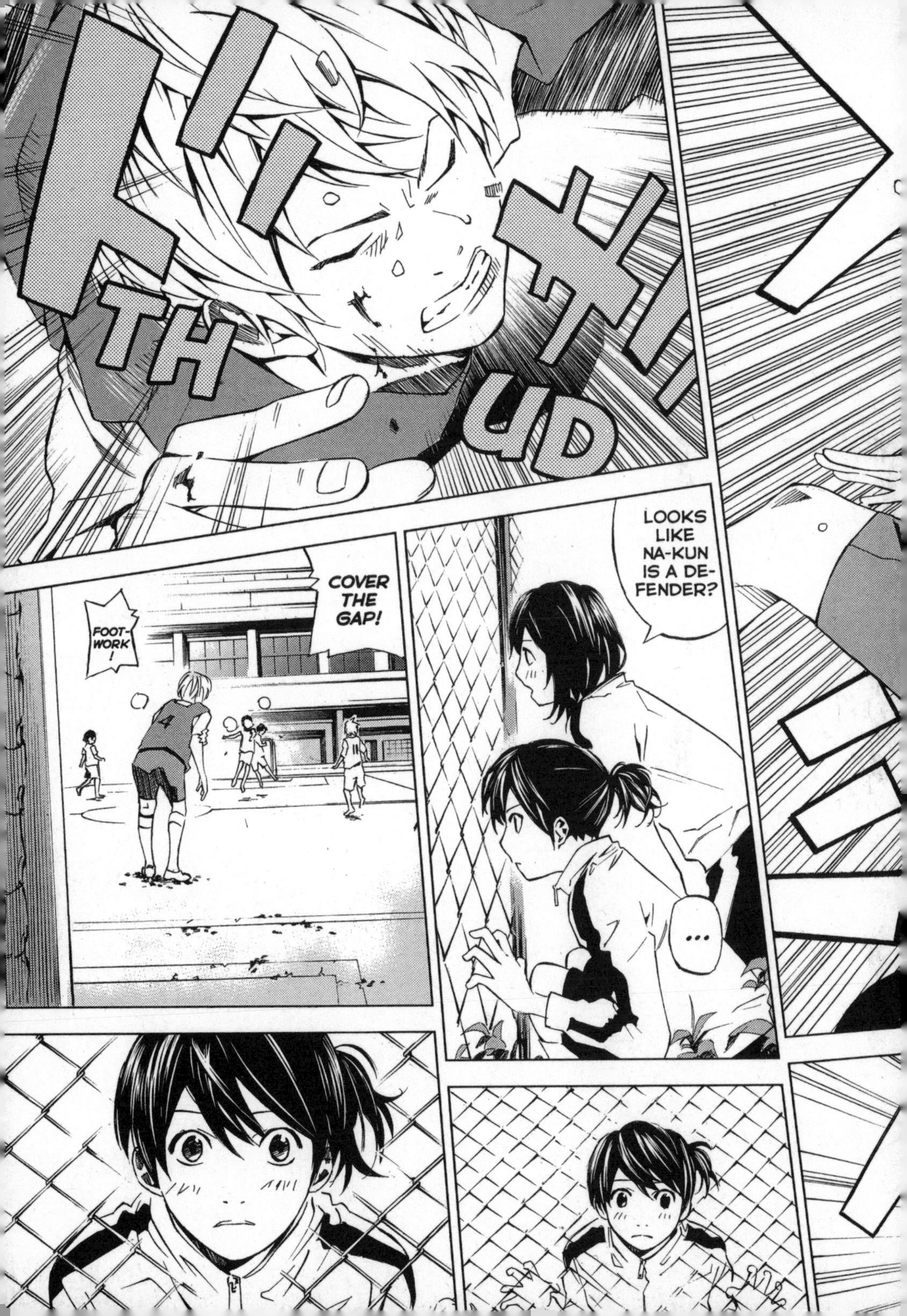
THUD
LOOKS LIKE NA-KUN IS A DEFENDER?
...
COVER THE GAP!
FOOT-WORK!

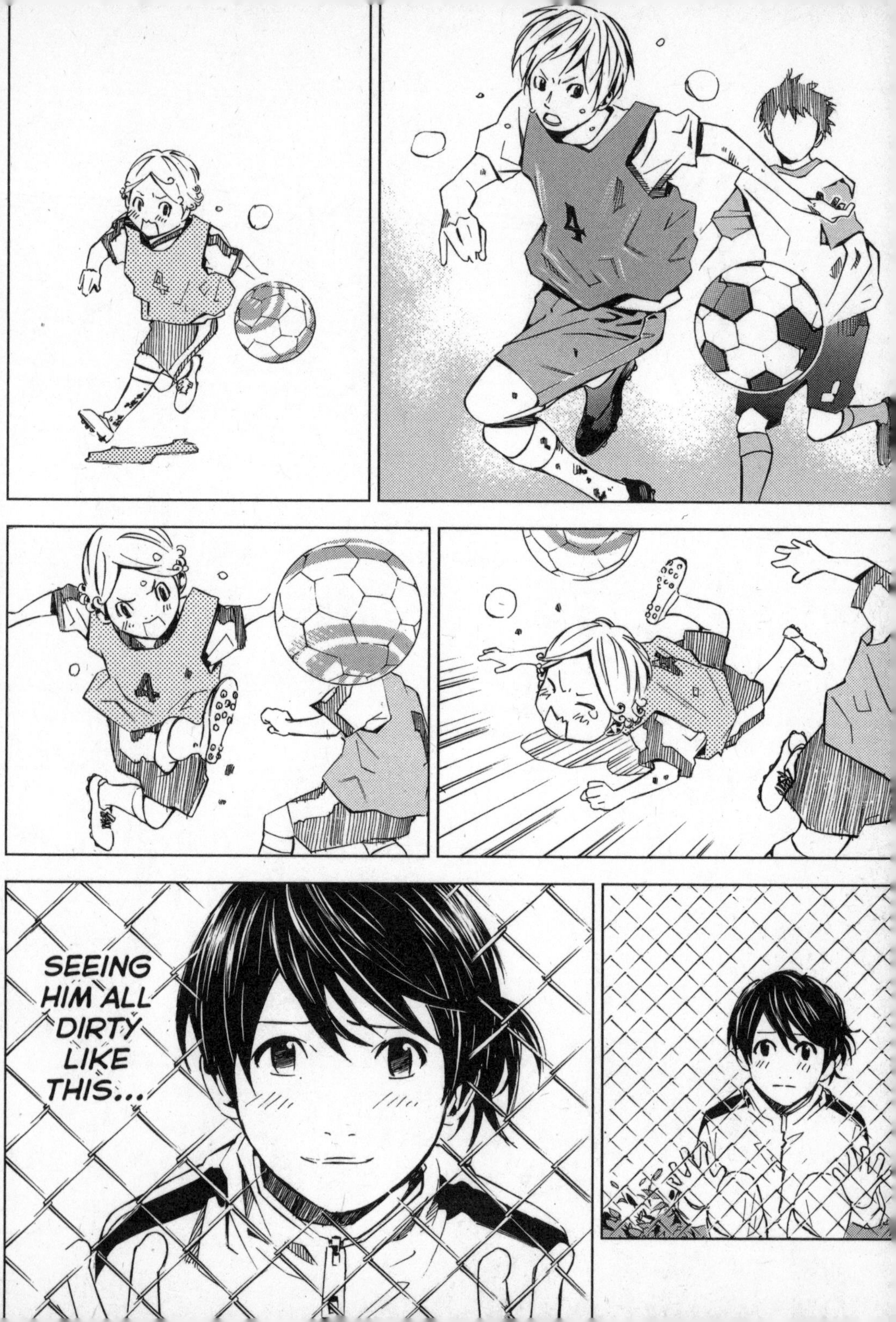
SEEING HIM ALL DIRTY LIKE THIS...

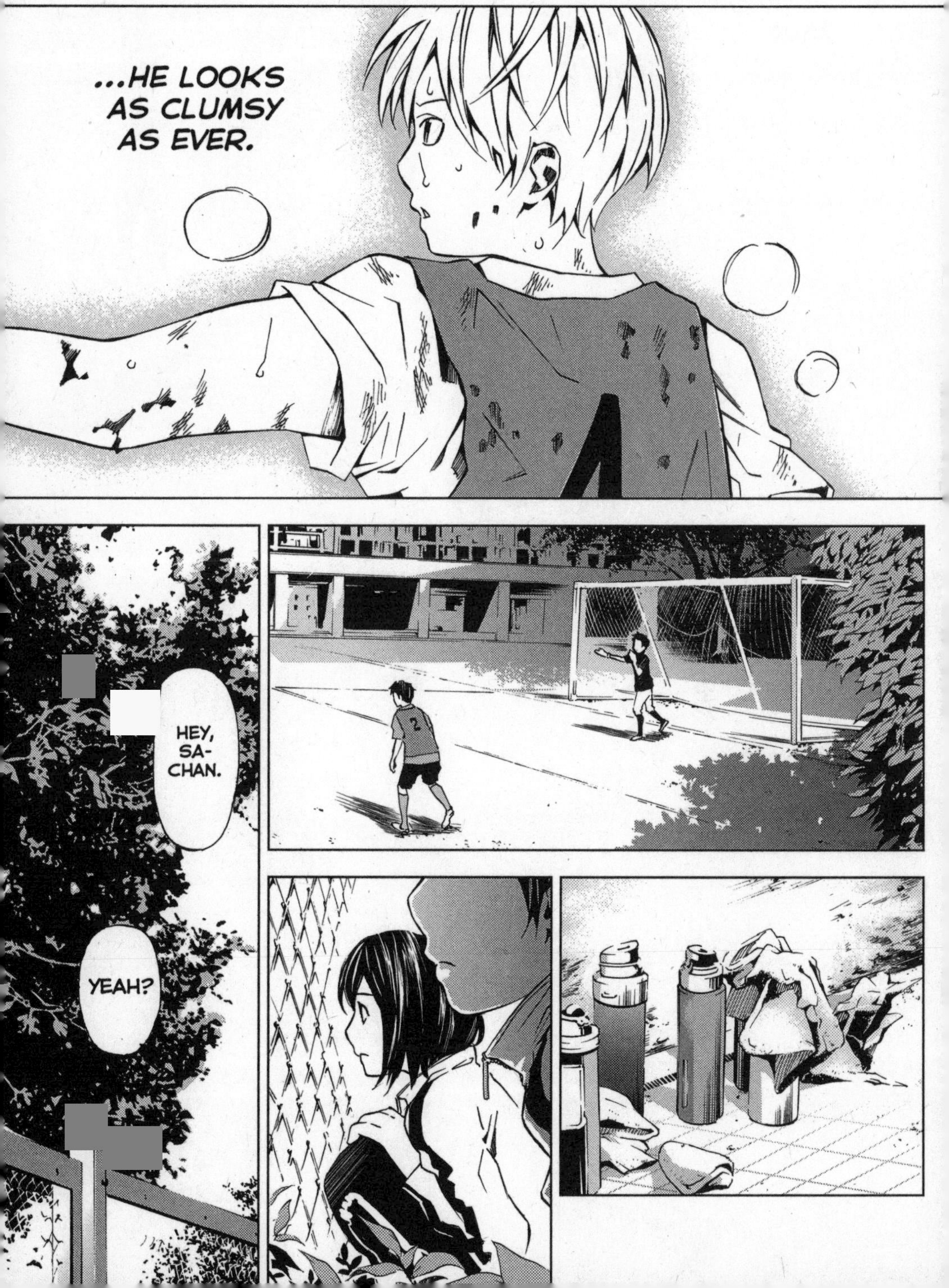
...HE LOOKS AS CLUMSY AS EVER.
HEY, SA-CHAN.
YEAH?

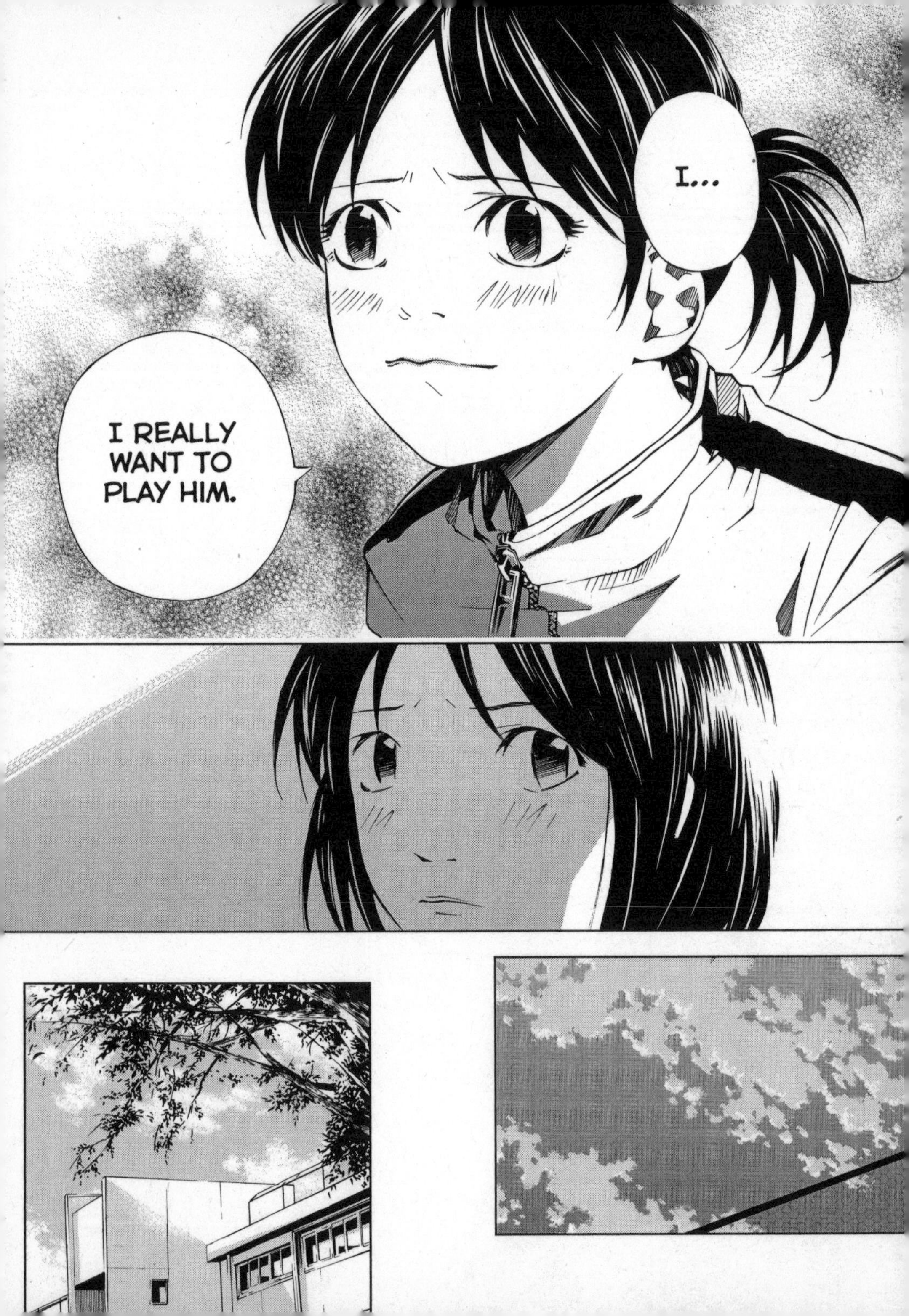
I...
I REALLY WANT TO PLAY HIM.

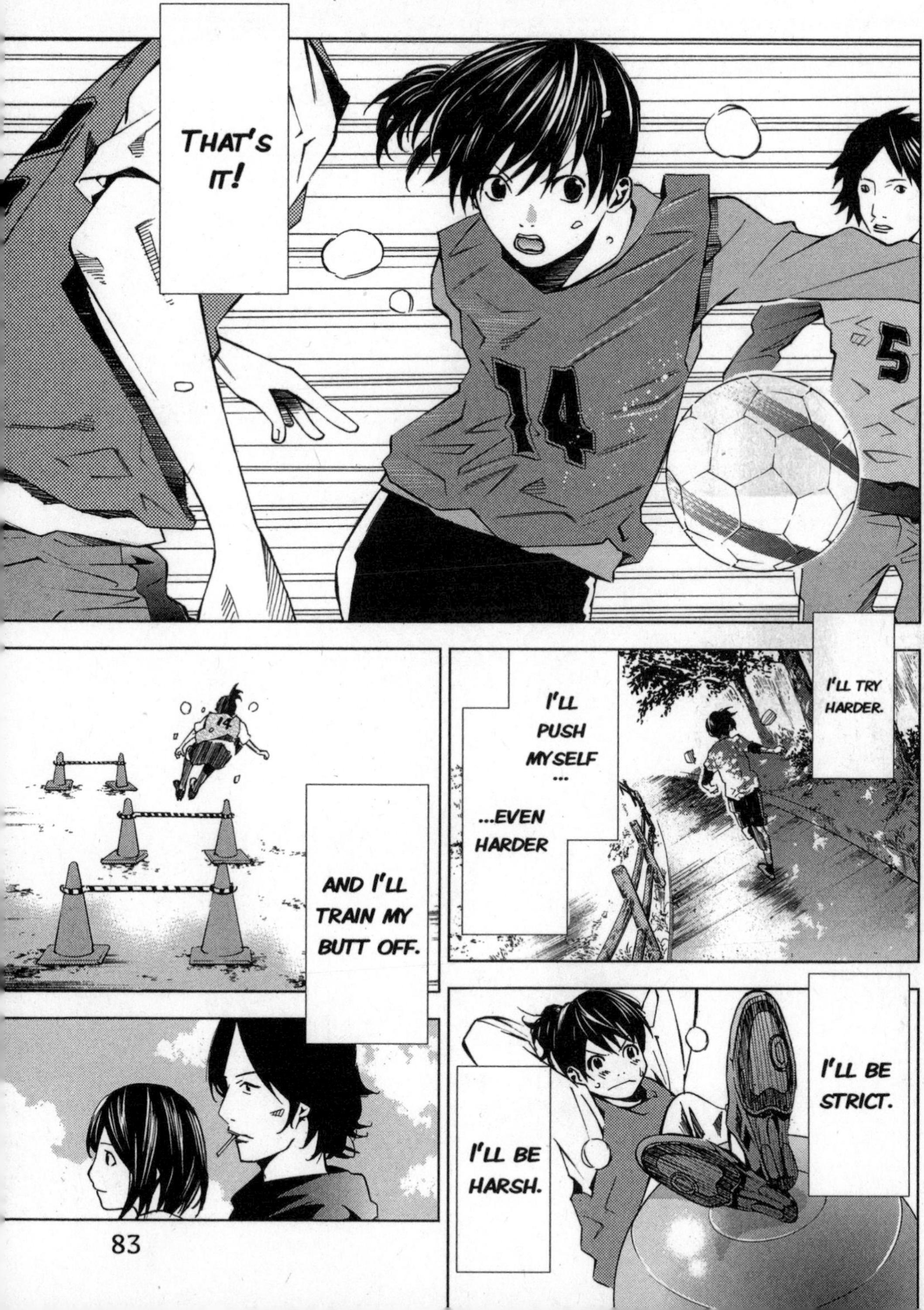
THAT'S IT!
I'LL TRY HARDER.
I'LL PUSH MYSELF...
...EVEN HARDER
AND I'LL TRAIN MY BUTT OFF.
I'LL BE STRICT.
I'LL BE HARSH.

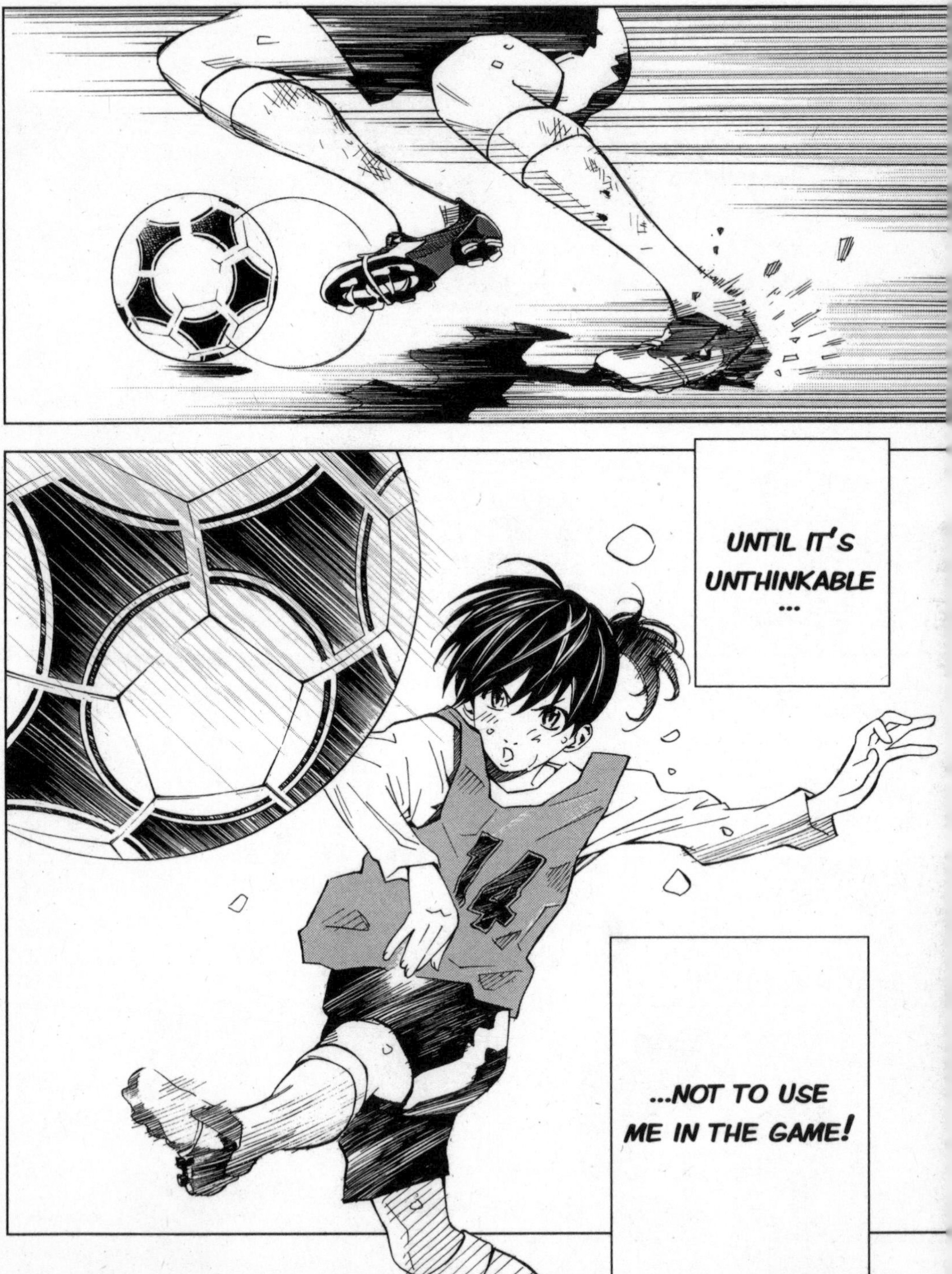
UNTIL IT'S UNTHINKABLE ...
...NOT TO USE ME IN THE GAME!

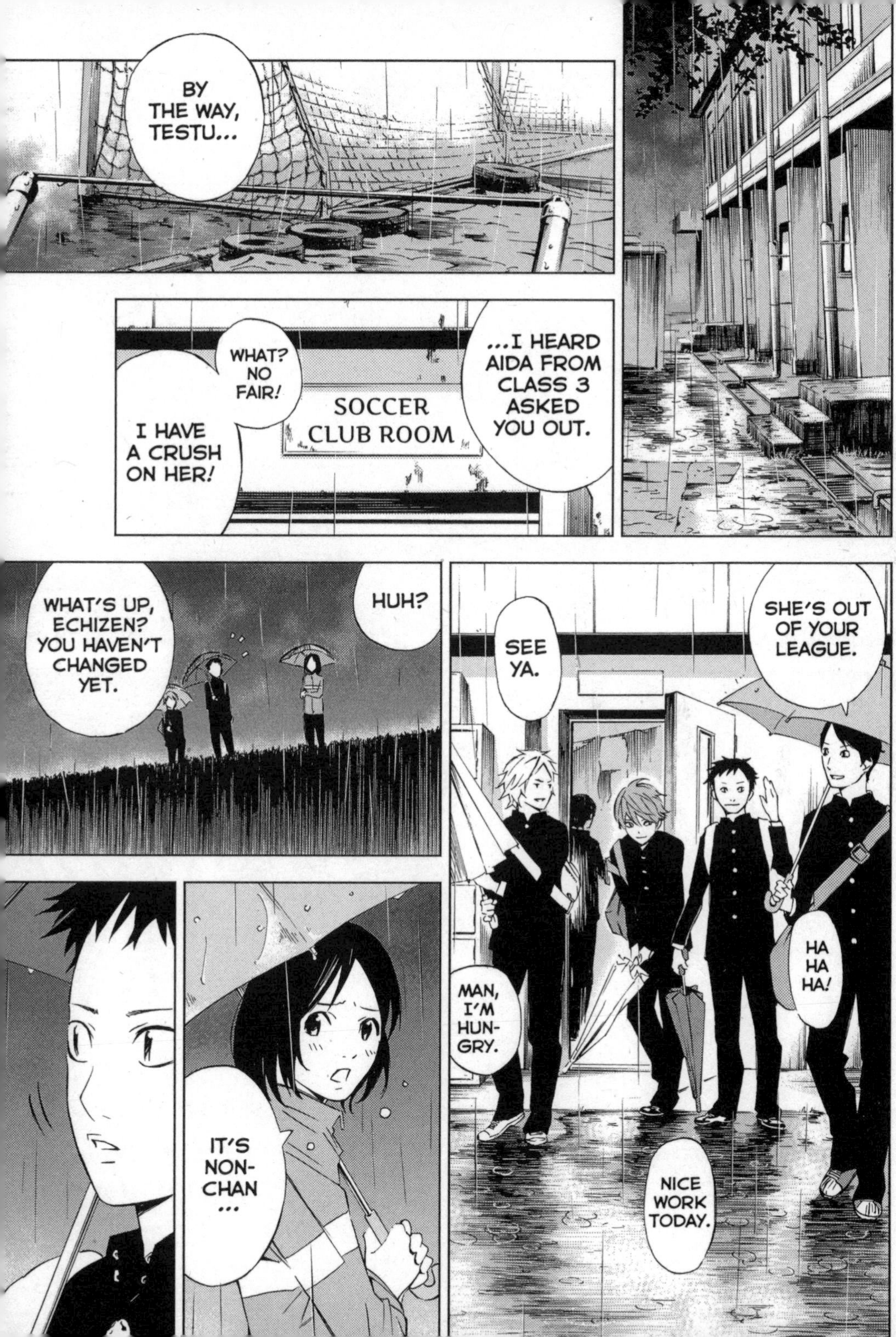
BY THE WAY, TESTU...
...I HEARD AIDA FROM CLASS 3 ASKED YOU OUT.
SOCCER CLUB ROOM
WHAT? NO FAIR!
I HAVE A CRUSH ON HER!
SHE'S OUT OF YOUR LEAGUE.
SEE YA.
HA HA HA!
MAN, I'M HUN-GRY.
NICE WORK TODAY.
HUH?
WHAT'S UP, ECHIZEN? YOU HAVEN'T CHANGED YET.
IT'S NON-CHAN...

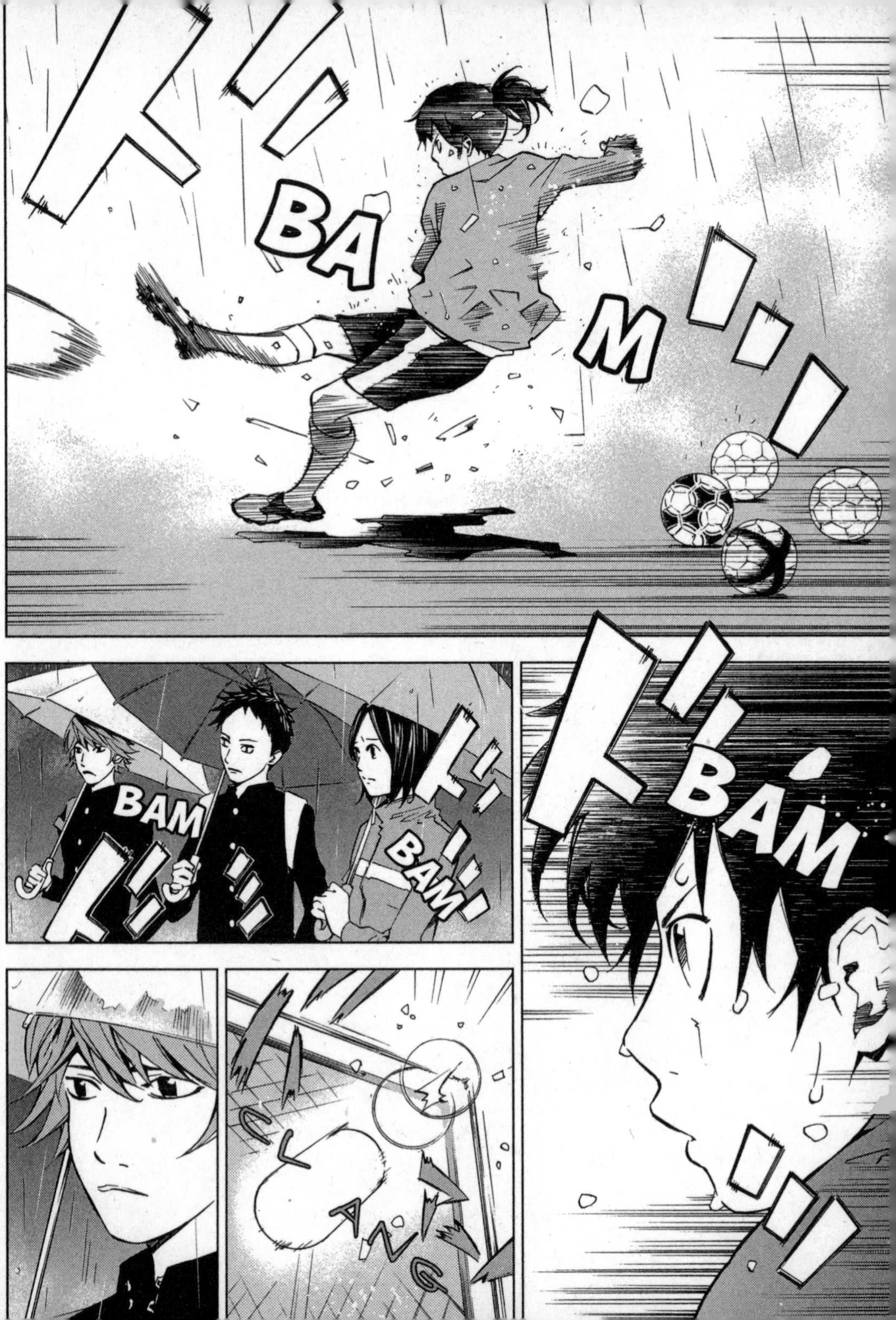
BAM
BAM
BAM
BAM
CLANG

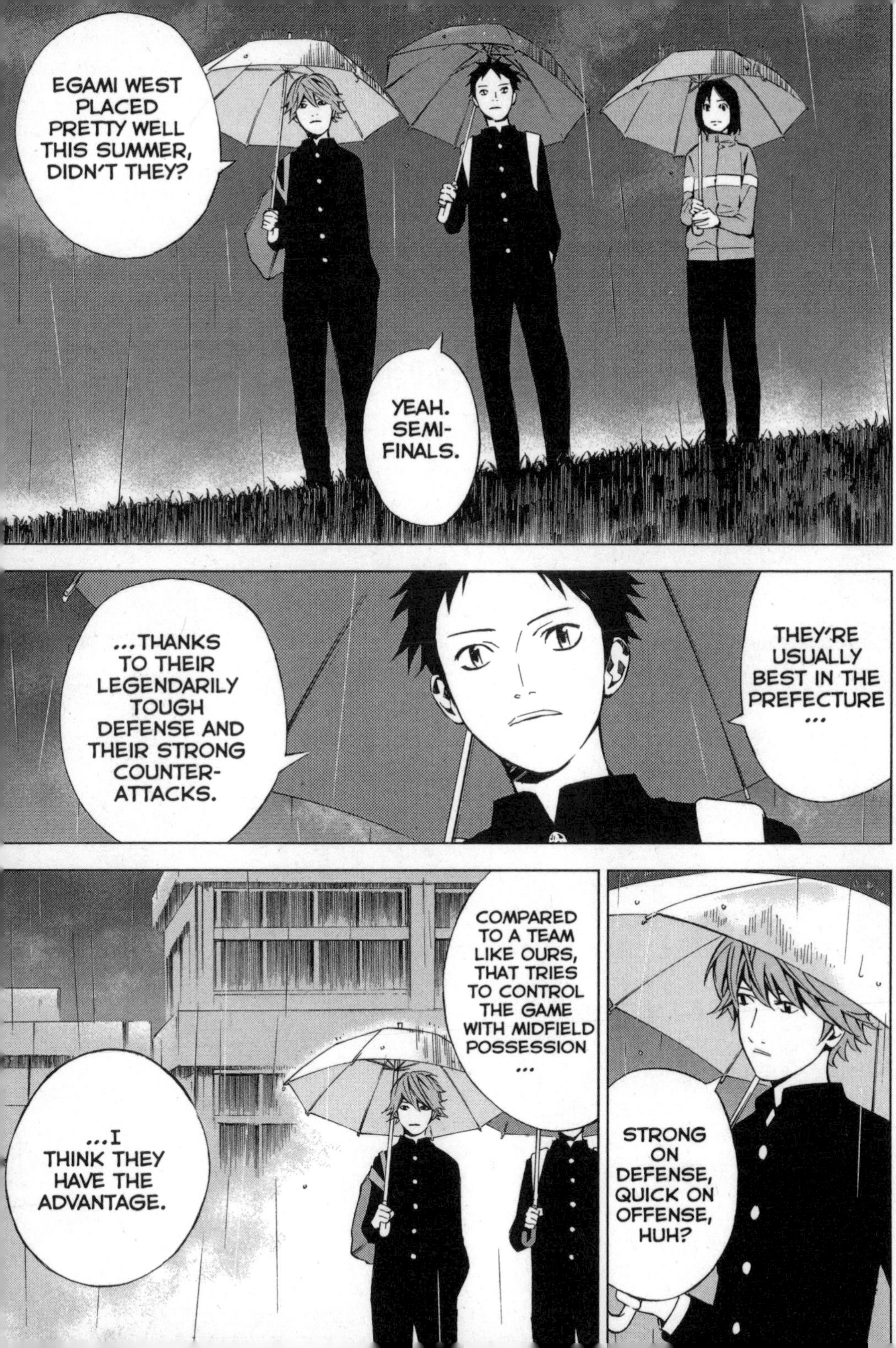
EGAMI WEST PLACED PRETTY WELL THIS SUMMER, DIDN'T THEY?
YEAH. SEMI-FINALS.
THEY'RE USUALLY BEST IN THE PREFECTURE ...
...THANKS TO THEIR LEGENDARILY TOUGH DEFENSE AND THEIR STRONG COUNTER-ATTACKS.
STRONG ON DEFENSE, QUICK ON OFFENSE, HUH?
COMPARED TO A TEAM LIKE OURS, THAT TRIES TO CONTROL THE GAME WITH MIDFIELD POSSESSION ...
...I THINK THEY HAVE THE ADVANTAGE.

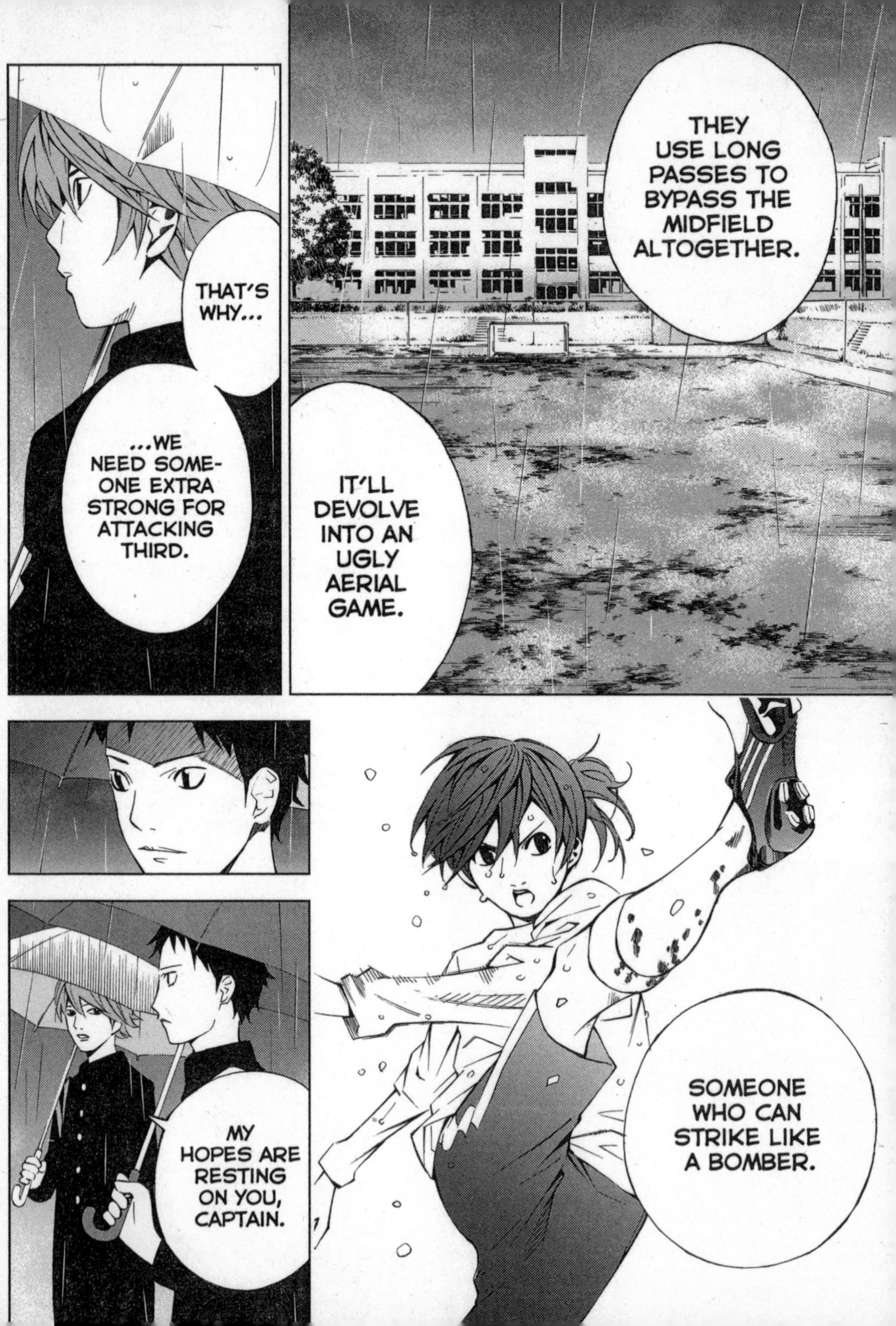
THEY USE LONG PASSES TO BYPASS THE MIDFIELD ALTOGETHER.
IT'LL DEVOLVE INTO AN UGLY AERIAL GAME.
THAT'S WHY...
...WE NEED SOME-ONE EXTRA STRONG FOR ATTACKING THIRD.
SOMEONE WHO CAN STRIKE LIKE A BOMBER.
MY HOPES ARE RESTING ON YOU, CAPTAIN.

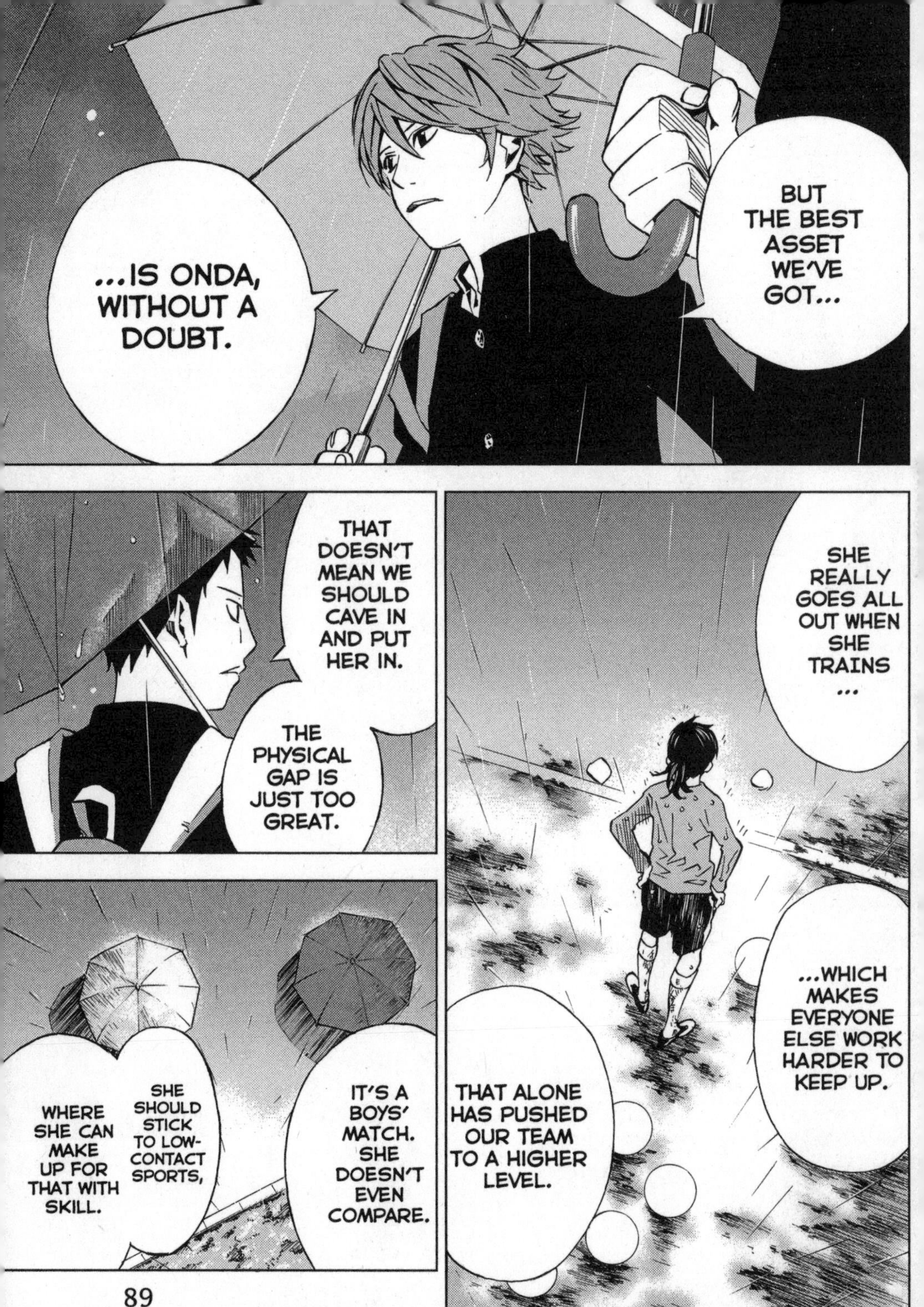
BUT THE BEST ASSET WE'VE GOT...
...IS ONDA, WITHOUT A DOUBT.
SHE REALLY GOES ALL OUT WHEN SHE TRAINS...
...WHICH MAKES EVERYONE ELSE WORK HARDER TO KEEP UP.
THAT ALONE HAS PUSHED OUR TEAM TO A HIGHER LEVEL.
THAT DOESN'T MEAN WE SHOULD CAVE IN AND PUT HER IN.
THE PHYSICAL GAP IS JUST TOO GREAT.
IT'S A BOYS' MATCH. SHE DOESN'T EVEN COMPARE.
SHE SHOULD STICK TO LOW-CONTACT SPORTS,
WHERE SHE CAN MAKE UP FOR THAT WITH SKILL.

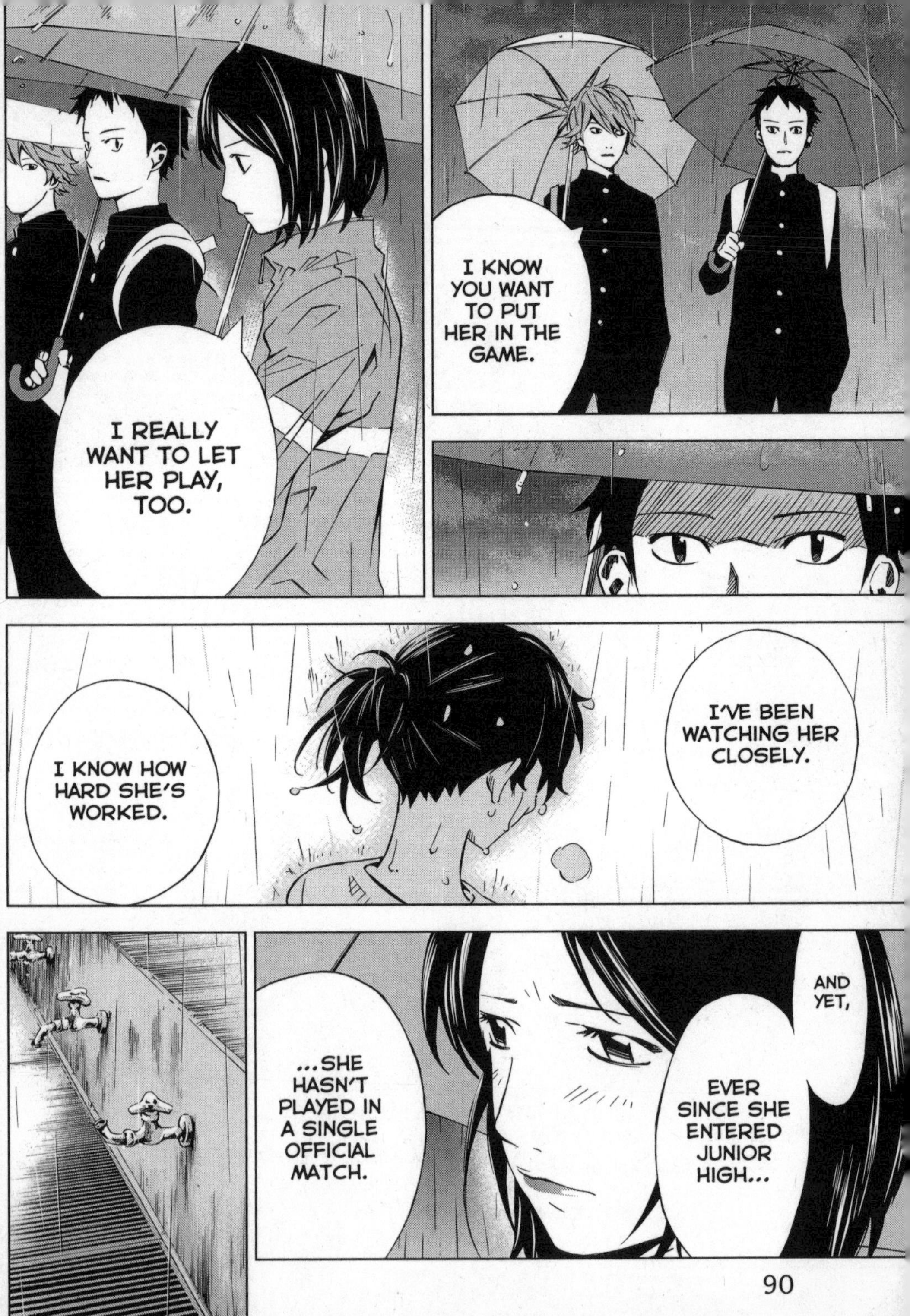
I KNOW YOU WANT TO PUT HER IN THE GAME.
I REALLY WANT TO LET HER PLAY, TOO.
I'VE BEEN WATCHING HER CLOSELY.
I KNOW HOW HARD SHE'S WORKED.
AND YET,
EVER SINCE SHE ENTERED JUNIOR HIGH...
...SHE HASN'T PLAYED IN A SINGLE OFFICIAL MATCH.

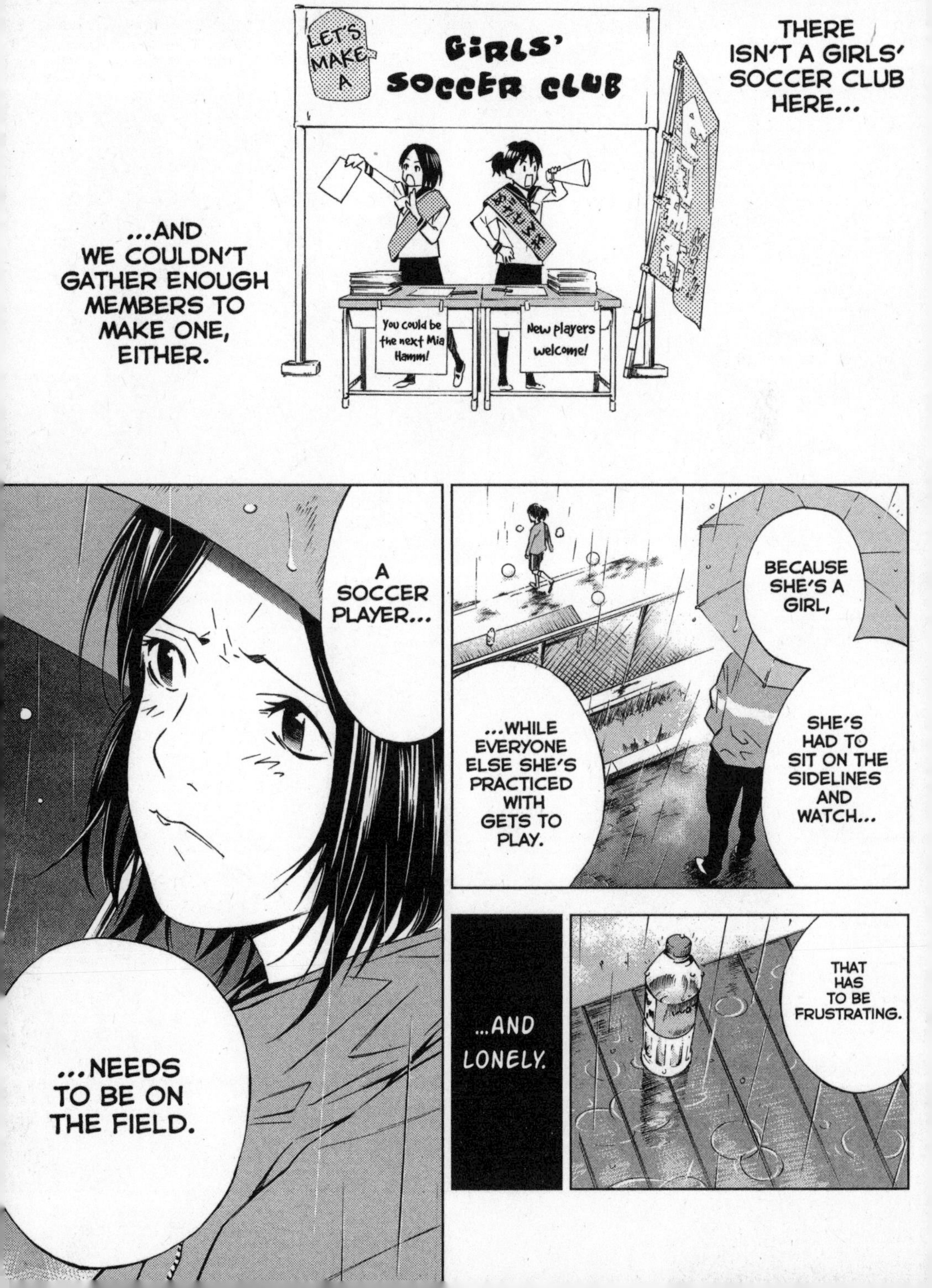
THERE ISN'T A GIRLS' SOCCER CLUB HERE...
LET'S MAKE A
GIRLS' SOCCER CLUB
New players welcome!
You could be the next Mia Hamm!
...AND WE COULDN'T GATHER ENOUGH MEMBERS TO MAKE ONE, EITHER.
BECAUSE SHE'S A GIRL,
SHE'S HAD TO SIT ON THE SIDELINES AND WATCH...
...WHILE EVERYONE ELSE SHE'S PRACTICED WITH GETS TO PLAY.
THAT HAS TO BE FRUSTRATING.
...AND LONELY.
A SOCCER PLAYER...
...NEEDS TO BE ON THE FIELD.

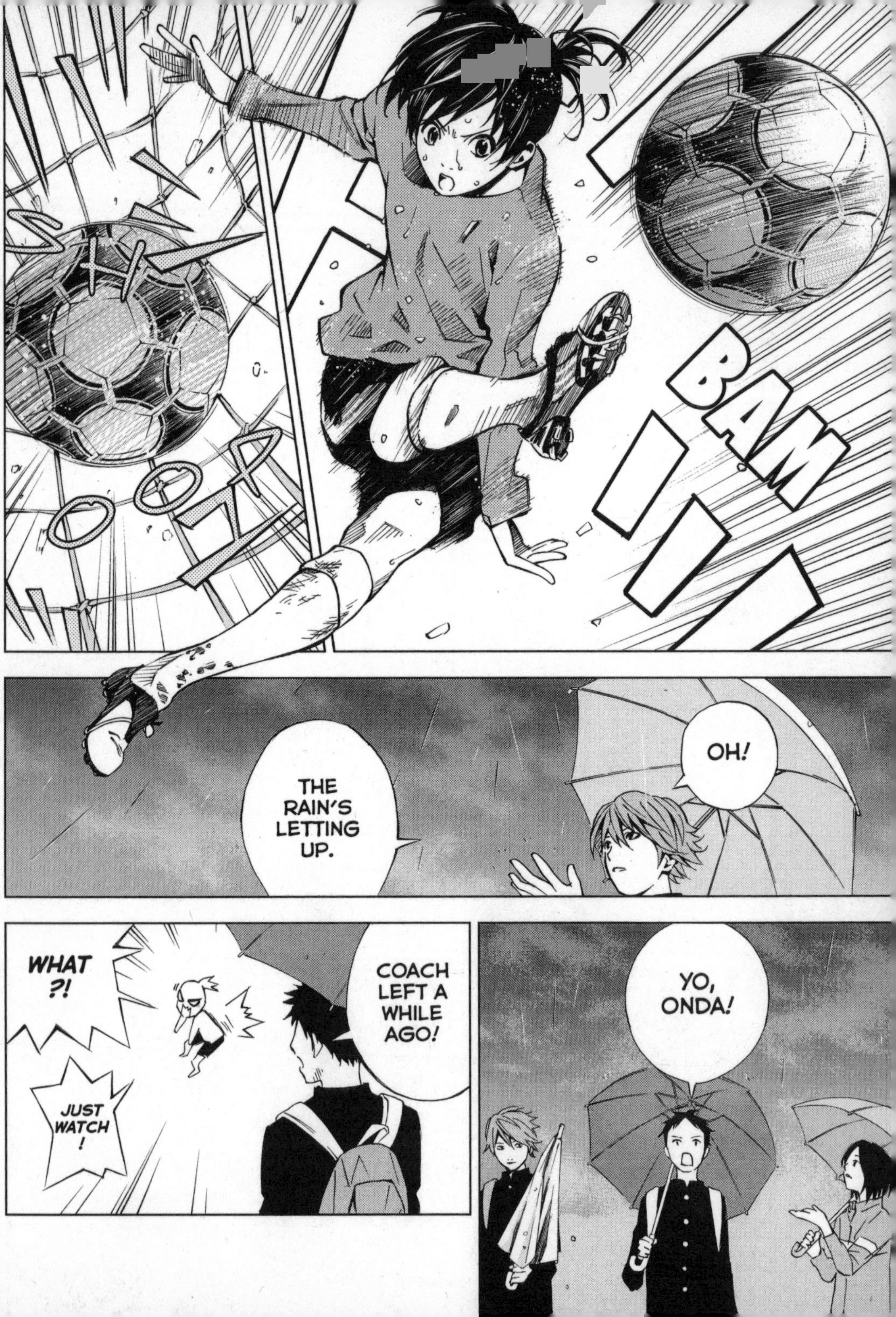
BAM
SHOOP
OH!
THE RAIN'S LETTING UP.
YO, ONDA!
COACH LEFT A WHILE AGO!
WHAT?!
JUST WATCH!

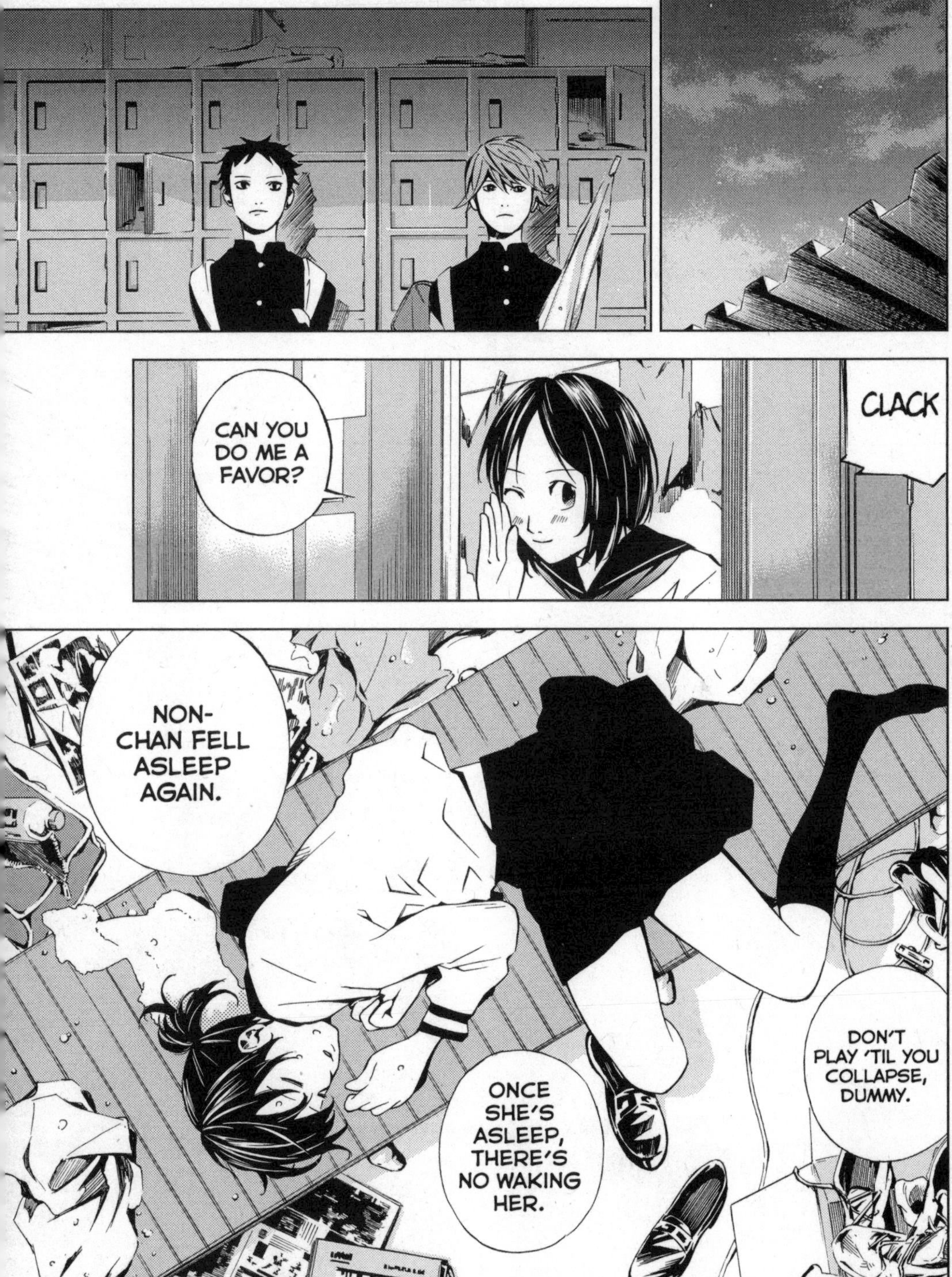
CLACK
CAN YOU DO ME A FAVOR?
NON-CHAN FELL ASLEEP AGAIN.
ONCE SHE'S ASLEEP, THERE'S NO WAKING HER.
DON'T PLAY 'TIL YOU COLLAPSE, DUMMY.

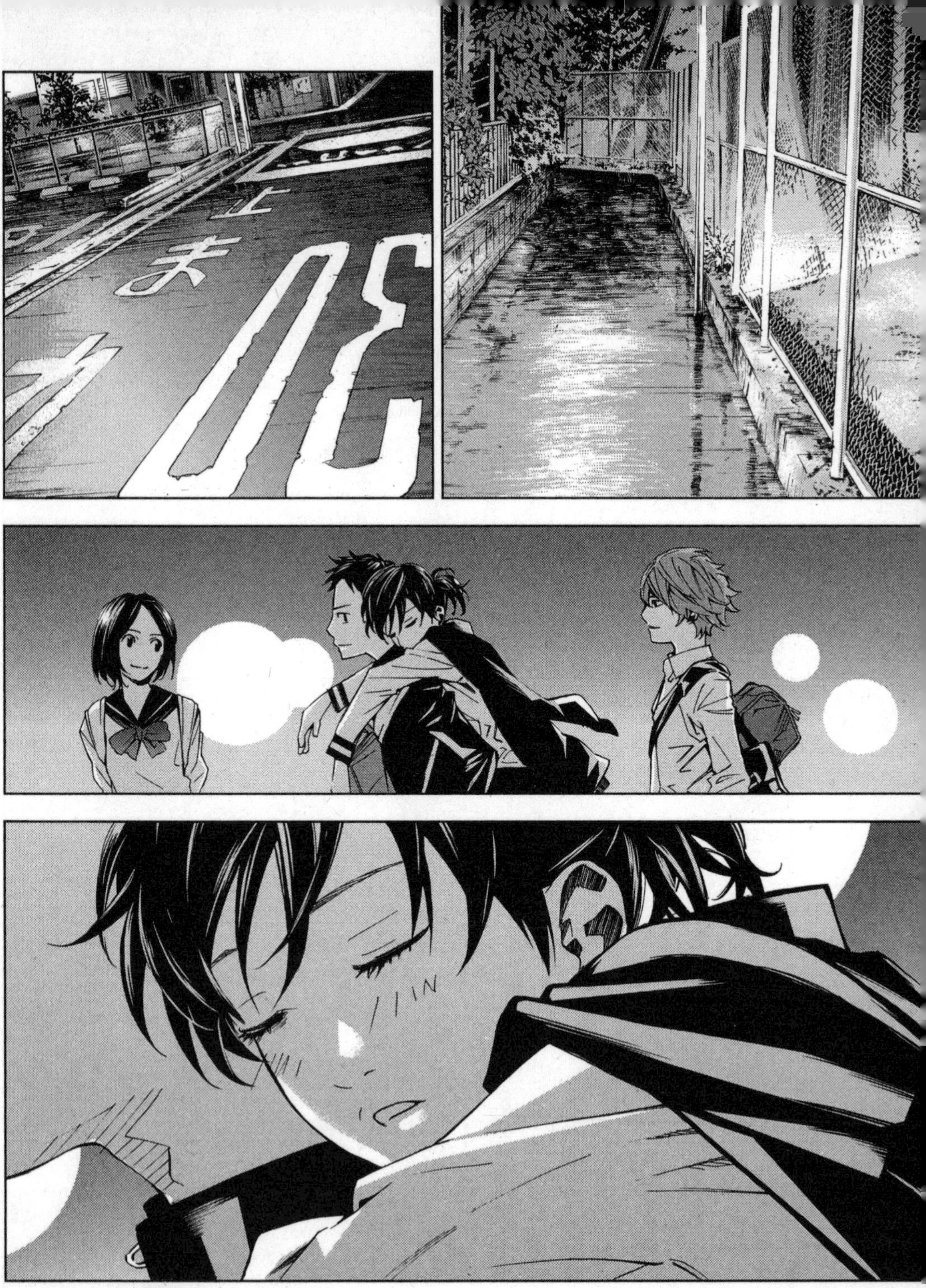

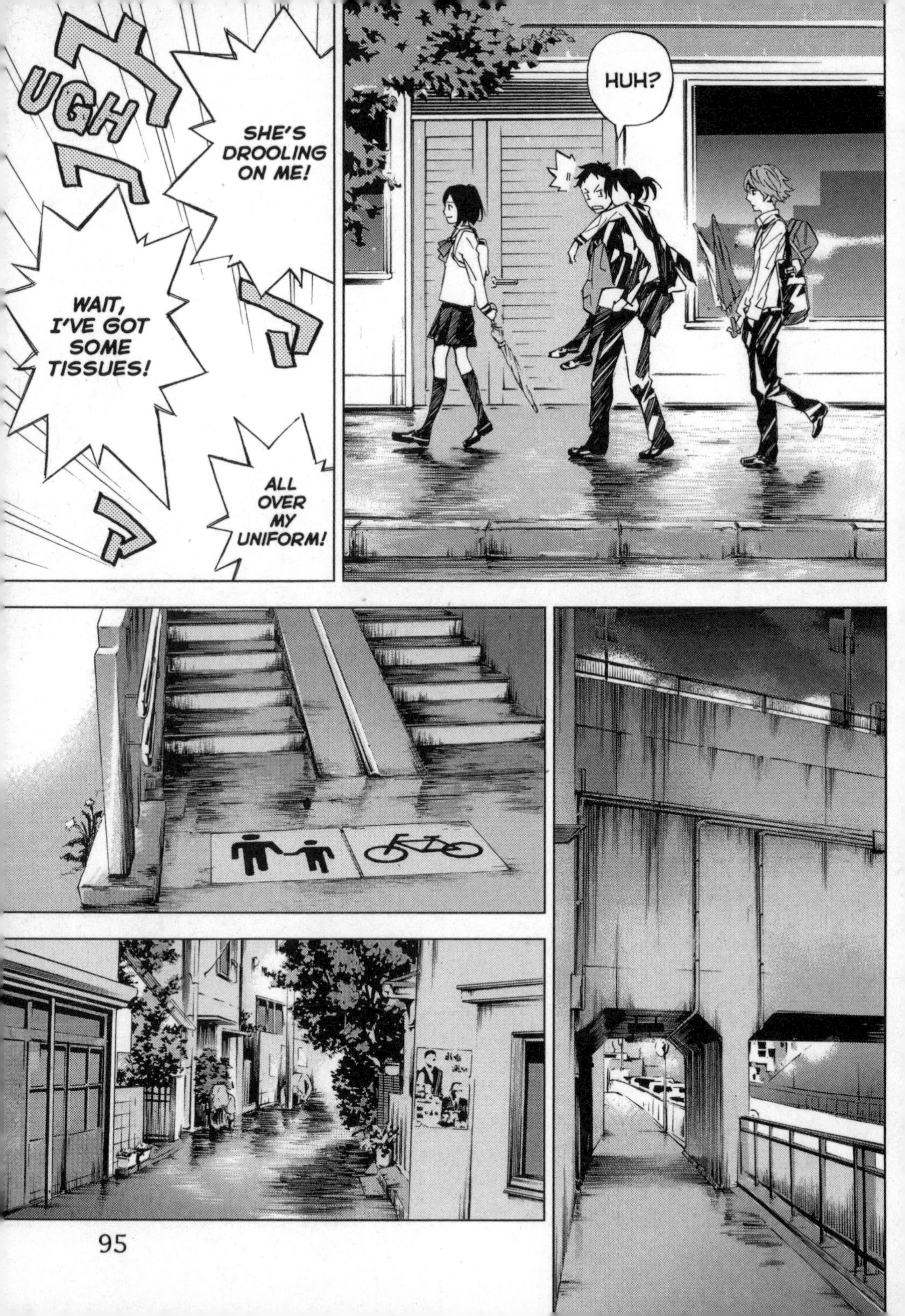
HUH?
UGH
SHE'S DROOLING ON ME!
WAIT, I'VE GOT SOME TISSUES!
ALL OVER MY UNIFORM!

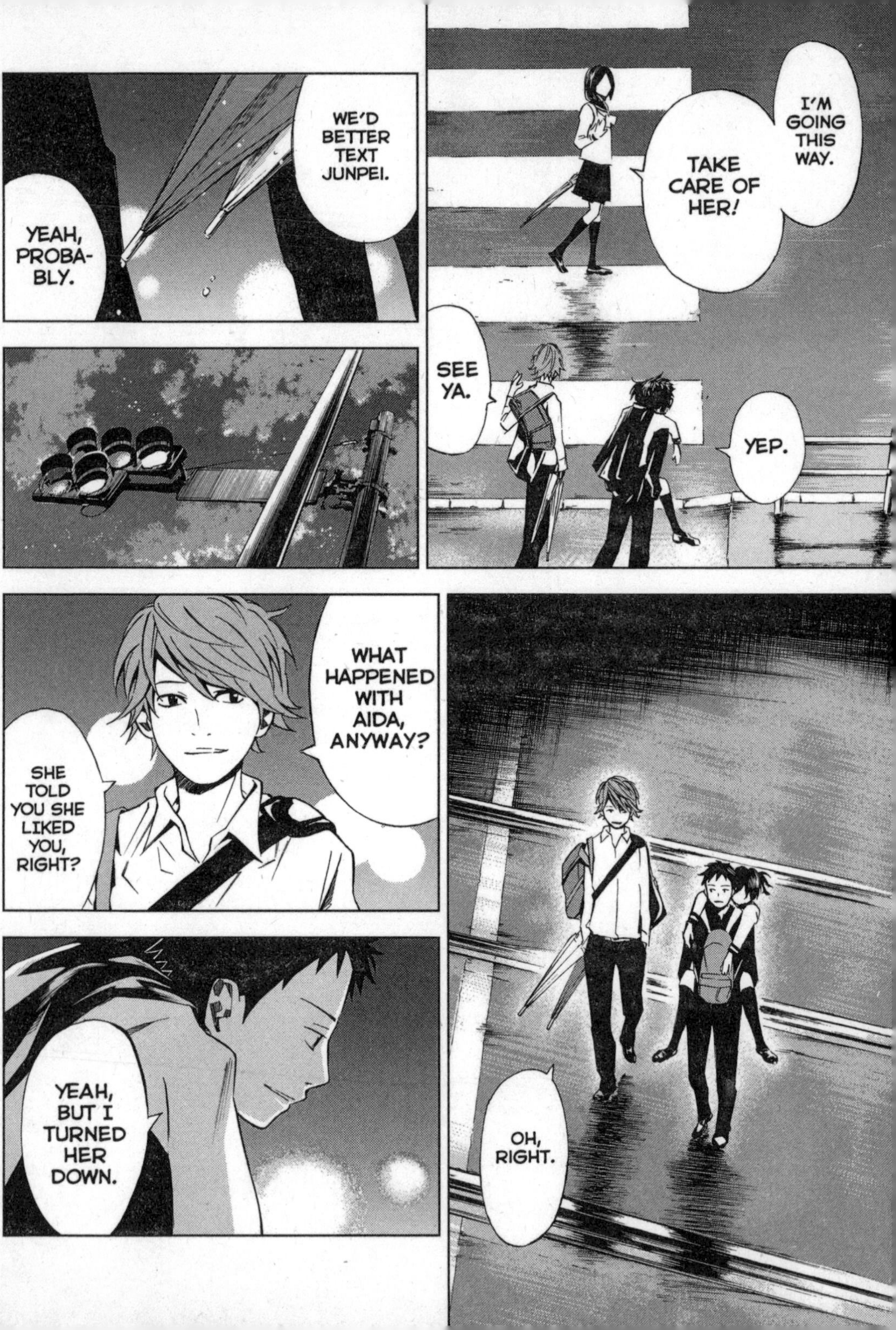
I'M GOING THIS WAY.
TAKE CARE OF HER!
SEE YA.
YEP.
WE'D BETTER TEXT JUNPEI.
YEAH, PROBABLY.
OH, RIGHT.
WHAT HAPPENED WITH AIDA, ANYWAY?
SHE TOLD YOU SHE LIKED YOU, RIGHT?
YEAH, BUT I TURNED HER DOWN.

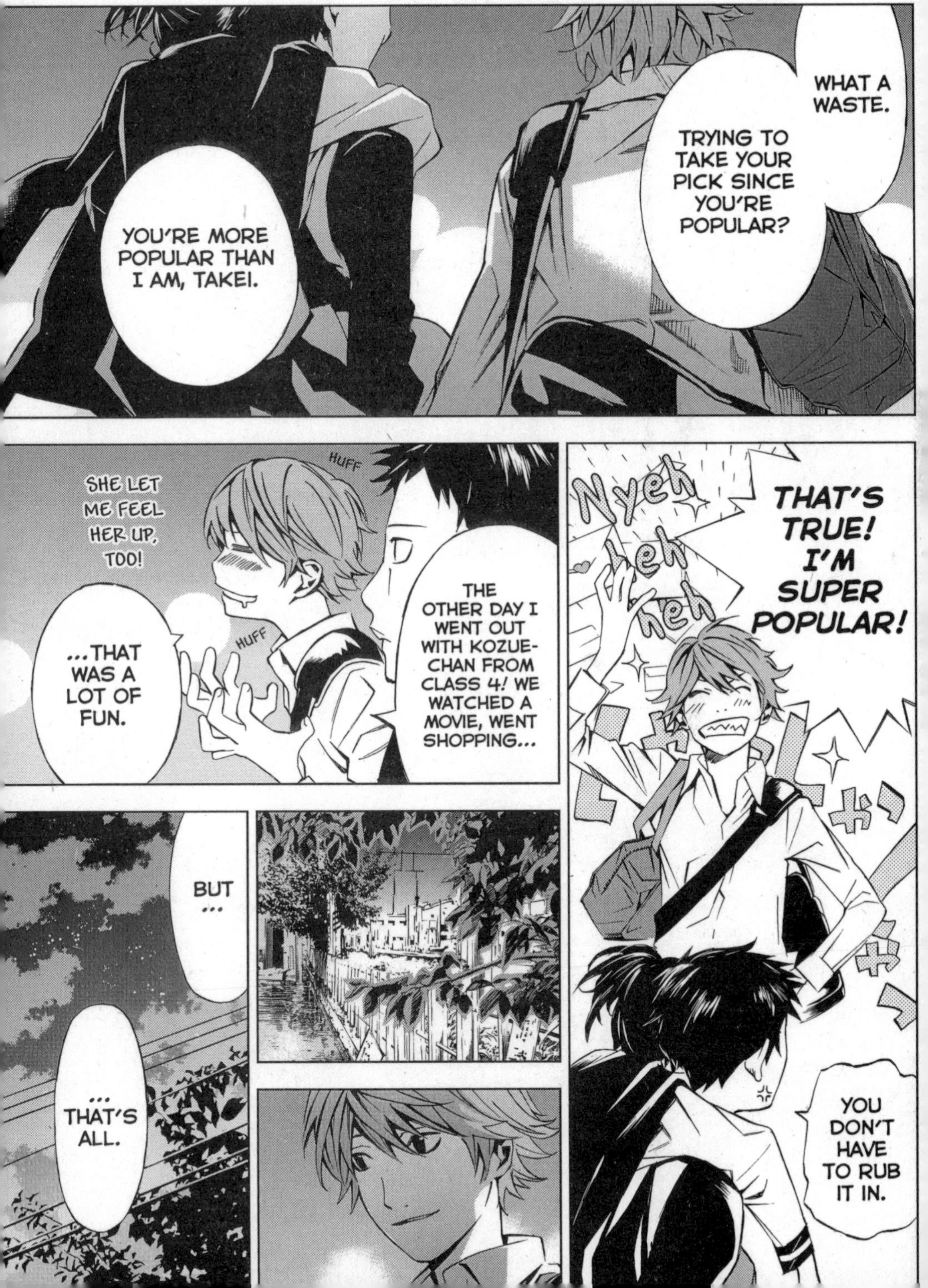
WHAT A WASTE.
TRYING TO TAKE YOUR PICK SINCE YOU'RE POPULAR?
YOU'RE MORE POPULAR THAN I AM, TAKEI.
Nyeh heh heh
THAT'S TRUE! I'M SUPER POPULAR!
YOU DON'T HAVE TO RUB IT IN.
HUFF
THE OTHER DAY I WENT OUT WITH KOZUE-CHAN FROM CLASS 4! WE WATCHED A MOVIE, WENT SHOPPING...
SHE LET ME FEEL HER UP, TOO!
HUFF
...THAT WAS A LOT OF FUN.
BUT...
...THAT'S ALL.

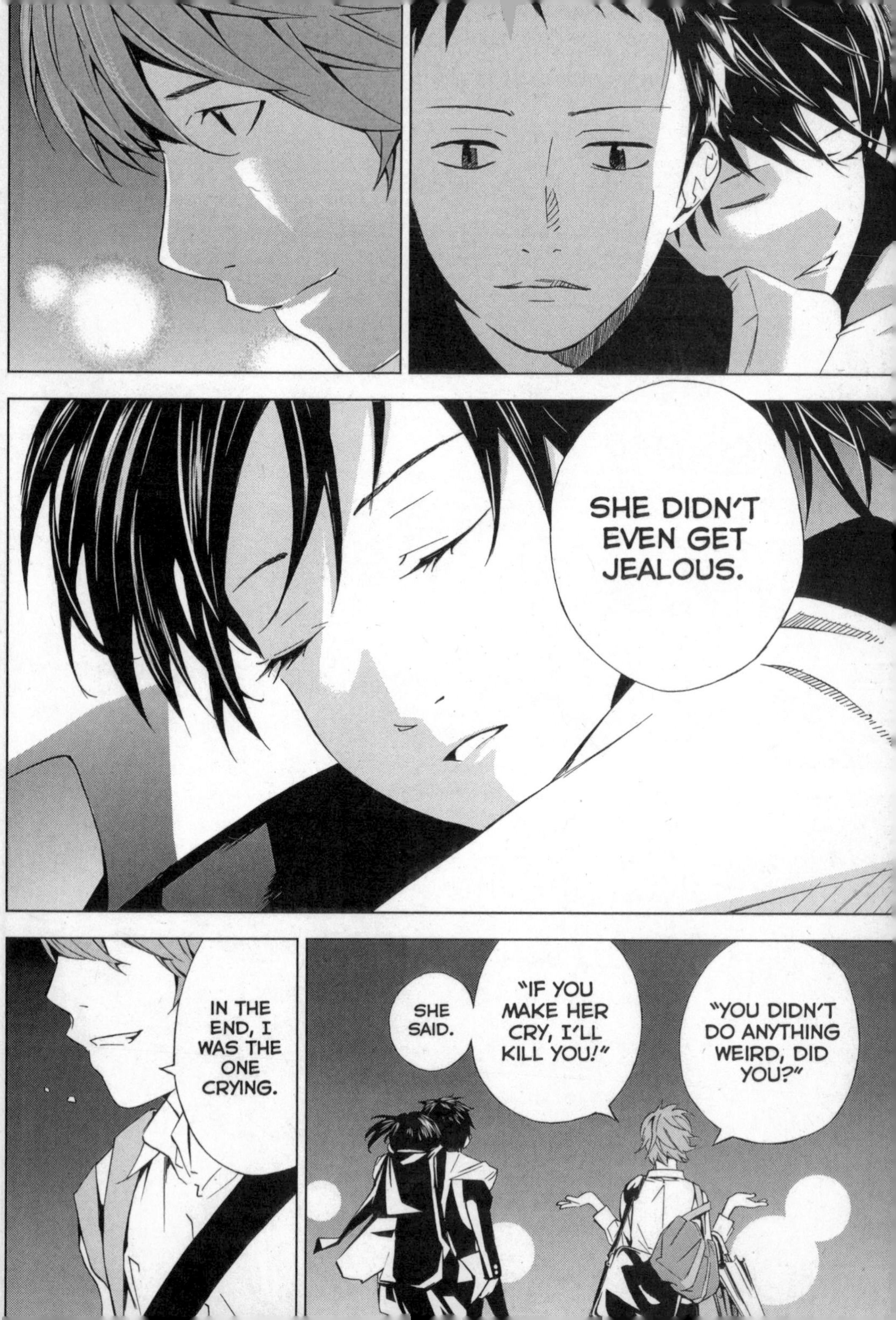
SHE DIDN'T EVEN GET JEALOUS.
"YOU DIDN'T DO ANYTHING WEIRD, DID YOU?"
"IF YOU MAKE HER CRY, I'LL KILL YOU!"
SHE SAID.
IN THE END, I WAS THE ONE CRYING.

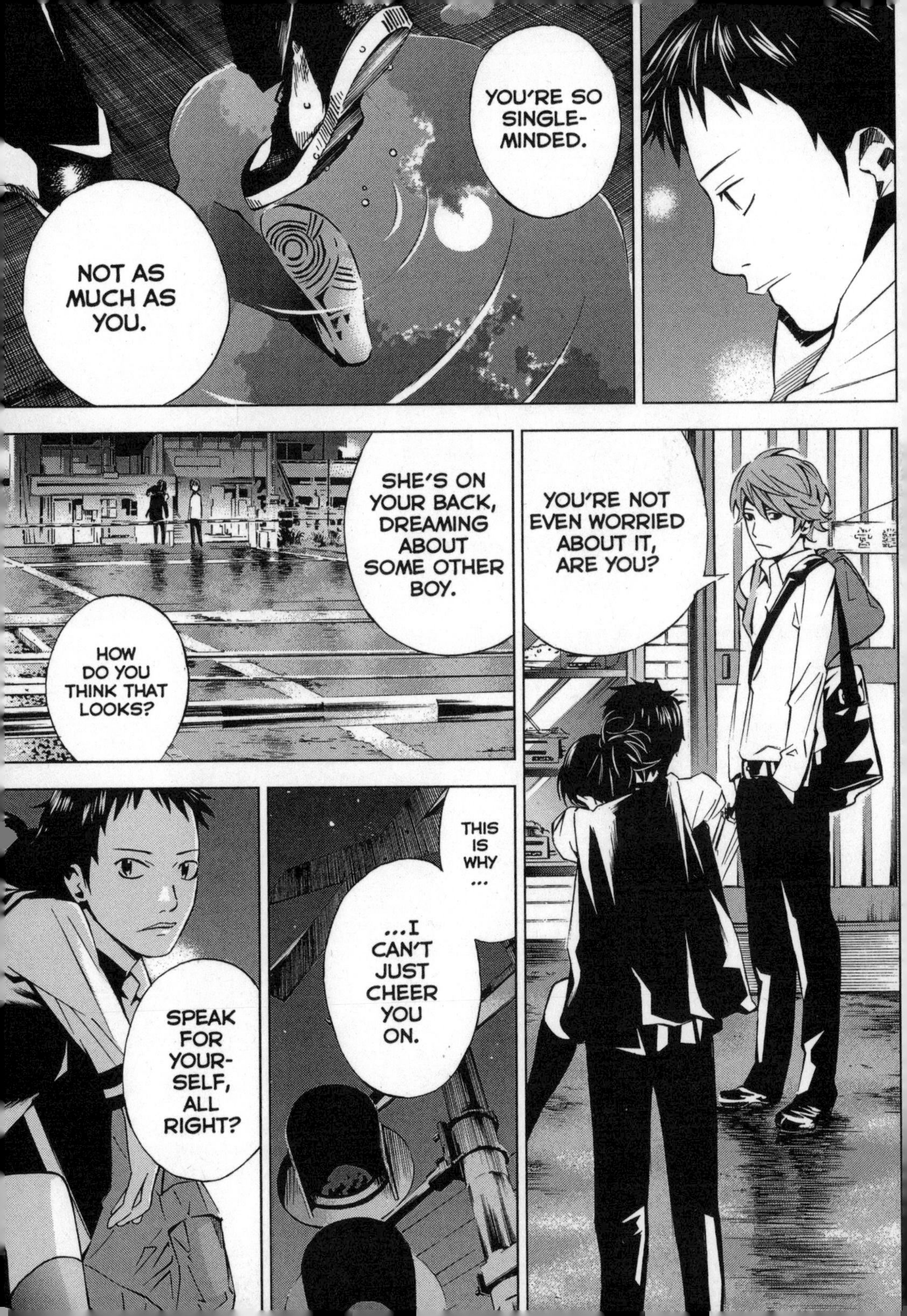
YOU'RE SO SINGLE-MINDED.
NOT AS MUCH AS YOU.
YOU'RE NOT EVEN WORRIED ABOUT IT, ARE YOU?
SHE'S ON YOUR BACK, DREAMING ABOUT SOME OTHER BOY.
HOW DO YOU THINK THAT LOOKS?
THIS IS WHY...
...I CAN'T JUST CHEER YOU ON.
SPEAK FOR YOUR-SELF, ALL RIGHT?

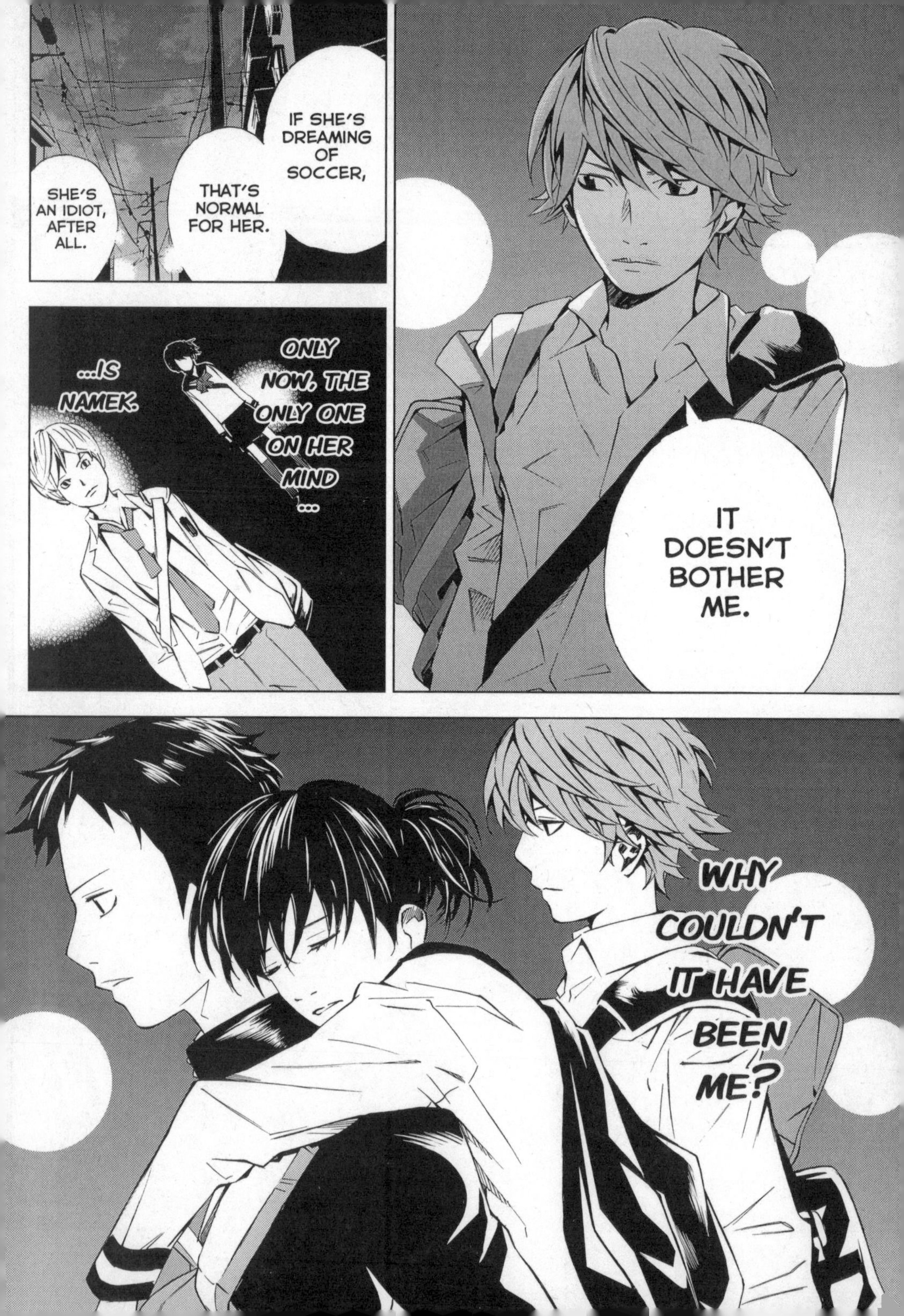
IT DOESN'T BOTHER ME.
IF SHE'S DREAMING OF SOCCER,
THAT'S NORMAL FOR HER.
SHE'S AN IDIOT, AFTER ALL.
ONLY NOW, THE ONLY ONE ON HER MIND...
...IS NAMEK.
WHY COULDN'T IT HAVE BEEN ME?

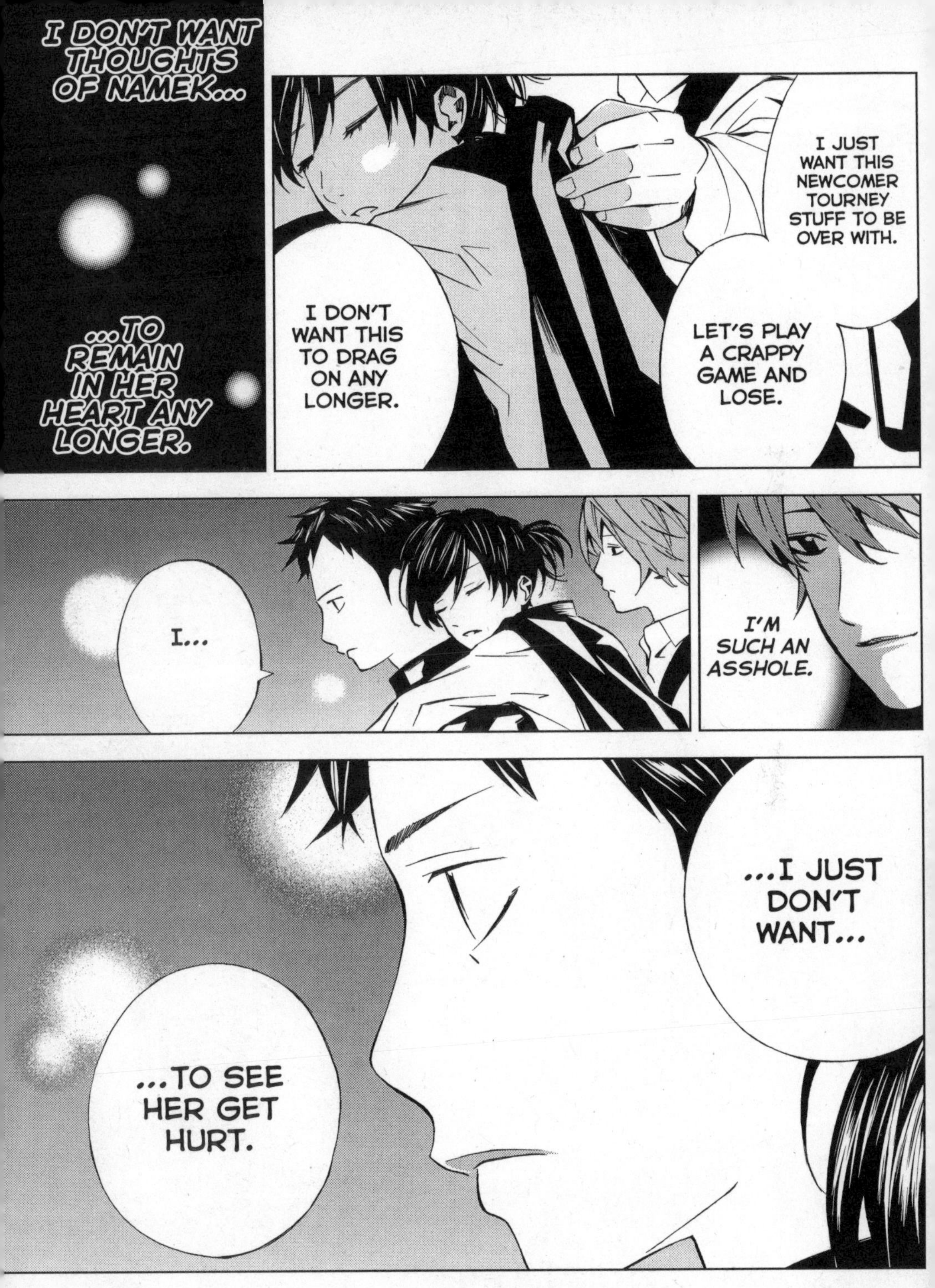
I JUST WANT THIS NEWCOMER TOURNEY STUFF TO BE OVER WITH.
LET'S PLAY A CRAPPY GAME AND LOSE.
I DON'T WANT THIS TO DRAG ON ANY LONGER.
I DON'T WANT THOUGHTS OF NAMEK...
...TO REMAIN IN HER HEART ANY LONGER.
I'M SUCH AN ASSHOLE.
I...
...I JUST DON'T WANT...
...TO SEE HER GET HURT.

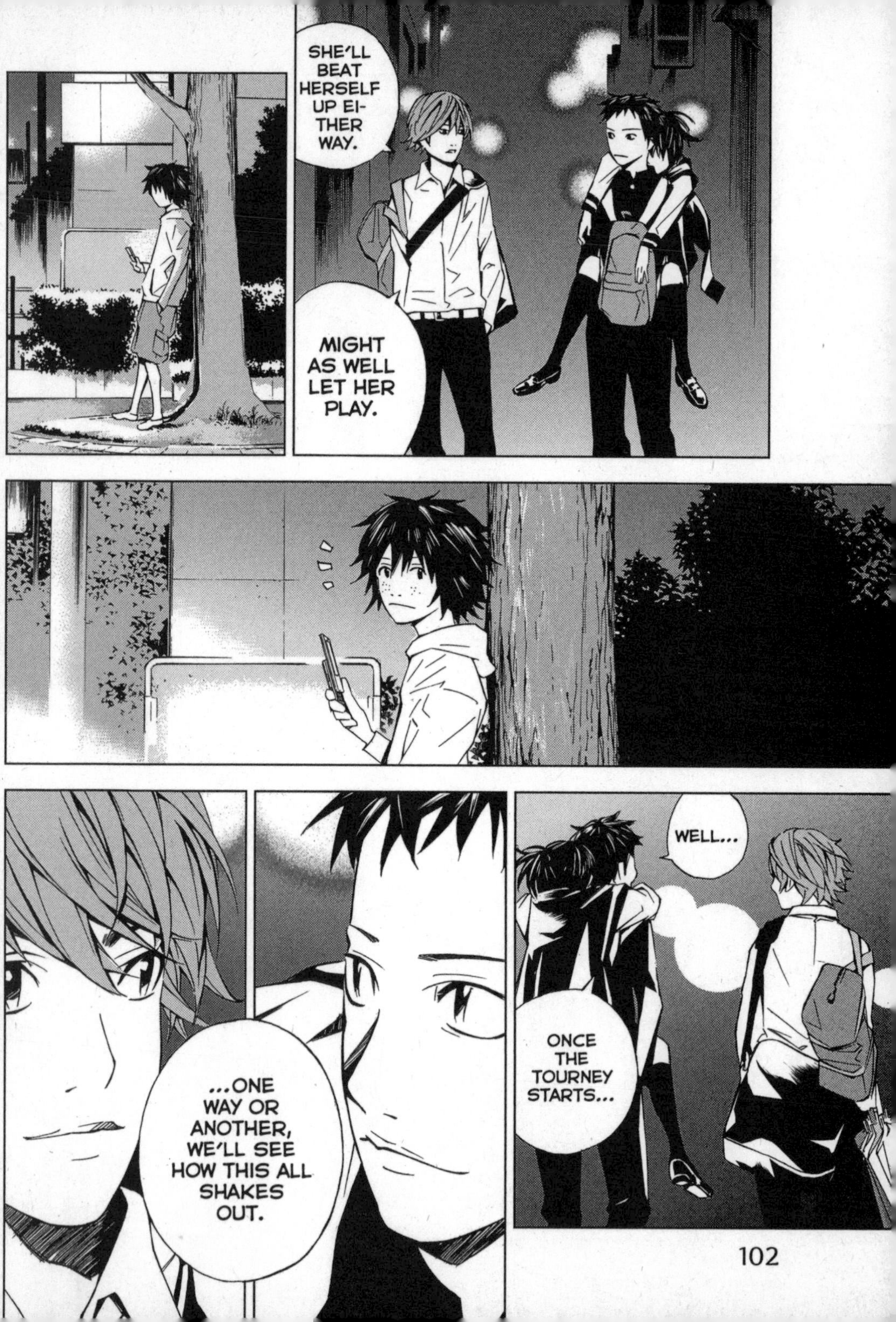
SHE'LL BEAT HERSELF UP EI- THER WAY.
MIGHT AS WELL LET HER PLAY.
WELL...
ONCE THE TOURNEY STARTS...
...ONE WAY OR ANOTHER, WE'LL SEE HOW THIS ALL SHAKES OUT.

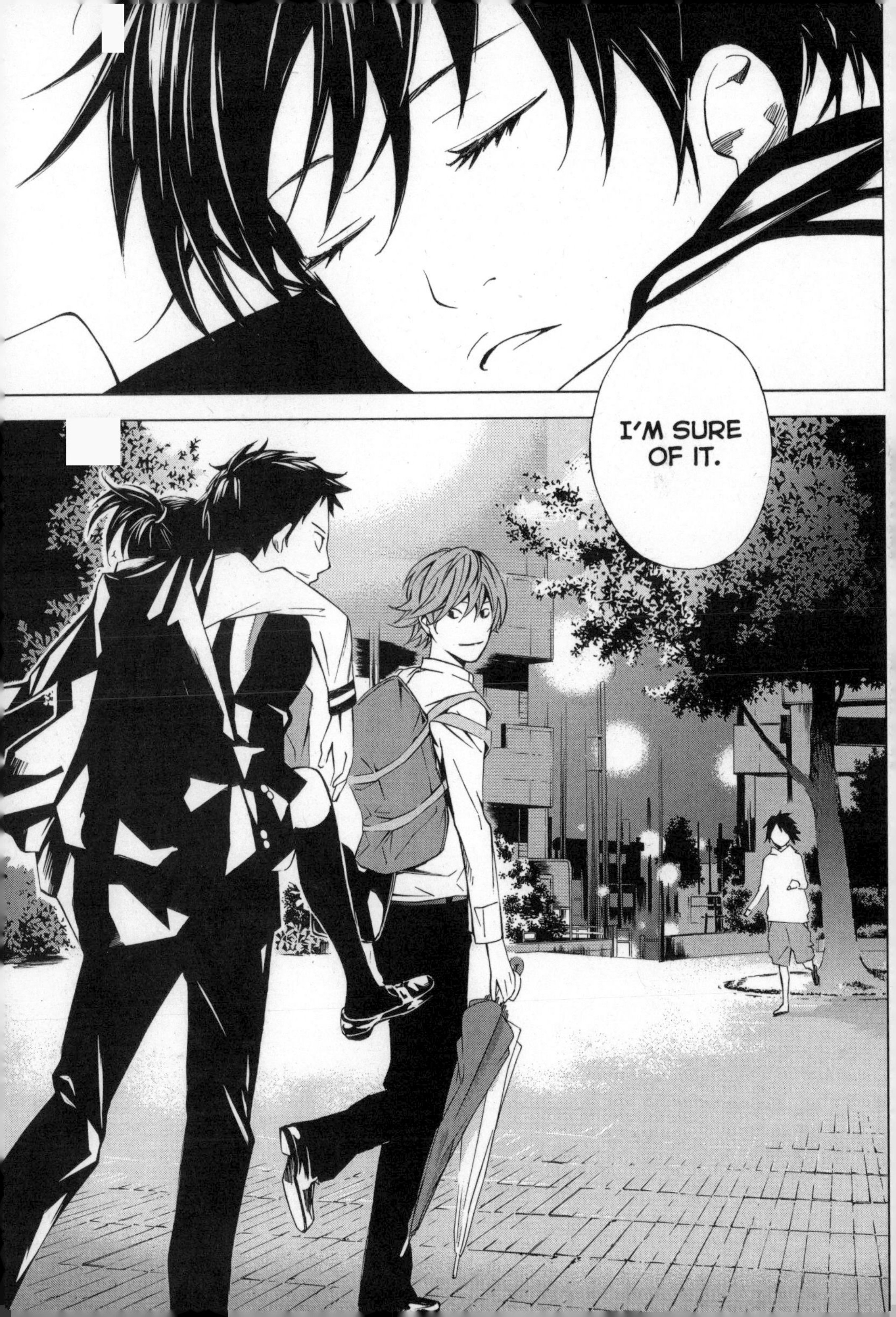
I'M SURE OF IT.

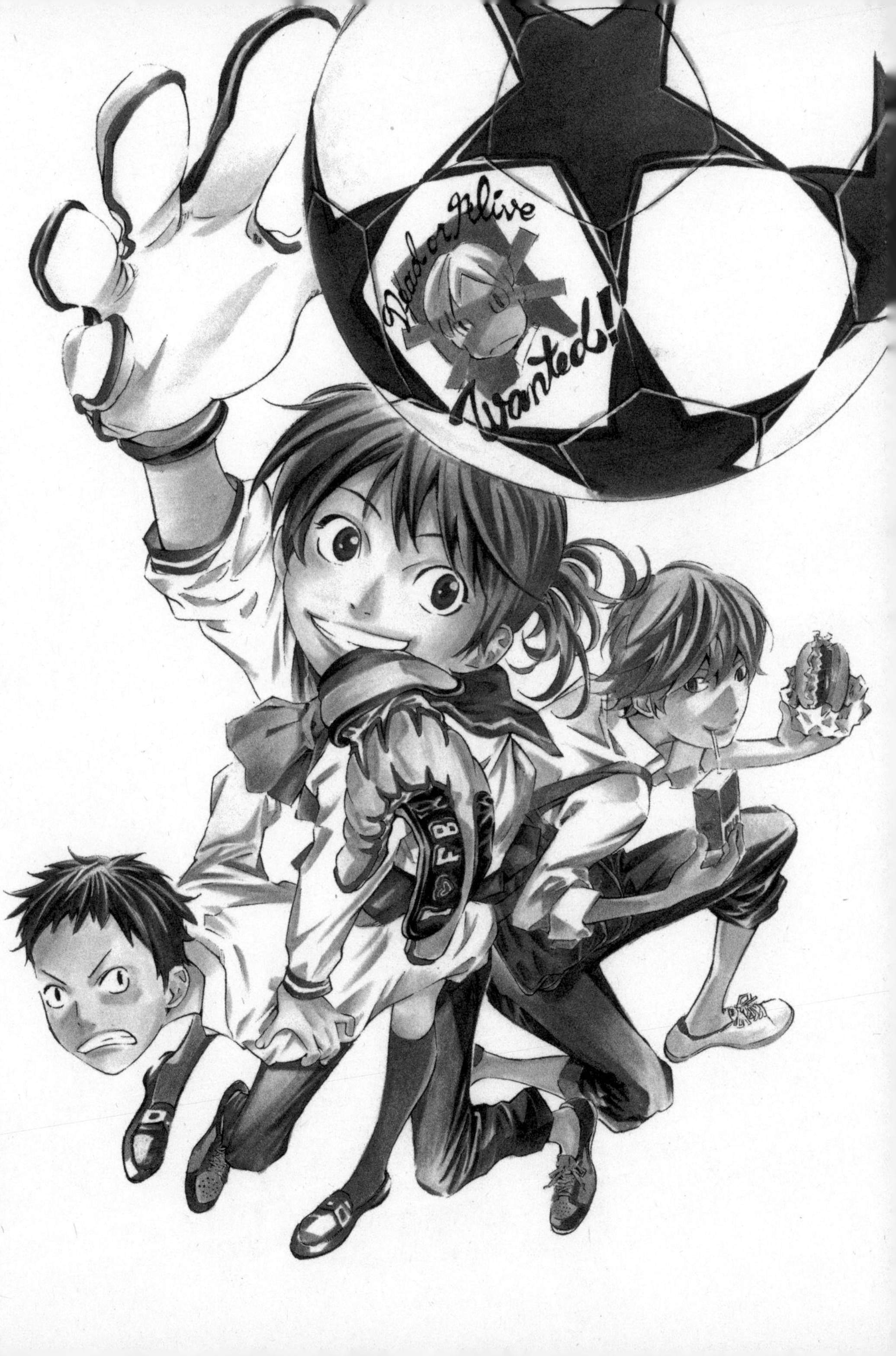
Dead or Alive
Wanted!

SAYONARA FOOTBALL

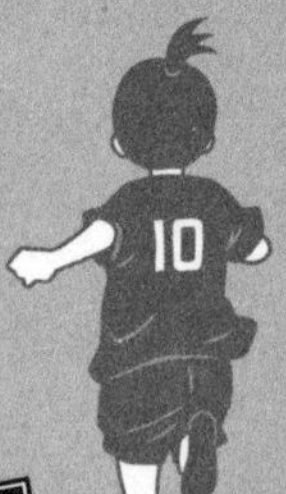
10

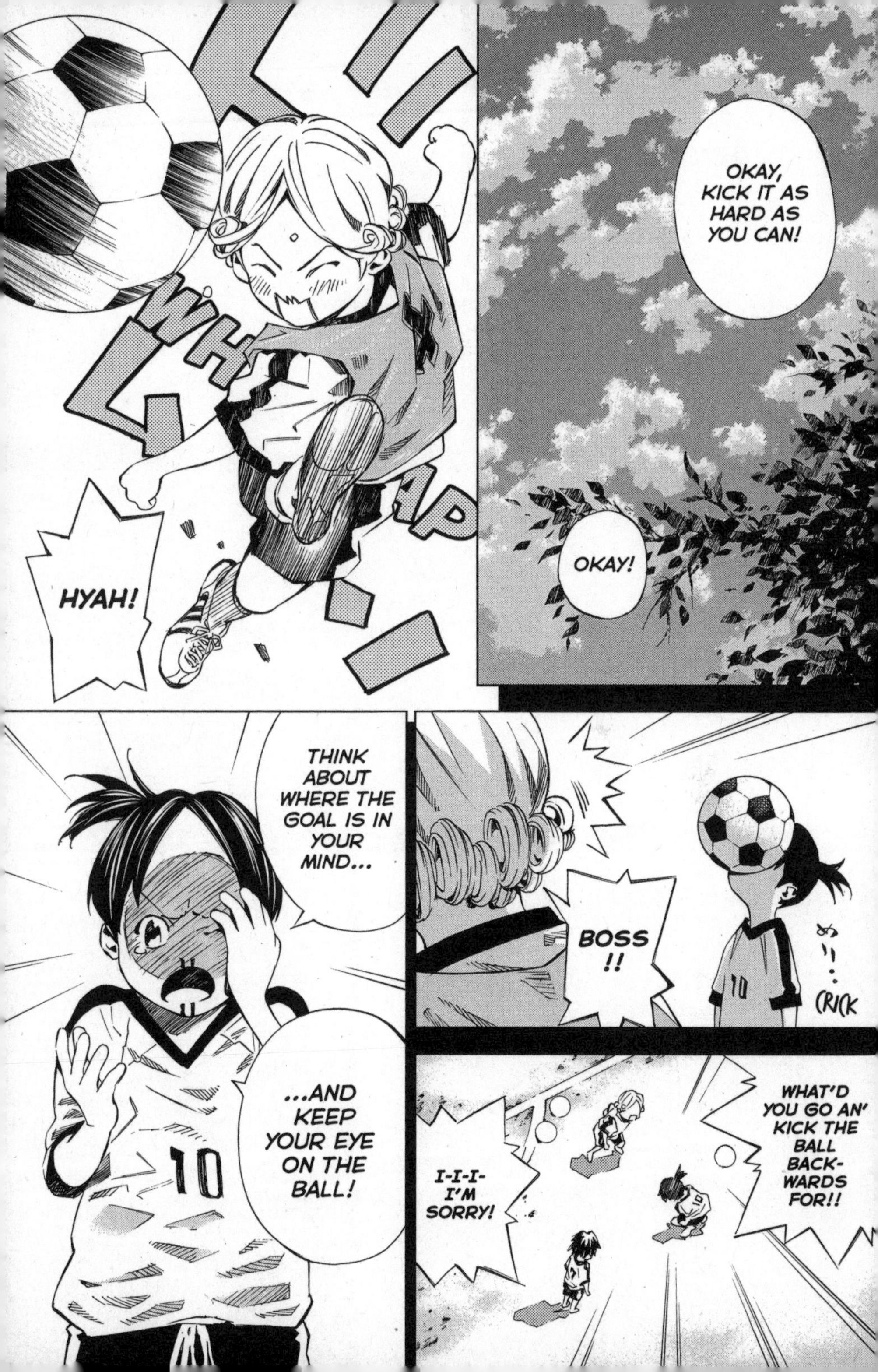
OKAY, KICK IT AS HARD AS YOU CAN!
OKAY!
HYAH!
BOSS !!
CRICK
WHAT'D YOU GO AN' KICK THE BALL BACKWARDS FOR!!
I-I-I-I'M SORRY!
THINK ABOUT WHERE THE GOAL IS IN YOUR MIND...
...AND KEEP YOUR EYE ON THE BALL!

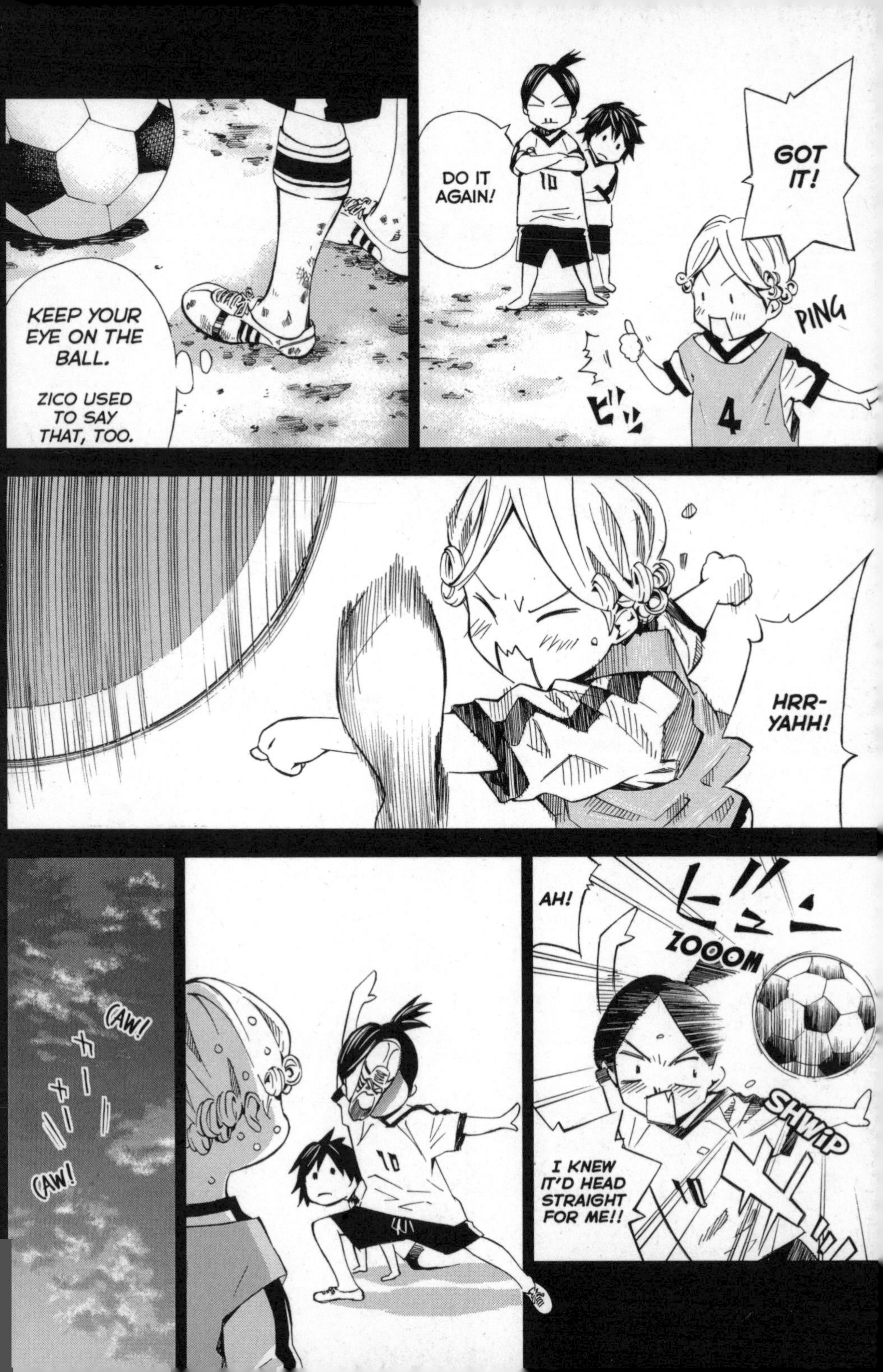
GOT IT!
DO IT AGAIN!
PING
ビッ
KEEP YOUR EYE ON THE BALL.
ZICO USED TO SAY THAT, TOO.
HRR-YAHH!
AH!
ZOOOM
SHWIP
I KNEW IT'D HEAD STRAIGHT FOR ME!!
CAW!
カー
カー
CAW!

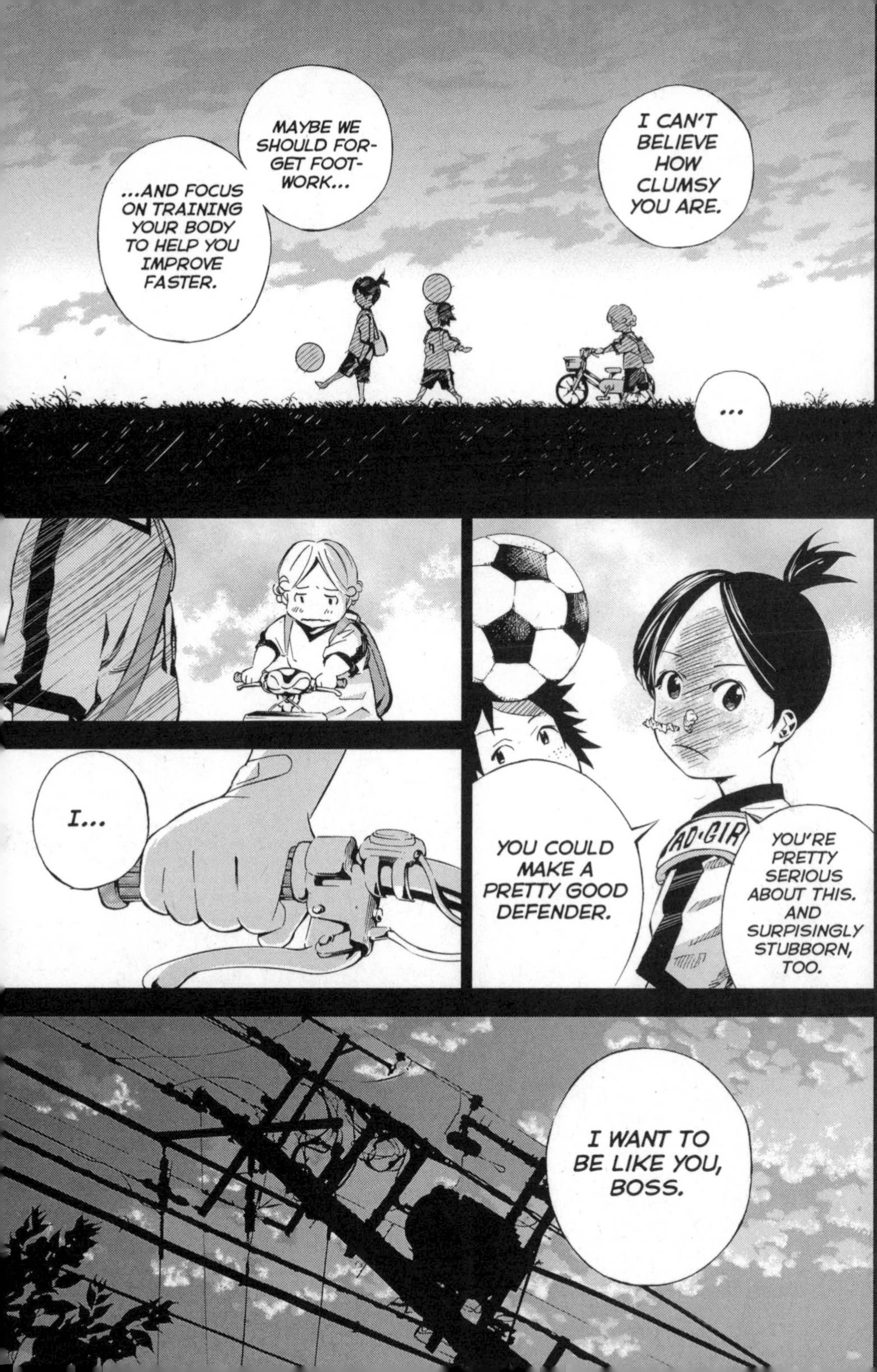
I CAN'T BELIEVE HOW CLUMSY YOU ARE.
MAYBE WE SHOULD FORGET FOOTWORK...
...AND FOCUS ON TRAINING YOUR BODY TO HELP YOU IMPROVE FASTER.
...
YOU'RE PRETTY SERIOUS ABOUT THIS. AND SURPISINGLY STUBBORN, TOO.
YOU COULD MAKE A PRETTY GOOD DEFENDER.
I...
I WANT TO BE LIKE YOU, BOSS.

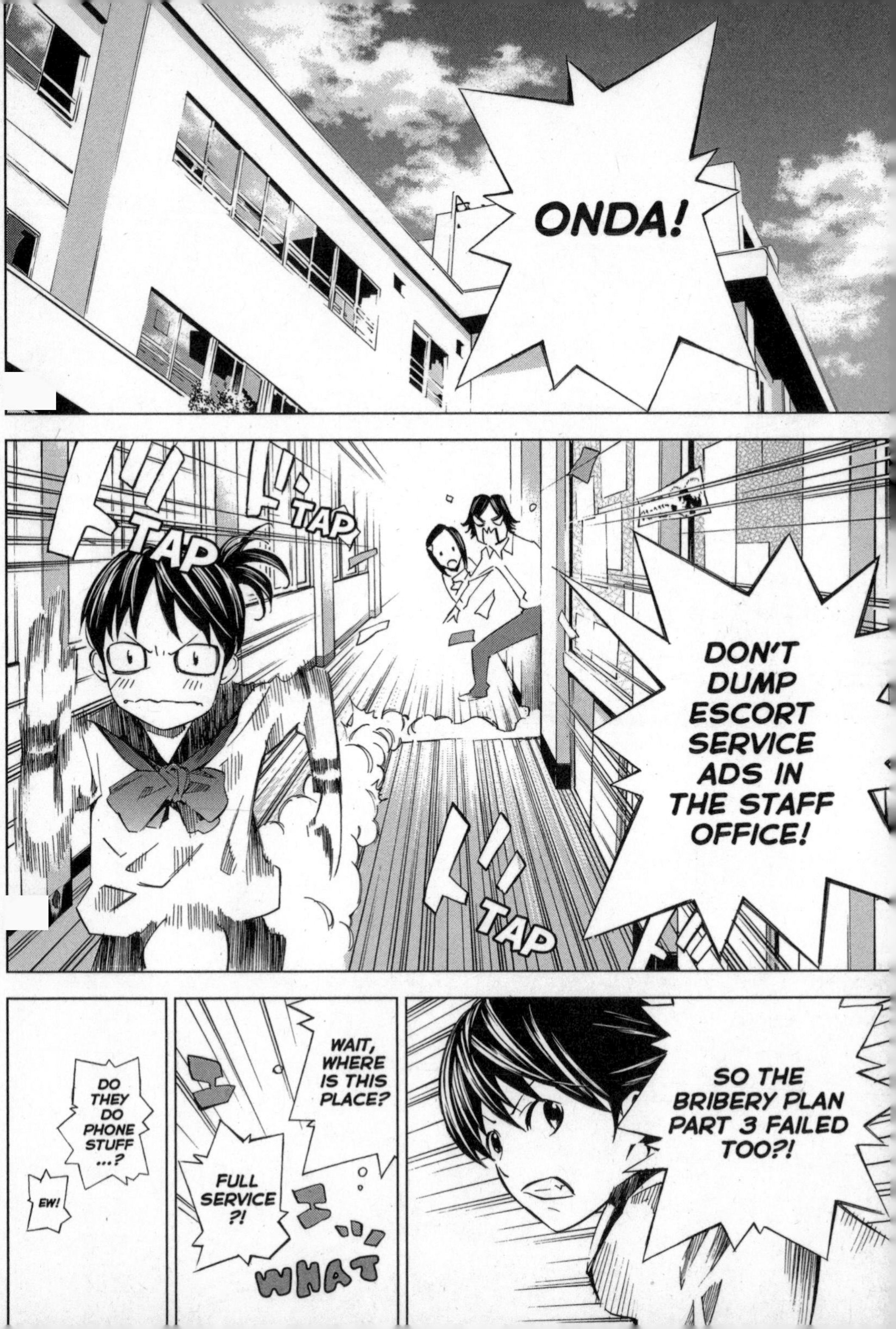
ONDA!
TAP
TAP
DON'T DUMP ESCORT SERVICE ADS IN THE STAFF OFFICE!
TAP
SO THE BRIBERY PLAN PART 3 FAILED TOO?!
WAIT, WHERE IS THIS PLACE?
FULL SERVICE ?!
WHAT
DO THEY DO PHONE STUFF ...?
EW!

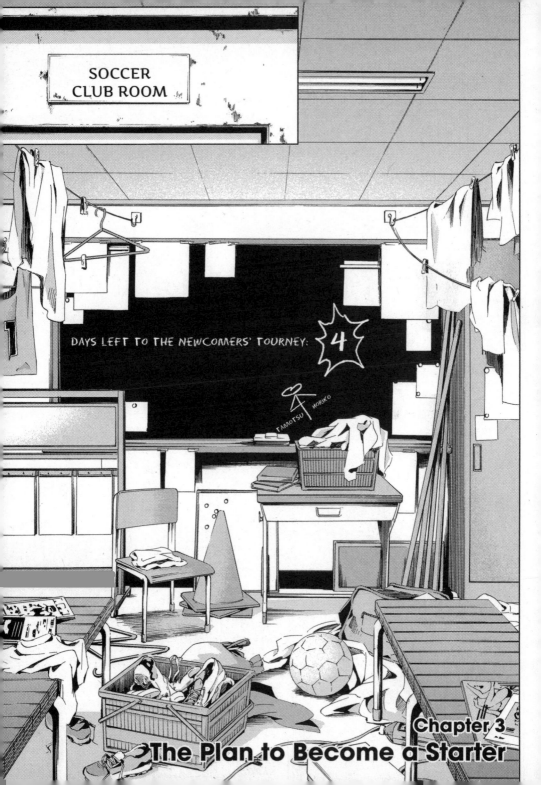

SOCCER CLUB ROOM

DAYS LEFT TO THE NEWCOMERS' TOURNEY: 4

Chapter 3
The Plan to Become a Starter

NEWCOMERS' TOURNEY: 4

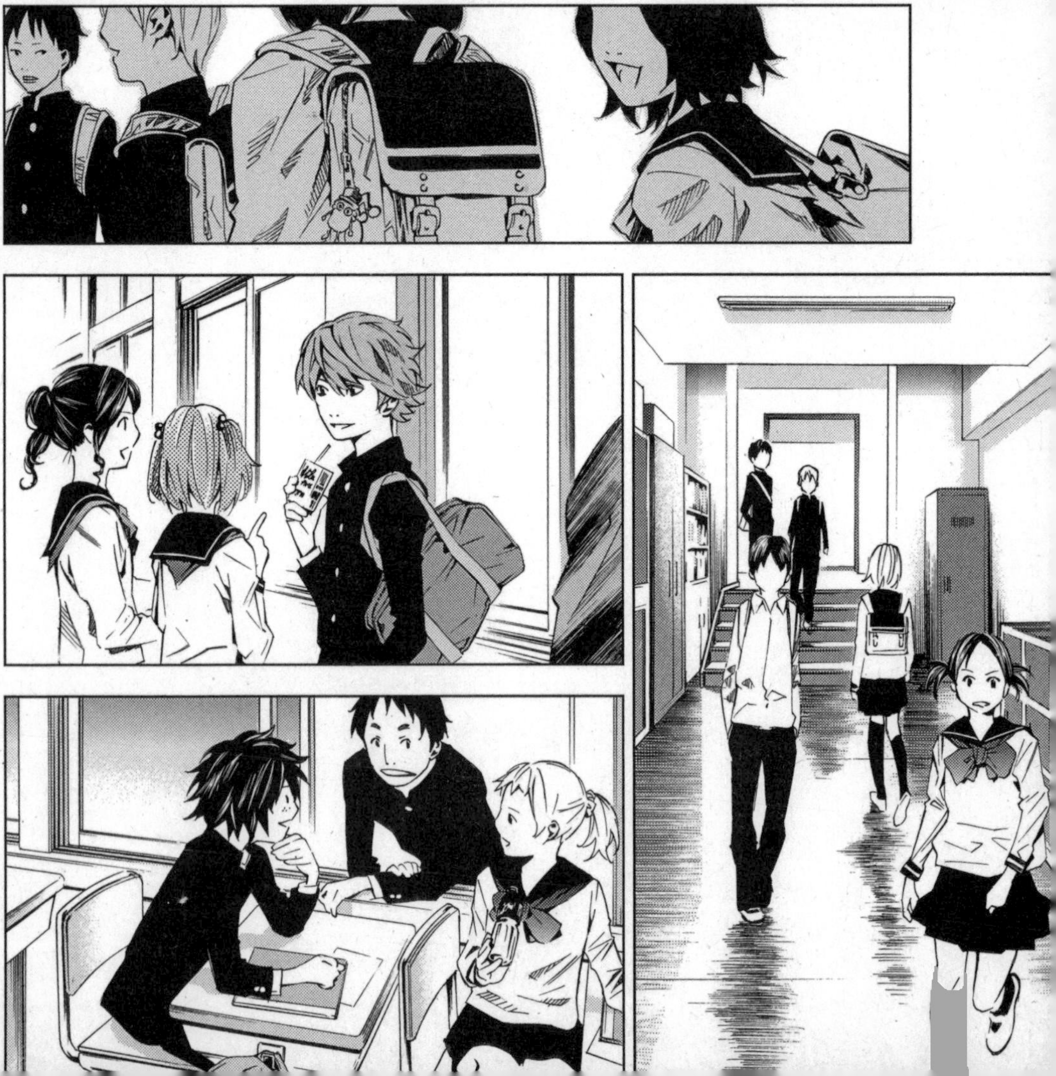

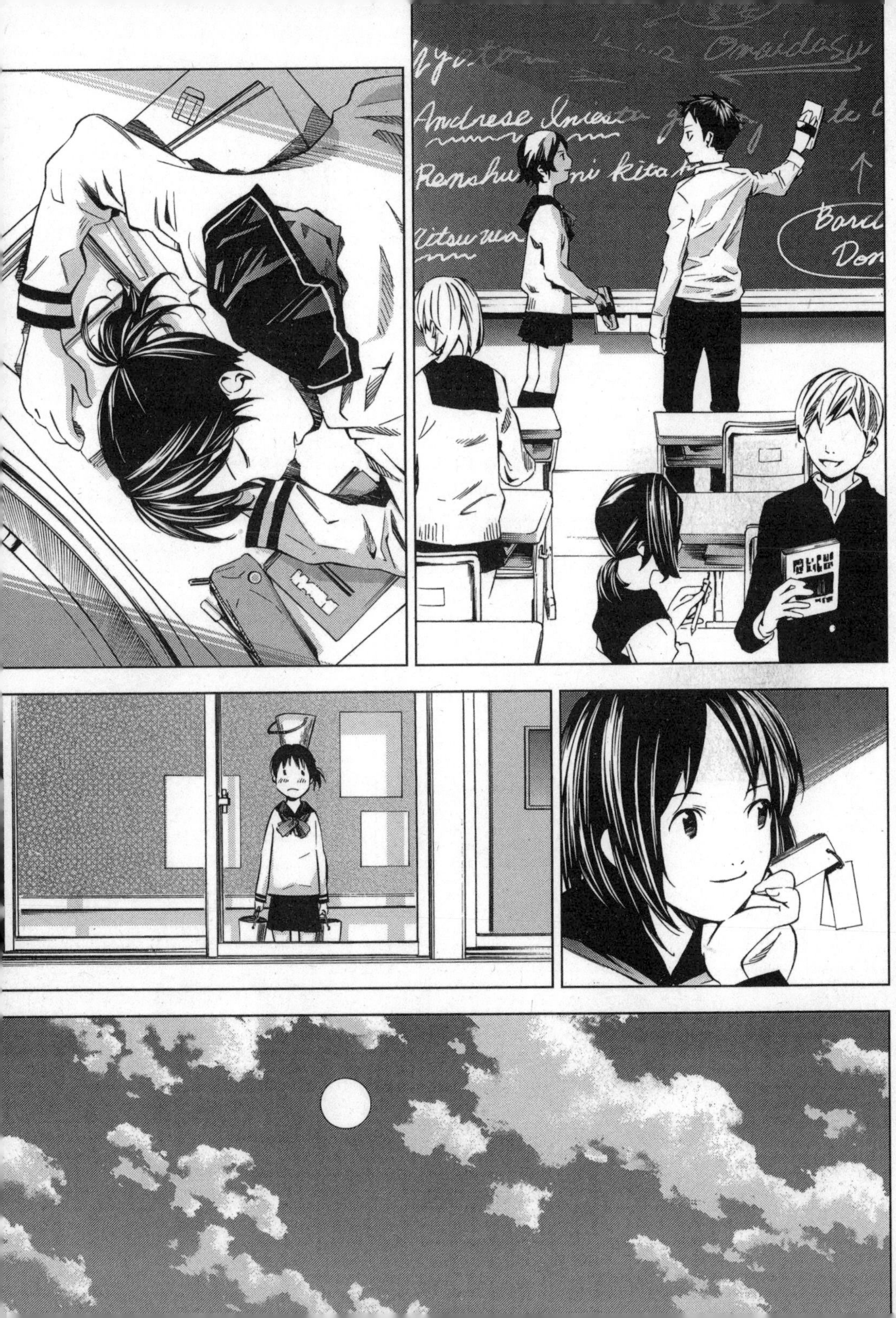

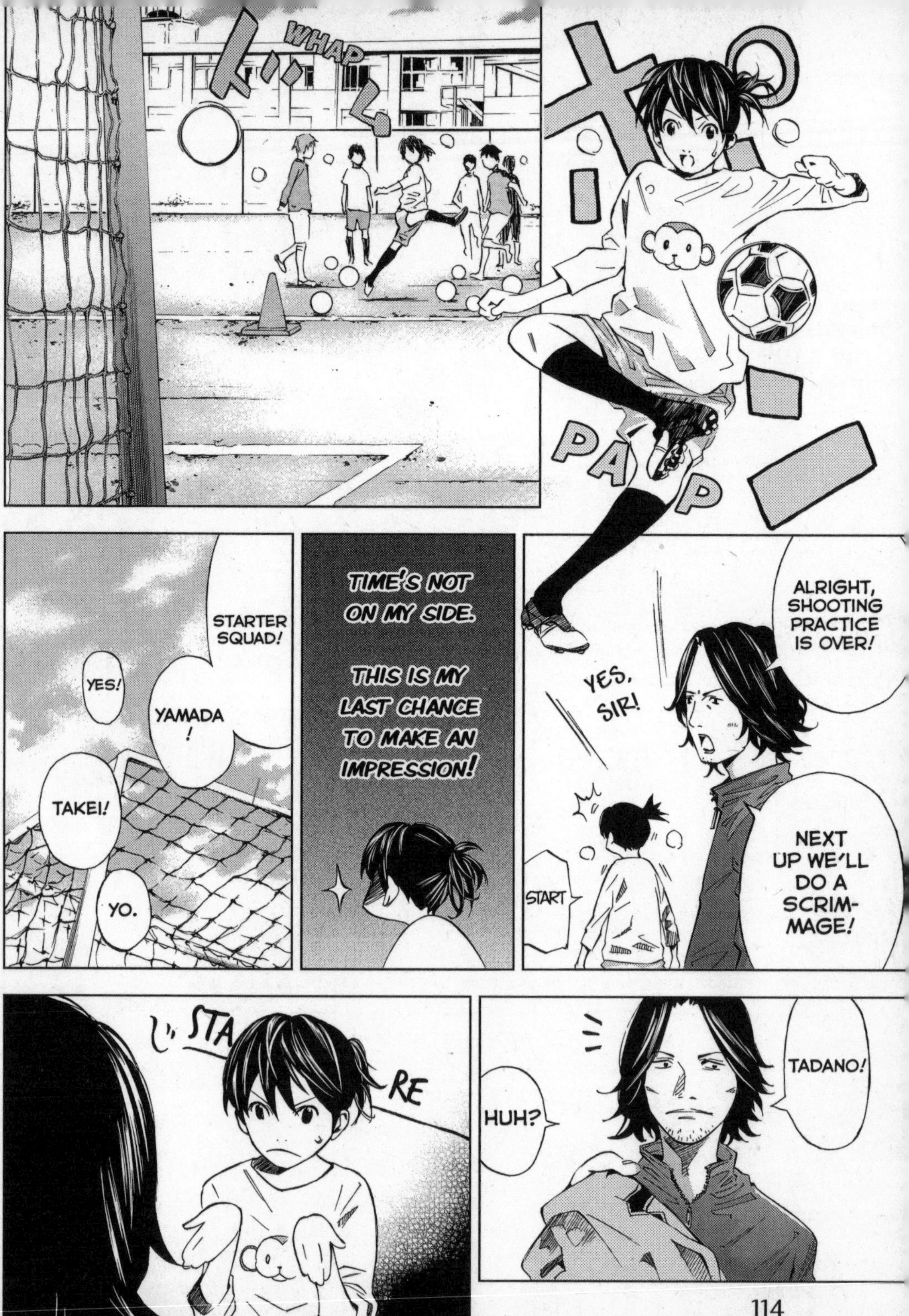
PAP
WHAP
ALRIGHT, SHOOTING PRACTICE IS OVER!
YES, SIR!
NEXT UP WE'LL DO A SCRIM-MAGE!
START
TIME'S NOT ON MY SIDE.
THIS IS MY LAST CHANCE TO MAKE AN IMPRESSION!
STARTER SQUAD!
YES!
YAMADA!
TAKEI!
YO.
TADANO!
HUH?
STARE

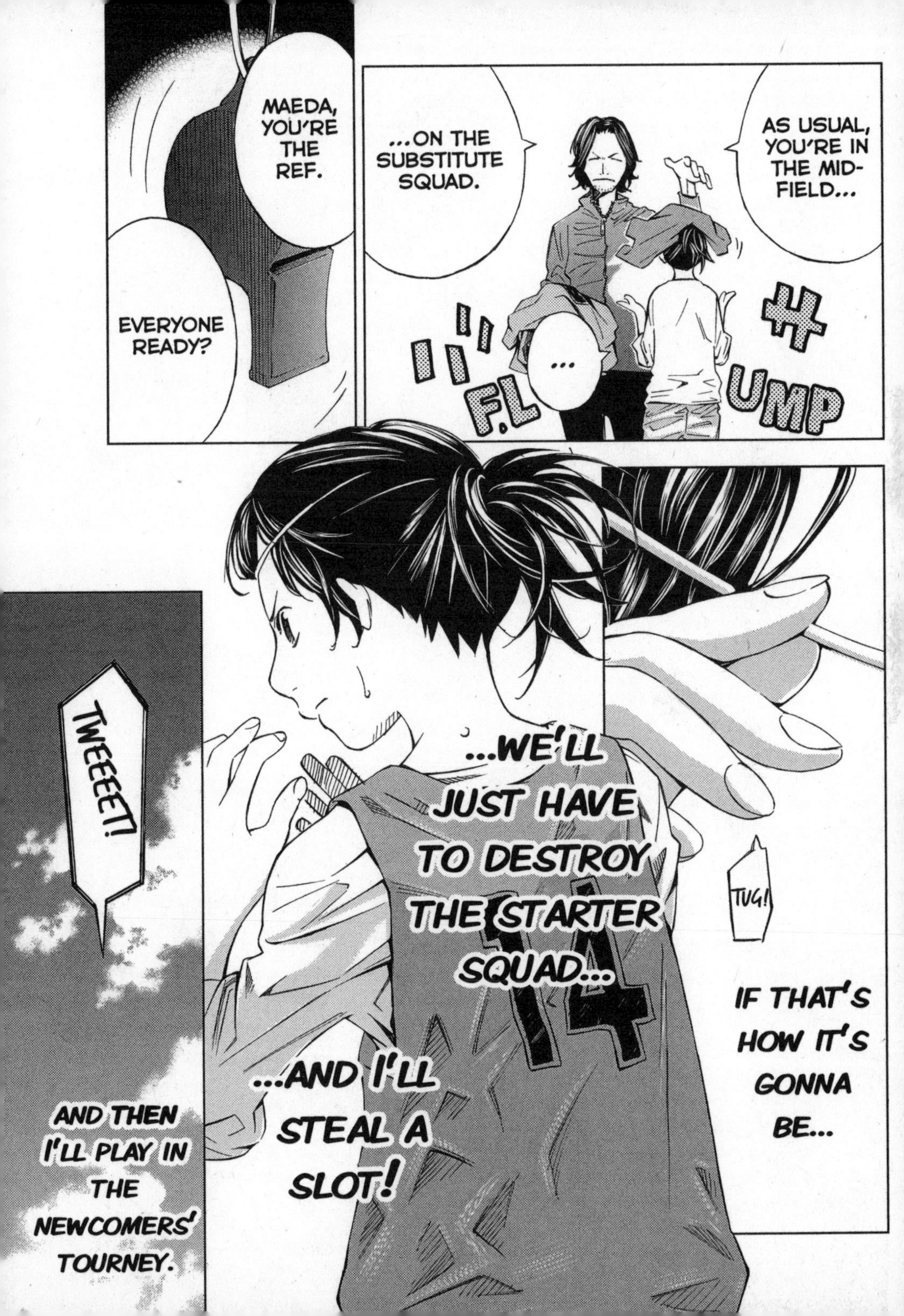
AS USUAL, YOU'RE IN THE MID-FIELD...
...ON THE SUBSTITUTE SQUAD.
FLUMP
...
MAEDA, YOU'RE THE REF.
EVERYONE READY?
TUG!
IF THAT'S HOW IT'S GONNA BE...
...WE'LL JUST HAVE TO DESTROY THE STARTER SQUAD...
...AND I'LL STEAL A SLOT!
AND THEN I'LL PLAY IN THE NEWCOMERS' TOURNEY.
TWEEEET!

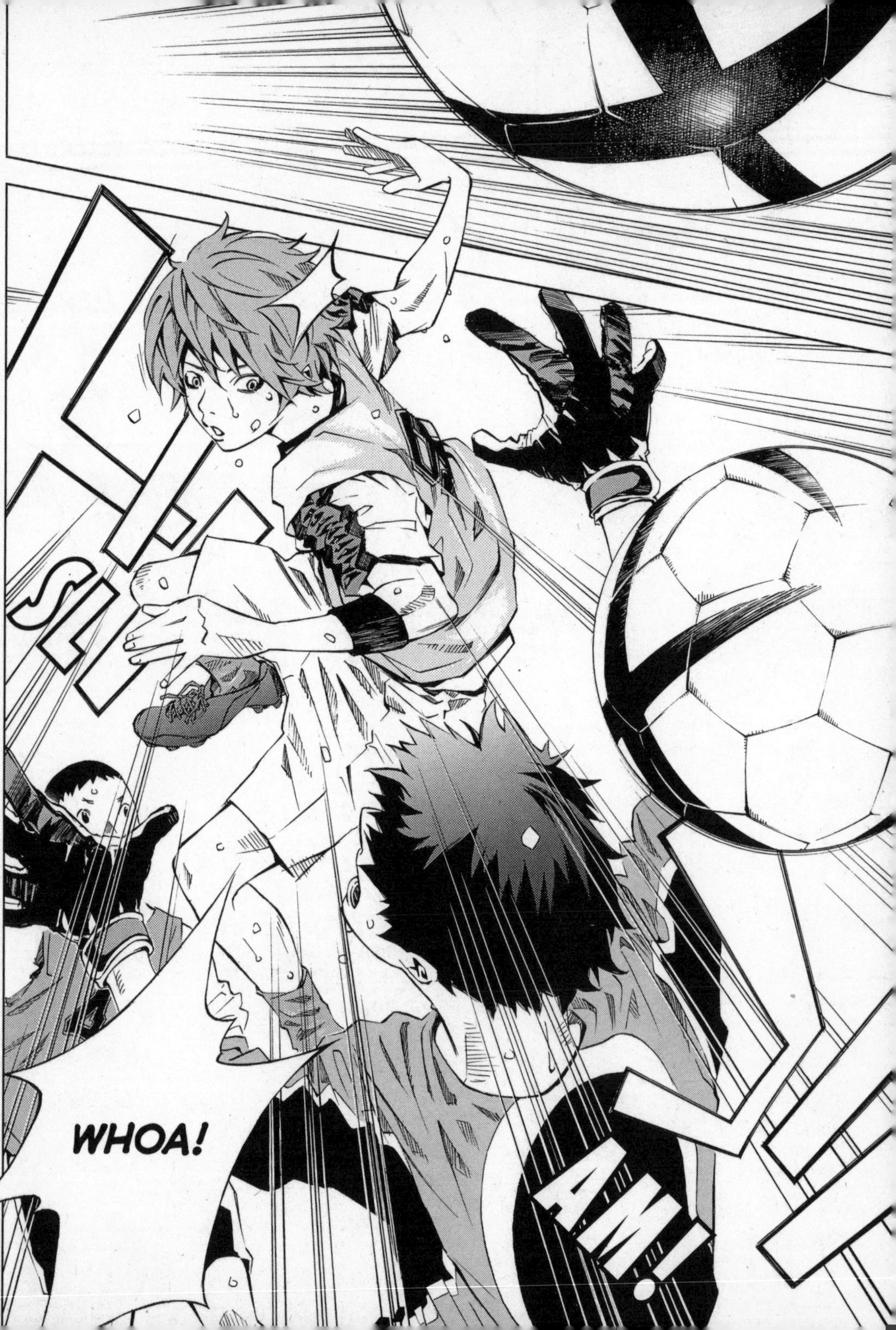
SL
AM!
WHOA!

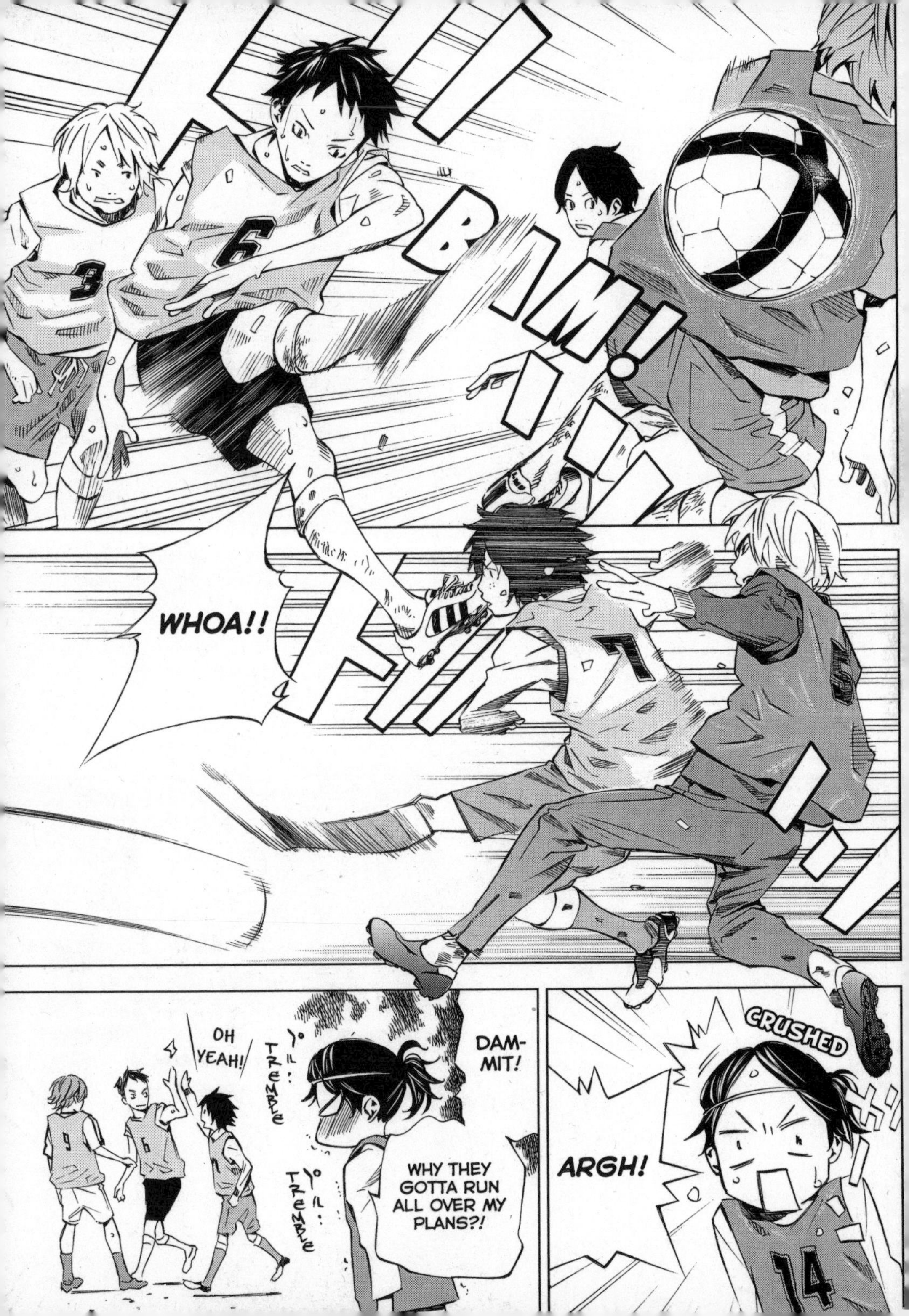
BAM!
WHOA!!
CRUSHED
ARGH!
DAM-MIT!
WHY THEY GOTTA RUN ALL OVER MY PLANS?!
TREMBLE
TREMBLE
OH YEAH!

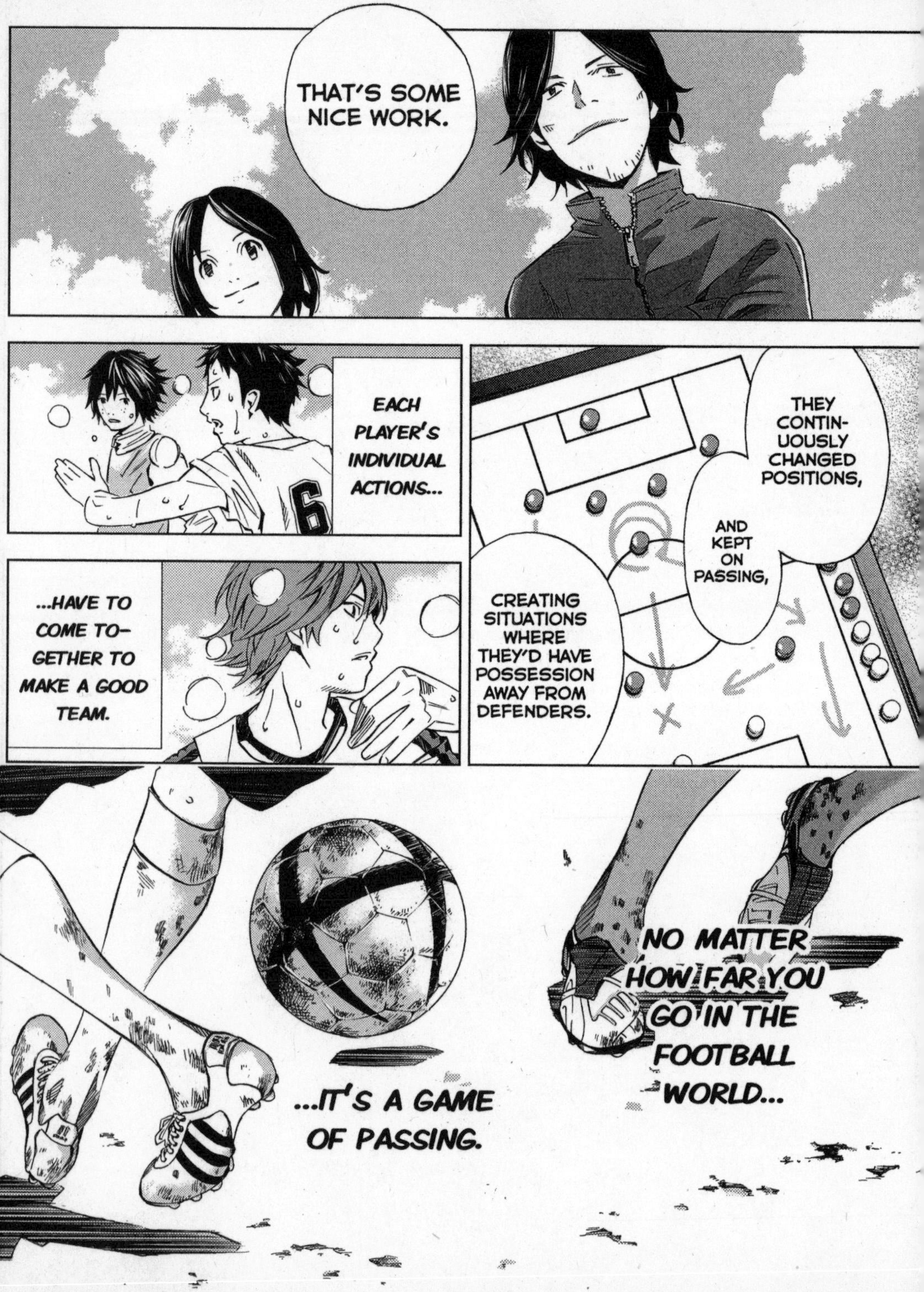
THAT'S SOME NICE WORK.
THEY CONTIN-UOUSLY CHANGED POSITIONS,
AND KEPT ON PASSING,
CREATING SITUATIONS WHERE THEY'D HAVE POSSESSION AWAY FROM DEFENDERS.
EACH PLAYER'S INDIVIDUAL ACTIONS...
...HAVE TO COME TO-GETHER TO MAKE A GOOD TEAM.
NO MATTER HOW FAR YOU GO IN THE FOOTBALL WORLD...
...IT'S A GAME OF PASSING.

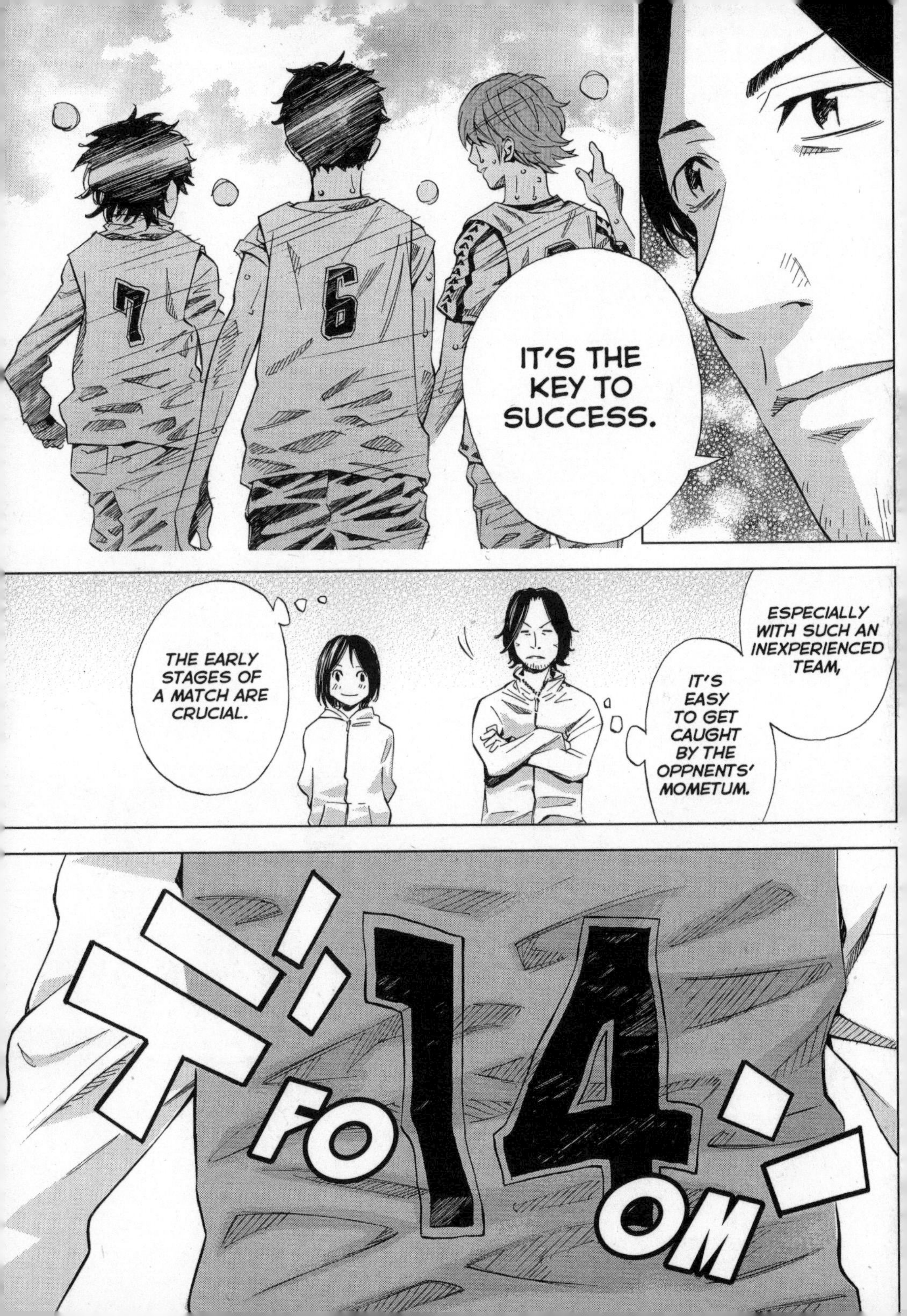
IT'S THE KEY TO SUCCESS.
ESPECIALLY WITH SUCH AN INEXPERIENCED TEAM,
IT'S EASY TO GET CAUGHT BY THE OPPNENTS' MOMETUM.
THE EARLY STAGES OF A MATCH ARE CRUCIAL.
14
FOOM

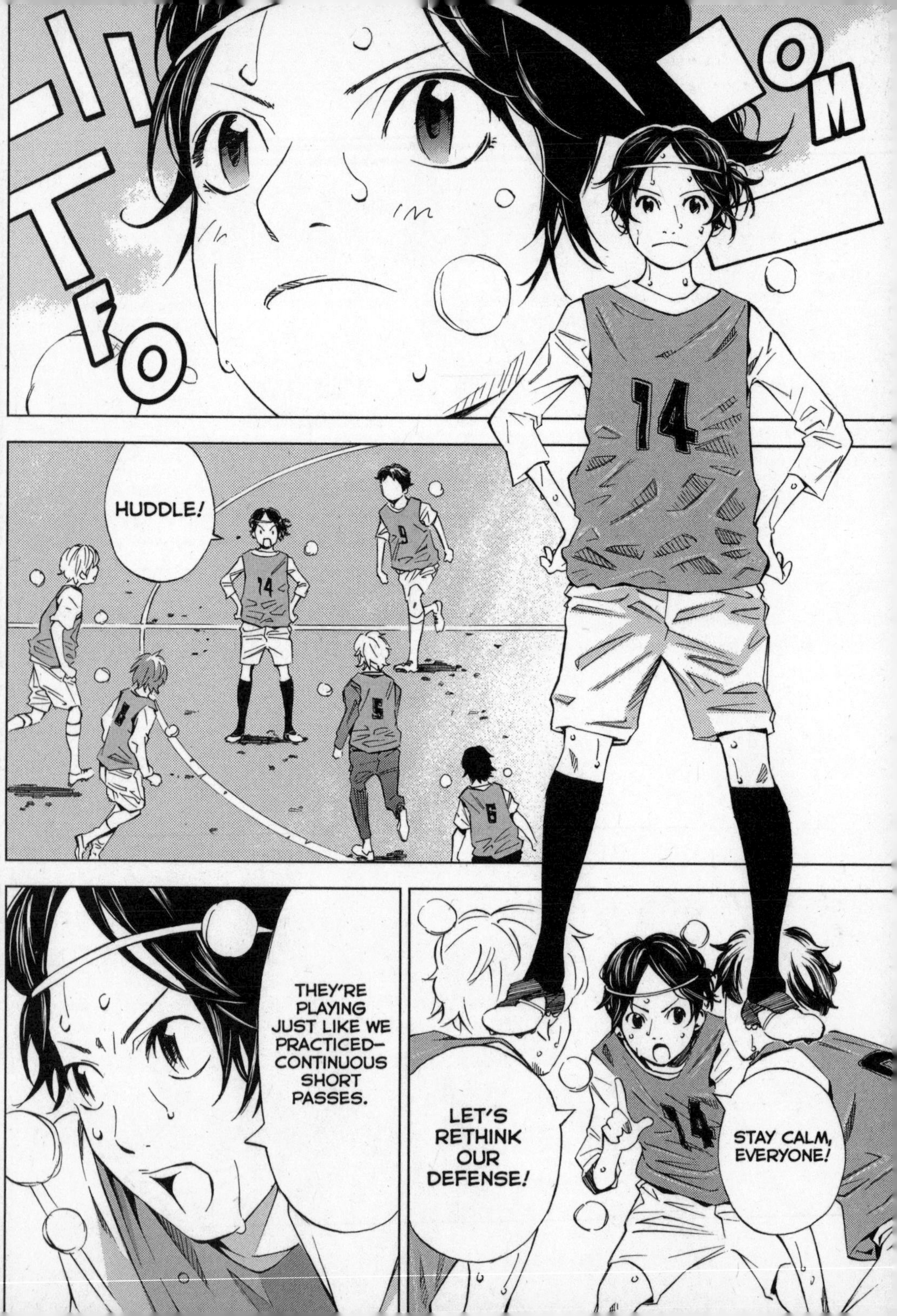
HUDDLE!
STAY CALM, EVERYONE!
LET'S RETHINK OUR DEFENSE!
THEY'RE PLAYING JUST LIKE WE PRACTICED—CONTINUOUS SHORT PASSES.

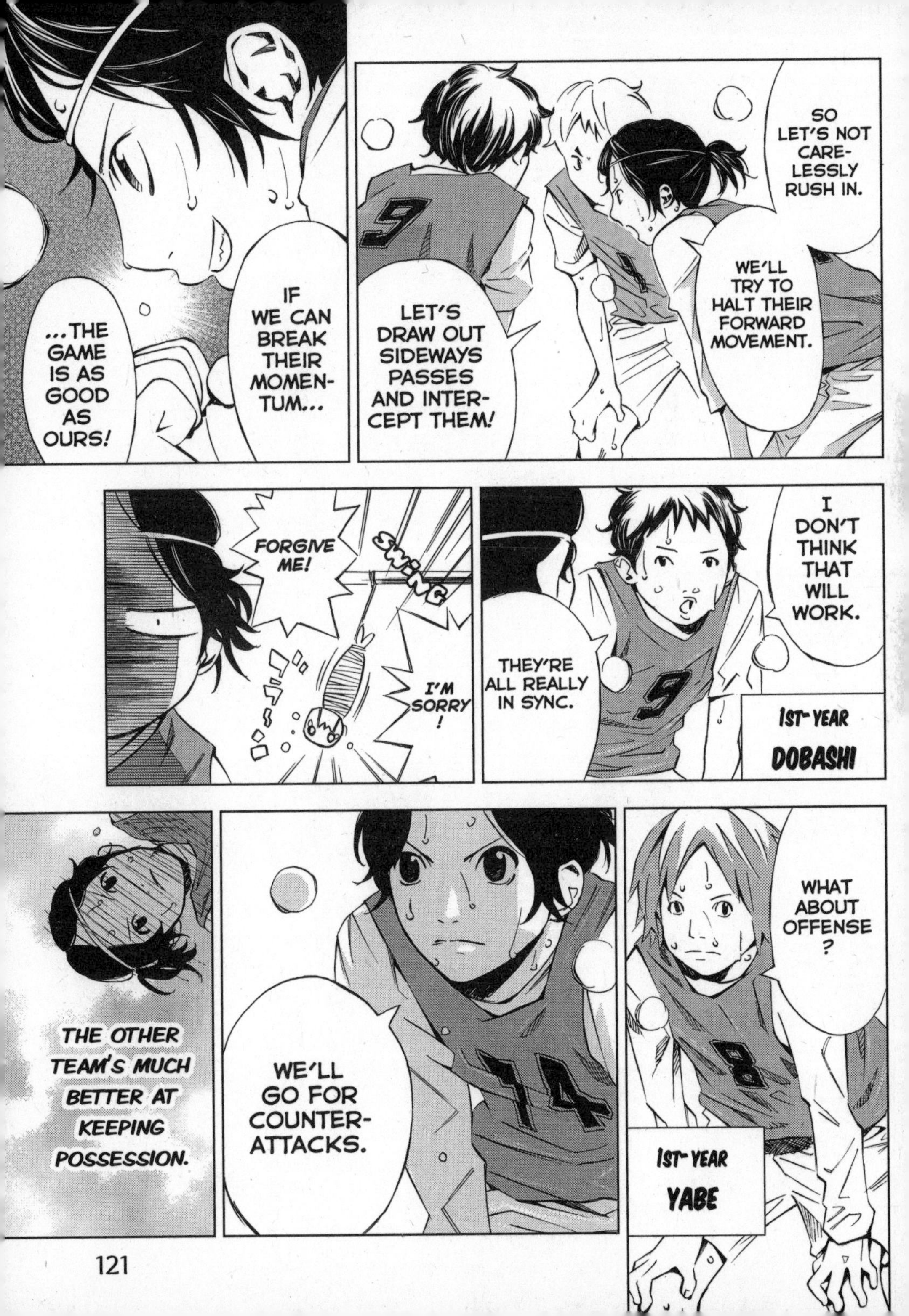
SO LET'S NOT CARELESSLY RUSH IN.
WE'LL TRY TO HALT THEIR FORWARD MOVEMENT.
LET'S DRAW OUT SIDEWAYS PASSES AND INTERCEPT THEM!
IF WE CAN BREAK THEIR MOMENTUM...
...THE GAME IS AS GOOD AS OURS!
I DON'T THINK THAT WILL WORK.
1ST-YEAR DOBASHI
THEY'RE ALL REALLY IN SYNC.
SWING
FORGIVE ME!
I'M SORRY!
WHAT ABOUT OFFENSE?
1ST-YEAR YABE
WE'LL GO FOR COUNTERATTACKS.
THE OTHER TEAM'S MUCH BETTER AT KEEPING POSSESSION.

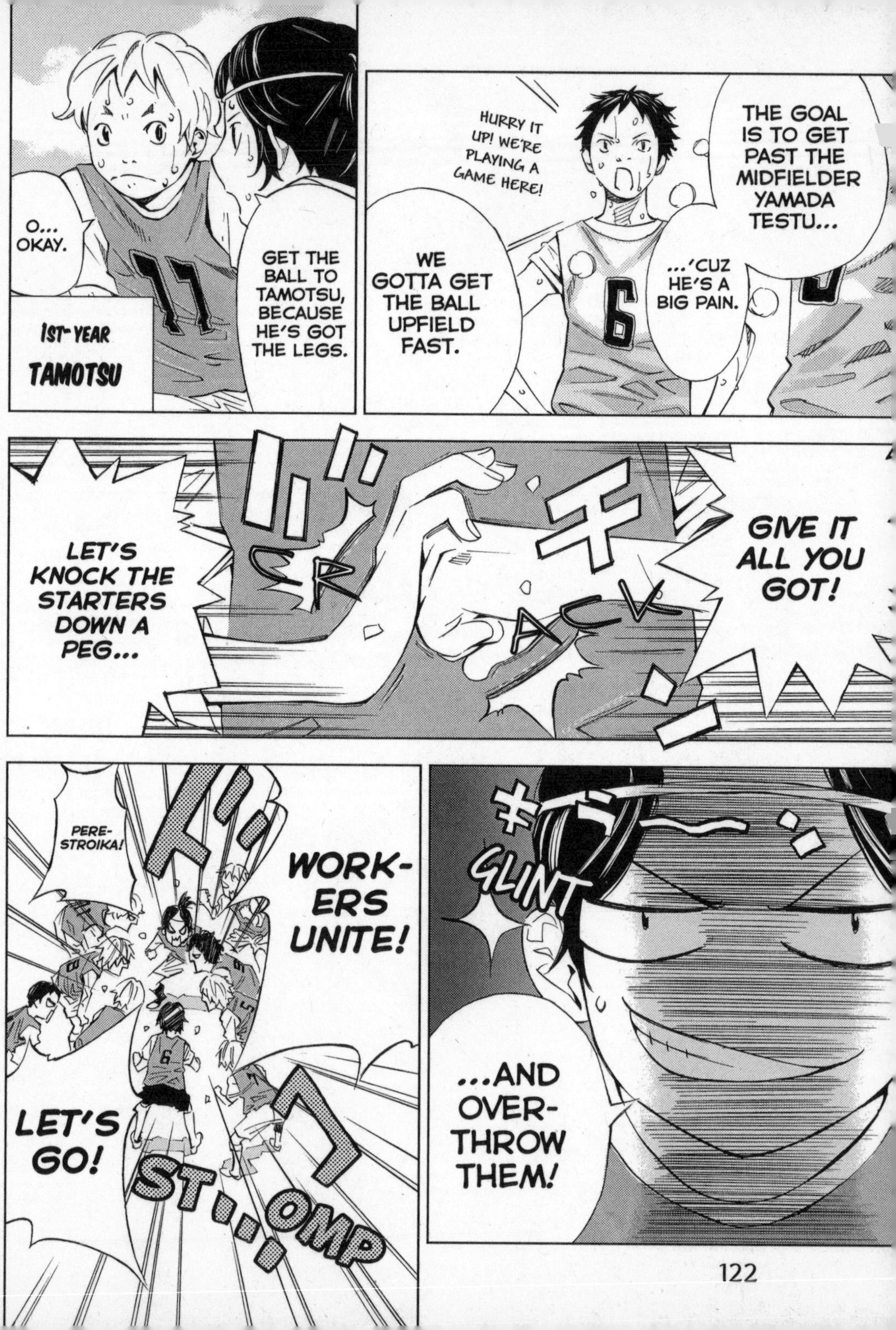
THE GOAL IS TO GET PAST THE MIDFIELDER YAMADA TESTU...
HURRY IT UP! WE'RE PLAYING A GAME HERE!
...'CUZ HE'S A BIG PAIN.
WE GOTTA GET THE BALL UPFIELD FAST.
GET THE BALL TO TAMOTSU, BECAUSE HE'S GOT THE LEGS.
O... OKAY.
1ST-YEAR TAMOTSU
GIVE IT ALL YOU GOT!
CRACK
LET'S KNOCK THE STARTERS DOWN A PEG...
GLINT
...AND OVER-THROW THEM!
PERE-STROIKA!
WORK-ERS UNITE!
LET'S GO!
ST...OMP

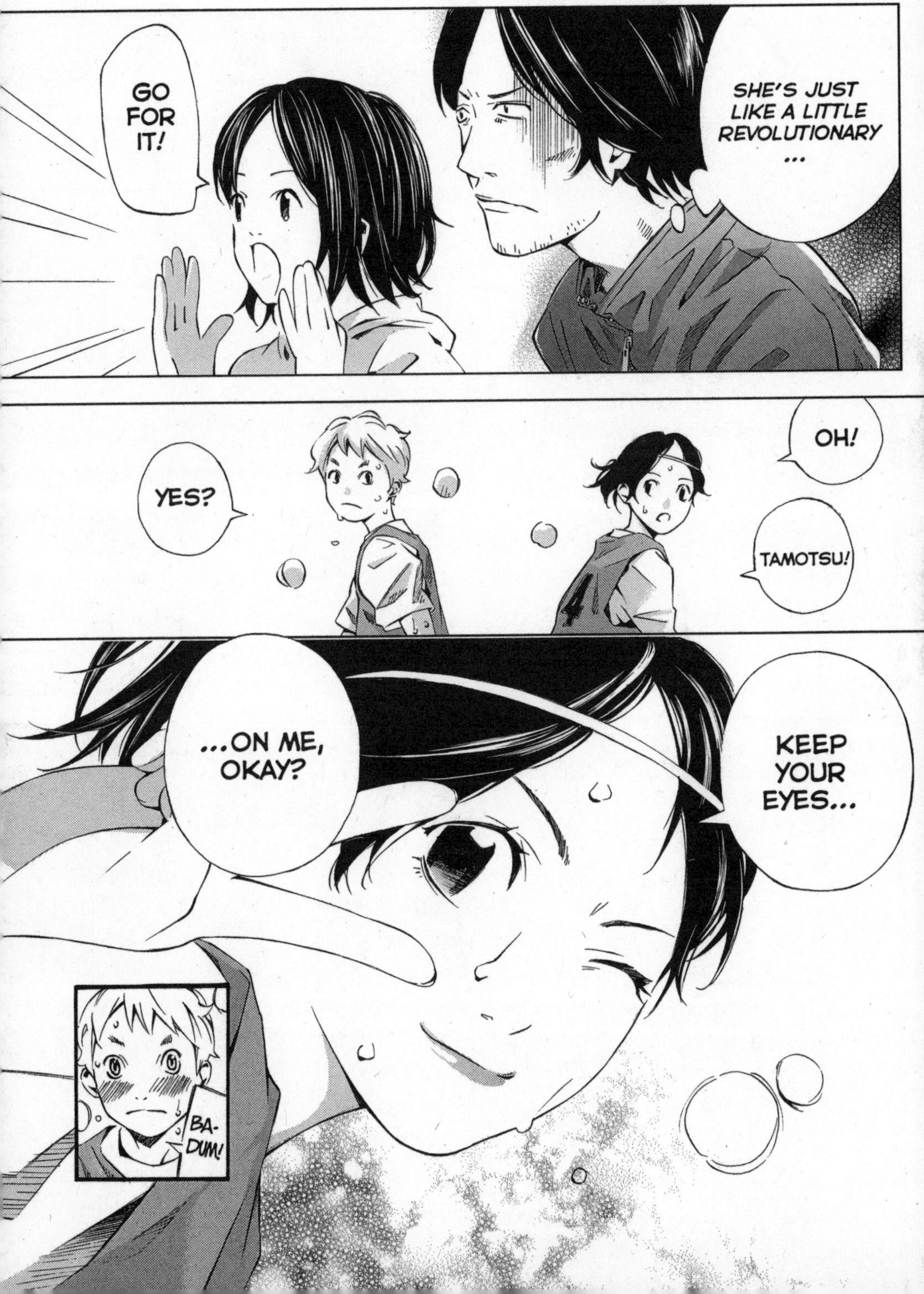
SHE'S JUST LIKE A LITTLE REVOLUTIONARY ...
GO FOR IT!
OH!
TAMOTSU!
YES?
KEEP YOUR EYES...
...ON ME, OKAY?
BA-DUM!

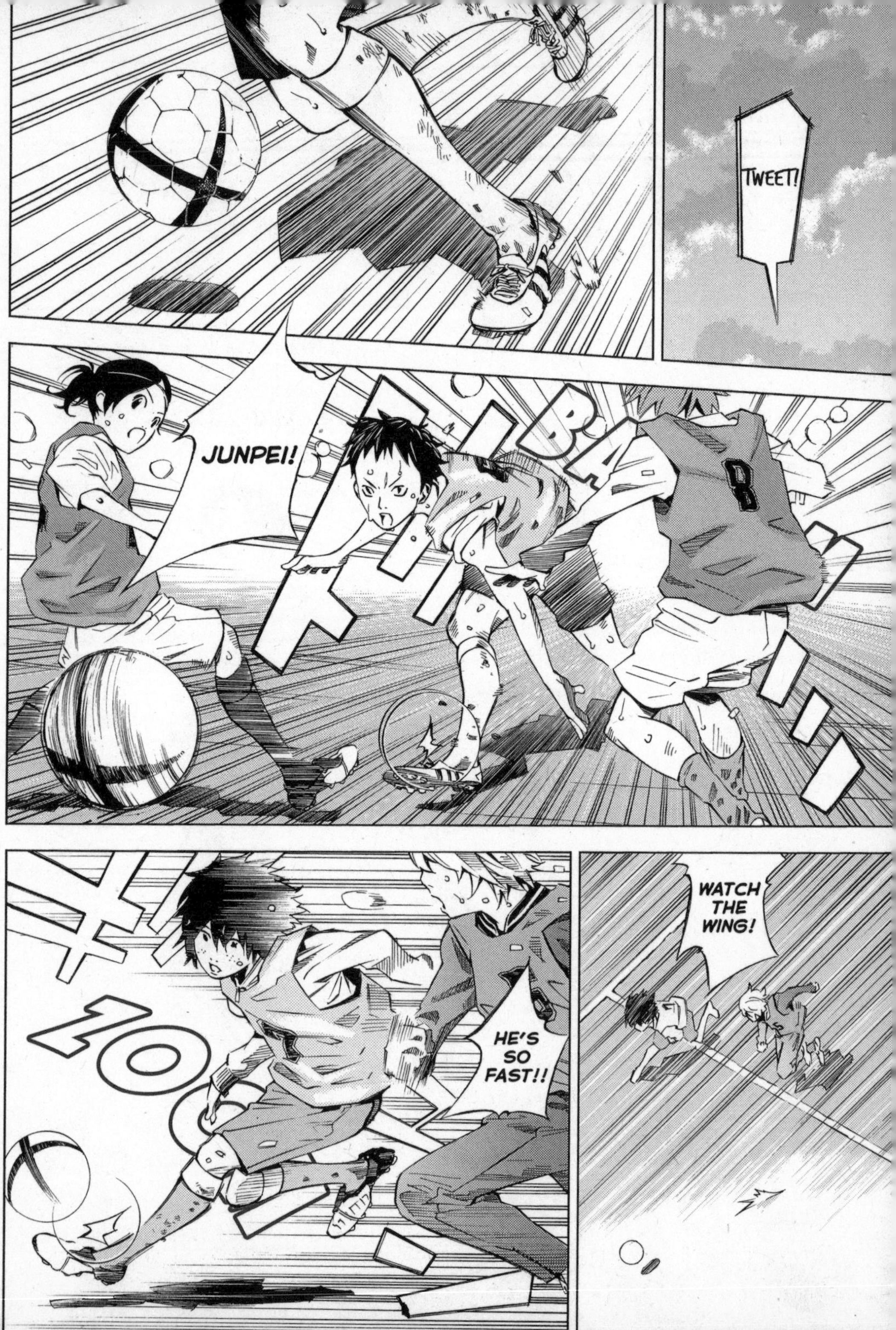
TWEET!
JUNPEI!
WATCH THE WING!
HE'S SO FAST!!

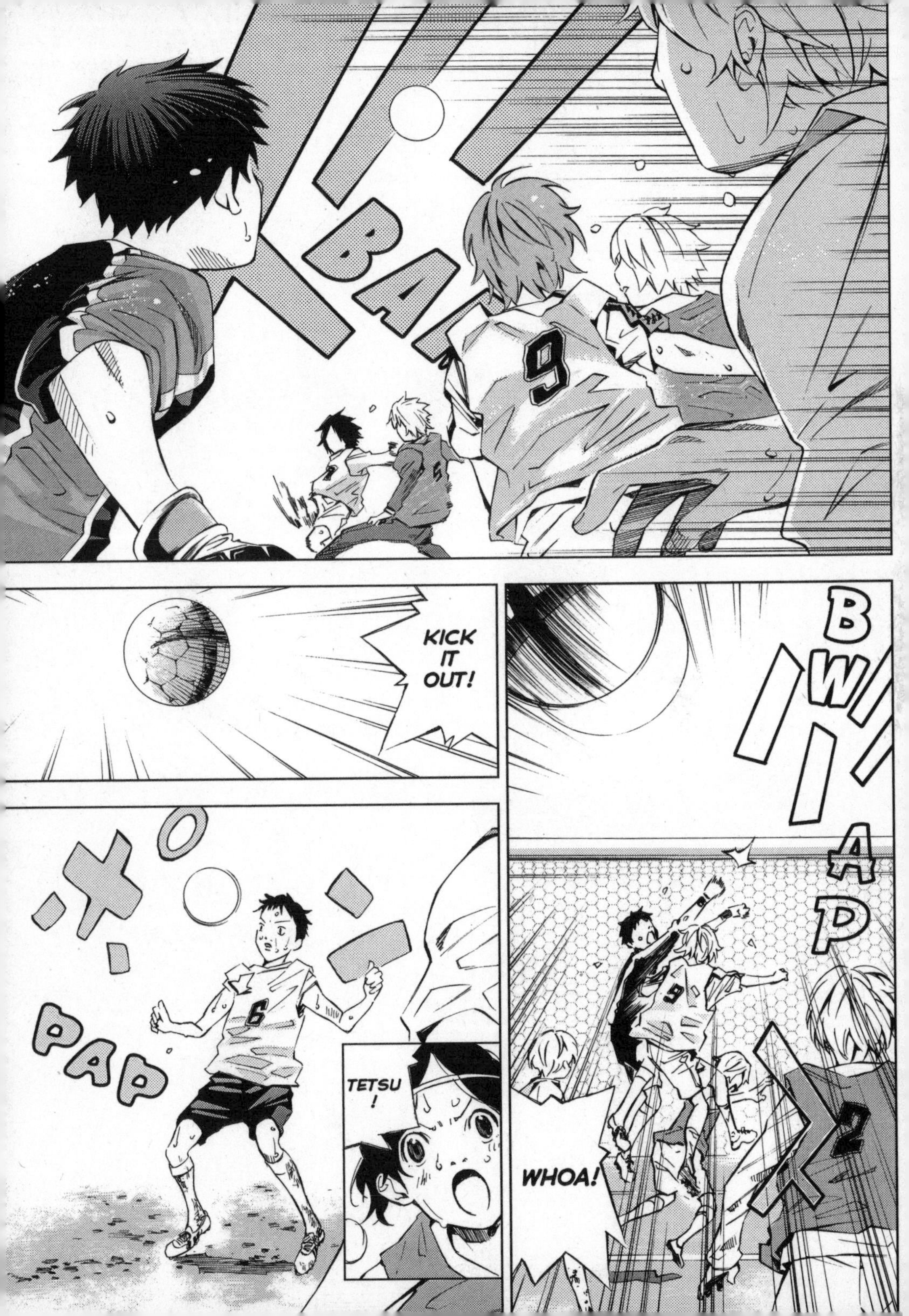
BA
BWAP
KICK IT OUT!
WHOA!
TETSU!
PAP

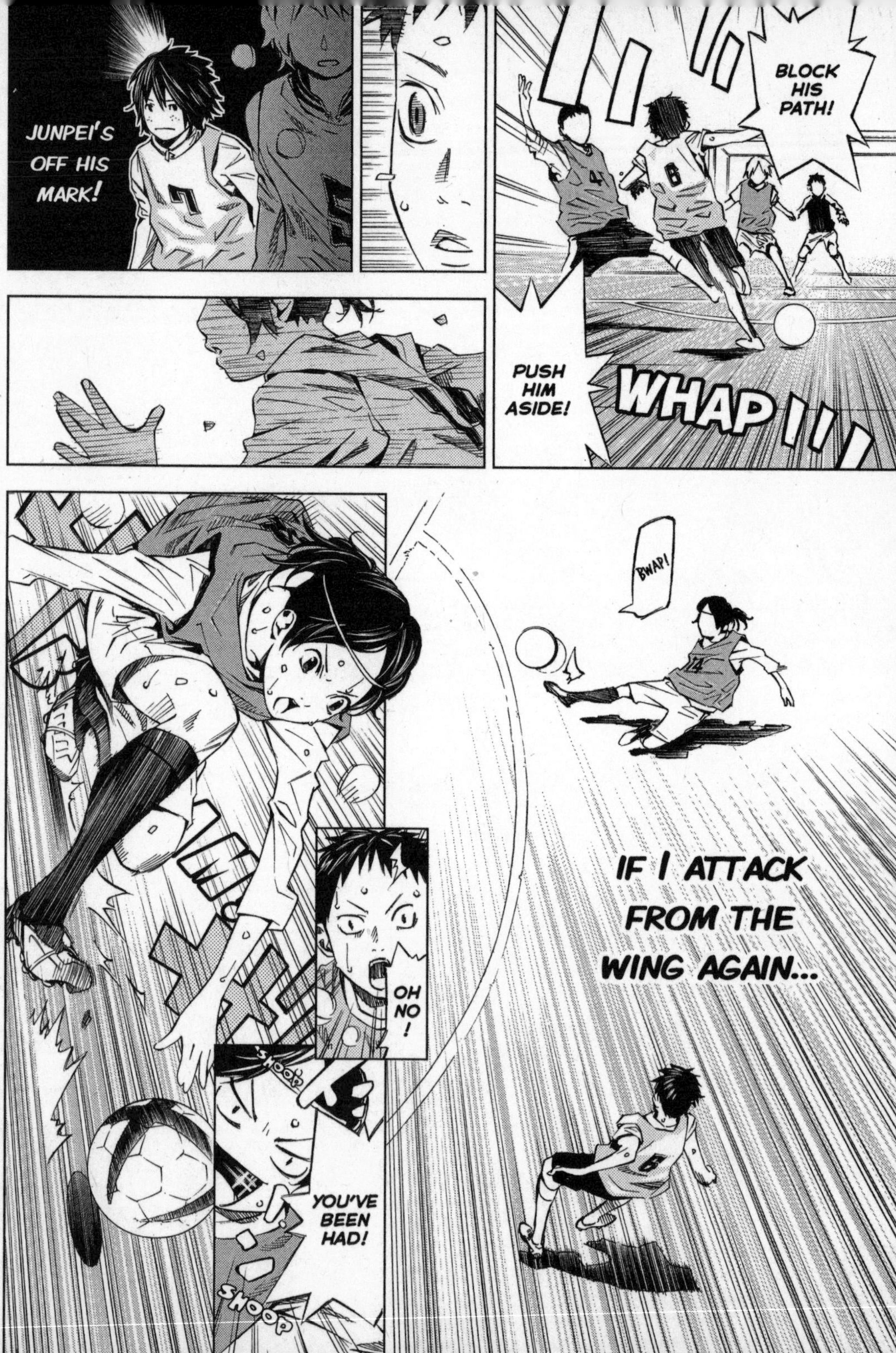
BLOCK HIS PATH!
PUSH HIM ASIDE!
WHAP!!!
JUNPEI'S OFF HIS MARK!
BWAP!
IF I ATTACK FROM THE WING AGAIN...
OH NO!
SHOOP
YOU'VE BEEN HAD!
SHOOP

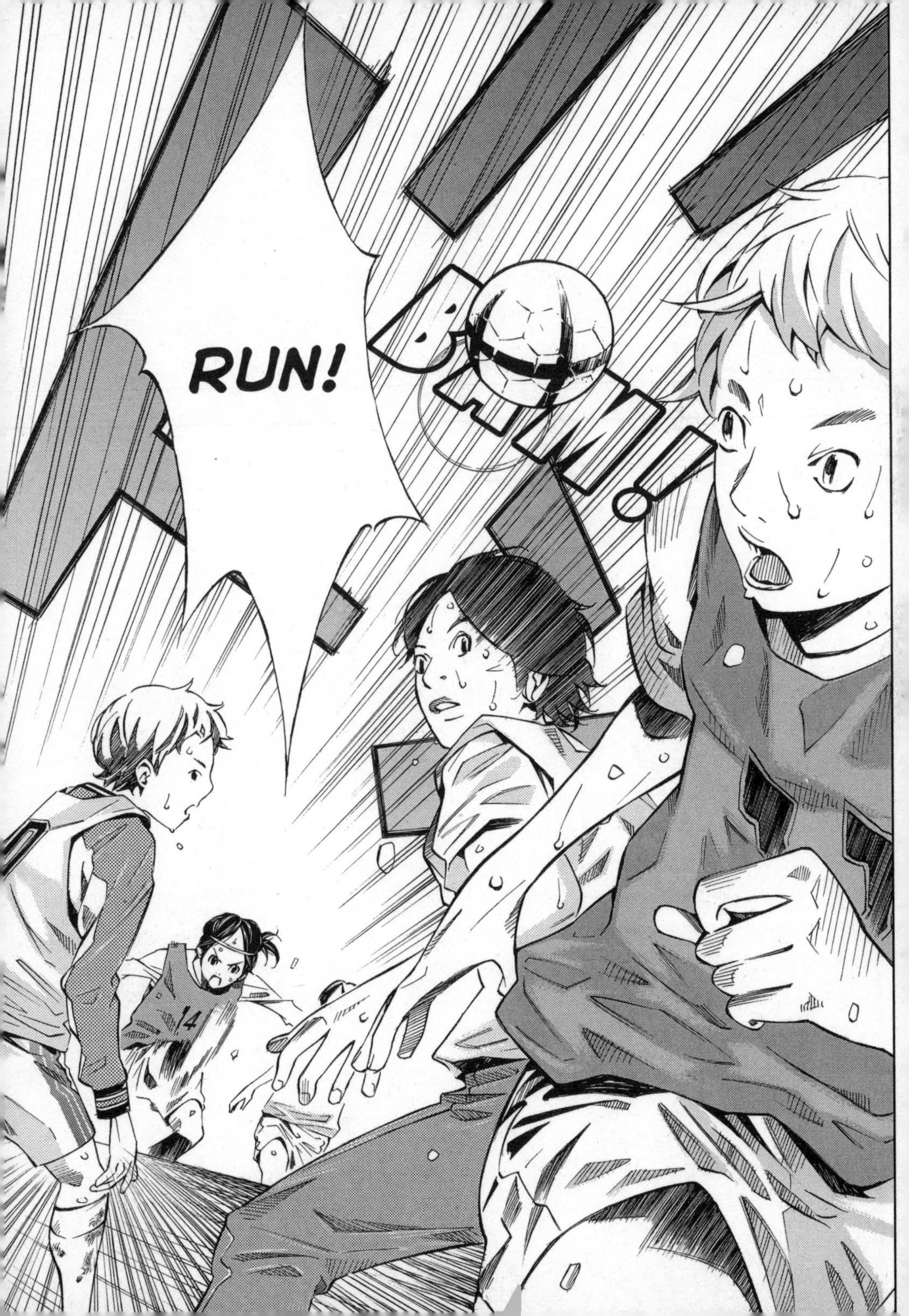
RUN!

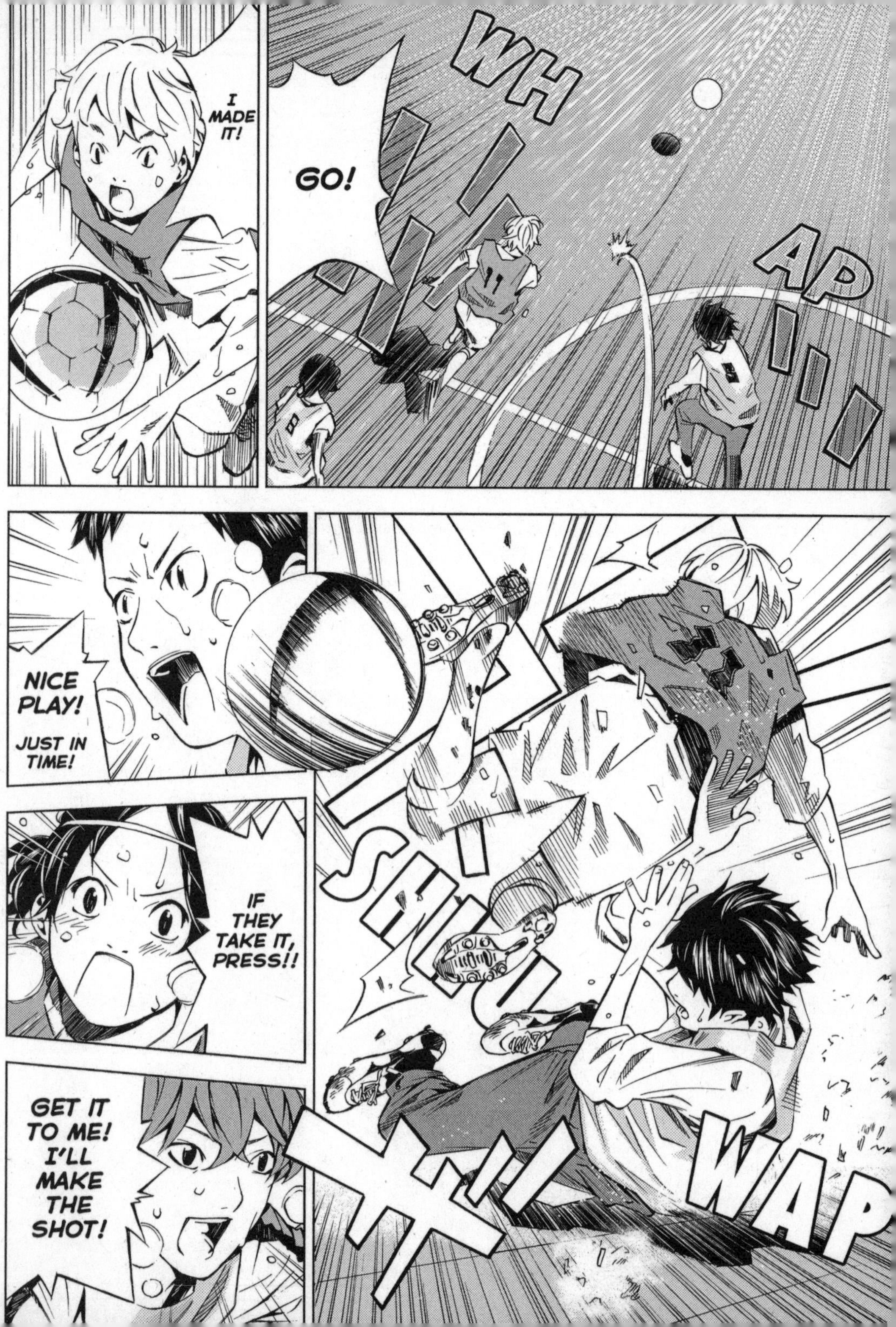
WH
GO!
AP
I MADE IT!
SHU
WAP
NICE PLAY!
JUST IN TIME!
IF THEY TAKE IT, PRESS!!
GET IT TO ME! I'LL MAKE THE SHOT!

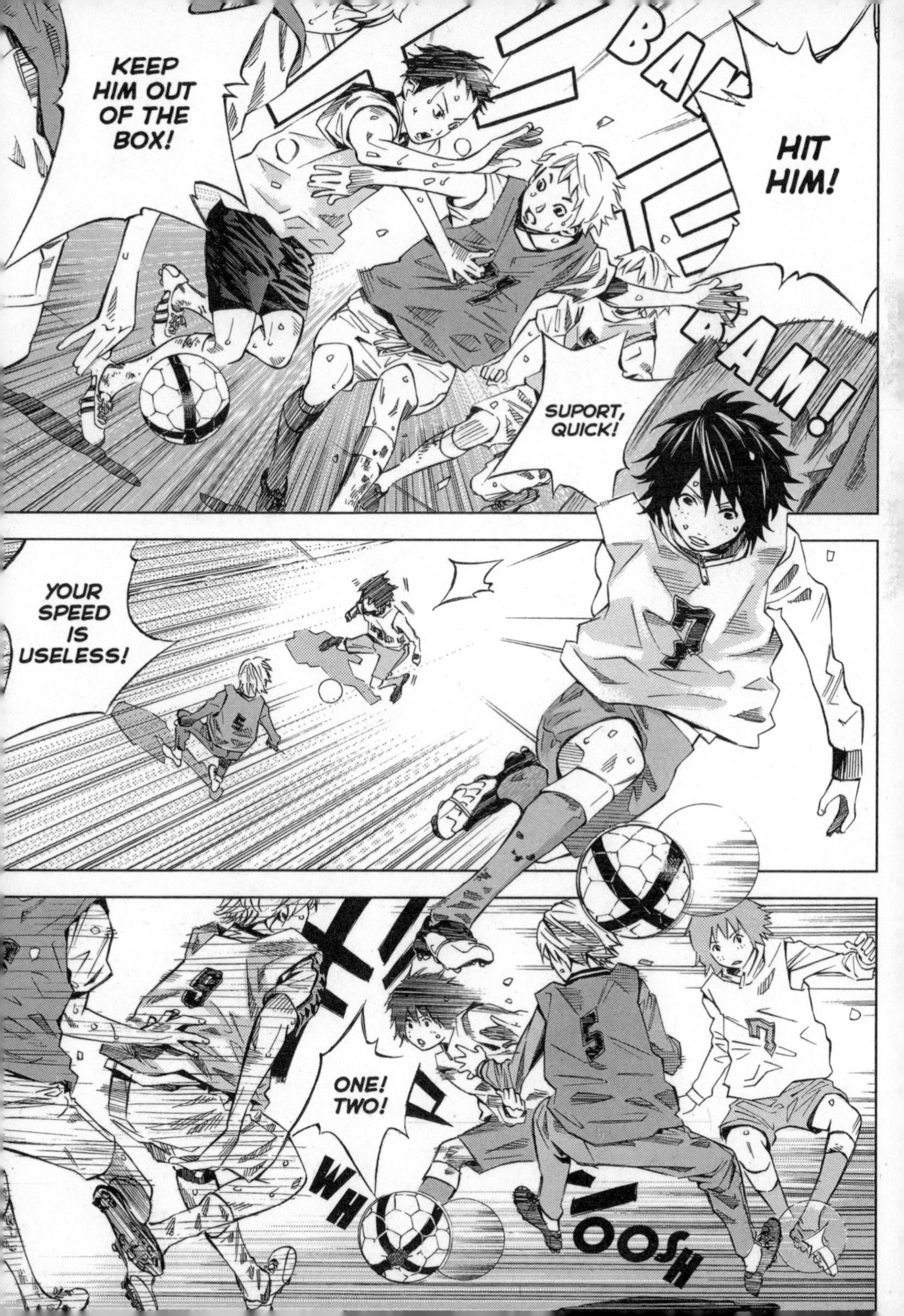
BA
HIT HIM!
BAM!
SUPORT, QUICK!
KEEP HIM OUT OF THE BOX!
YOUR SPEED IS USELESS!
ONE! TWO!
WHOOSH

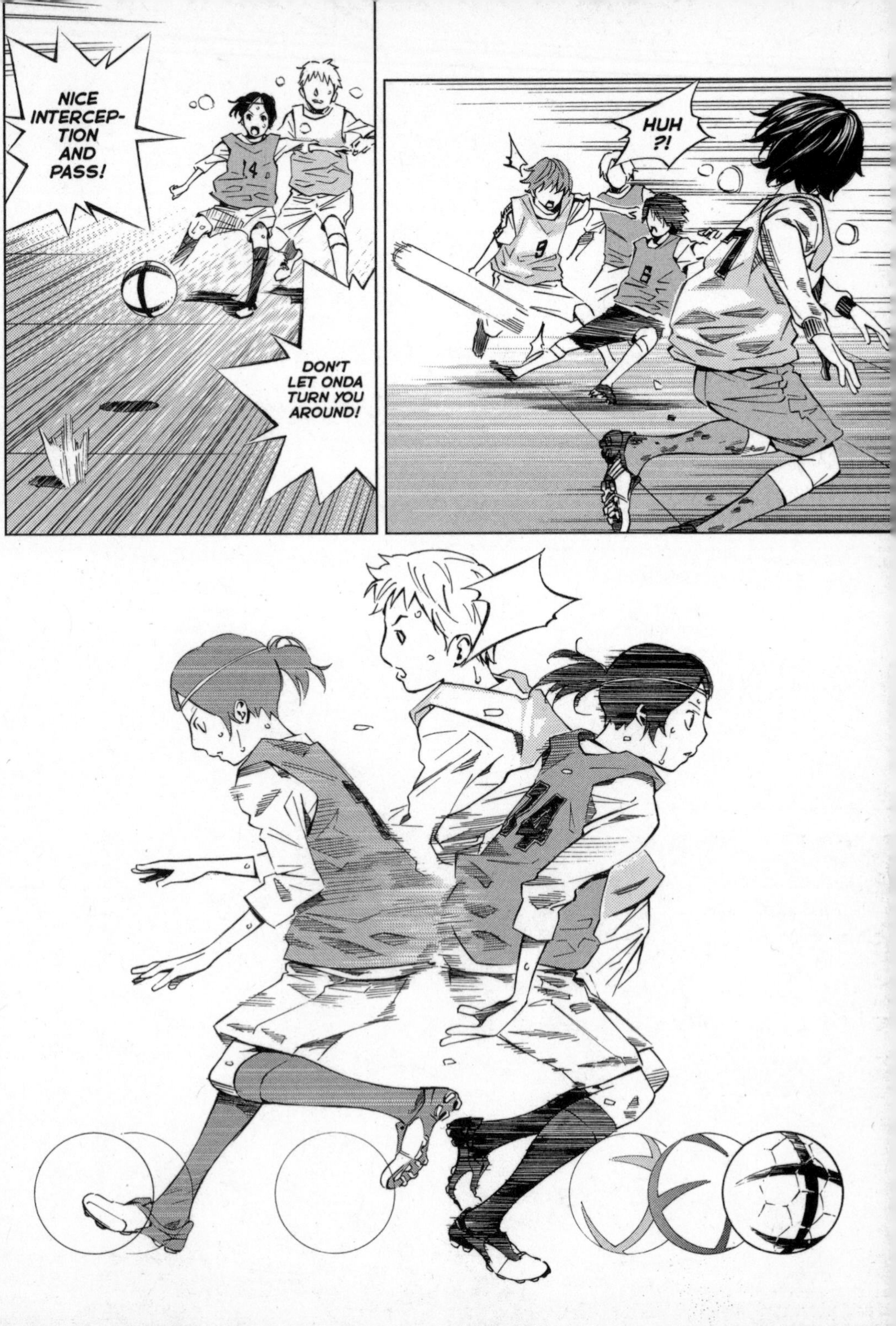
HUH ?!
NICE INTERCEPTION AND PASS!
DON'T LET ONDA TURN YOU AROUND!

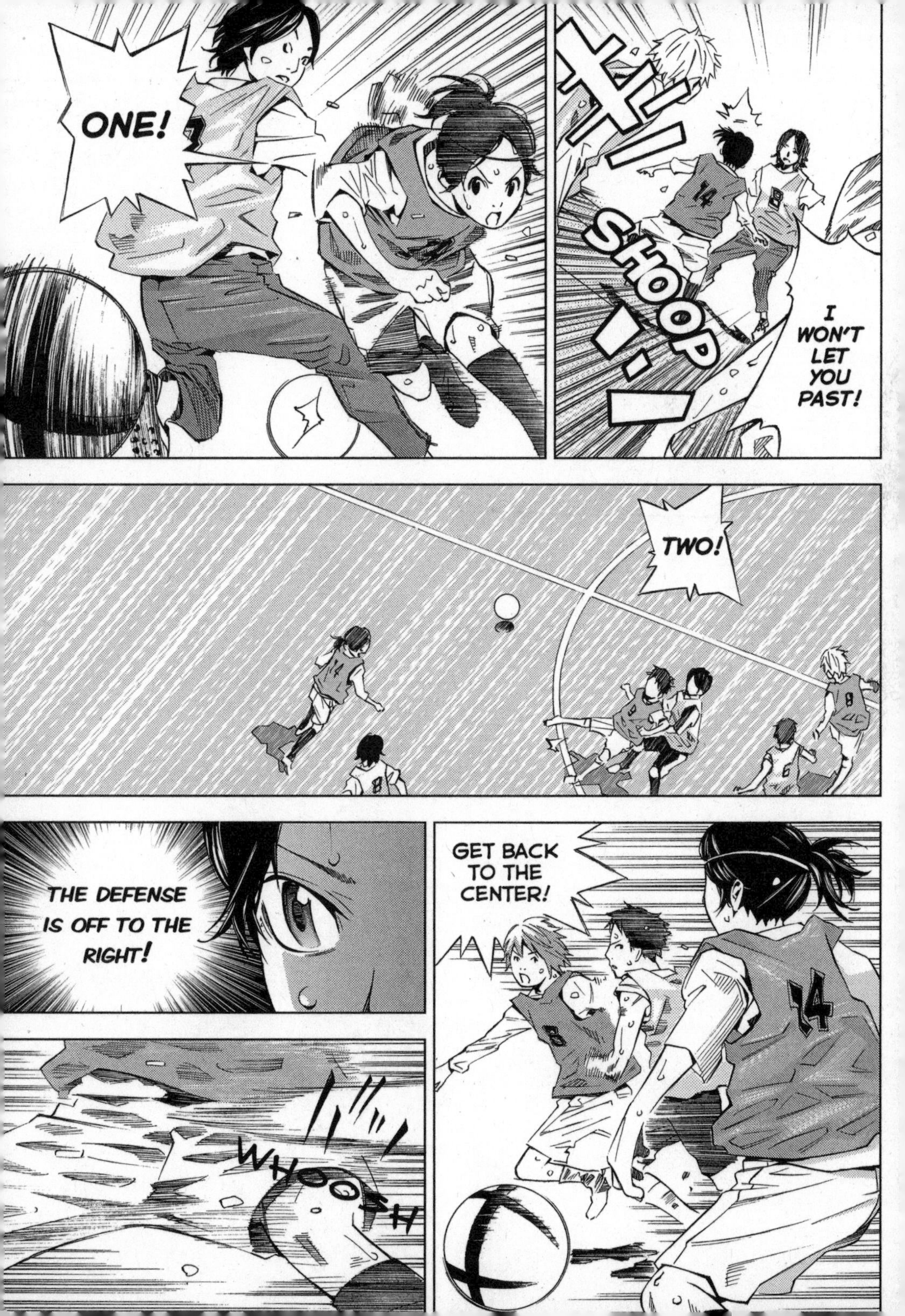
SHOOP!!
I WON'T LET YOU PAST!
ONE!
TWO!
GET BACK TO THE CENTER!
THE DEFENSE IS OFF TO THE RIGHT!
WHOOSH

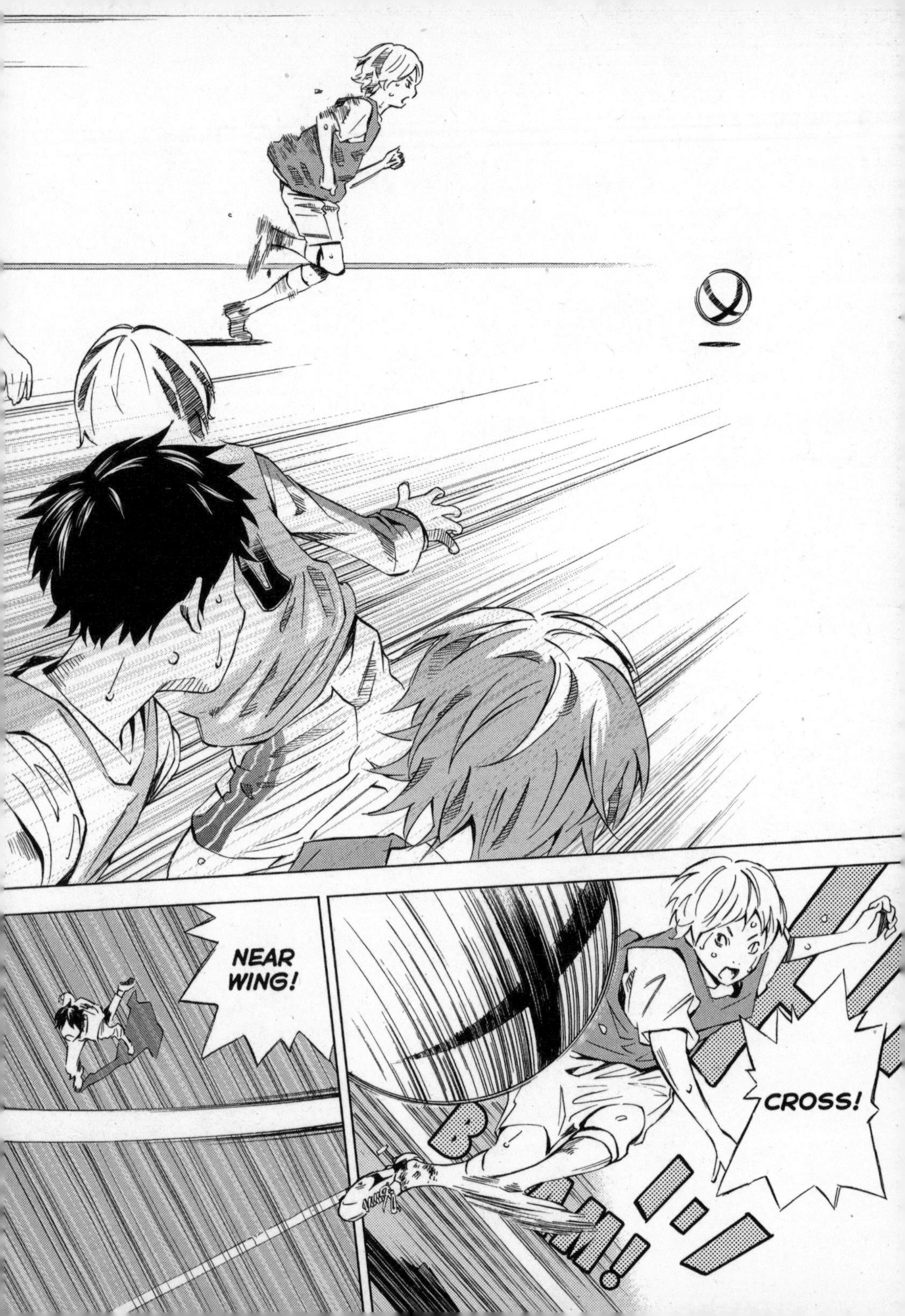
CROSS!
NEAR WING!

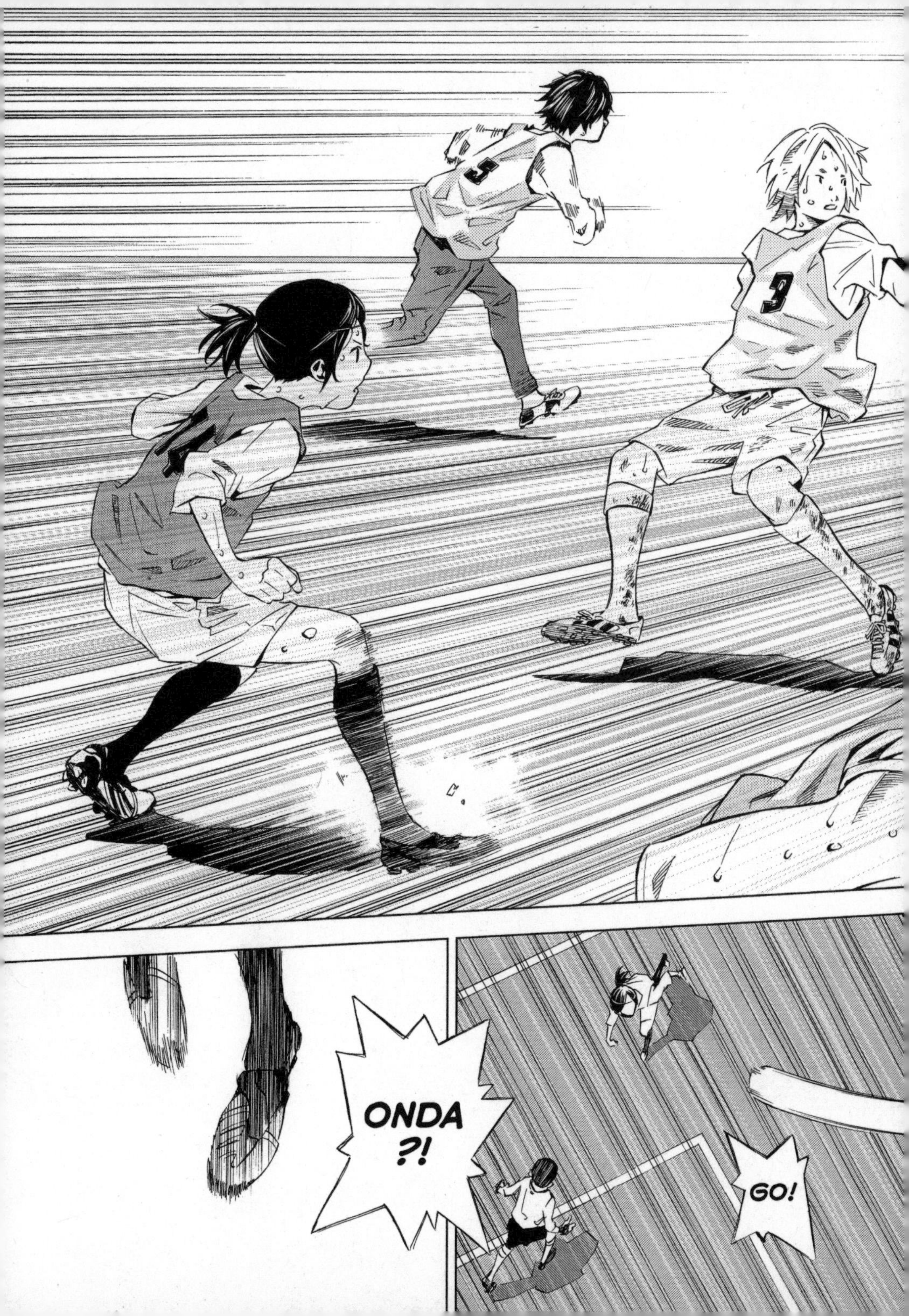
GO!
ONDA ?!

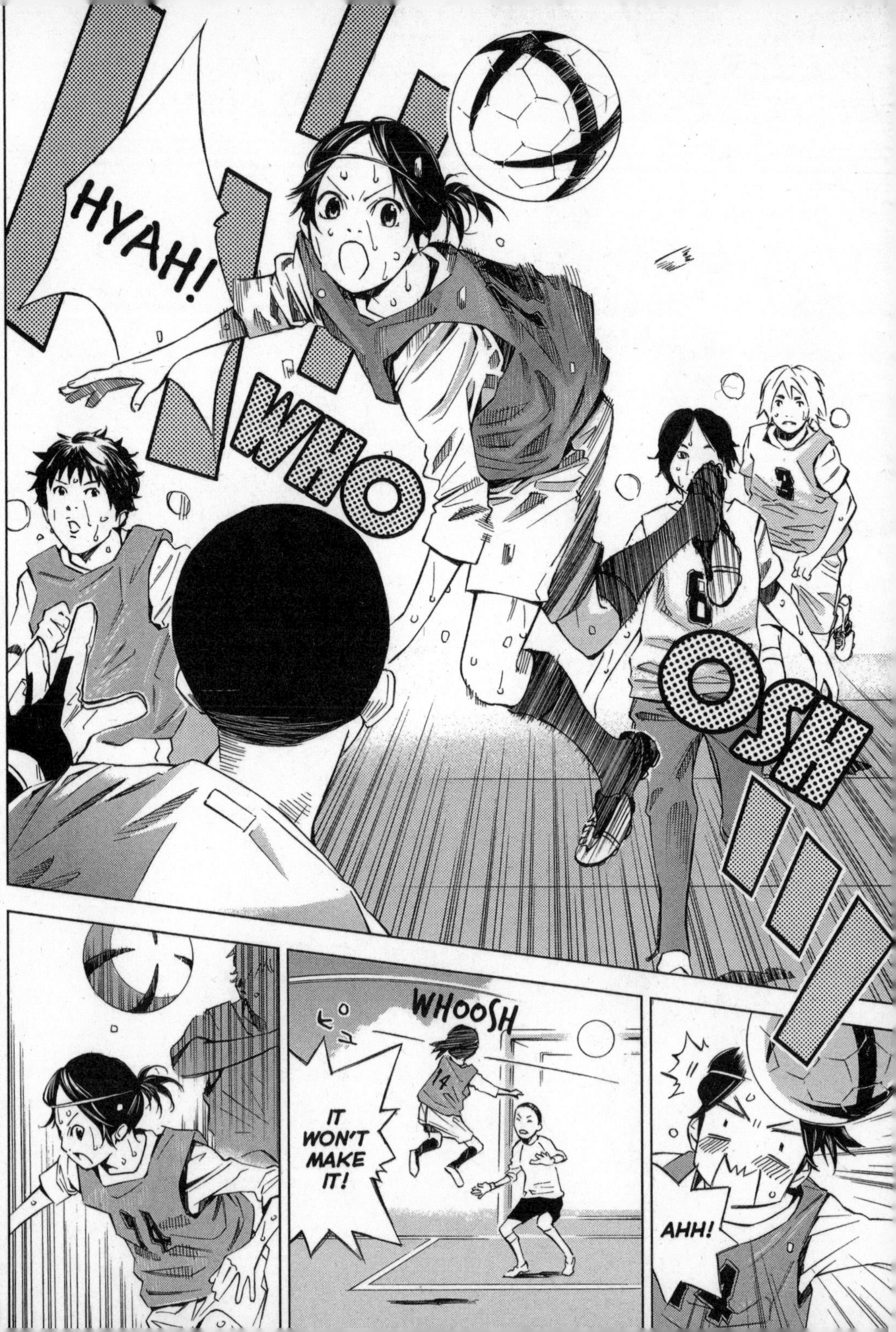
HYAH!
WHOOSH
AHH!
WHOOSH
IT WON'T MAKE IT!

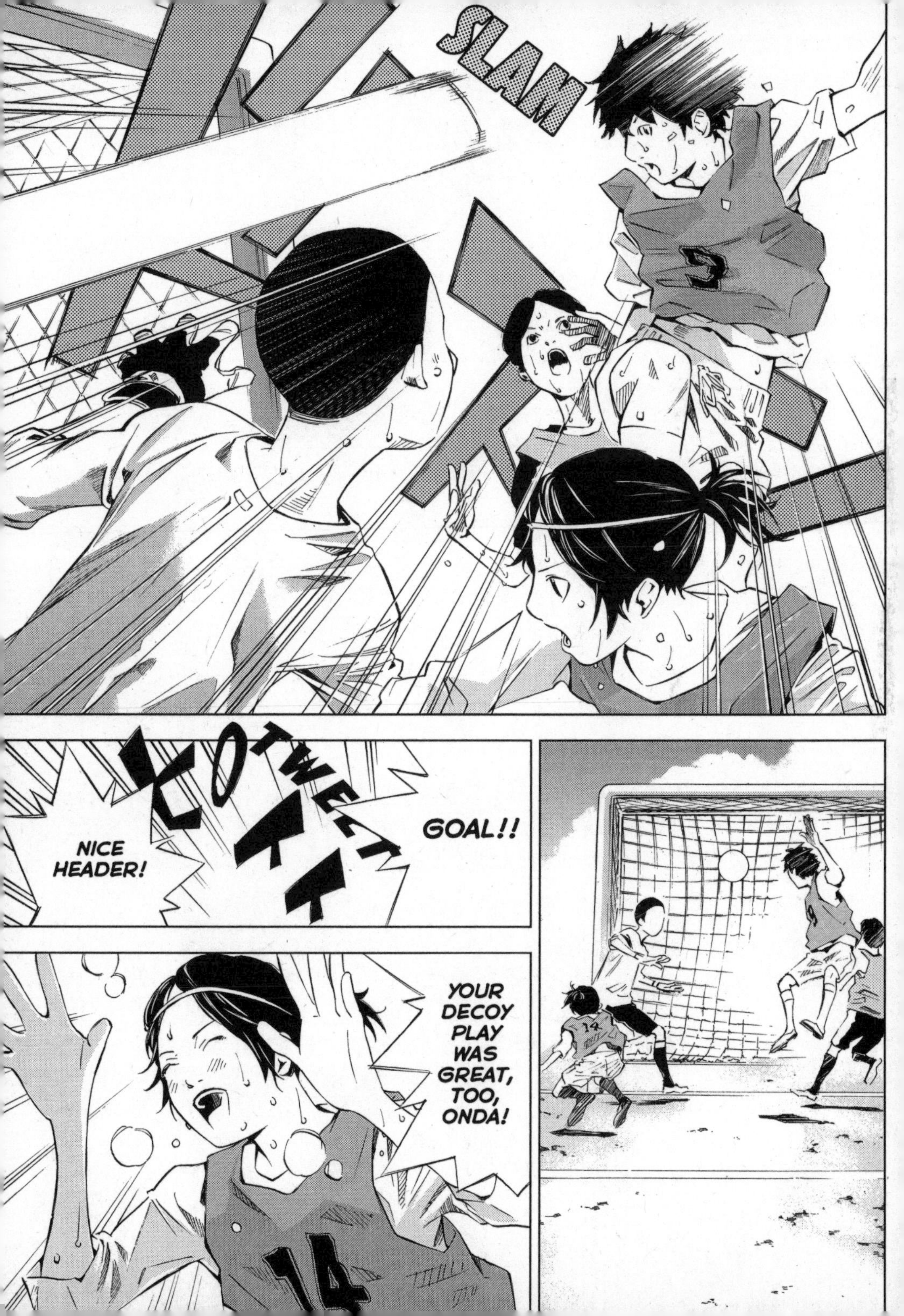
SLAM
GOAL!!
TWEET
NICE HEADER!
YOUR DECOY PLAY WAS GREAT, TOO, ONDA!

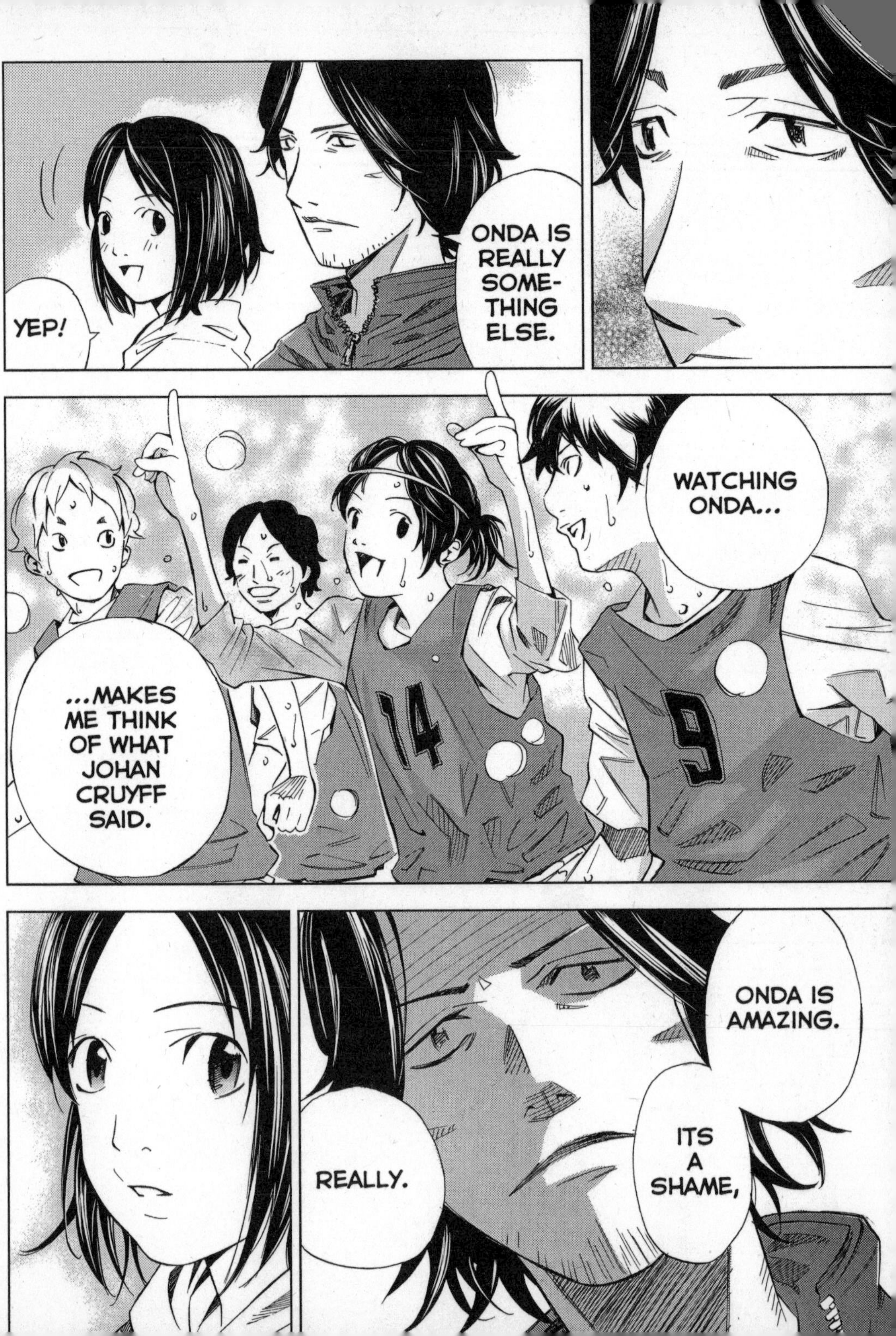
ONDA IS REALLY SOME-THING ELSE.
YEP!
WATCHING ONDA...
...MAKES ME THINK OF WHAT JOHAN CRUYFF SAID.
ONDA IS AMAZING.
ITS A SHAME,
REALLY.

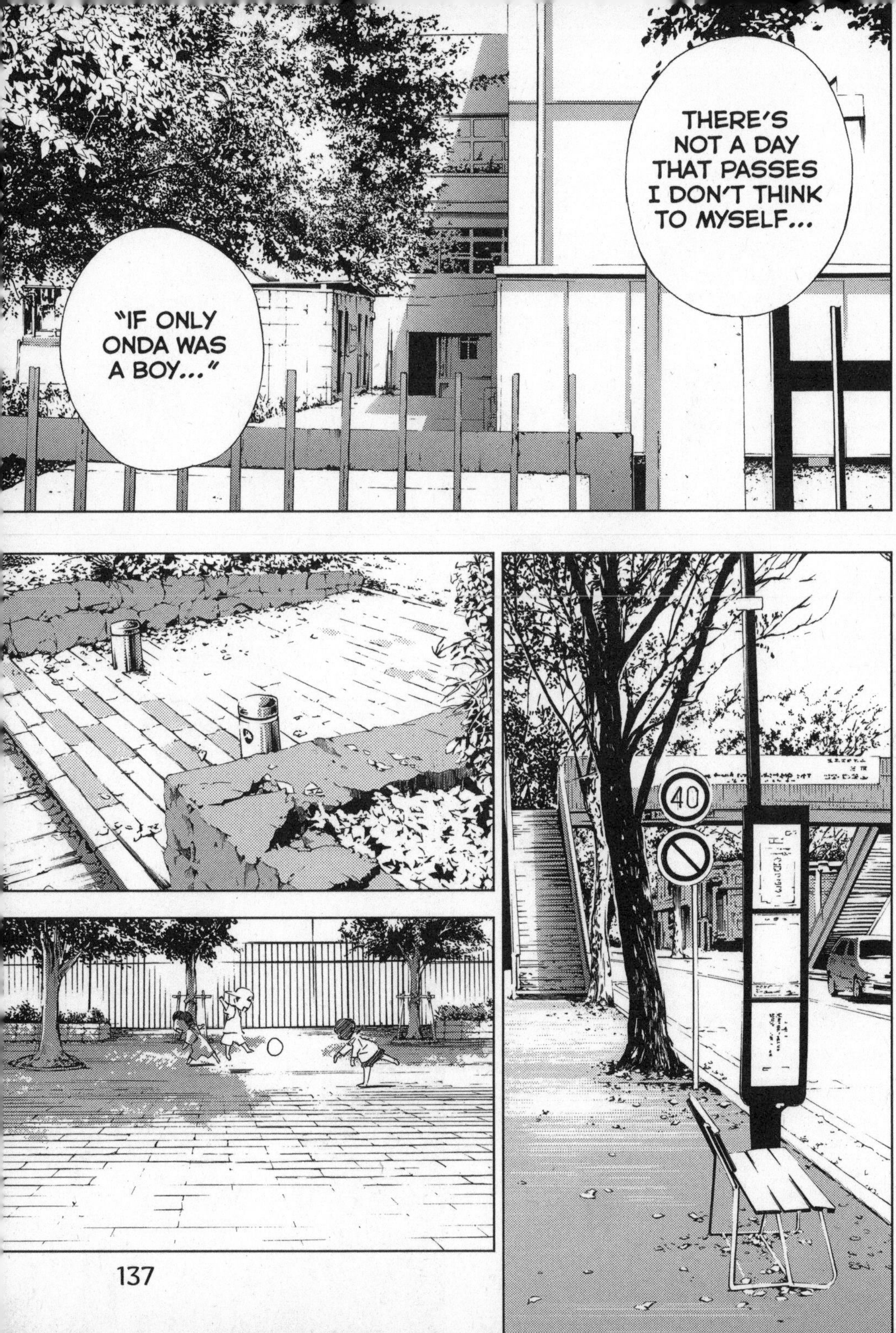
THERE'S NOT A DAY THAT PASSES I DON'T THINK TO MYSELF...
"IF ONLY ONDA WAS A BOY..."
40

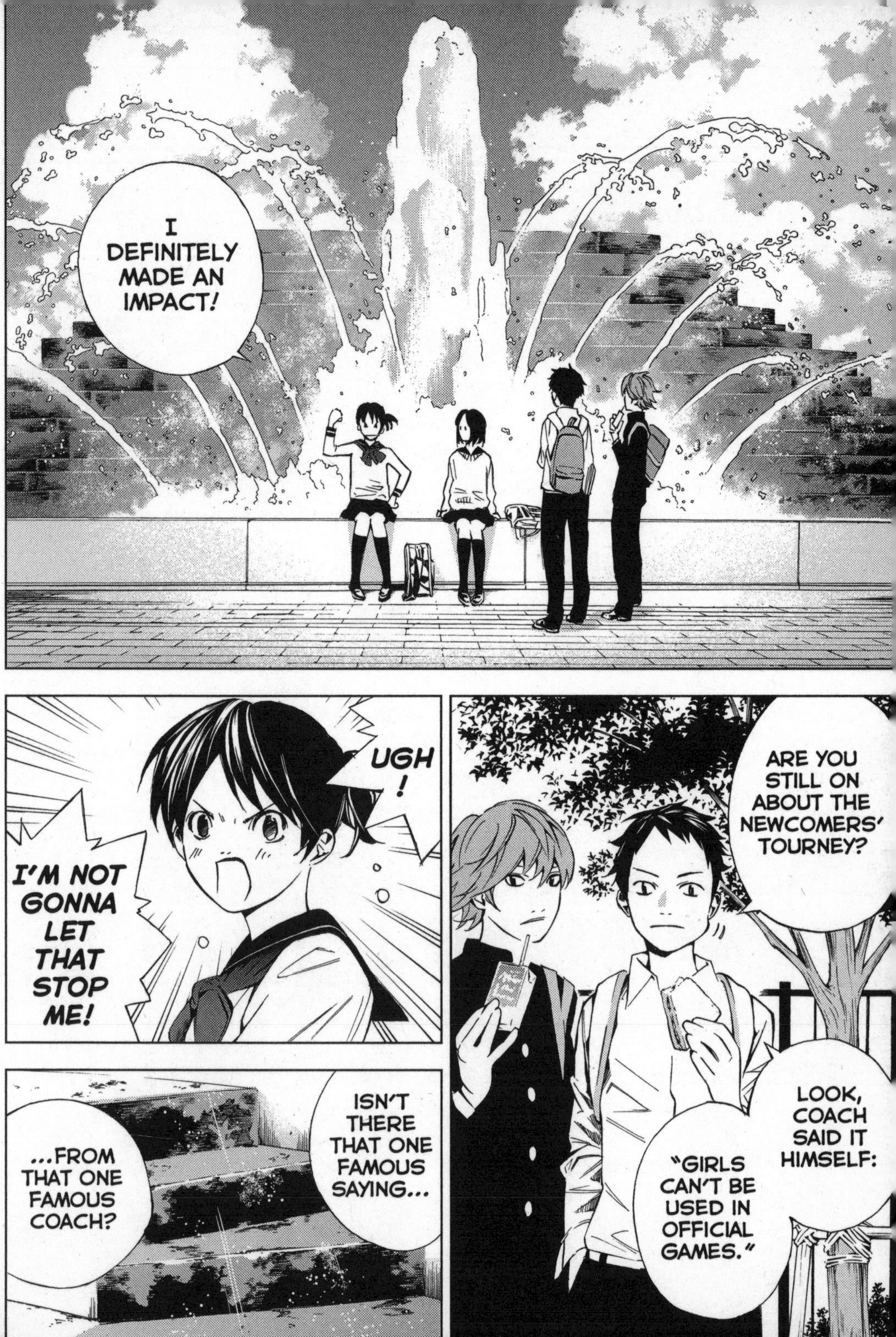
I DEFINITELY MADE AN IMPACT!
ARE YOU STILL ON ABOUT THE NEWCOMERS' TOURNEY?
LOOK, COACH SAID IT HIMSELF:
"GIRLS CAN'T BE USED IN OFFICIAL GAMES."
UGH!
I'M NOT GONNA LET THAT STOP ME!
ISN'T THERE THAT ONE FAMOUS SAYING...
...FROM THAT ONE FAMOUS COACH?

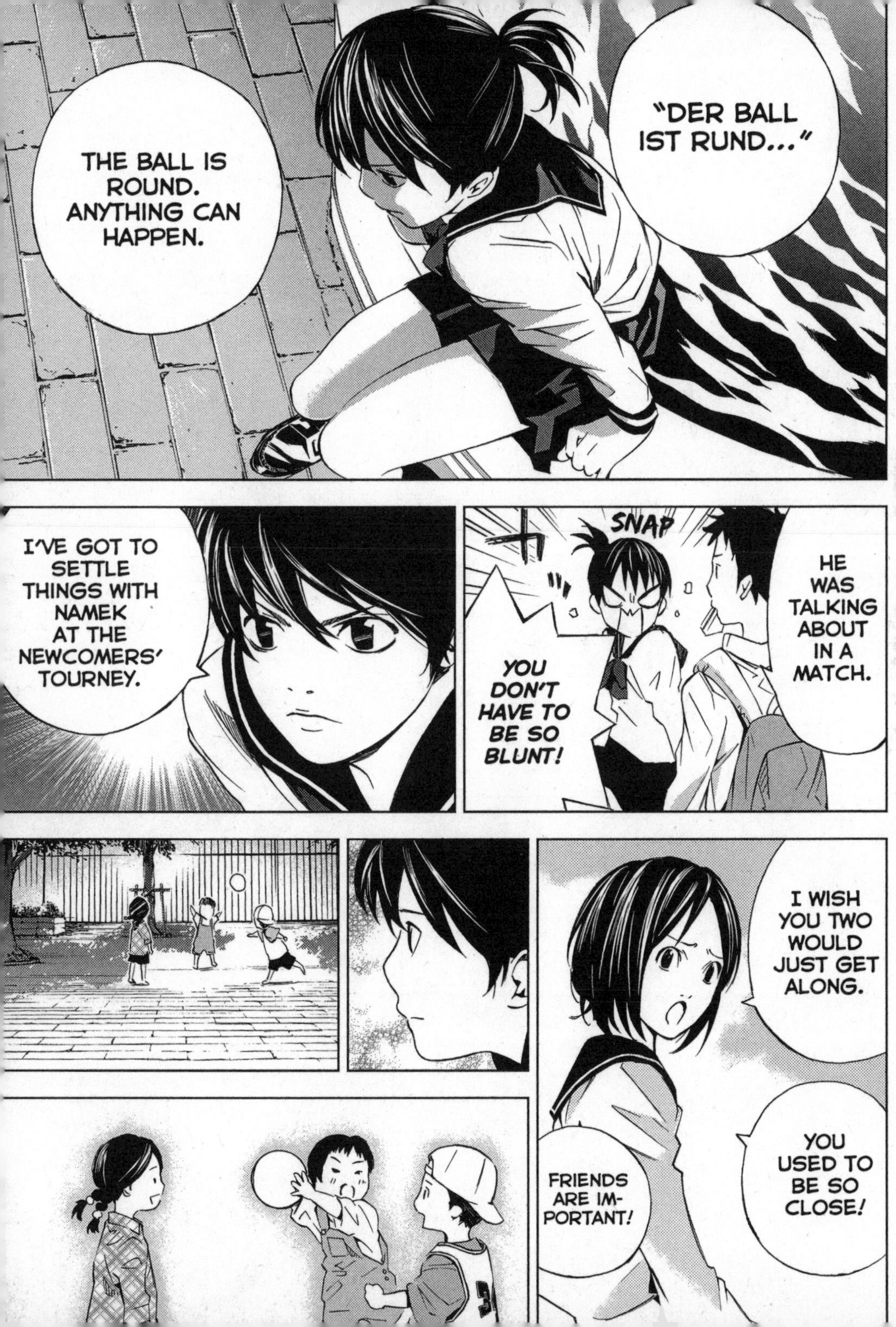
"DER BALL IST RUND..."
THE BALL IS ROUND. ANYTHING CAN HAPPEN.
HE WAS TALKING ABOUT IN A MATCH.
SNAP
YOU DON'T HAVE TO BE SO BLUNT!
I'VE GOT TO SETTLE THINGS WITH NAMEK AT THE NEWCOMERS' TOURNEY.
I WISH YOU TWO WOULD JUST GET ALONG.
YOU USED TO BE SO CLOSE!
FRIENDS ARE IM-PORTANT!

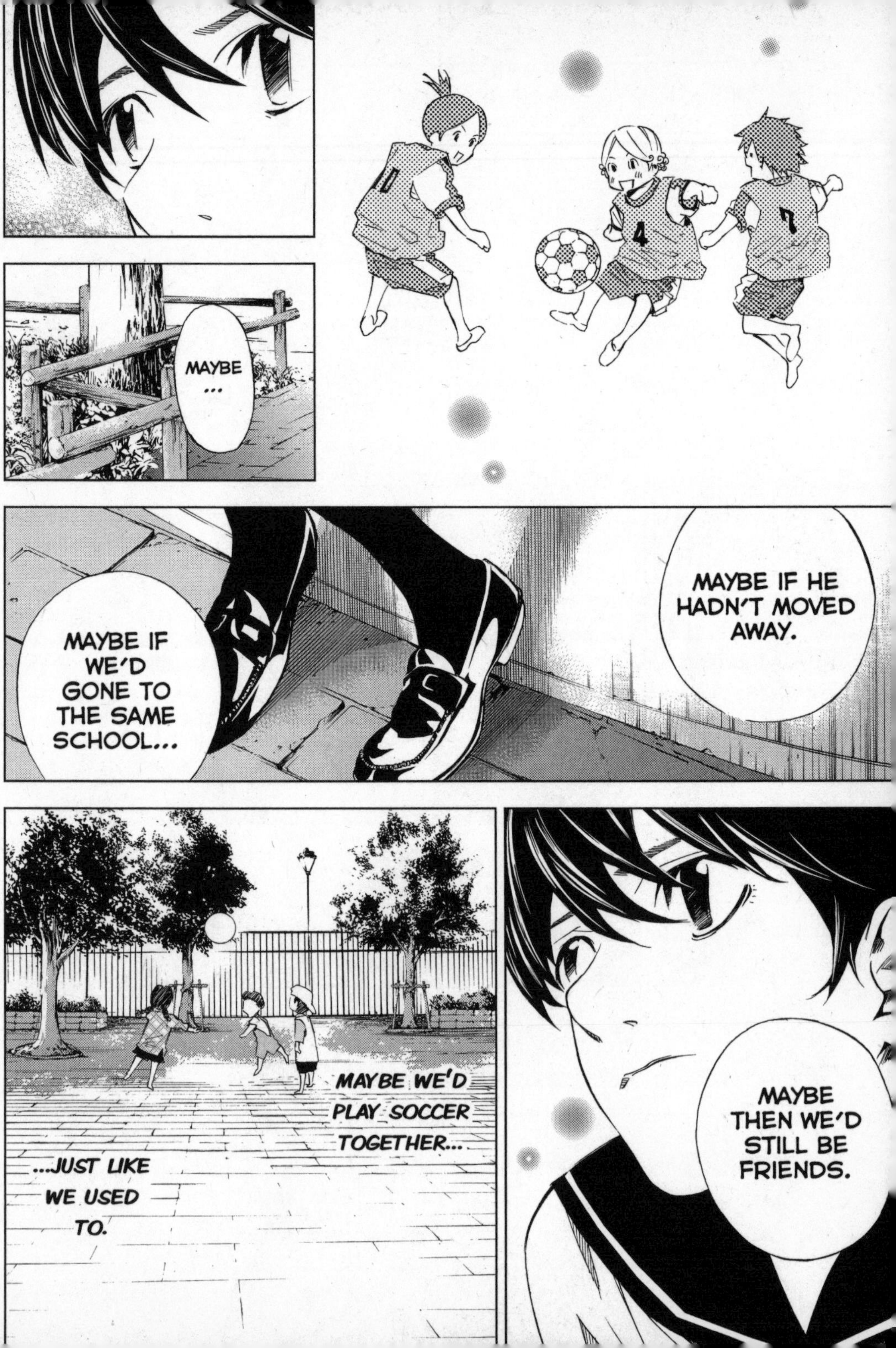
MAYBE ...
MAYBE IF HE HADN'T MOVED AWAY.
MAYBE IF WE'D GONE TO THE SAME SCHOOL...
MAYBE THEN WE'D STILL BE FRIENDS.
MAYBE WE'D PLAY SOCCER TOGETHER...
...JUST LIKE WE USED TO.

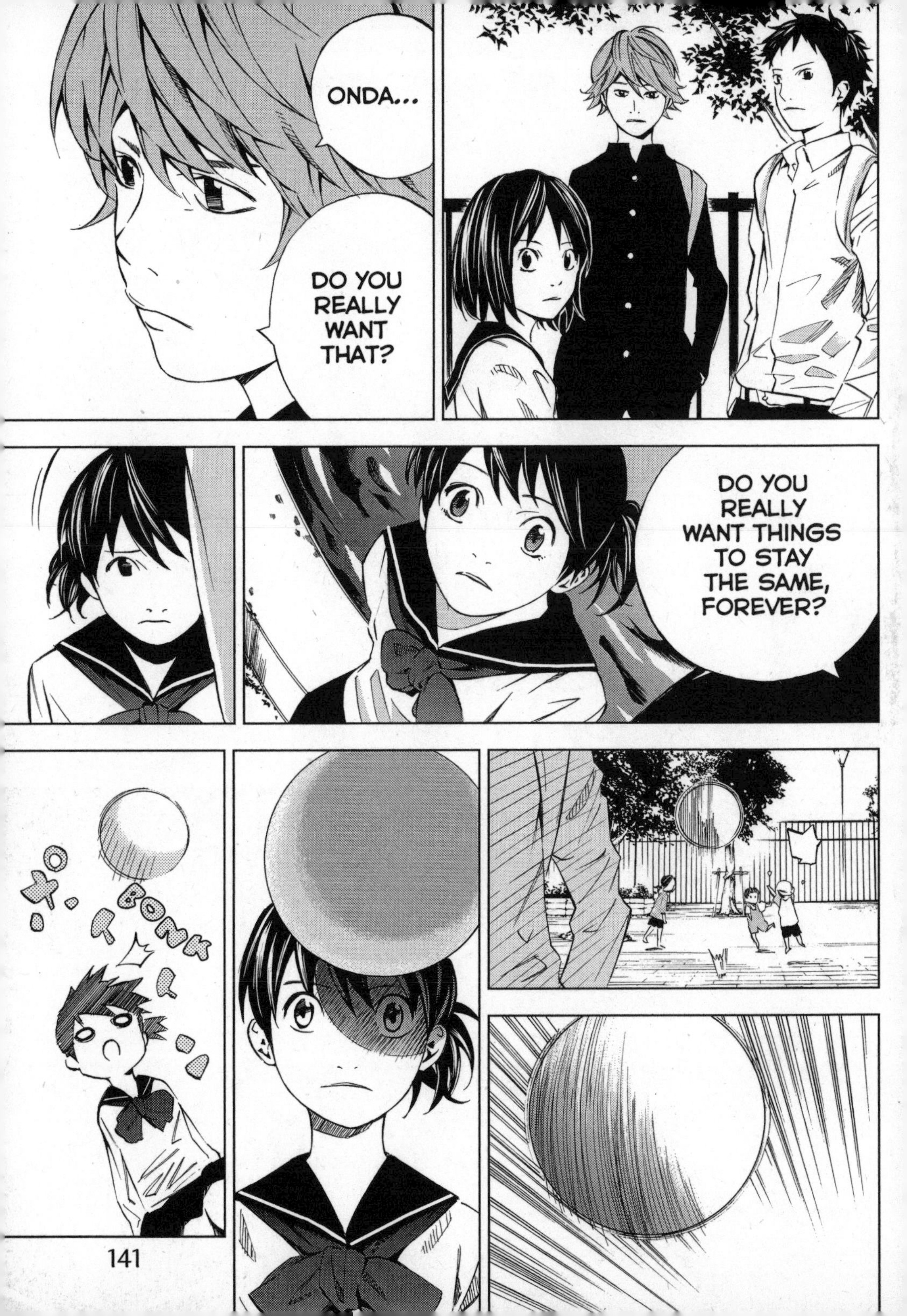
ONDA...
DO YOU REALLY WANT THAT?
DO YOU REALLY WANT THINGS TO STAY THE SAME, FOREVER?
BONK

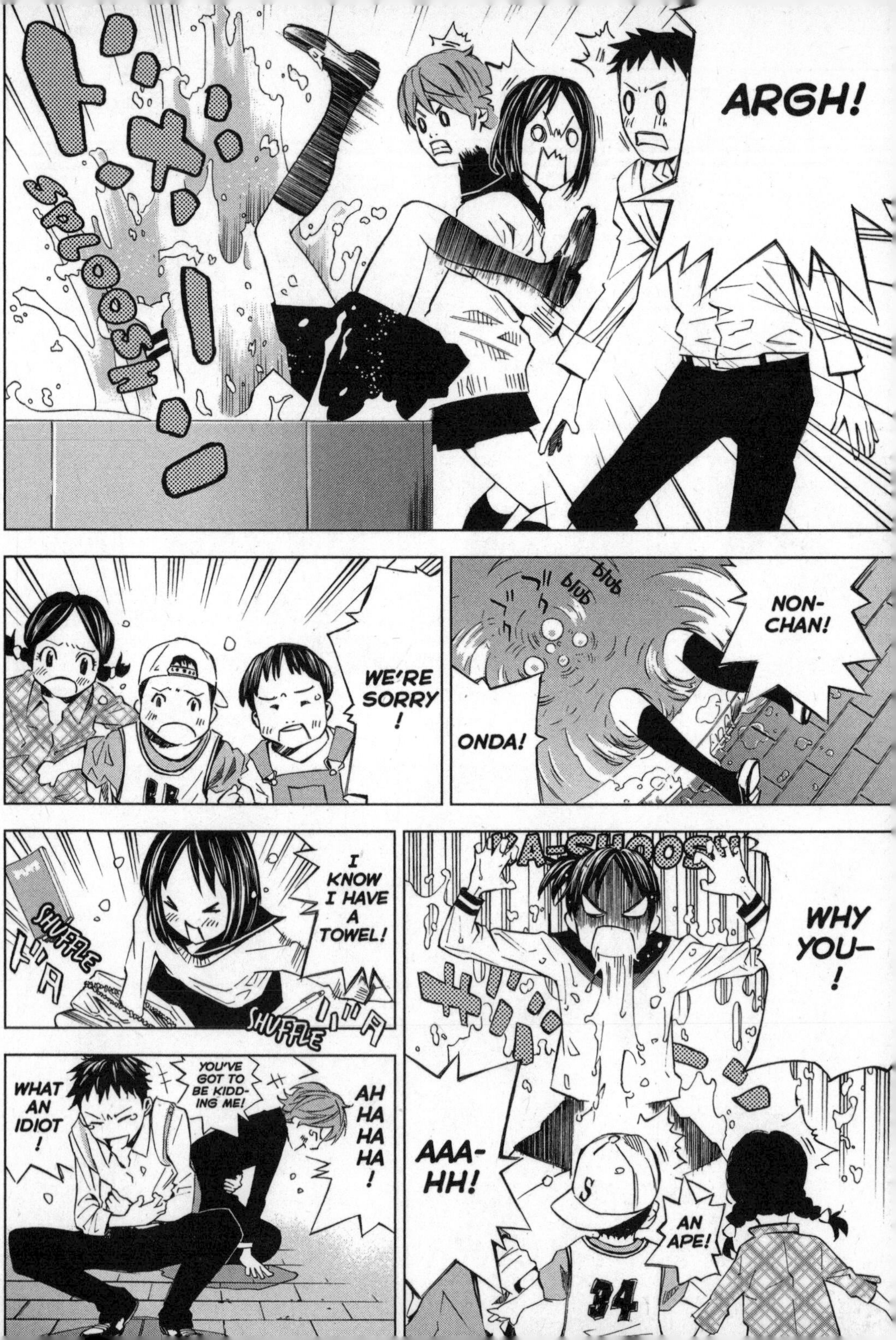
ARGH!
SPLOOSH
NON-CHAN!
blub
blub
ONDA!
WE'RE SORRY!
WHY YOU-!
AAA-HH!
AN APE!
I KNOW I HAVE A TOWEL!
SHUFFLE
SHUFFLE
AH HA HA HA!
YOU'VE GOT TO BE KIDDING ME!
WHAT AN IDIOT!

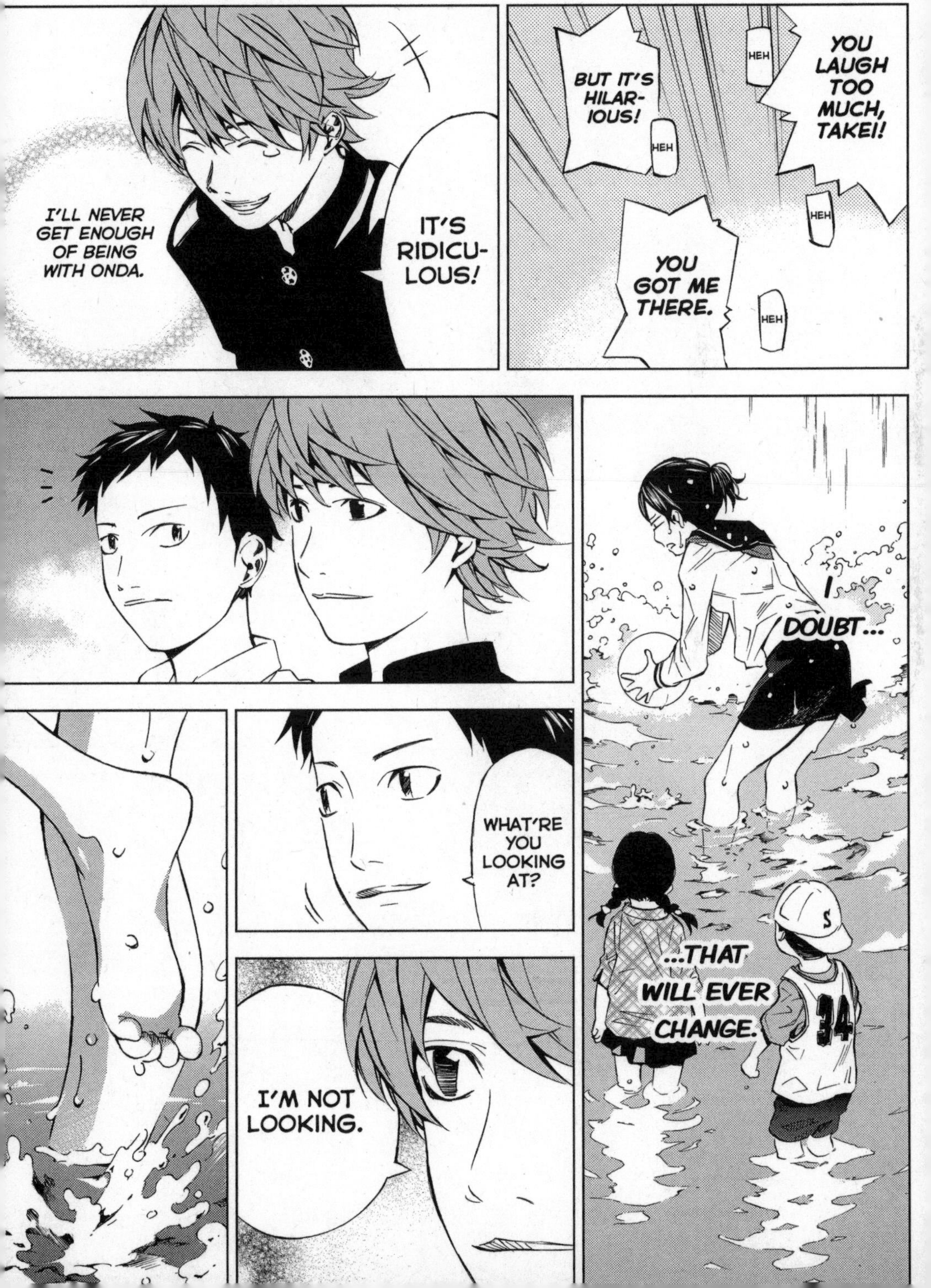
YOU LAUGH TOO MUCH, TAKEI!
HEH
BUT IT'S HILAR-IOUS!
HEH
HEH
YOU GOT ME THERE.
HEH
IT'S RIDICU-LOUS!
I'LL NEVER GET ENOUGH OF BEING WITH ONDA.
I DOUBT...
...THAT WILL EVER CHANGE.
WHAT'RE YOU LOOKING AT?
I'M NOT LOOKING.

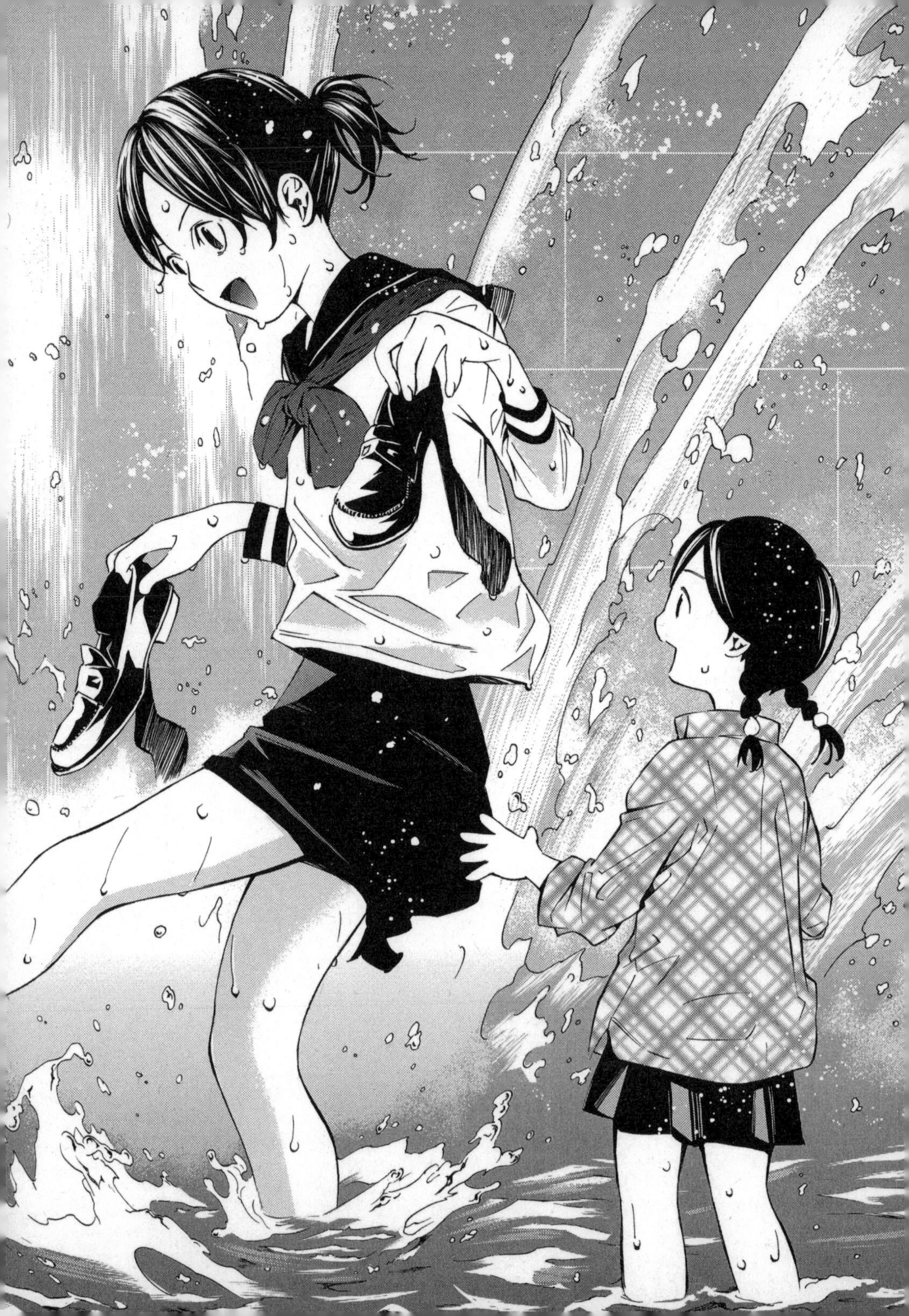

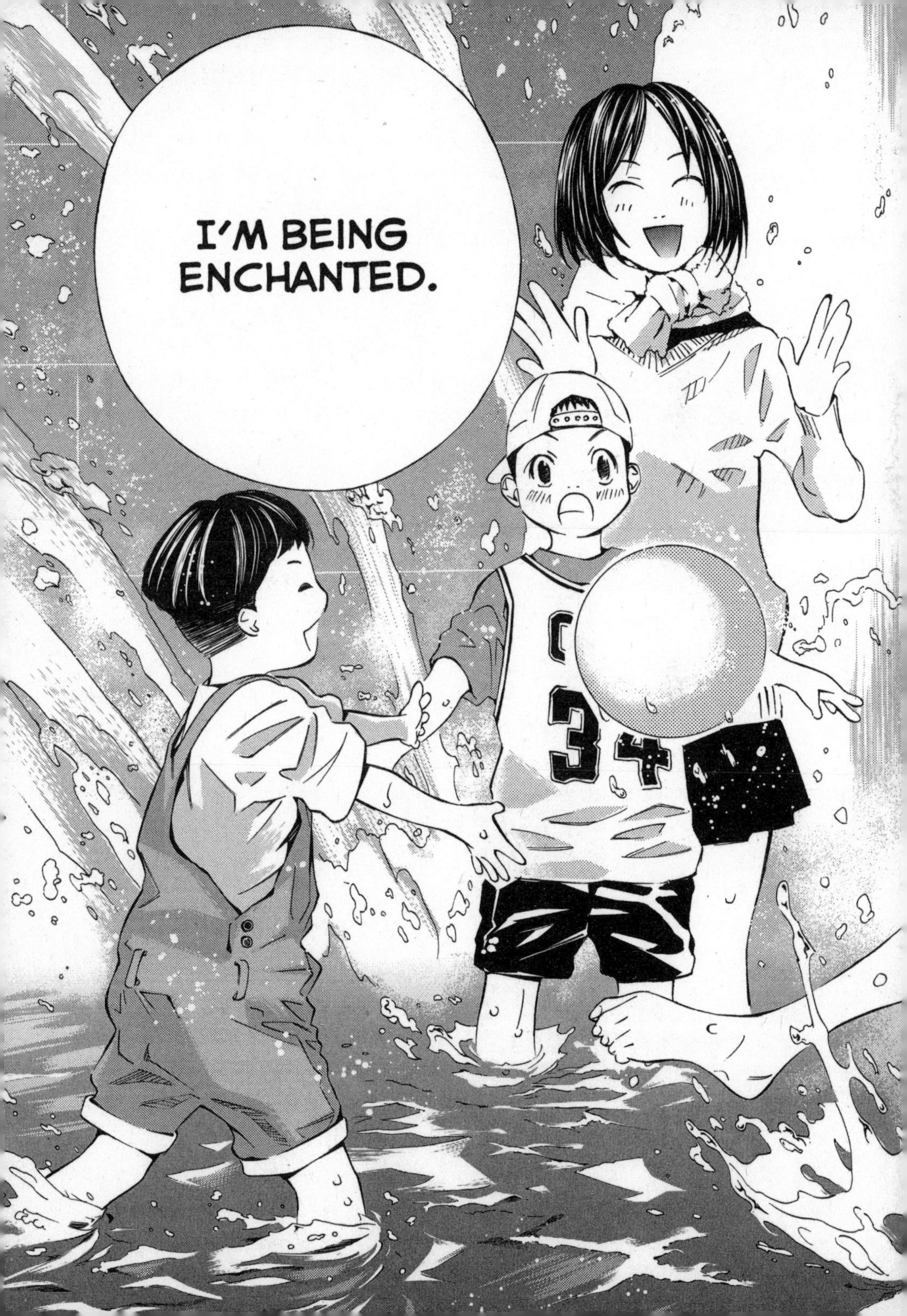
I'M BEING ENCHANTED.

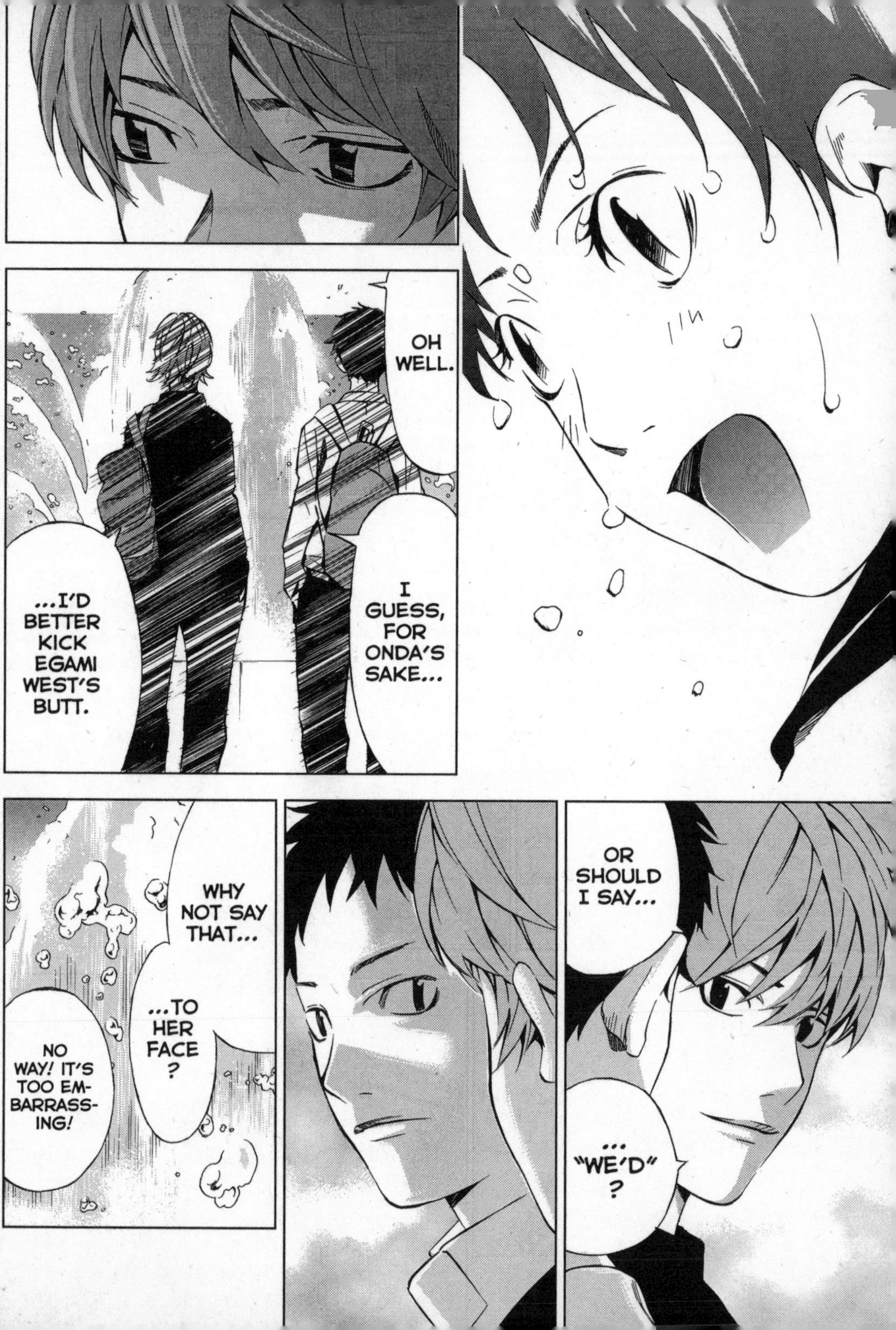
OH WELL.
I GUESS, FOR ONDA'S SAKE...
...I'D BETTER KICK EGAMI WEST'S BUTT.
OR SHOULD I SAY...
..."WE'D"?
WHY NOT SAY THAT...
...TO HER FACE?
NO WAY! IT'S TOO EM-BARRASS-ING!

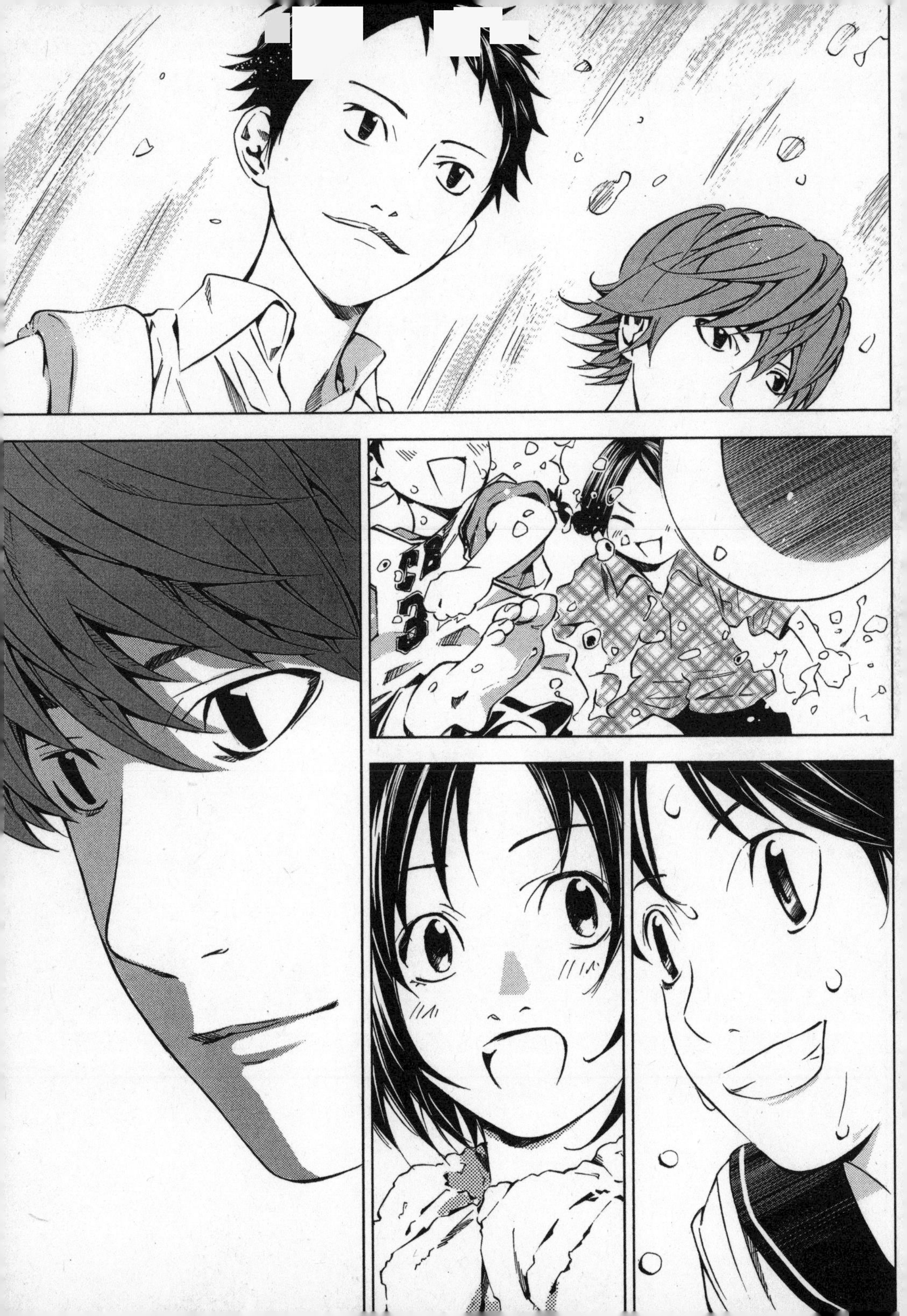
CB
3

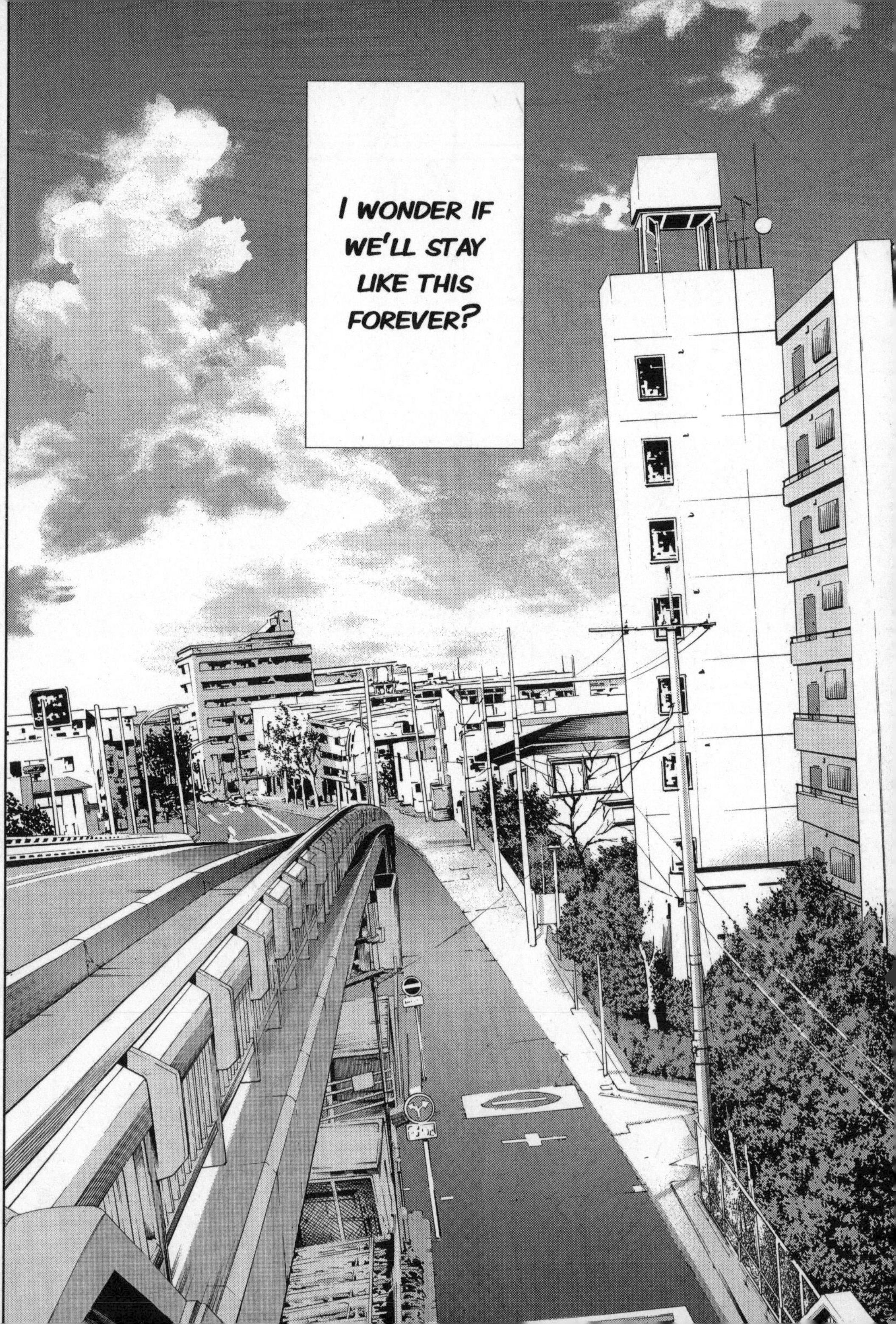
I WONDER IF WE'LL STAY LIKE THIS FOREVER?

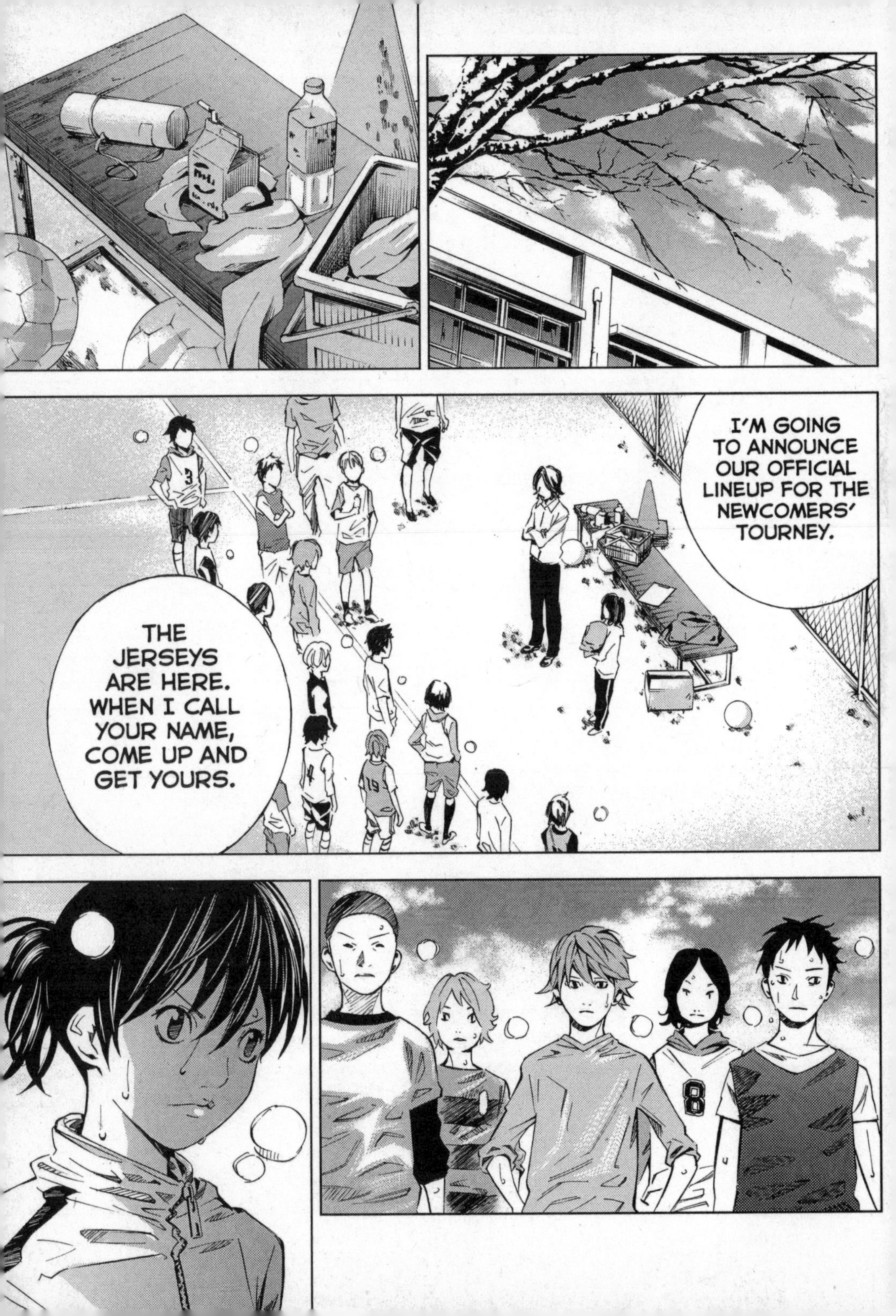
I'M GOING TO ANNOUNCE OUR OFFICIAL LINEUP FOR THE NEWCOMERS' TOURNEY.
THE JERSEYS ARE HERE. WHEN I CALL YOUR NAME, COME UP AND GET YOURS.

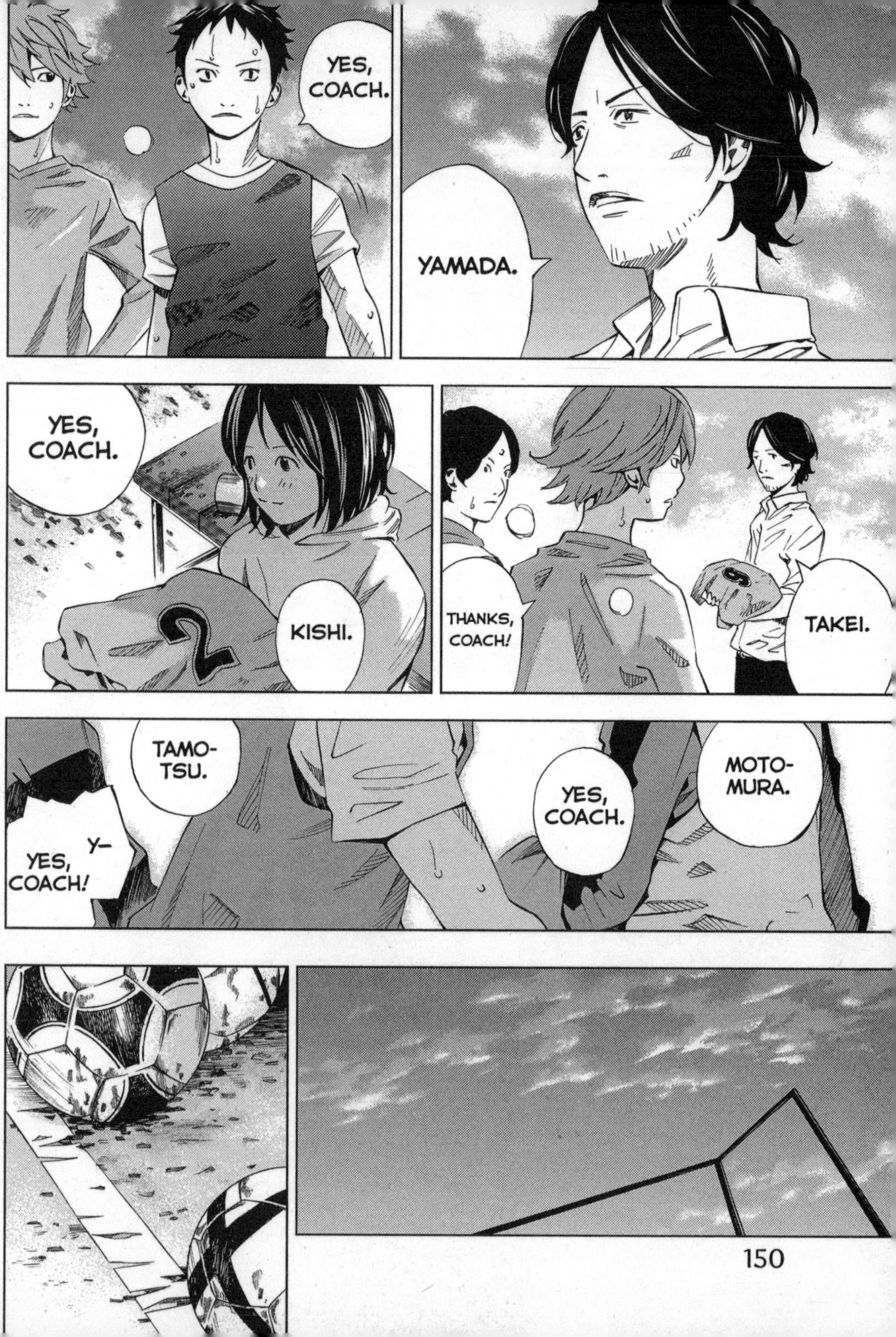
YAMADA.
YES, COACH.
TAKEI.
THANKS, COACH!
KISHI.
YES, COACH.
MOTO-MURA.
YES, COACH.
TAMO-TSU.
Y— YES, COACH!

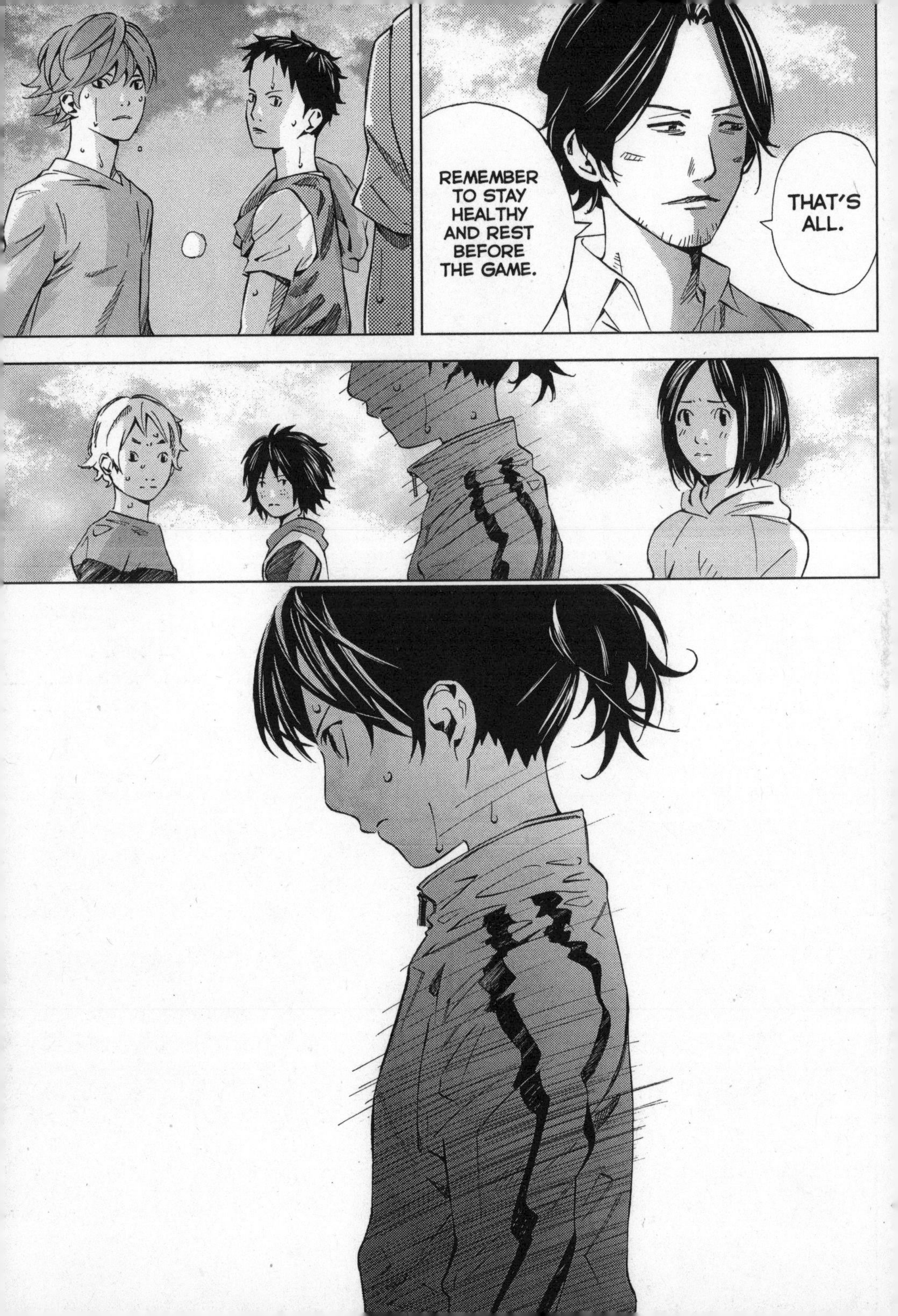
THAT'S ALL.
REMEMBER TO STAY HEALTHY AND REST BEFORE THE GAME.

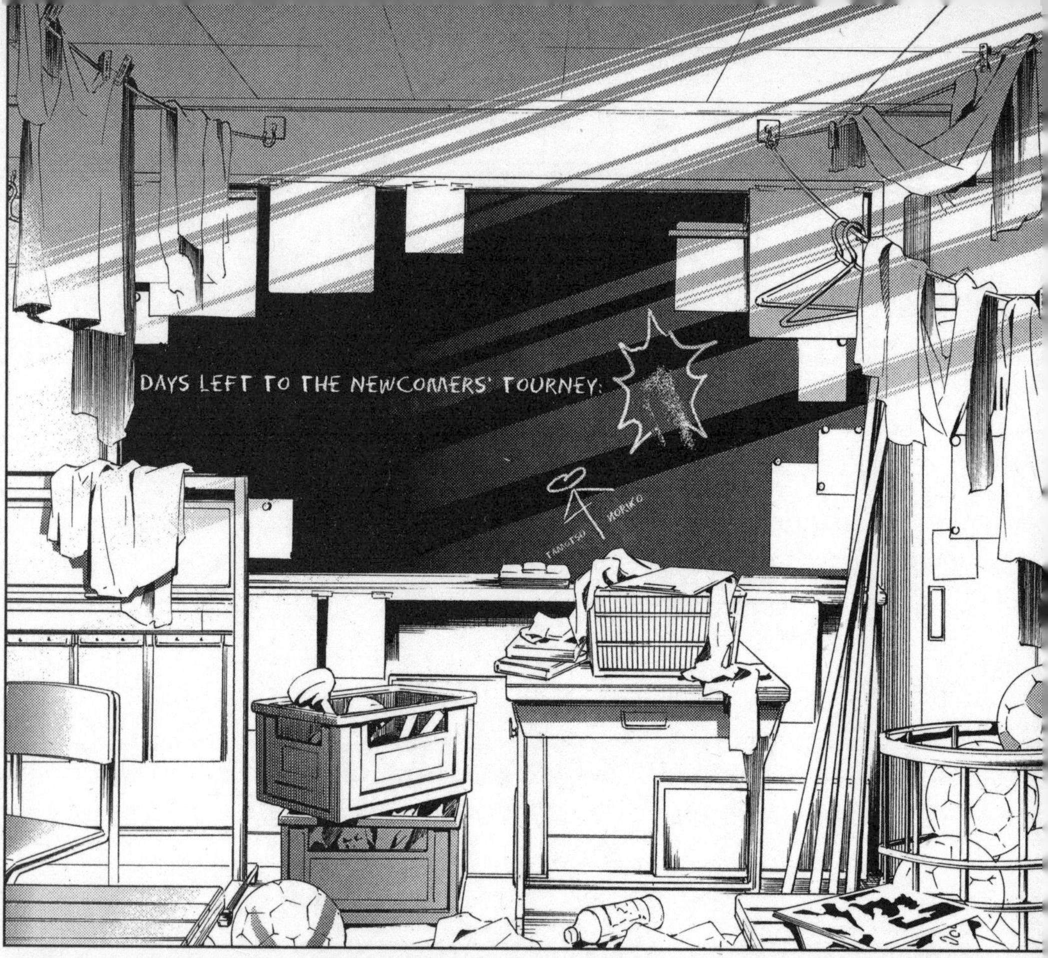
DAYS LEFT TO THE NEWCOMERS' TOURNEY:
TAMOTSU
NORIKO
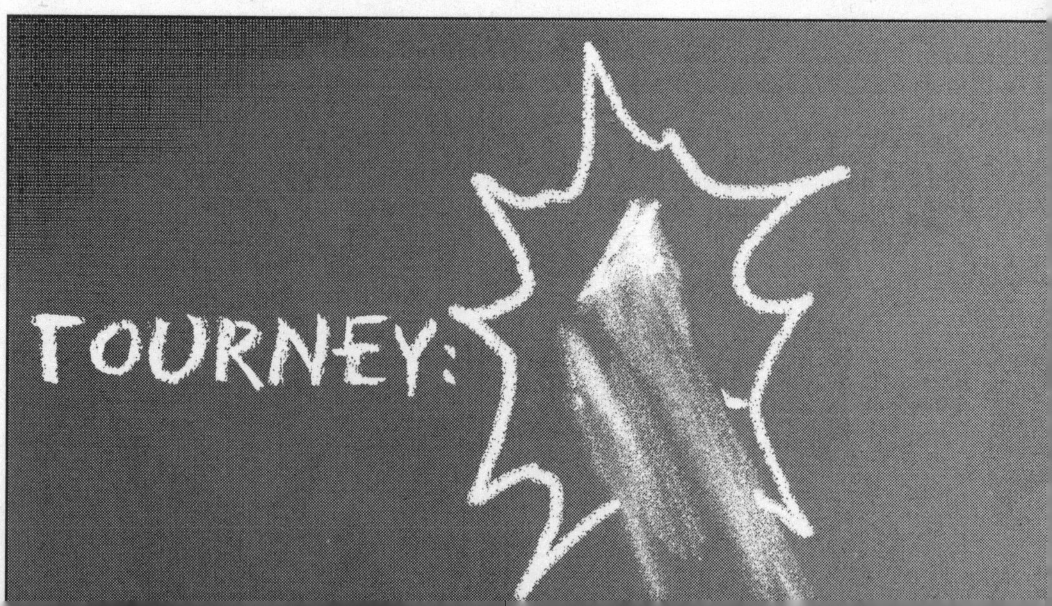
TOURNEY:

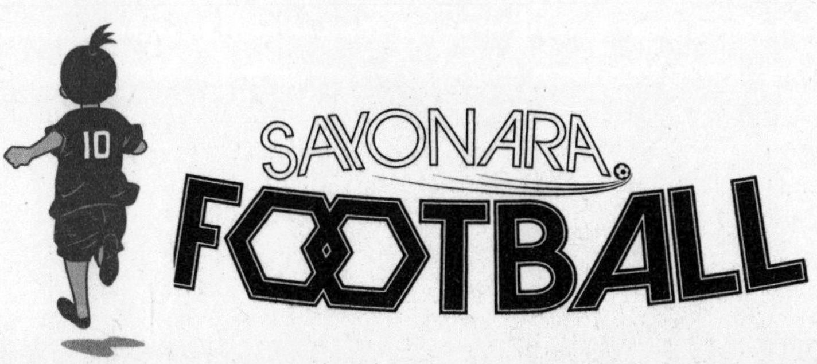
10

SAYONARA
FOOTBALL

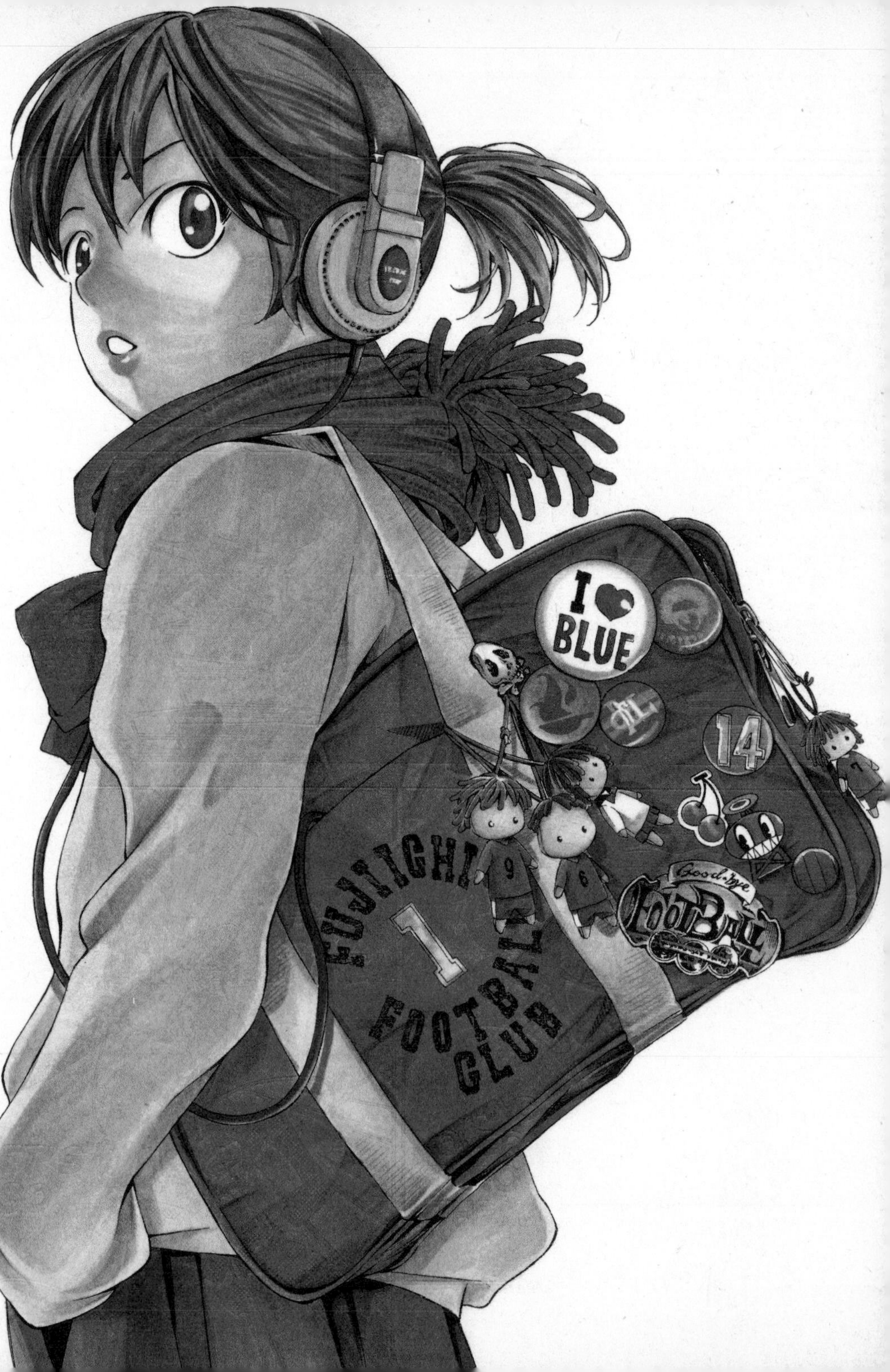
I ♥ BLUE
14
FUJIICHI FOOTBALL CLUB
1
Good-bye
FOOTBALL

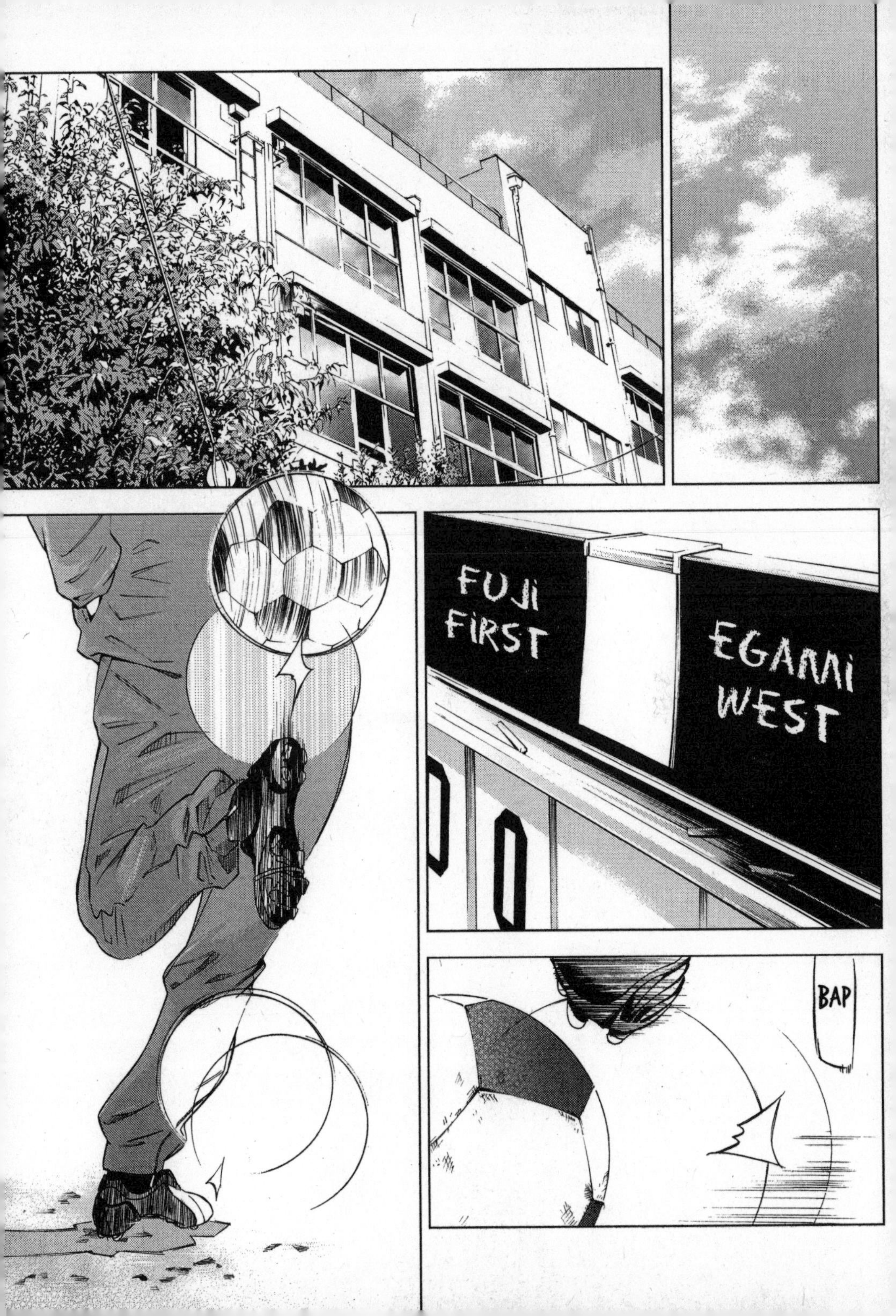
FUJI FIRST
EGAMI WEST
BAP

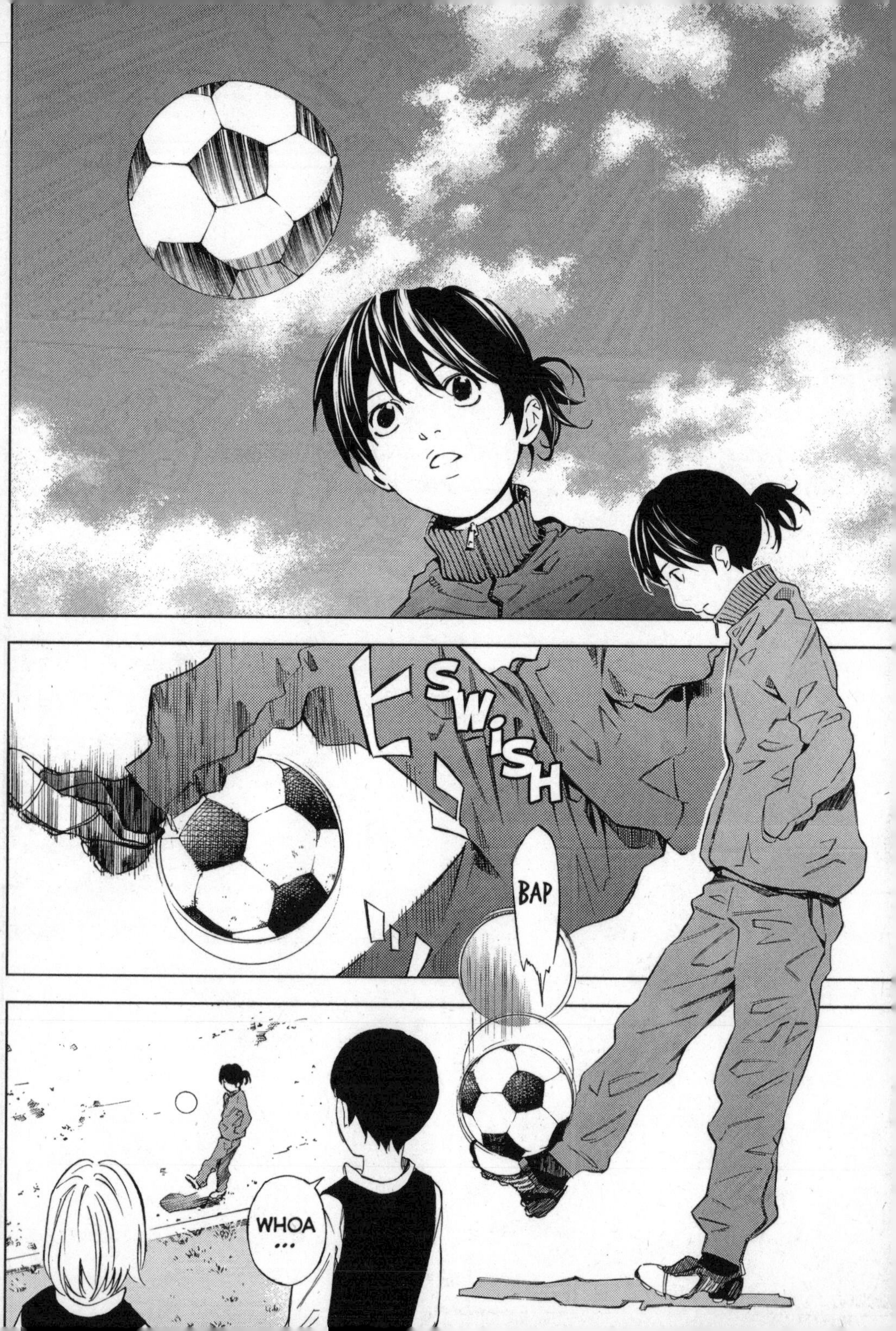
SWISH
BAP
WHOA ...

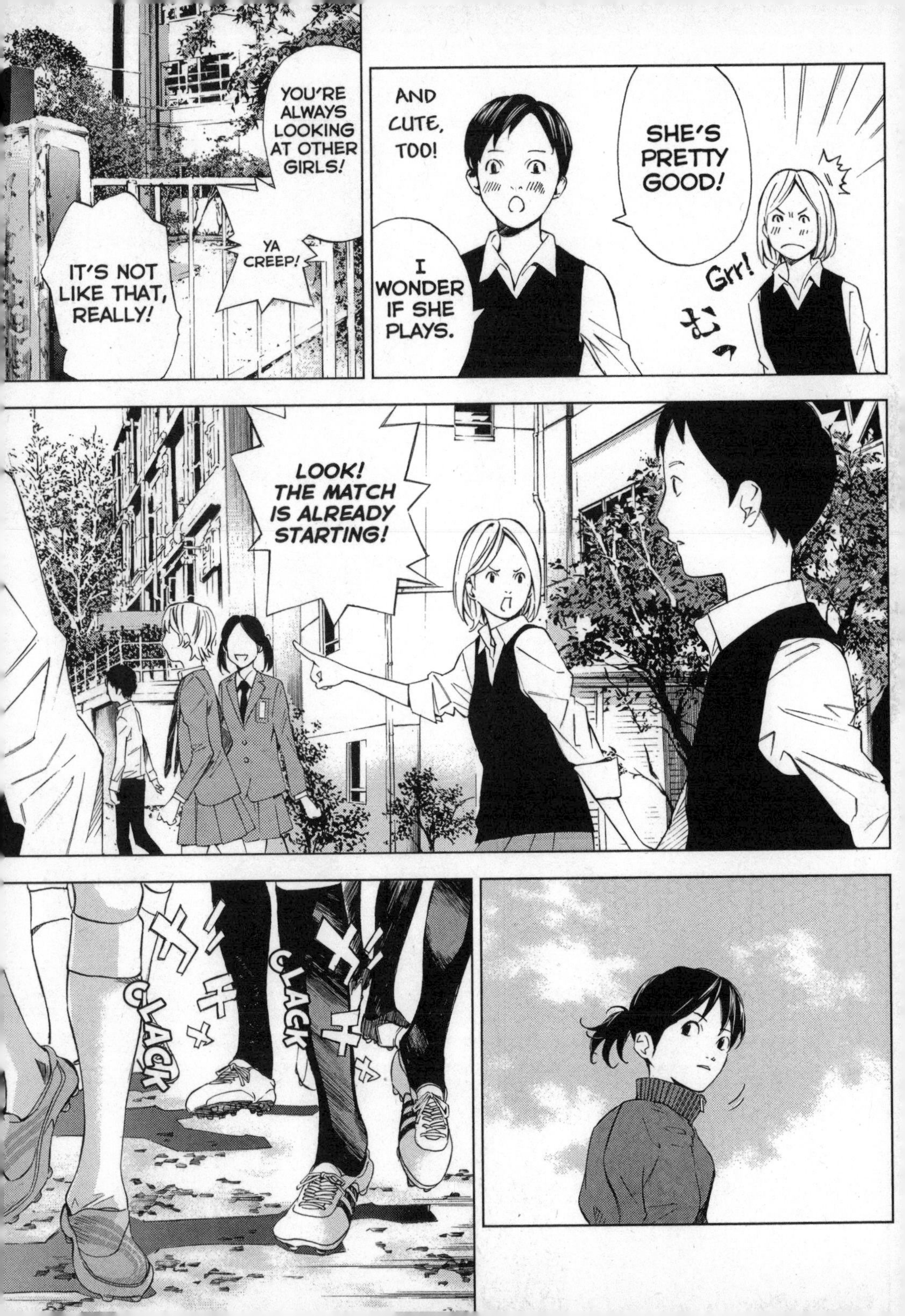

SHE'S PRETTY GOOD!
AND CUTE, TOO!
Grr!
むっ
I WONDER IF SHE PLAYS.
YOU'RE ALWAYS LOOKING AT OTHER GIRLS!
YA CREEP!
IT'S NOT LIKE THAT, REALLY!
LOOK! THE MATCH IS ALREADY STARTING!
CLACK
CLACK
CLACK

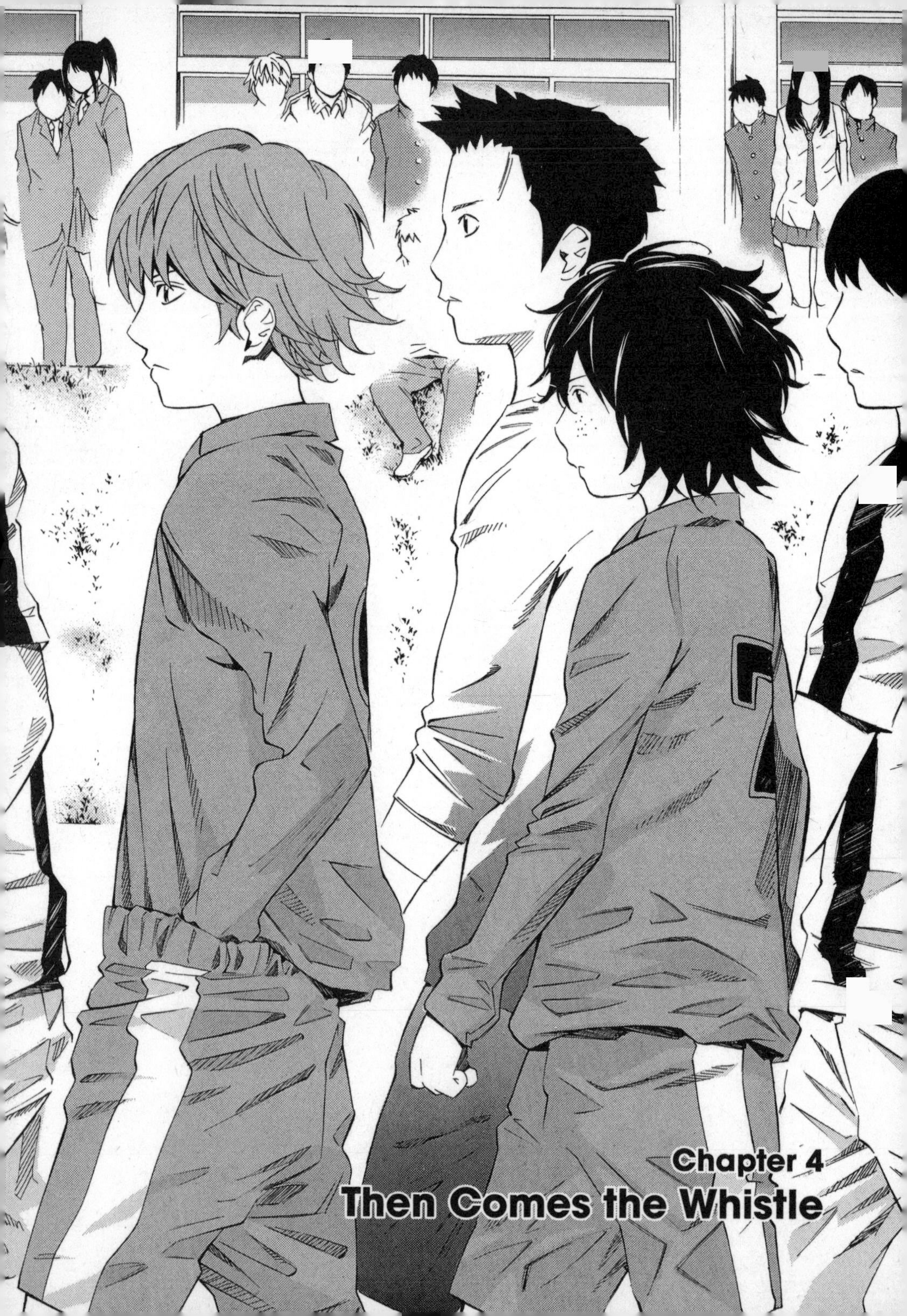
Chapter 4
Then Comes the Whistle

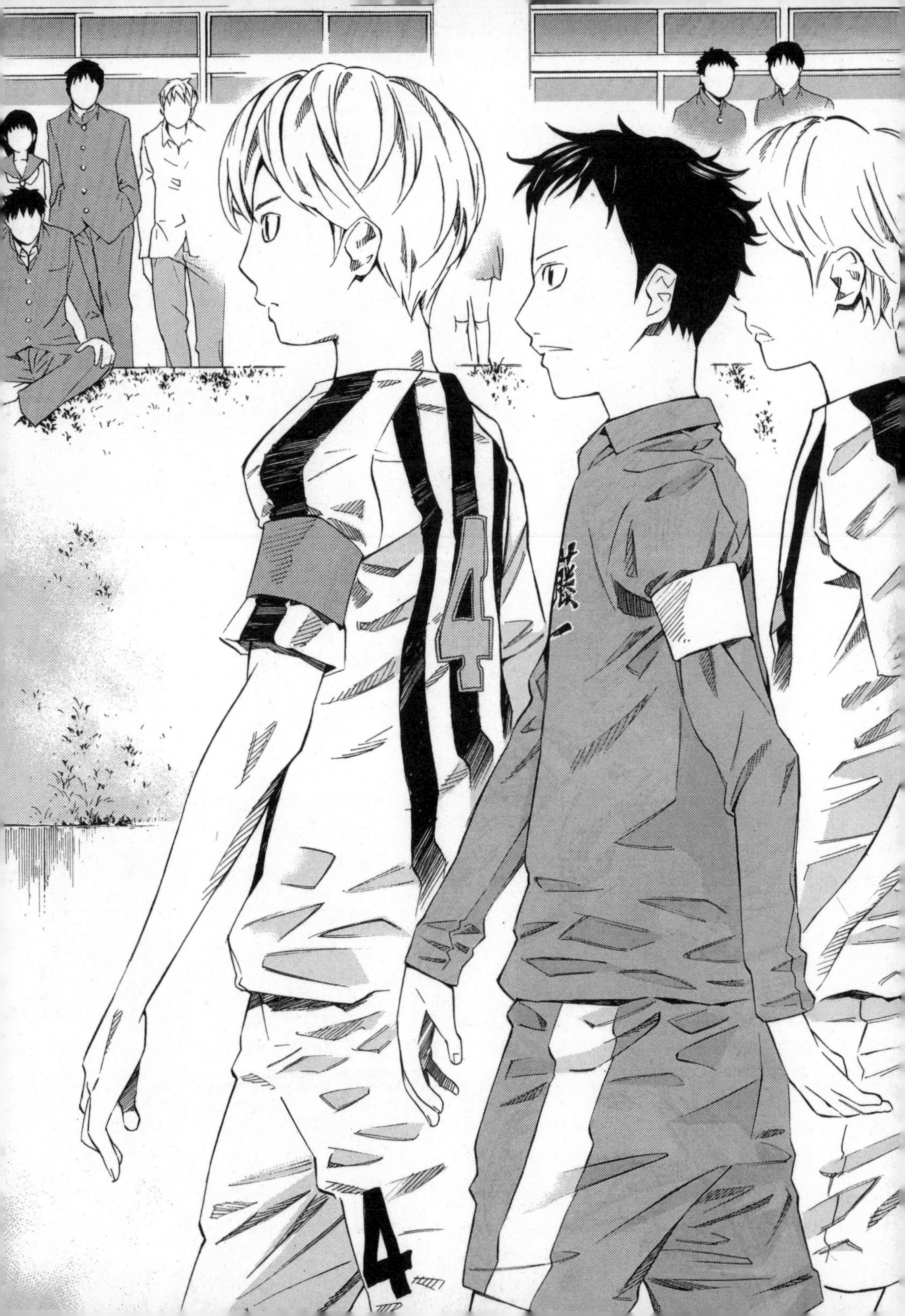

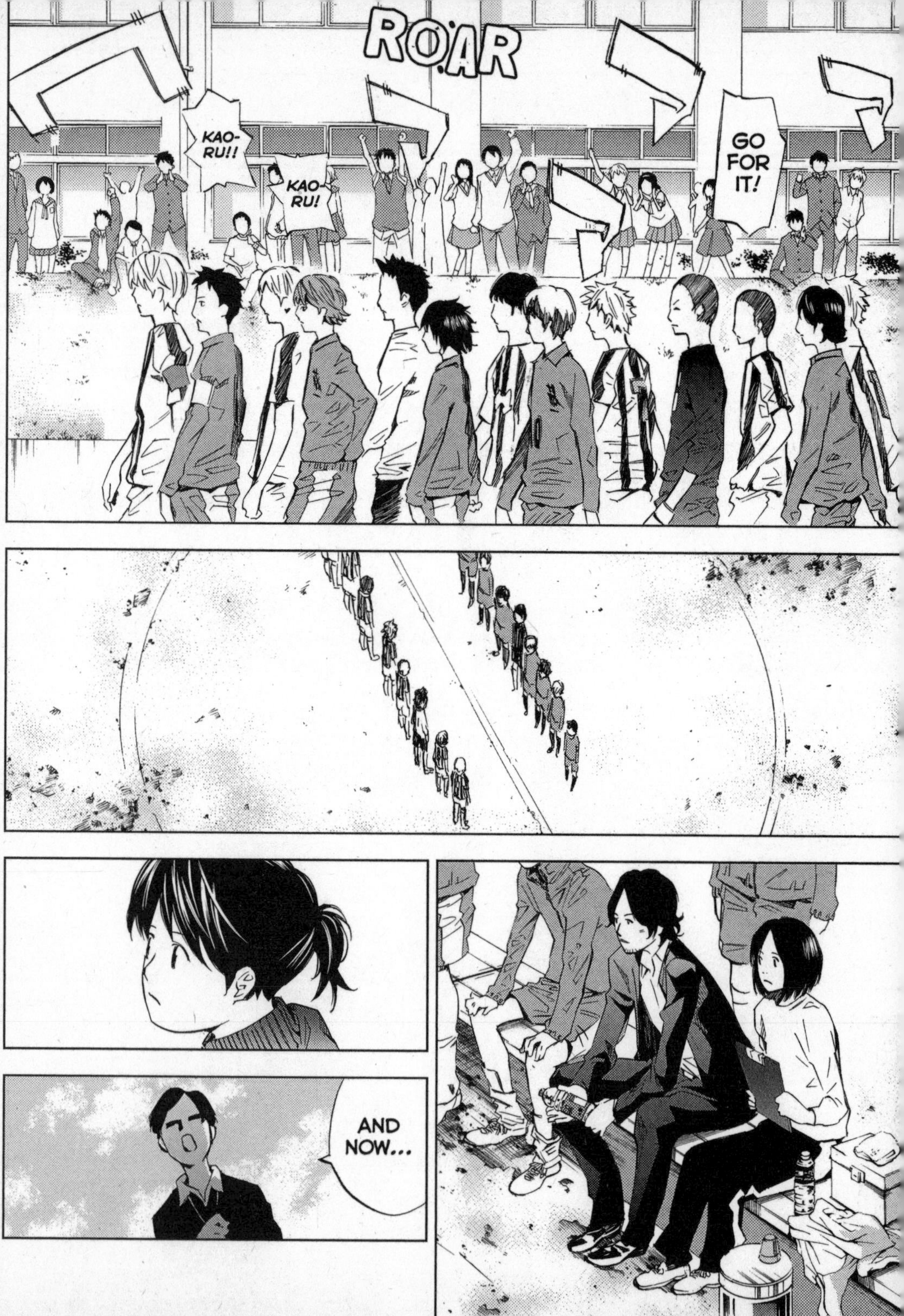
ROAR
GO FOR IT!
KAO-RU!
KAO-RU!!
AND NOW...

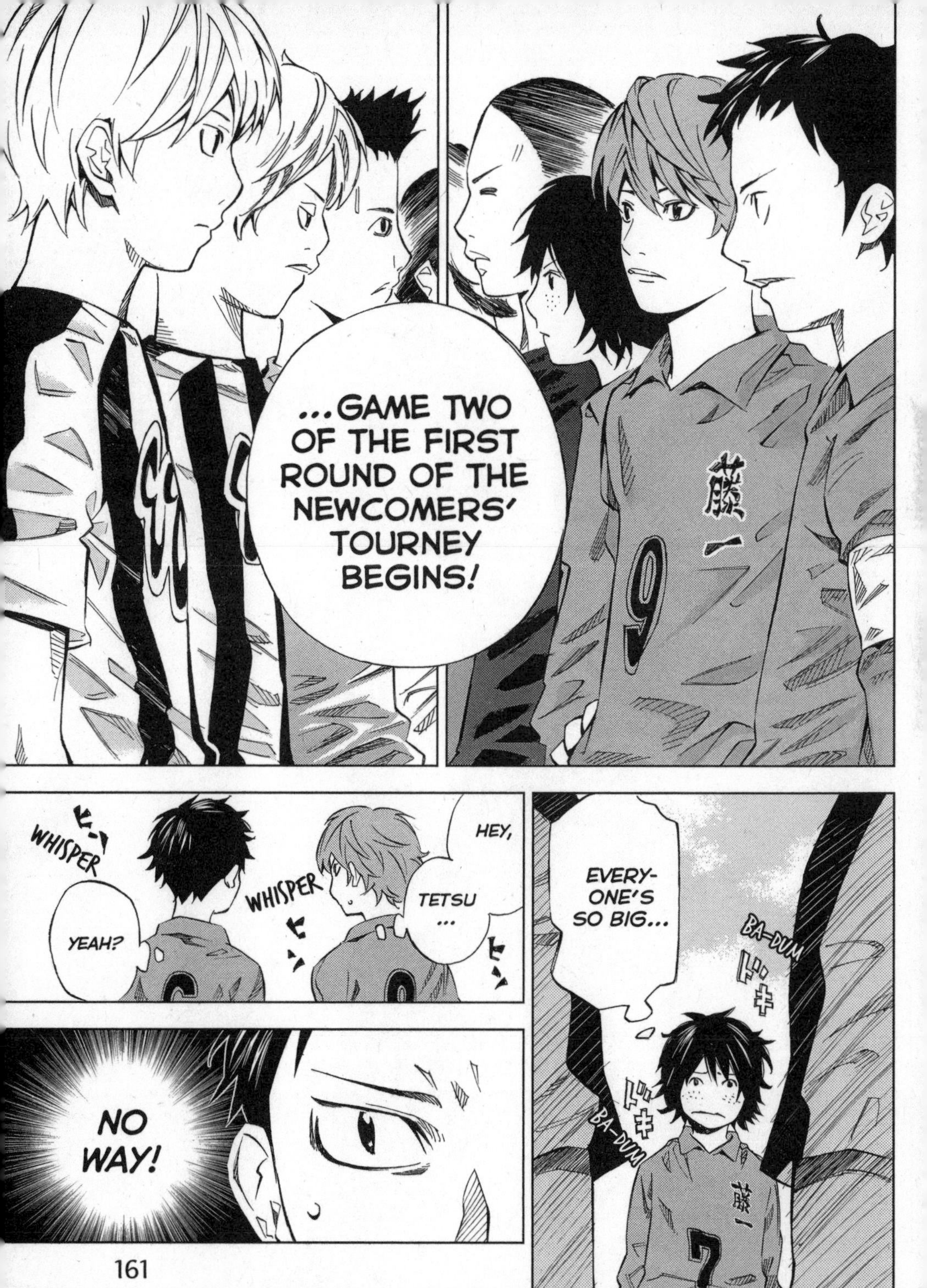
...GAME TWO OF THE FIRST ROUND OF THE NEWCOMERS' TOURNEY BEGINS!
EVERY-ONE'S SO BIG...
BA-DUM
BA-DUM
HEY, TETSU...
WHISPER
WHISPER
YEAH?
NO WAY!

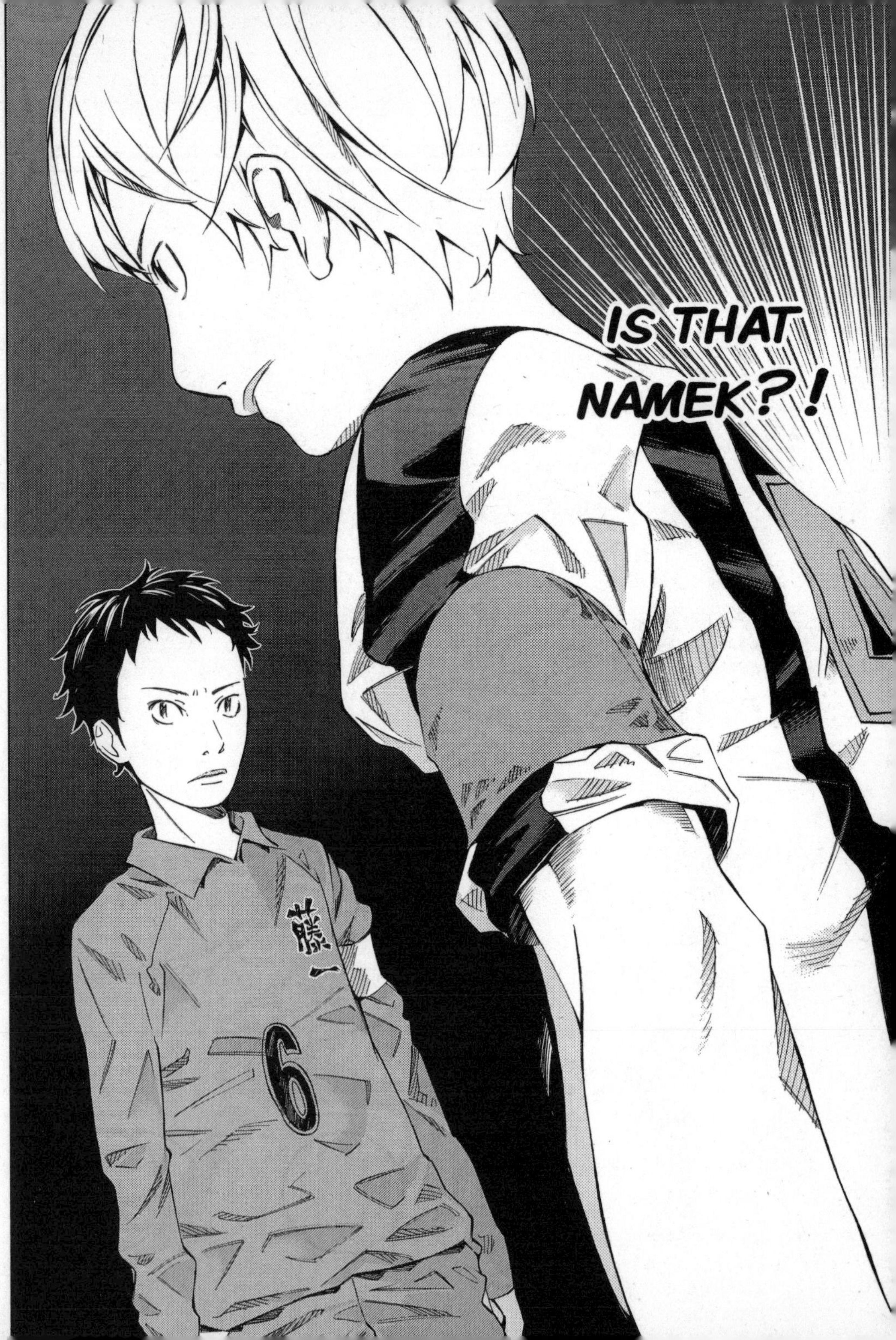
IS THAT NAMEK?!
藤一
6

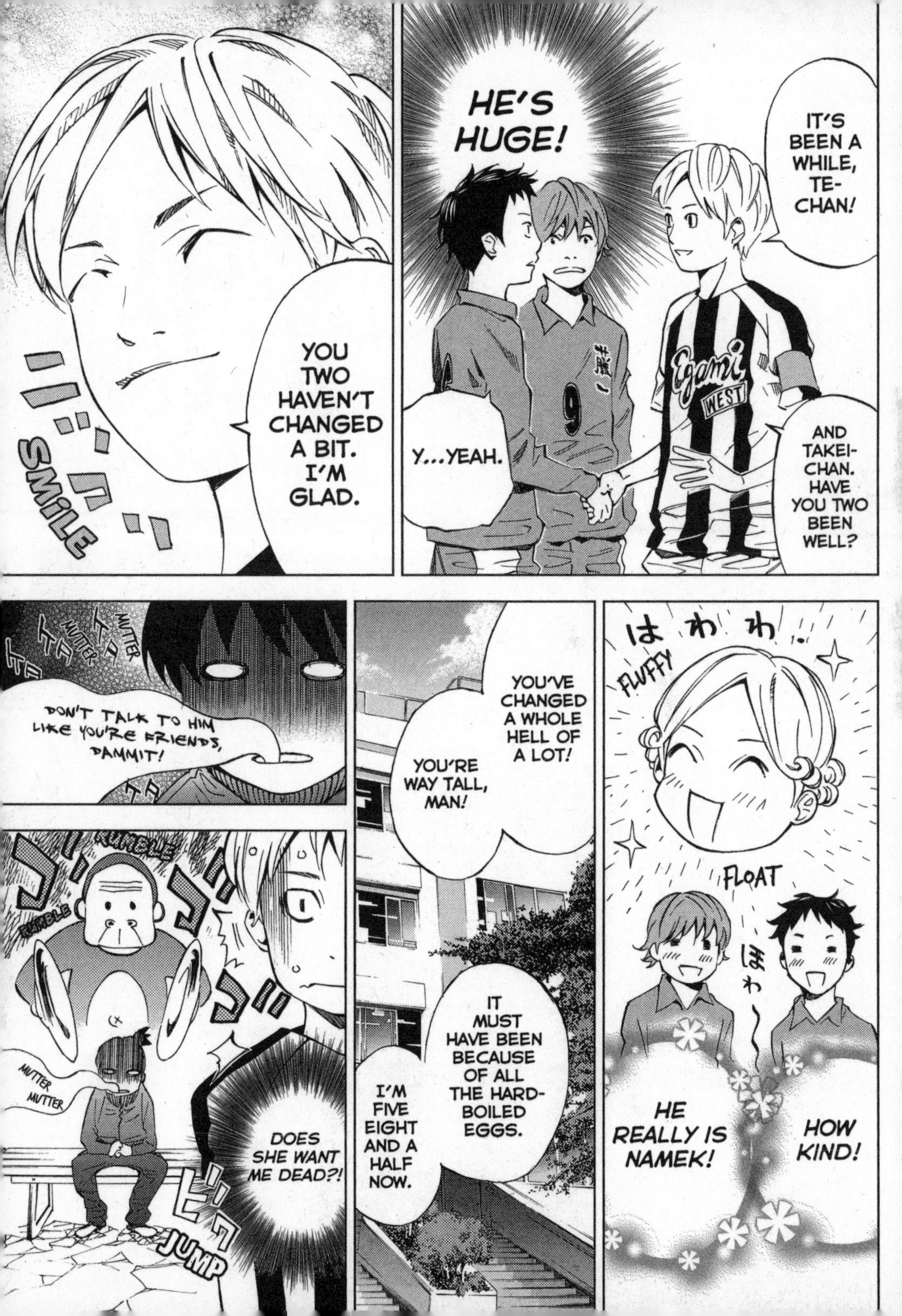
IT'S BEEN A WHILE, TE-CHAN!
HE'S HUGE!
AND TAKEI-CHAN. HAVE YOU TWO BEEN WELL?
Y...YEAH.
YOU TWO HAVEN'T CHANGED A BIT. I'M GLAD.
SMILE
はわわ..
FLUFFY
FLOAT
ほわ~
HOW KIND!
HE REALLY IS NAMEK!
YOU'VE CHANGED A WHOLE HELL OF A LOT!
YOU'RE WAY TALL, MAN!
IT MUST HAVE BEEN BECAUSE OF ALL THE HARD-BOILED EGGS.
I'M FIVE EIGHT AND A HALF NOW.
MUTTER
MUTTER
DON'T TALK TO HIM LIKE YOU'RE FRIENDS, DAMMIT!
RUMBLE
RUMBLE
MUTTER
MUTTER
DOES SHE WANT ME DEAD?!
JUMP

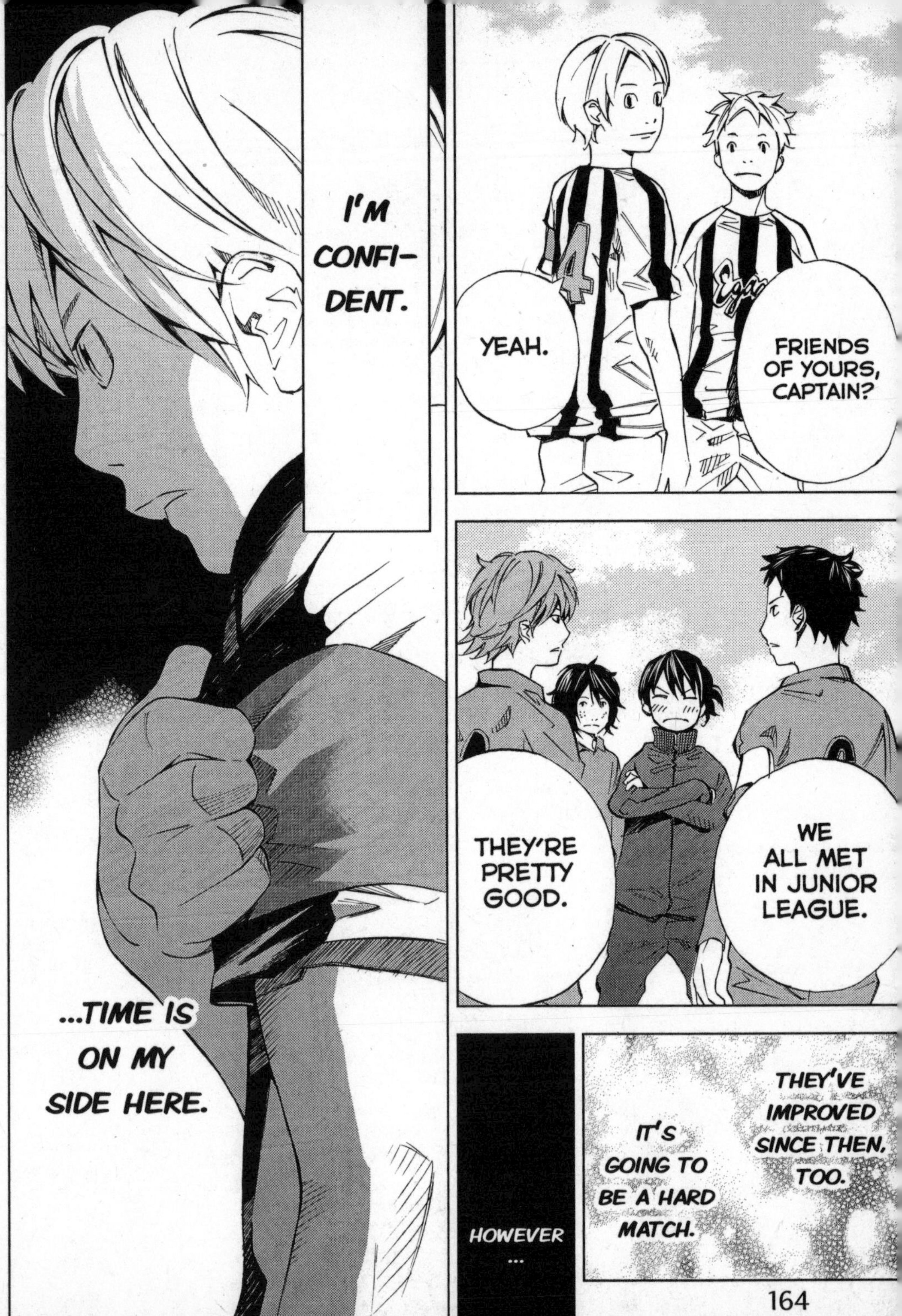
FRIENDS OF YOURS, CAPTAIN?
YEAH.
WE ALL MET IN JUNIOR LEAGUE.
THEY'RE PRETTY GOOD.
THEY'VE IMPROVED SINCE THEN, TOO.
IT'S GOING TO BE A HARD MATCH.
HOWEVER...
I'M CONFI-DENT.
...TIME IS ON MY SIDE HERE.

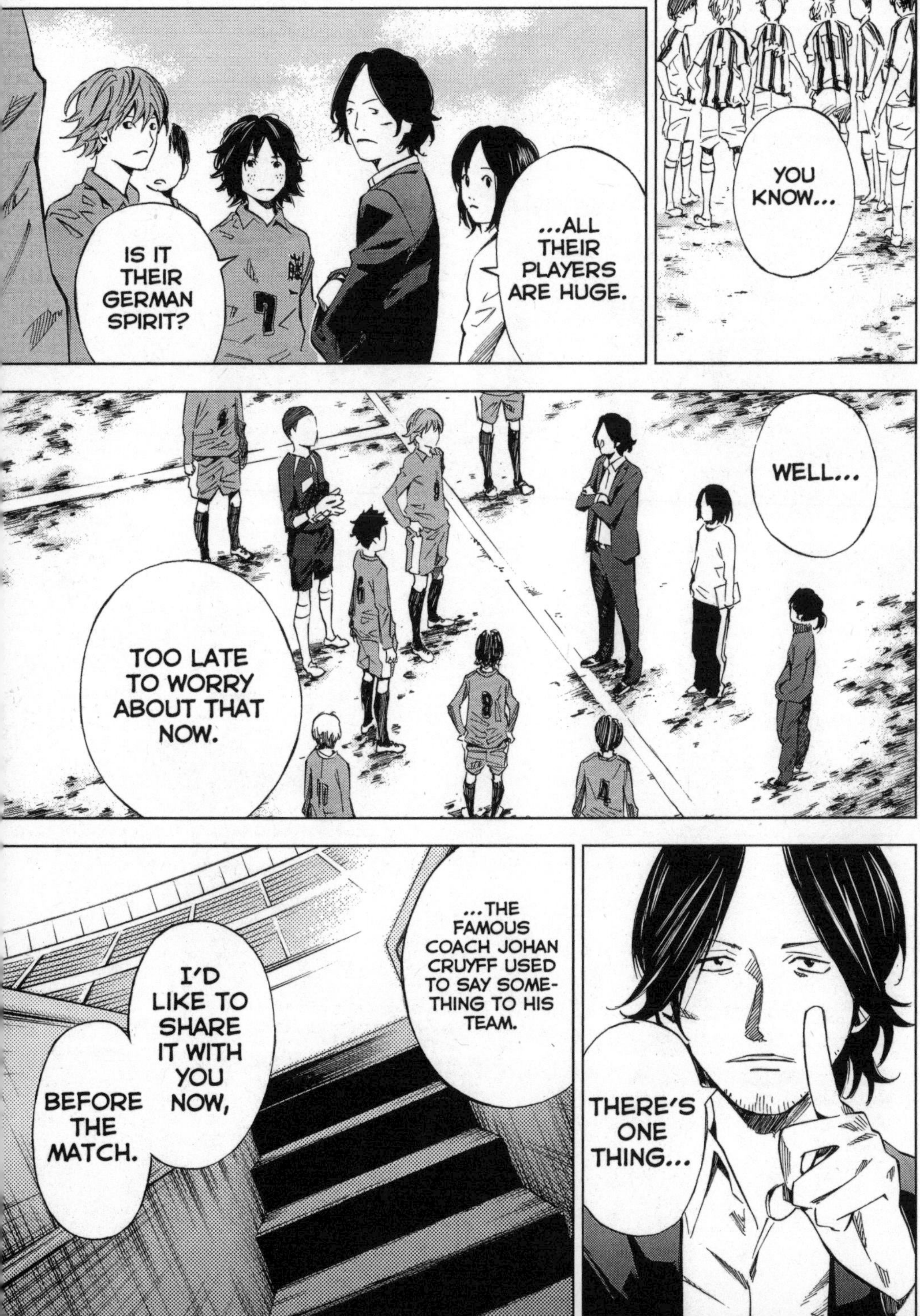
YOU KNOW...
...ALL THEIR PLAYERS ARE HUGE.
IS IT THEIR GERMAN SPIRIT?
WELL...
TOO LATE TO WORRY ABOUT THAT NOW.
THERE'S ONE THING...
...THE FAMOUS COACH JOHAN CRUYFF USED TO SAY SOME-THING TO HIS TEAM.
I'D LIKE TO SHARE IT WITH YOU NOW,
BEFORE THE MATCH.

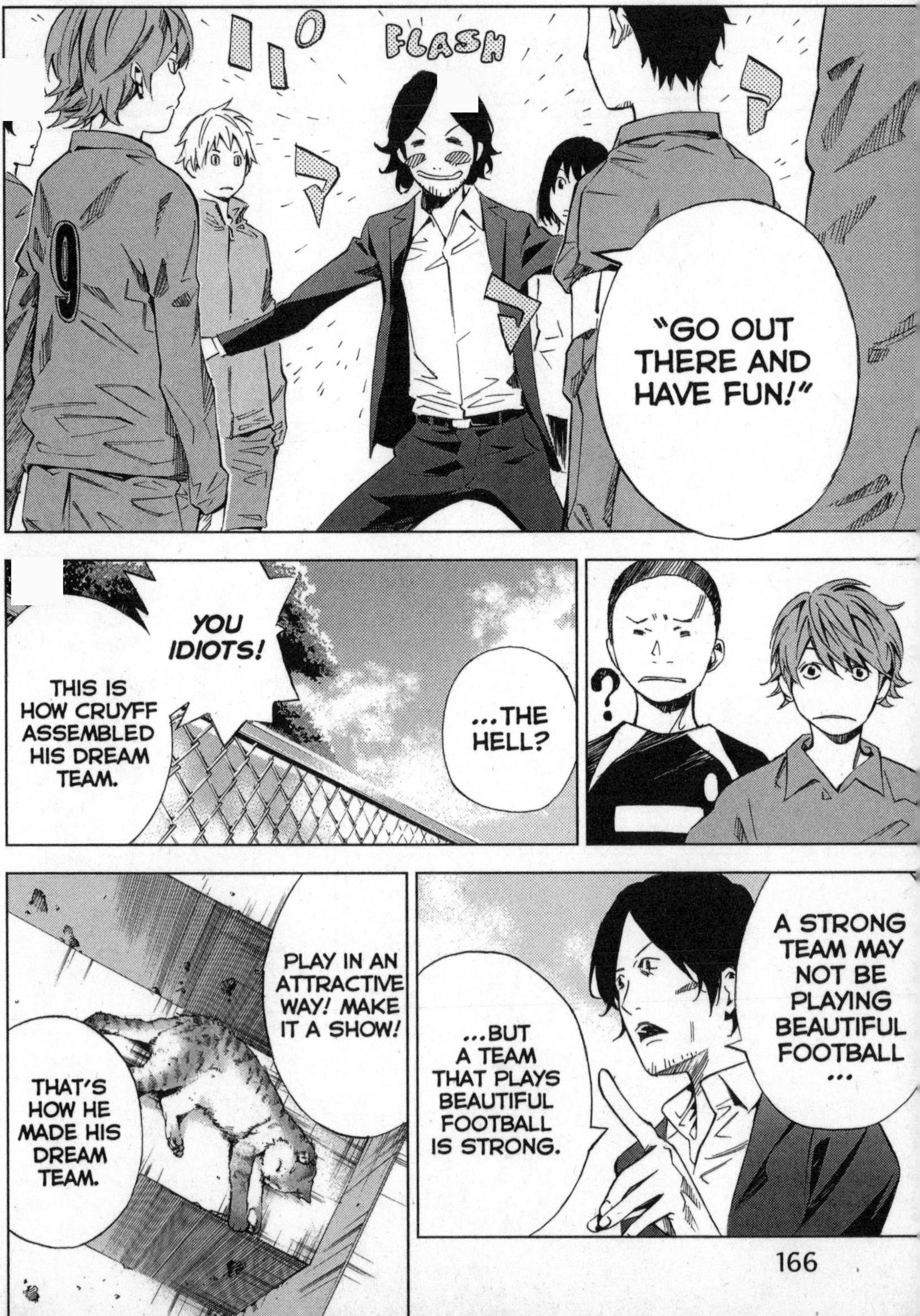
FLASH
"GO OUT THERE AND HAVE FUN!"
YOU IDIOTS!
THIS IS HOW CRUYFF ASSEMBLED HIS DREAM TEAM.
...THE HELL?
A STRONG TEAM MAY NOT BE PLAYING BEAUTIFUL FOOTBALL ...
...BUT A TEAM THAT PLAYS BEAUTIFUL FOOTBALL IS STRONG.
PLAY IN AN ATTRACTIVE WAY! MAKE IT A SHOW!
THAT'S HOW HE MADE HIS DREAM TEAM.

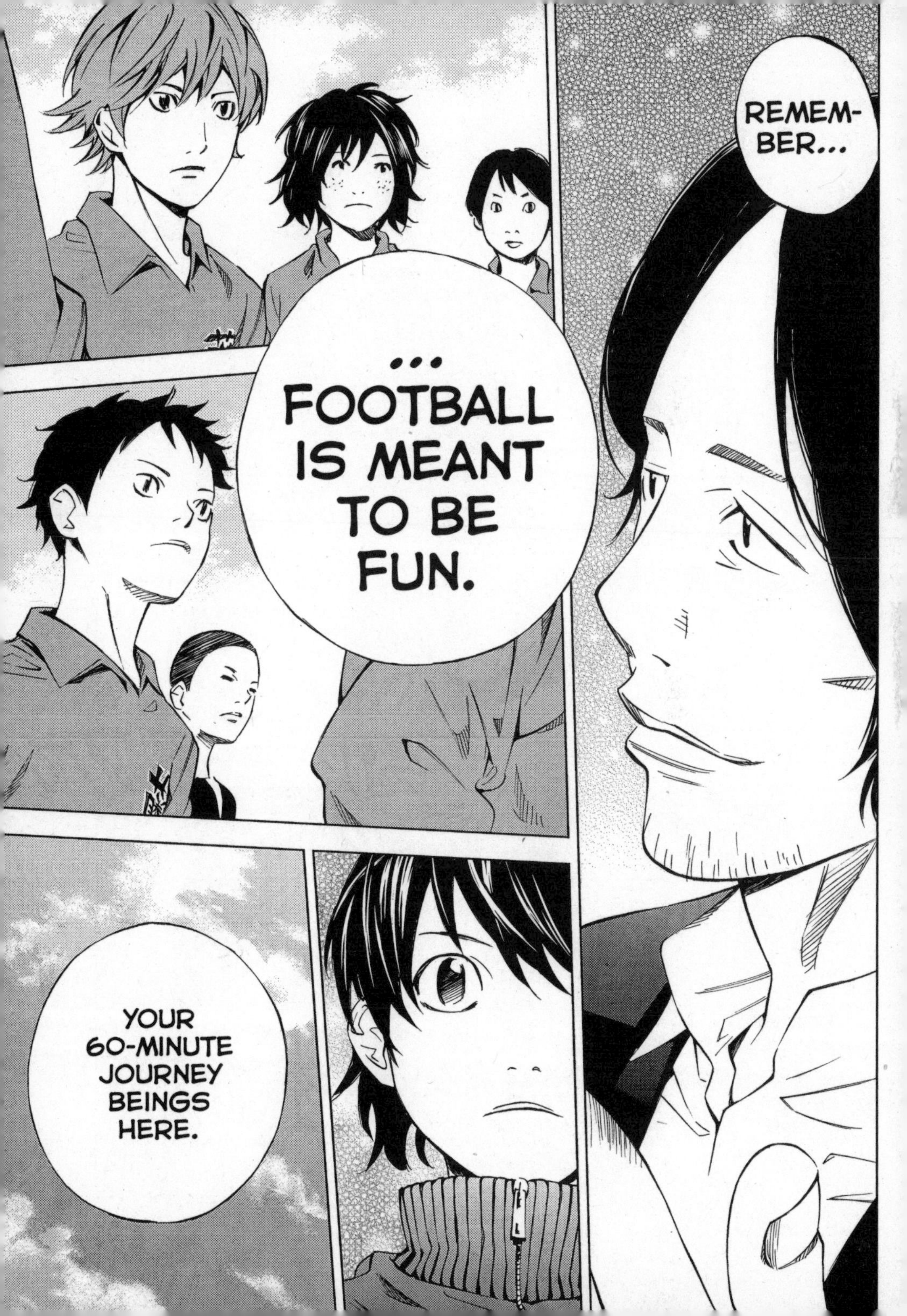
REMEM-BER...
...FOOTBALL IS MEANT TO BE FUN.
YOUR 60-MINUTE JOURNEY BEINGS HERE.

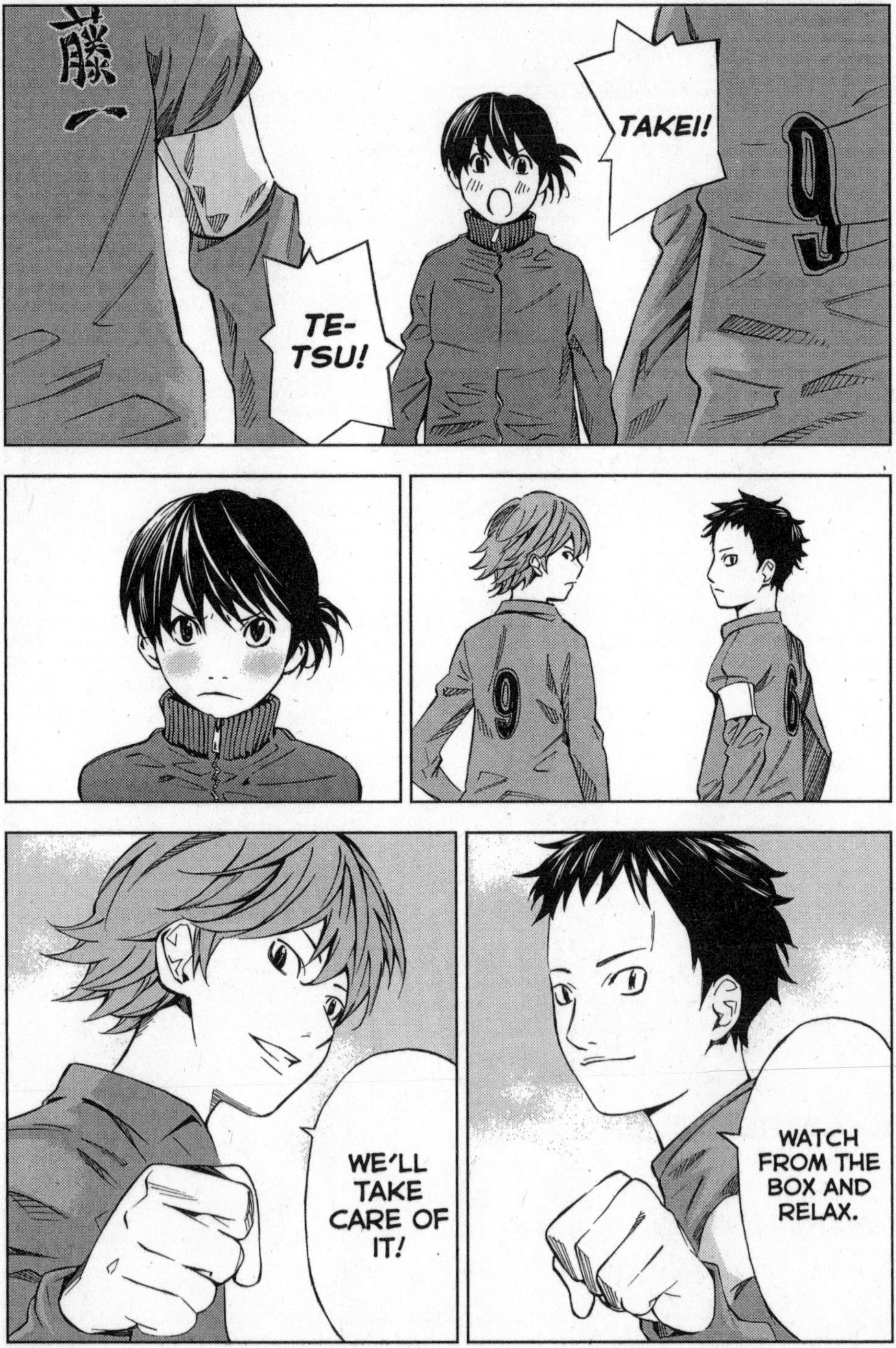
TAKEI!
TE-TSU!
WATCH FROM THE BOX AND RELAX.
WE'LL TAKE CARE OF IT!

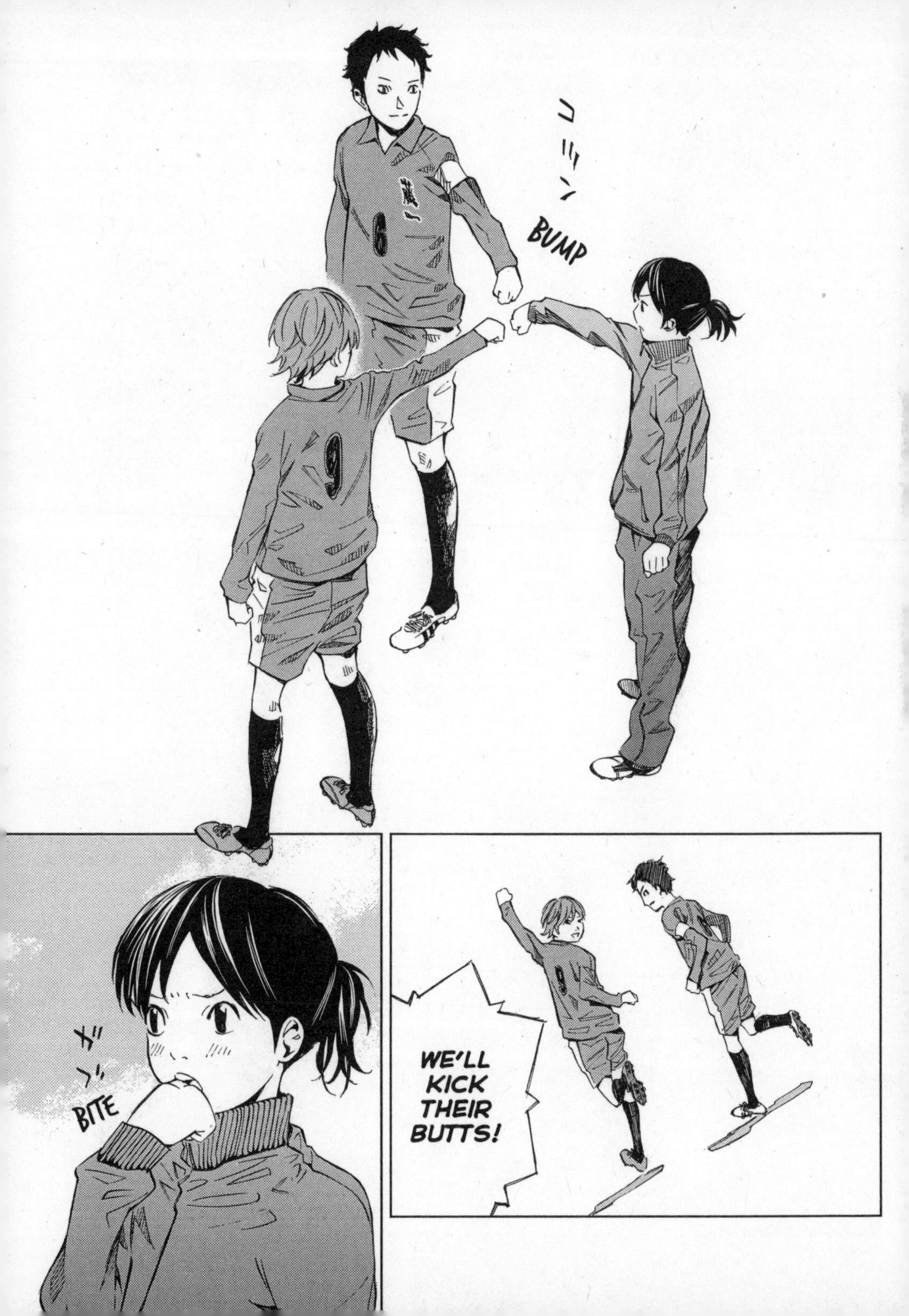
BUMP
WE'LL KICK THEIR BUTTS!
BITE

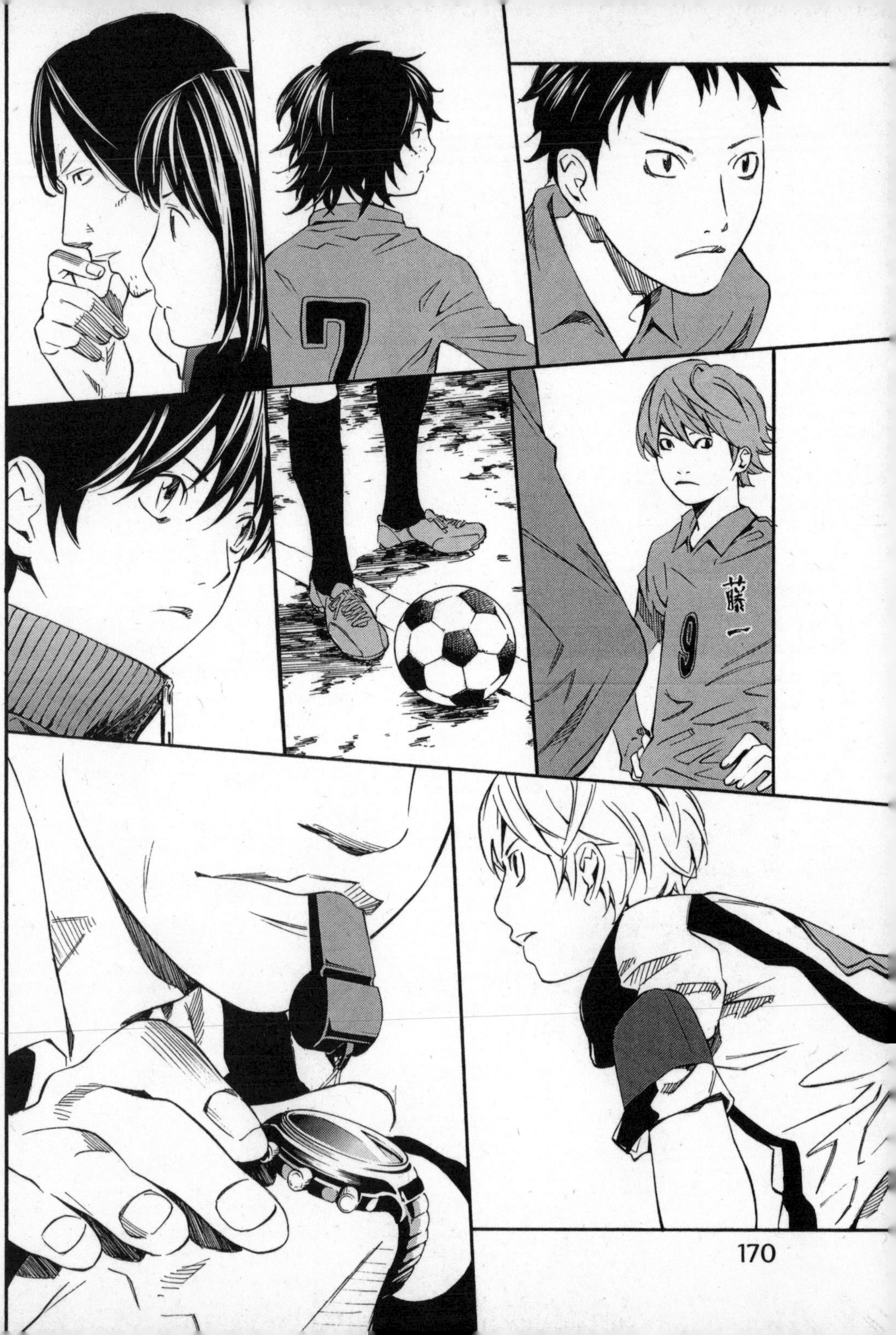
藤一

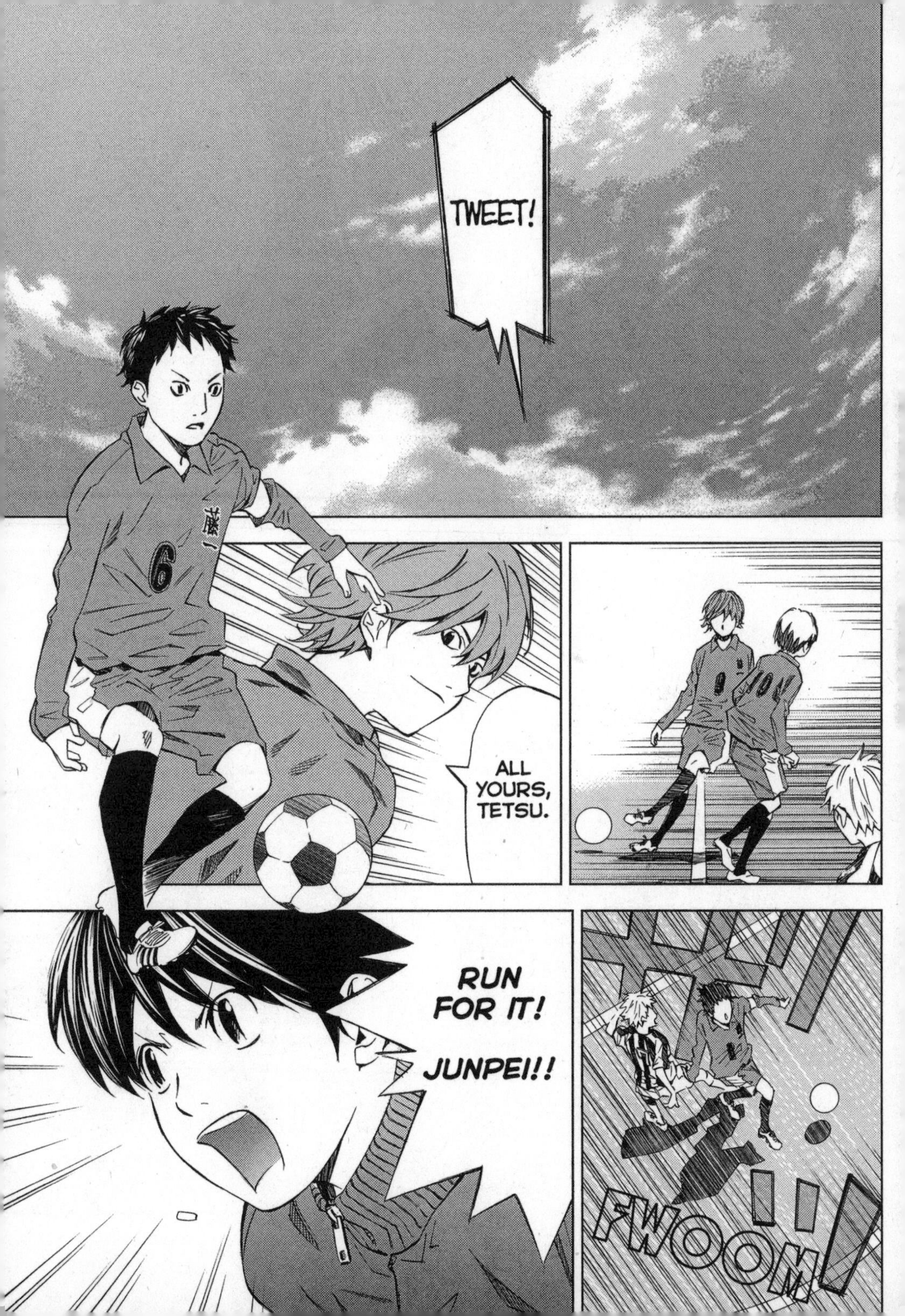
TWEET!
ALL YOURS, TETSU.
FWOOM!!
RUN FOR IT!
JUNPEI!!

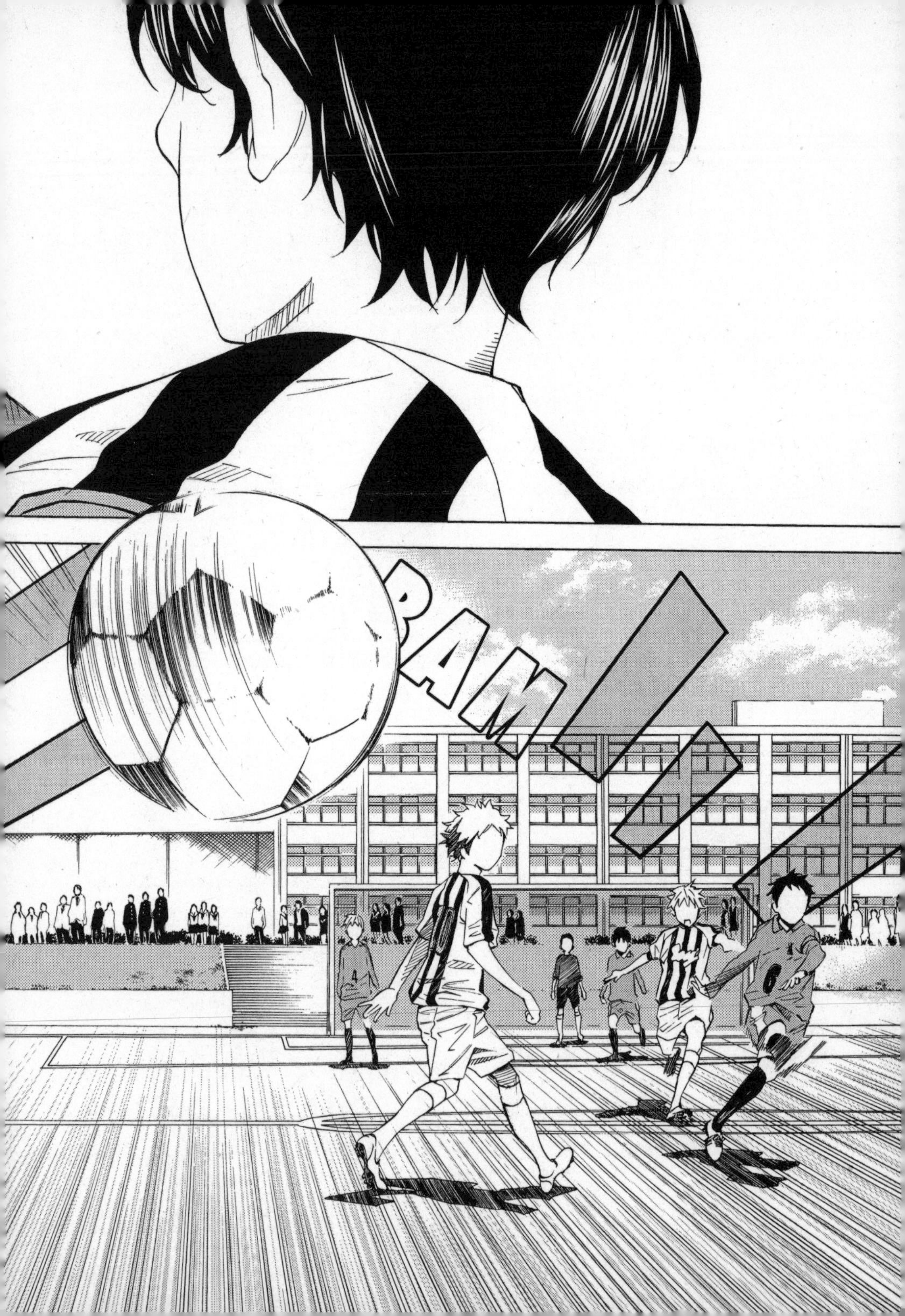
BAM

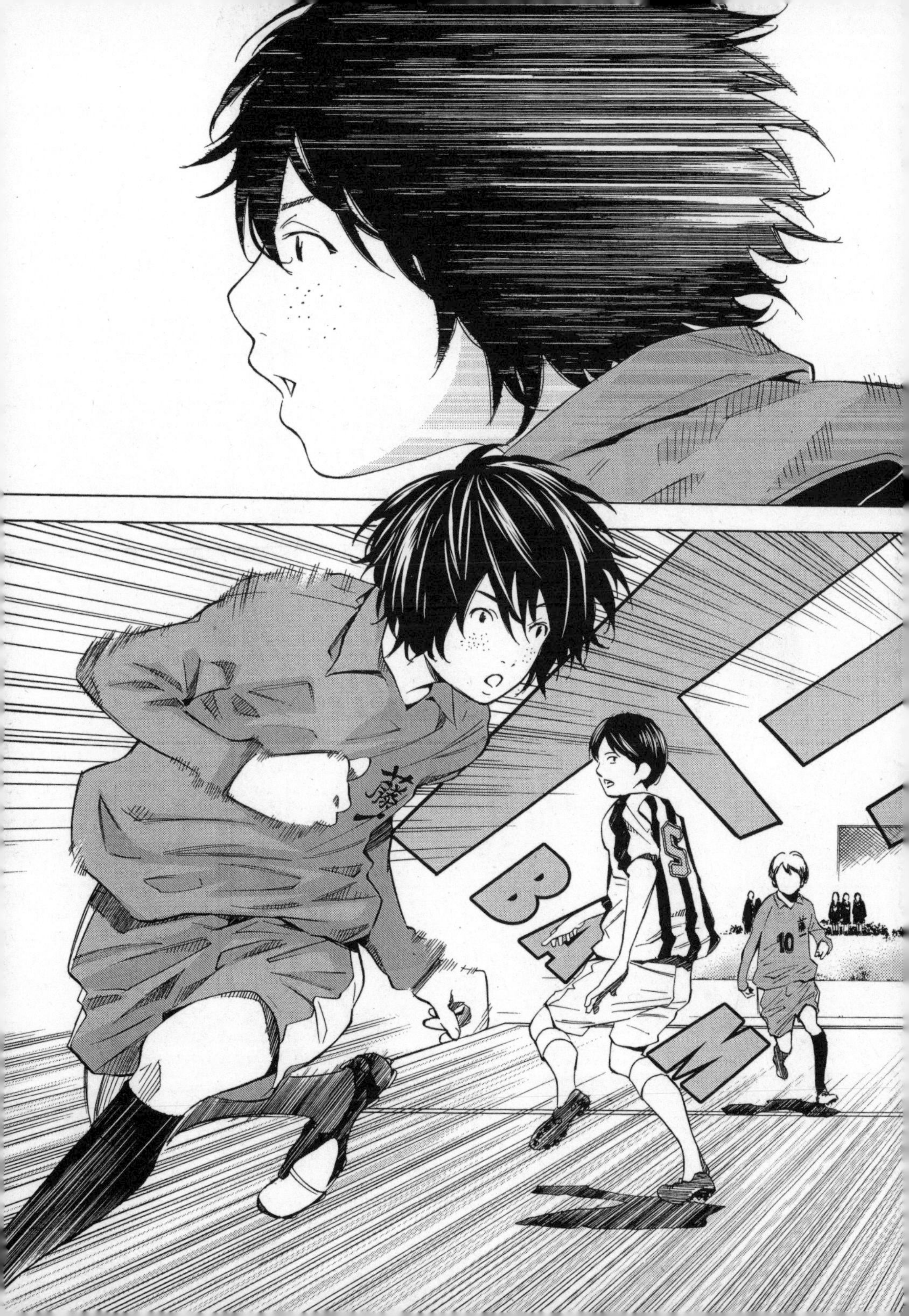
BAM

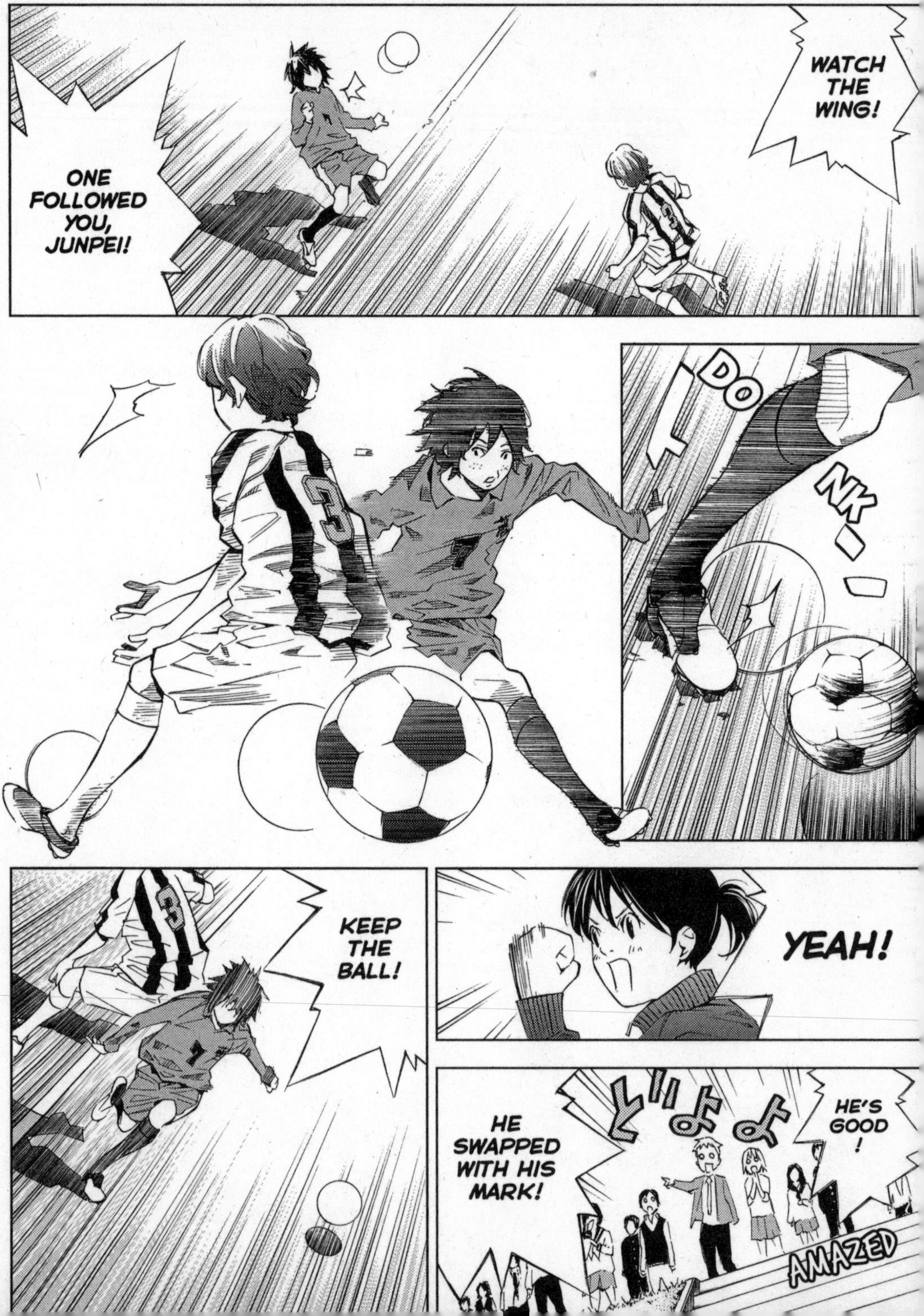
WATCH THE WING!
ONE FOLLOWED YOU, JUNPEI!
DONK--
YEAH!
HE'S GOOD!
HE SWAPPED WITH HIS MARK!
AMAZED
KEEP THE BALL!

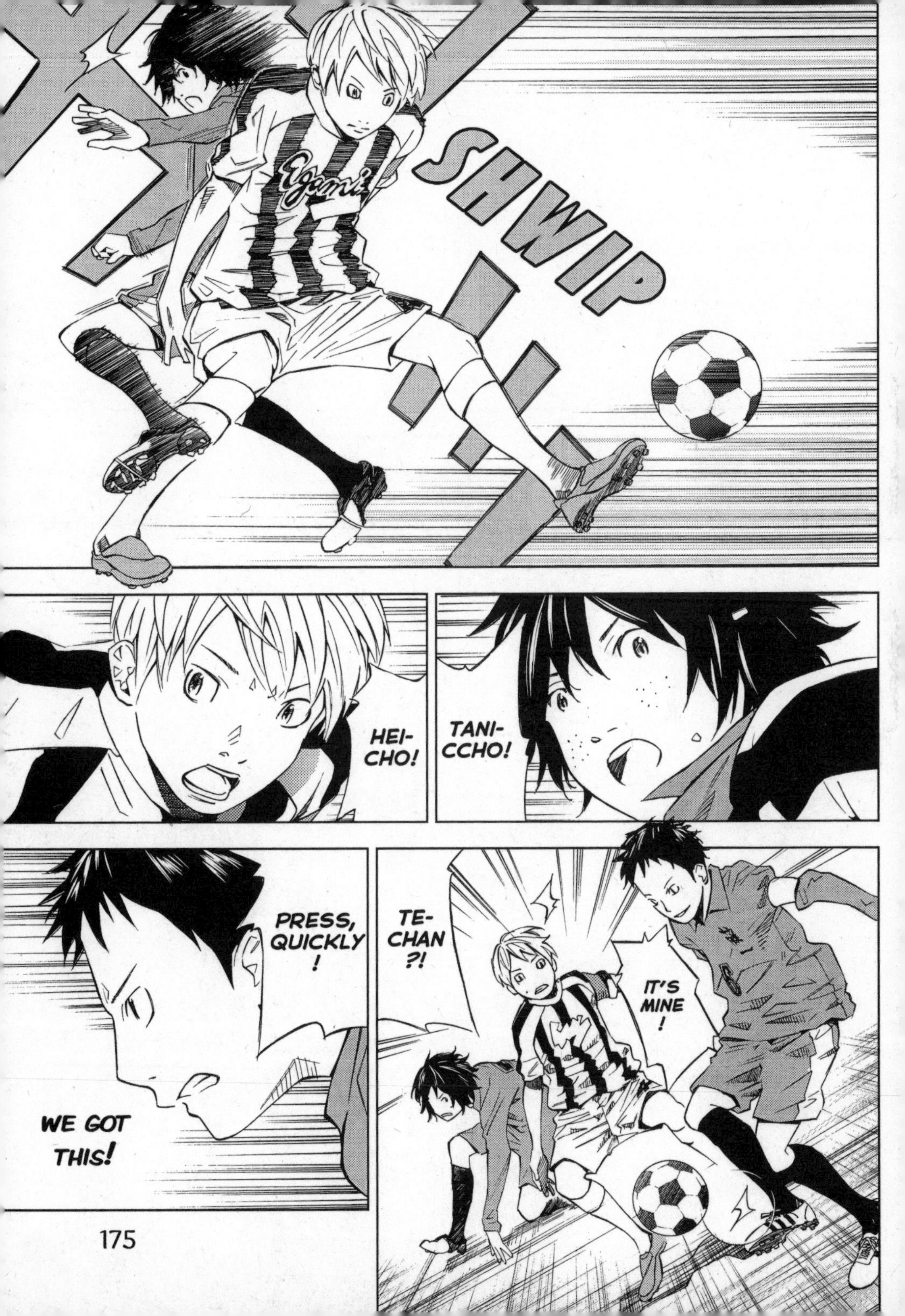
SHWIP
TANI-CCHO!
HEI-CHO!
TE-CHAN ?!
IT'S MINE !
PRESS, QUICKLY !
WE GOT THIS!

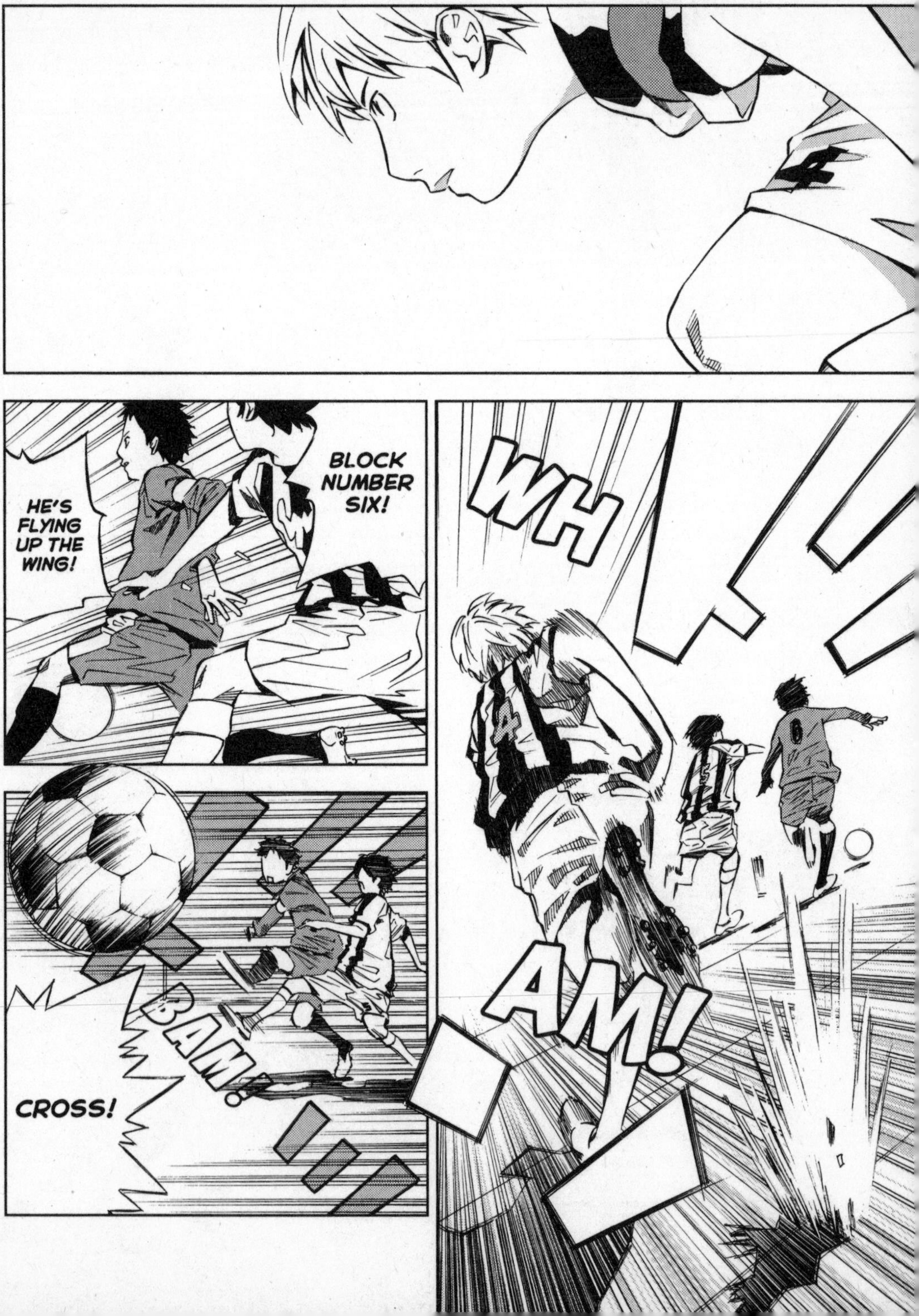
WH
AM!
BLOCK NUMBER SIX!
HE'S FLYING UP THE WING!
BAM!
CROSS!

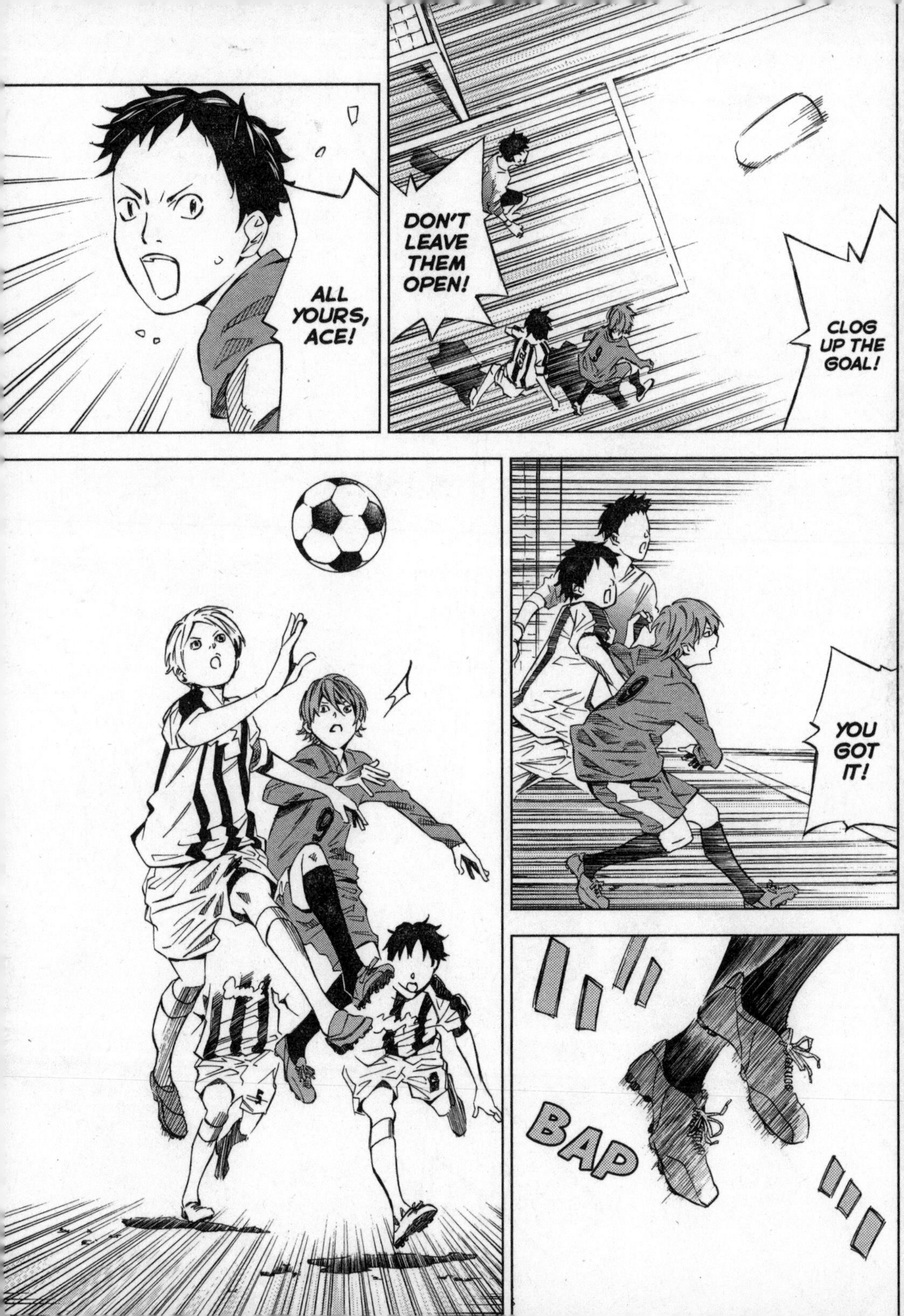

CLOG UP THE GOAL!
DON'T LEAVE THEM OPEN!
ALL YOURS, ACE!
YOU GOT IT!
BAP

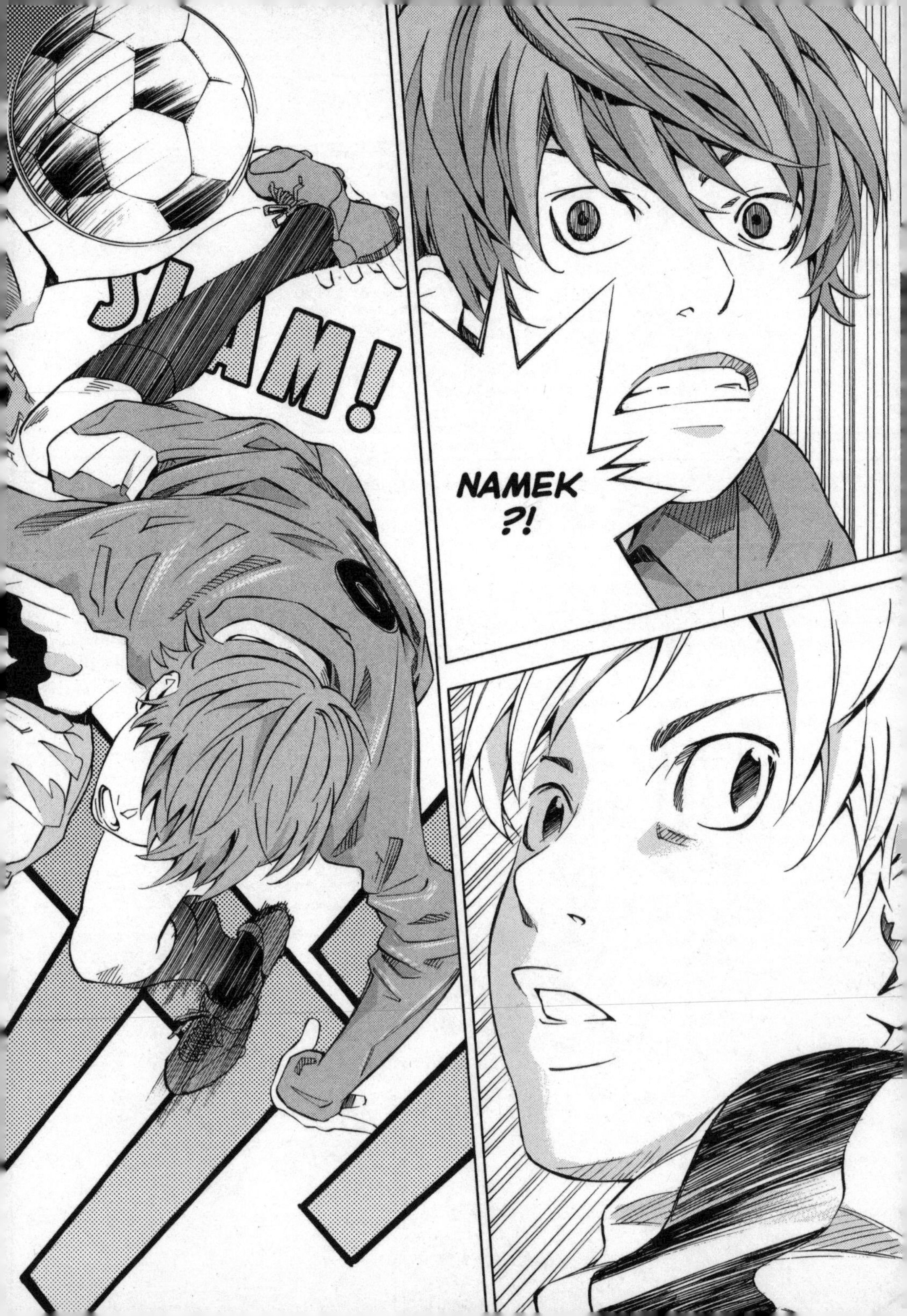
NAMEK
?!

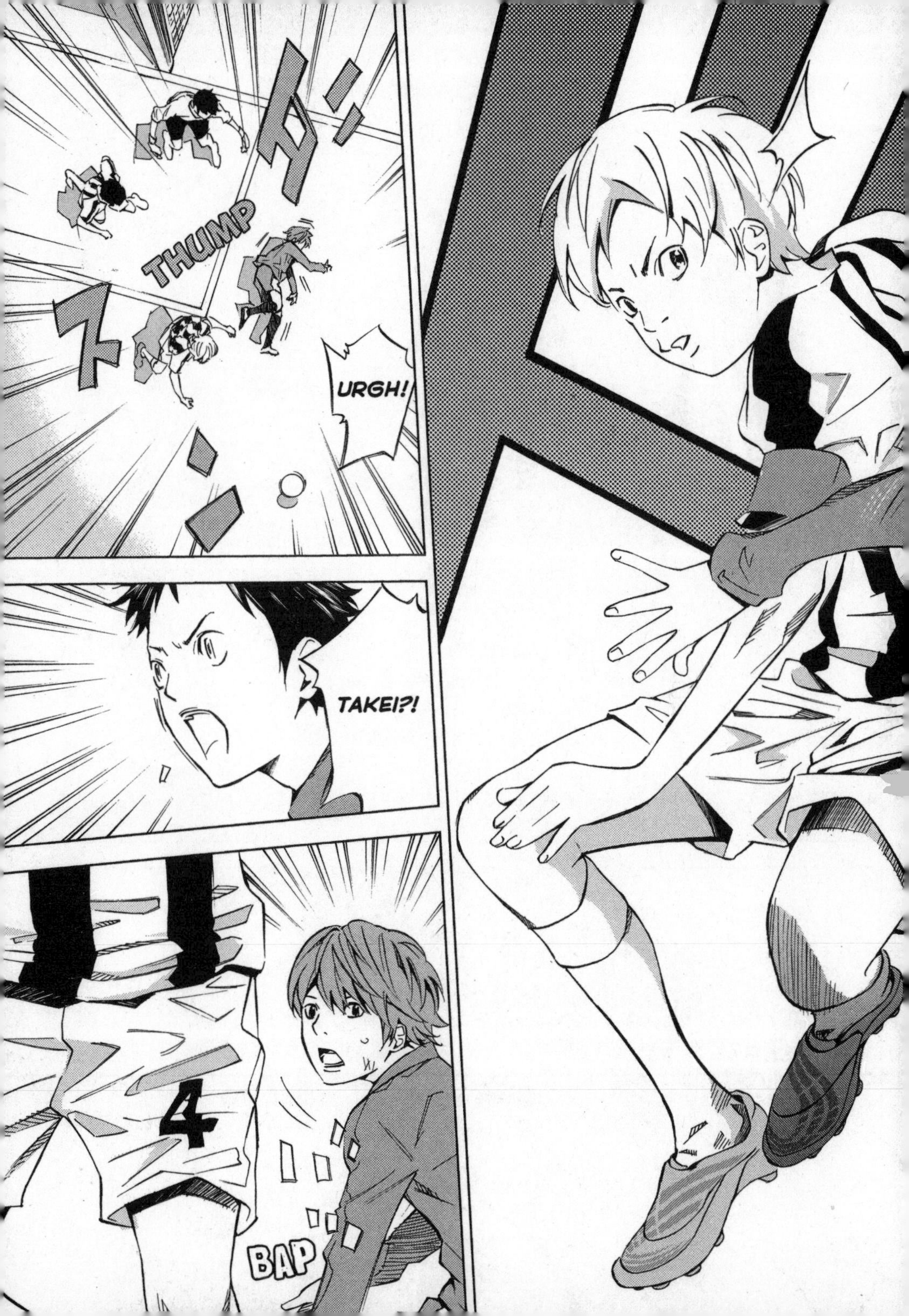
URGH!
THUMP
TAKEI?!
BAP

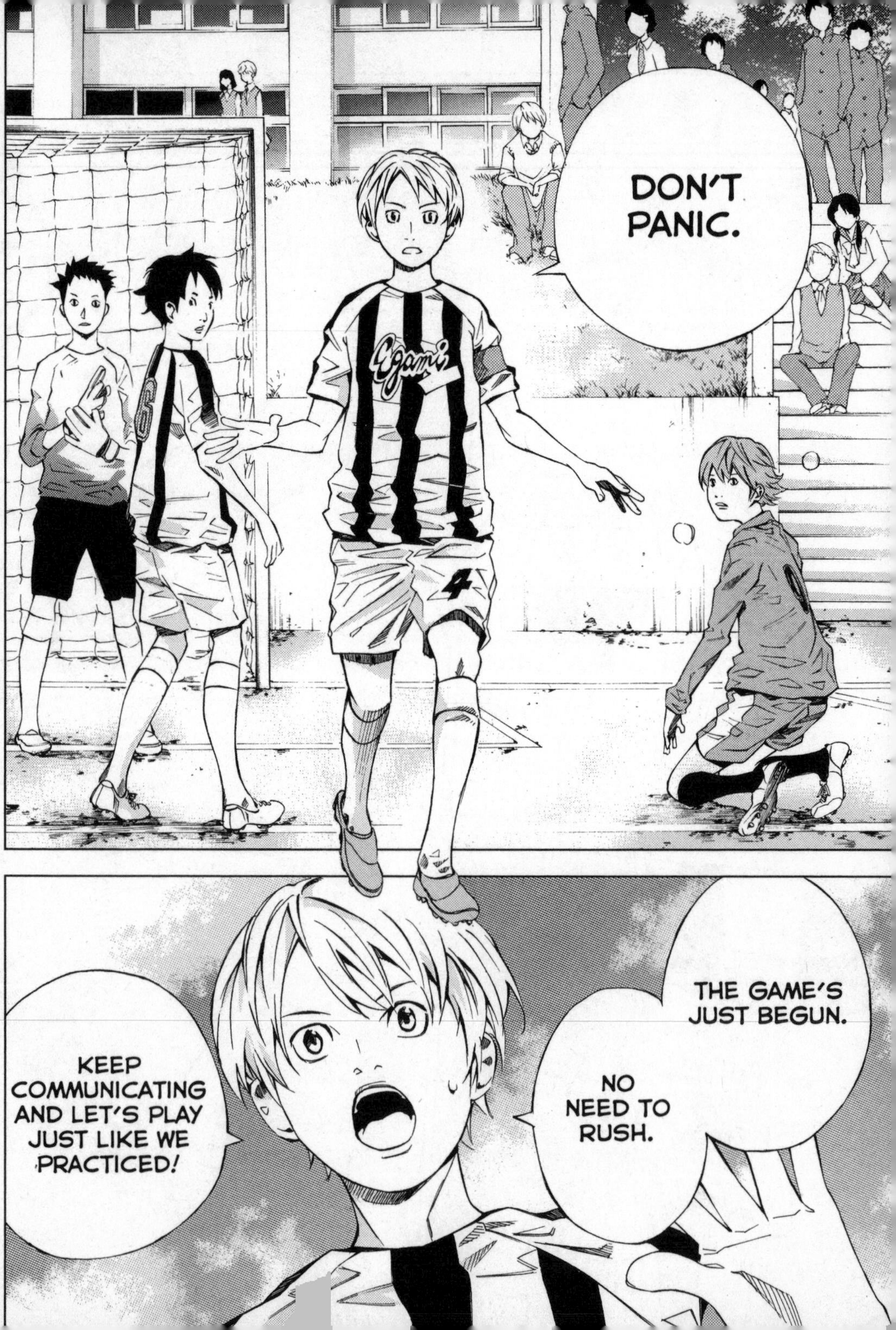
DON'T PANIC.
THE GAME'S JUST BEGUN.
NO NEED TO RUSH.
KEEP COMMUNICATING AND LET'S PLAY JUST LIKE WE PRACTICED!

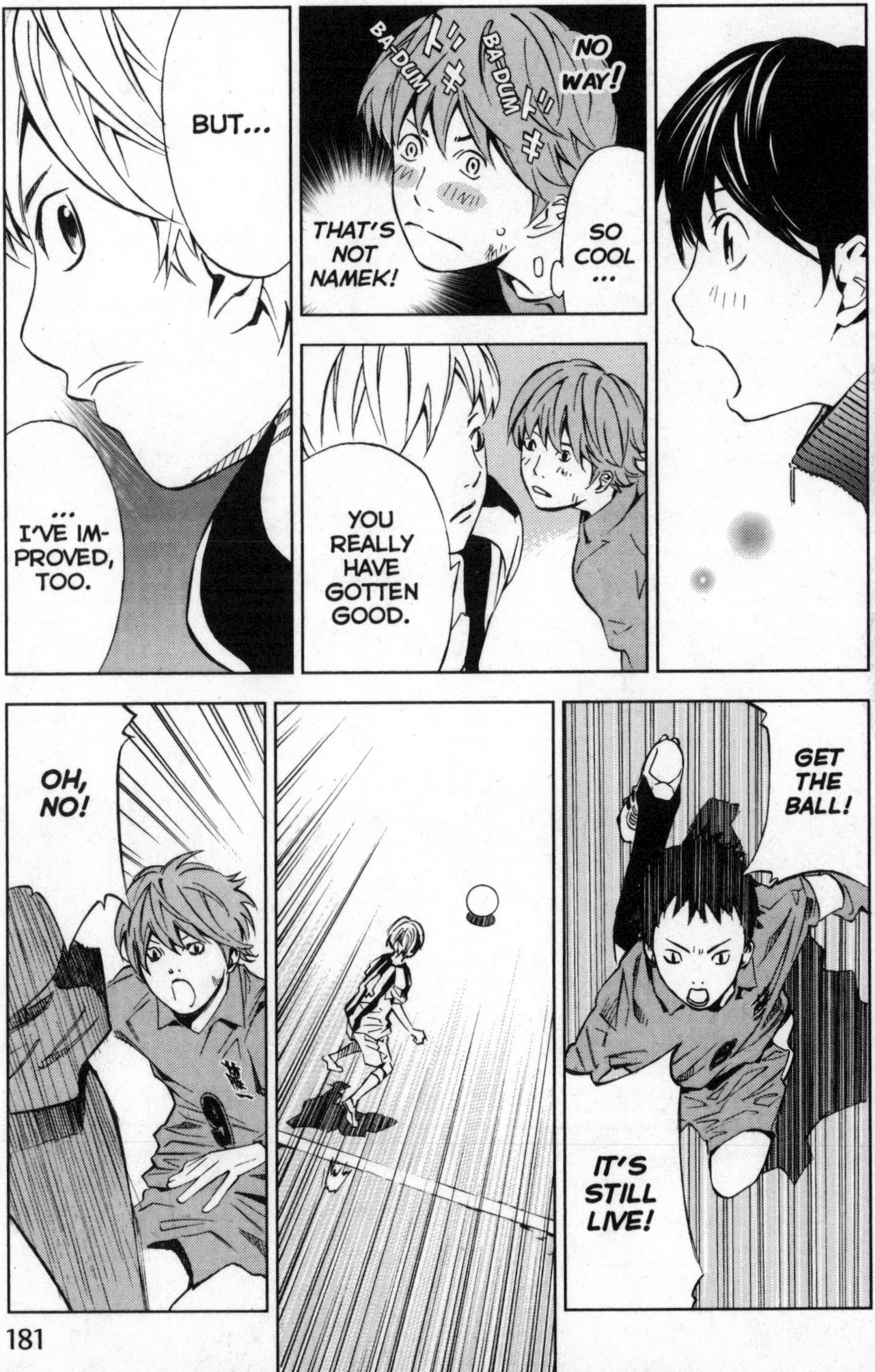
NO WAY!
BA-DUM
BA-DUM
SO COOL ...
THAT'S NOT NAMEK!
YOU REALLY HAVE GOTTEN GOOD.
BUT...
... I'VE IMPROVED, TOO.
GET THE BALL!
IT'S STILL LIVE!
OH, NO!

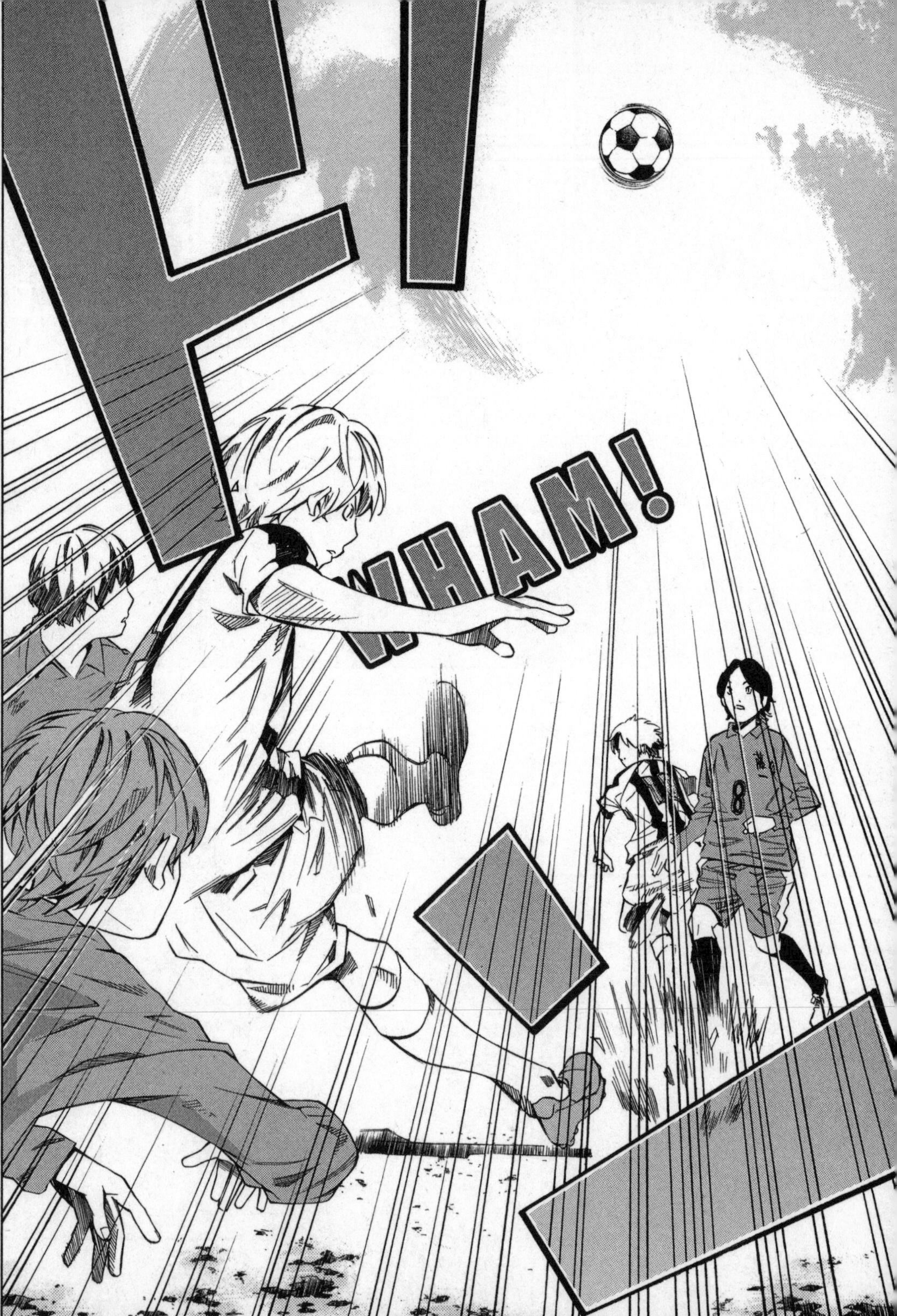

WHAM!

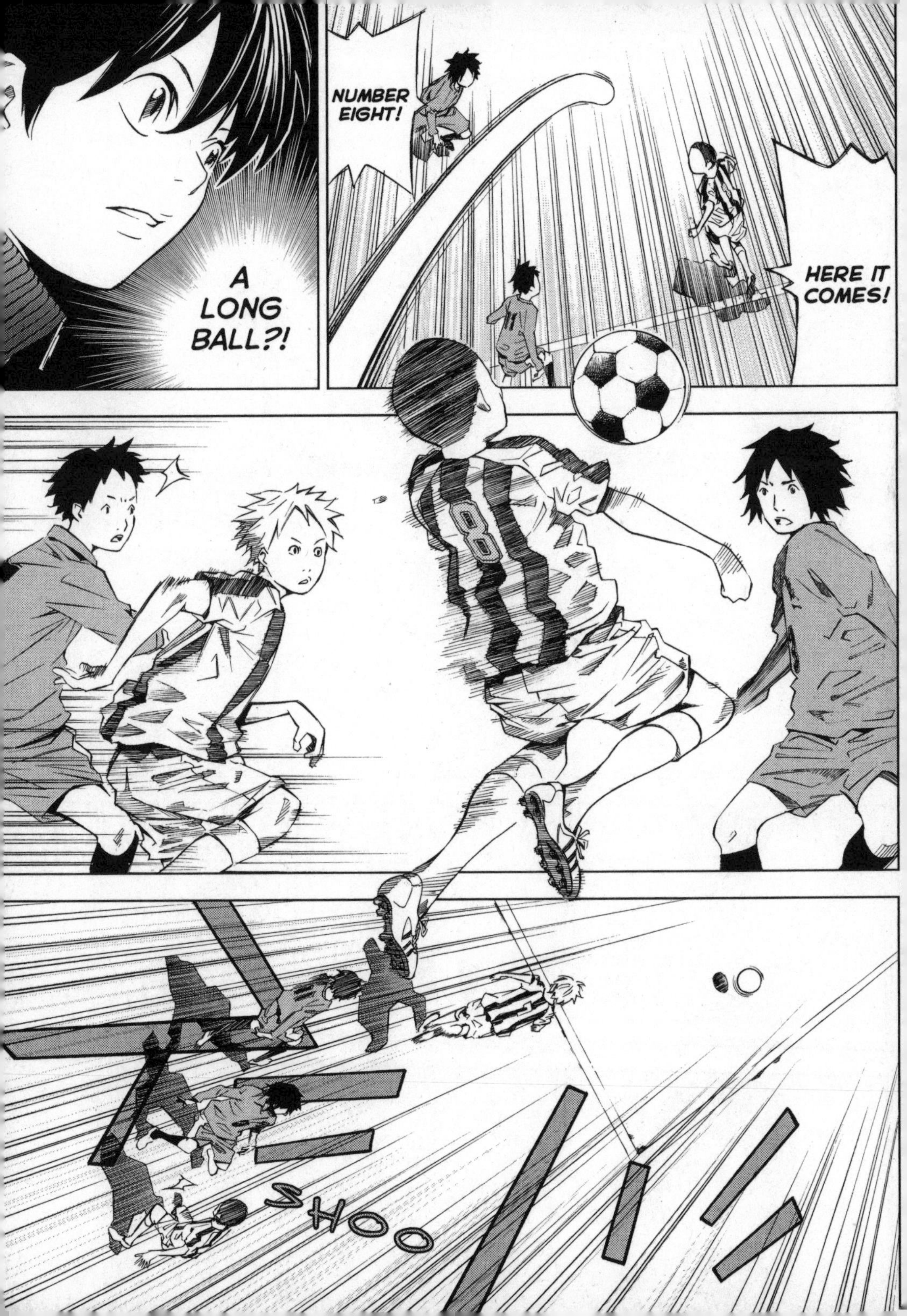
NUMBER EIGHT!
HERE IT COMES!
A LONG BALL?!
SHOO

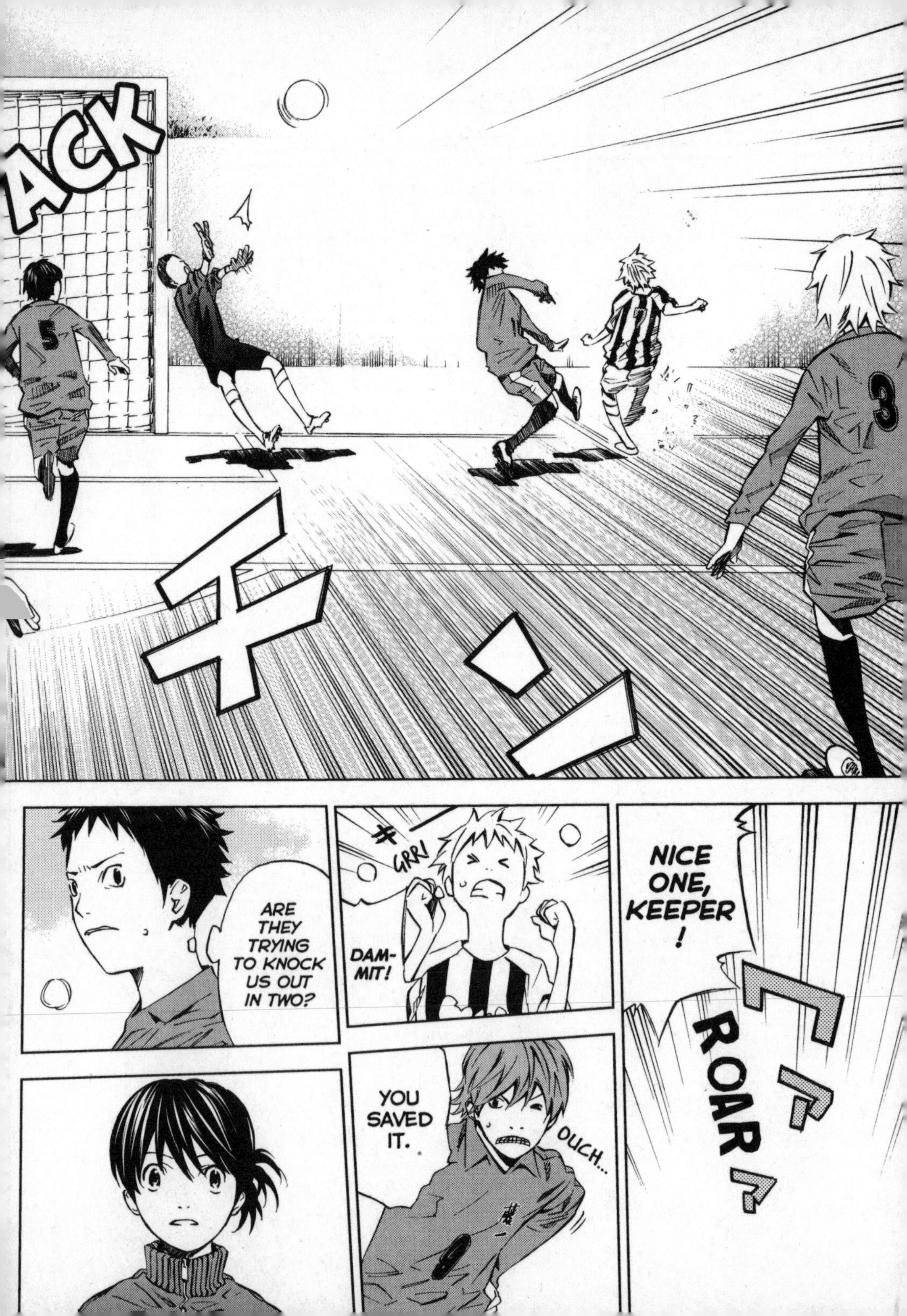
ACK
NICE ONE, KEEPER!
ROAR
GRR!
DAM-MIT!
ARE THEY TRYING TO KNOCK US OUT IN TWO?
YOU SAVED IT.
OUCH...

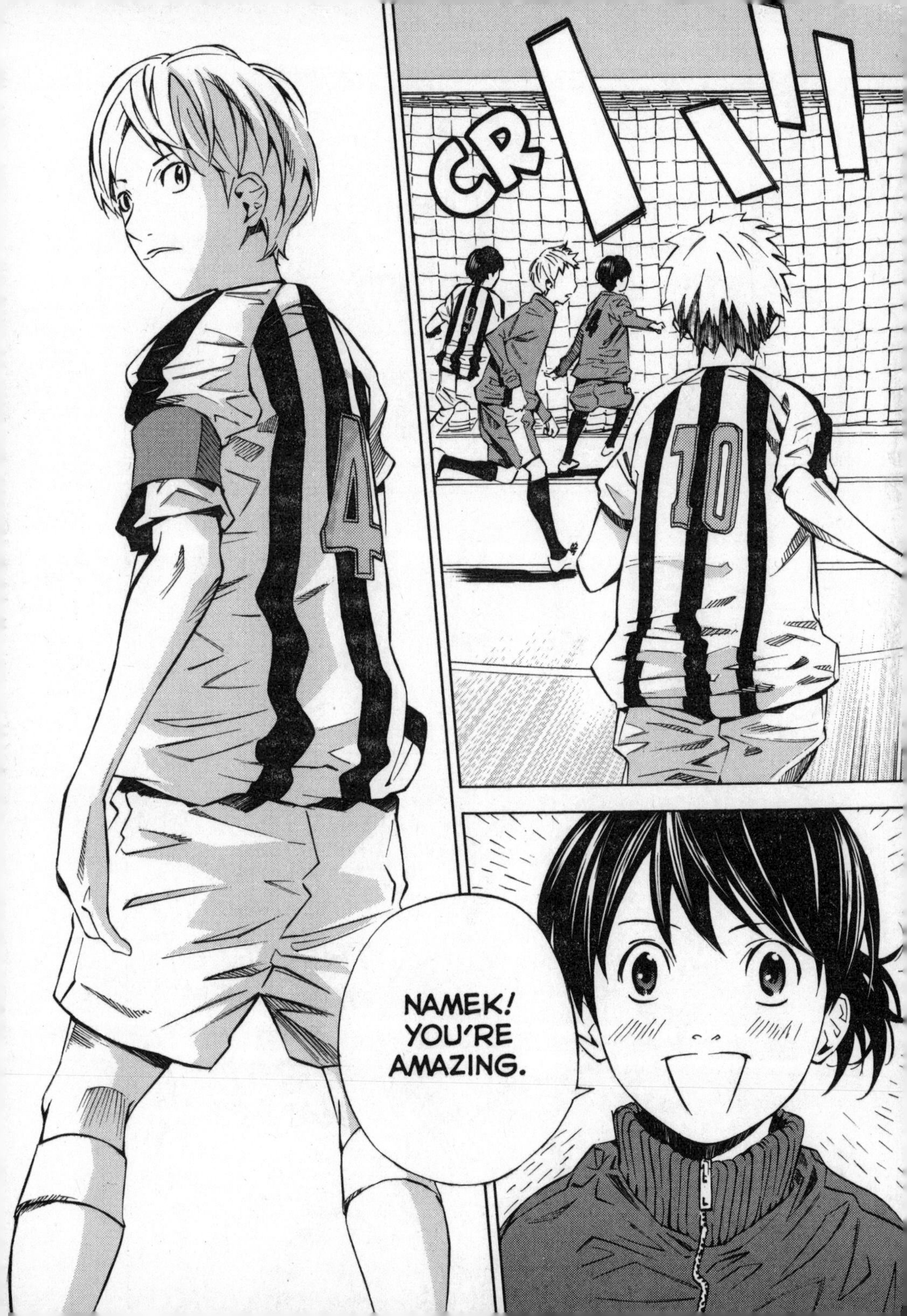
CR
NAMEK! YOU'RE AMAZING.

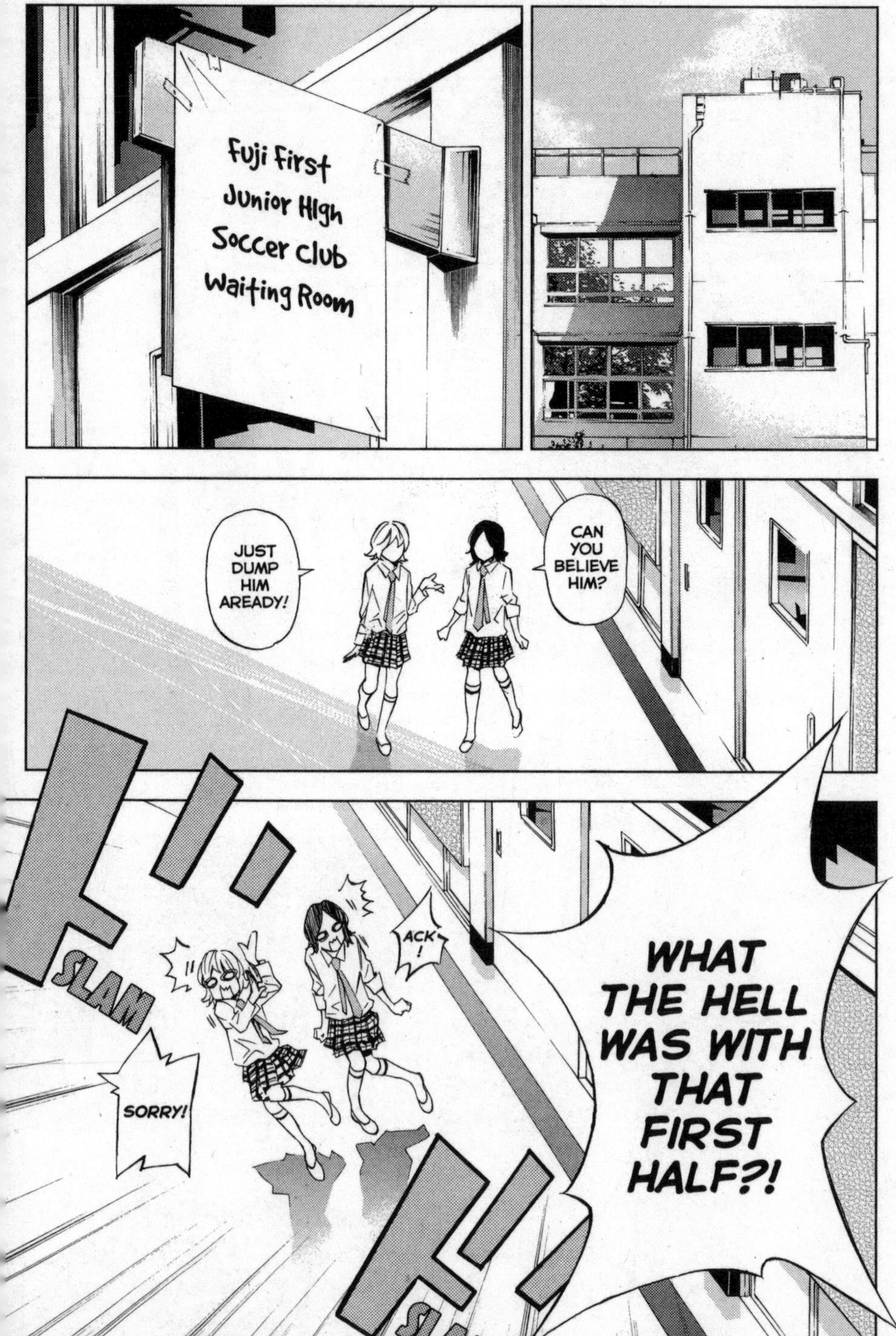
Fuji First Junior High Soccer Club Waiting Room
CAN YOU BELIEVE HIM?
JUST DUMP HIM AREADY!
WHAT THE HELL WAS WITH THAT FIRST HALF?!
ACK!
SLAM
SORRY!
SLAM

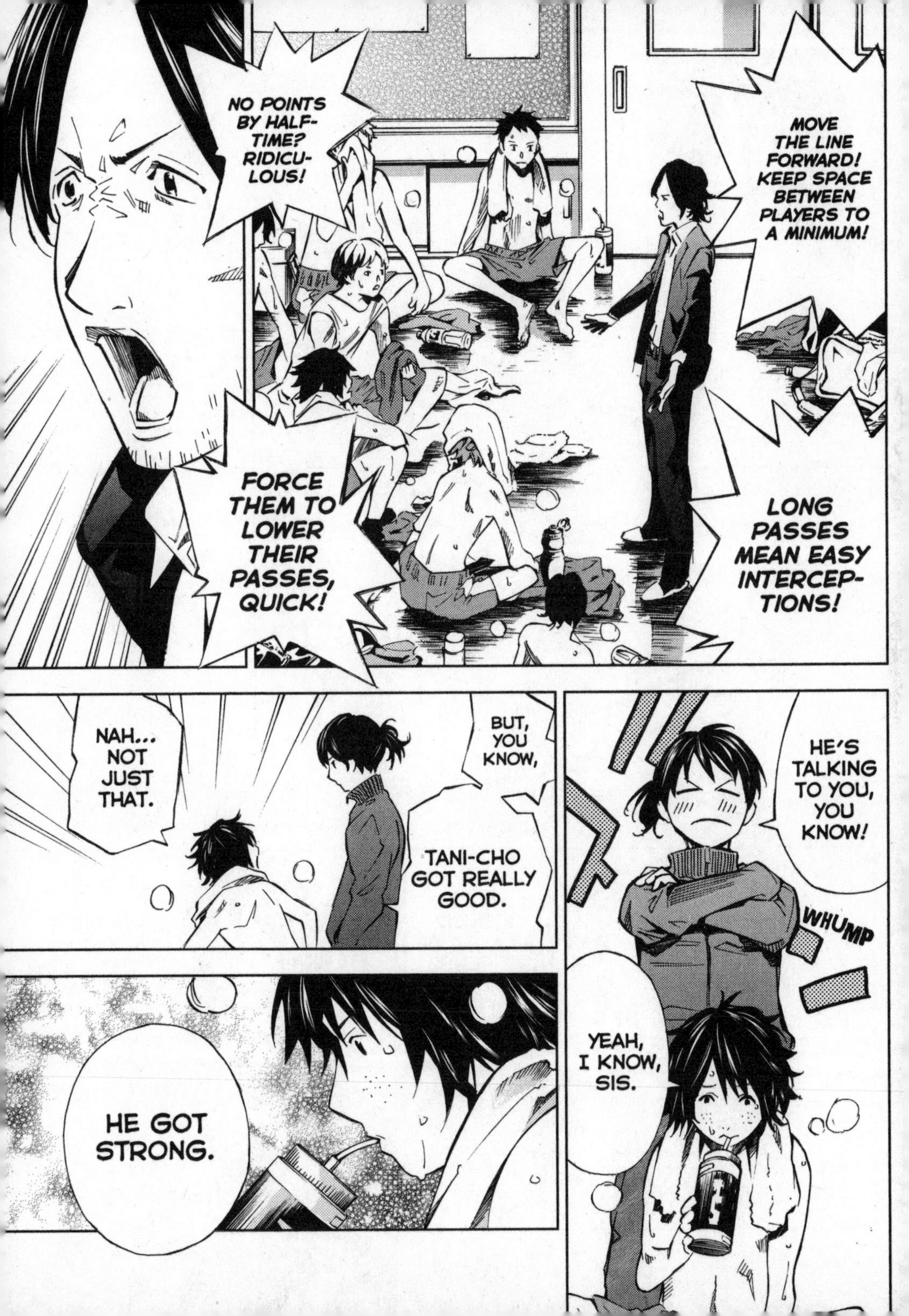
MOVE THE LINE FORWARD! KEEP SPACE BETWEEN PLAYERS TO A MINIMUM!
LONG PASSES MEAN EASY INTERCEP-TIONS!
NO POINTS BY HALF-TIME? RIDICU-LOUS!
FORCE THEM TO LOWER THEIR PASSES, QUICK!
HE'S TALKING TO YOU, YOU KNOW!
WHUMP
YEAH, I KNOW, SIS.
BUT, YOU KNOW,
TANI-CHO GOT REALLY GOOD.
NAH... NOT JUST THAT.
HE GOT STRONG.

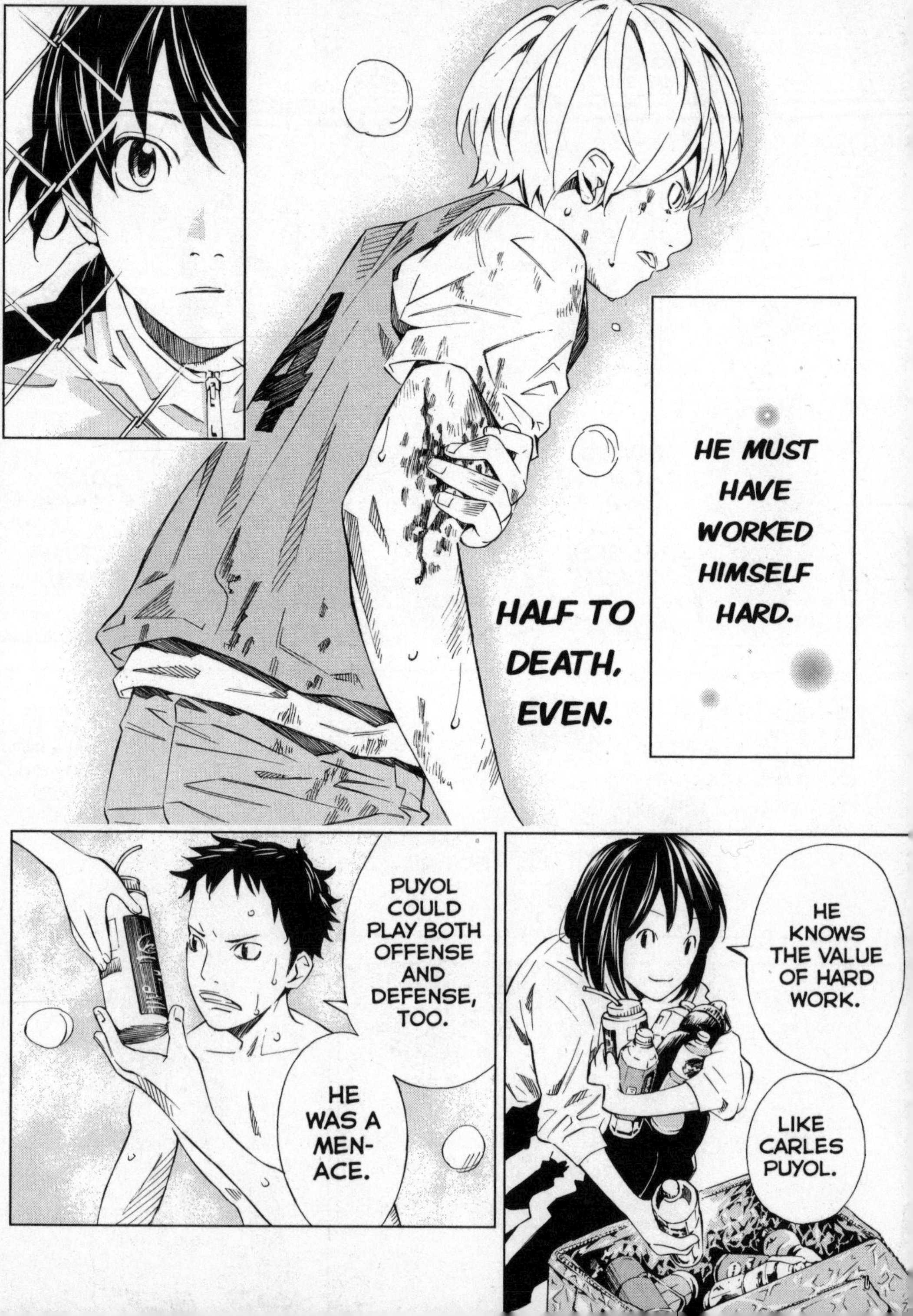
HE MUST HAVE WORKED HIMSELF HARD.
HALF TO DEATH, EVEN.
HE KNOWS THE VALUE OF HARD WORK.
LIKE CARLES PUYOL.
PUYOL COULD PLAY BOTH OFFENSE AND DEFENSE, TOO.
HE WAS A MEN-ACE.

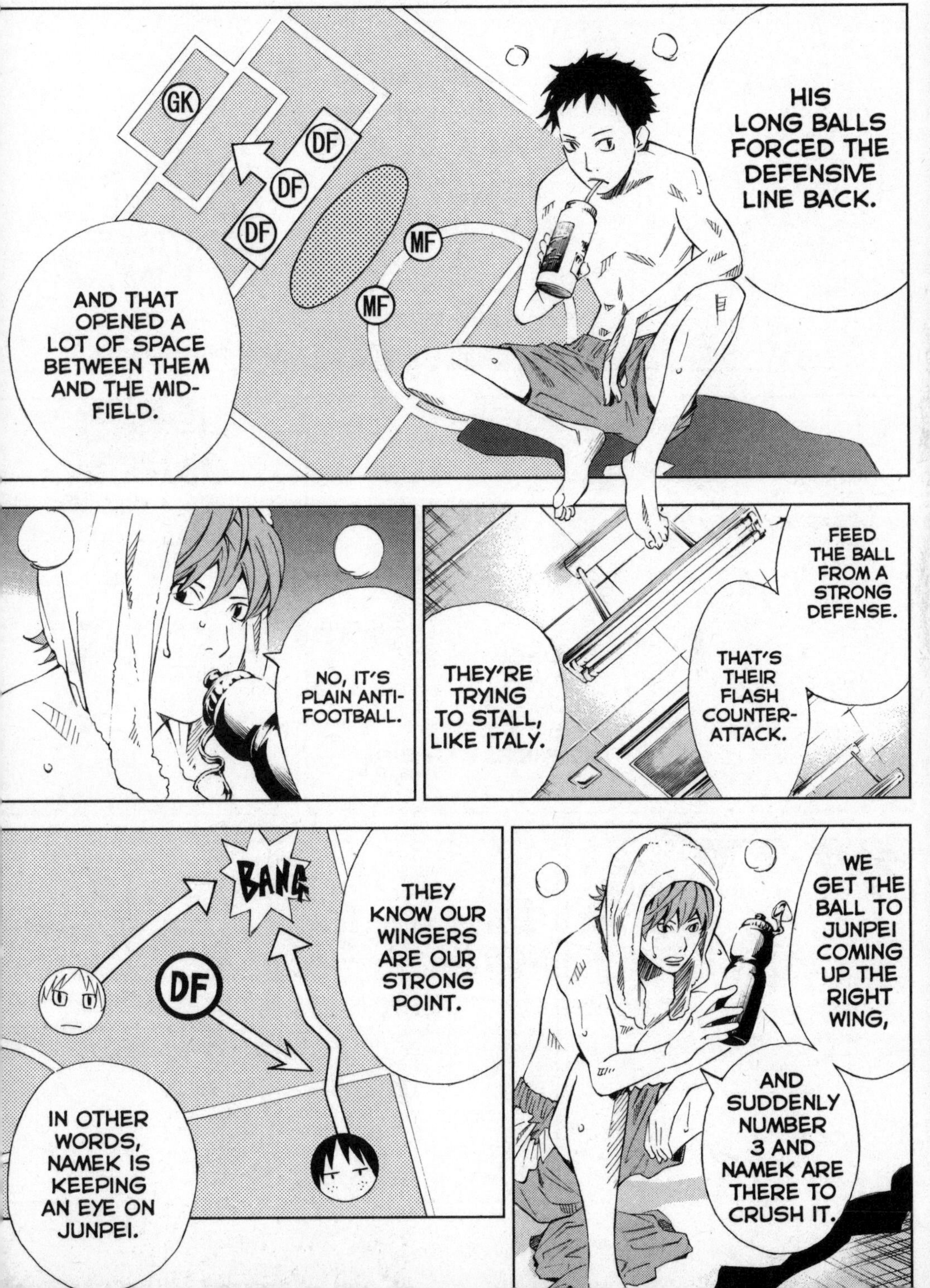
HIS LONG BALLS FORCED THE DEFENSIVE LINE BACK.
GK
DF
DF
DF
MF
MF
AND THAT OPENED A LOT OF SPACE BETWEEN THEM AND THE MID-FIELD.
FEED THE BALL FROM A STRONG DEFENSE.
THAT'S THEIR FLASH COUNTER-ATTACK.
THEY'RE TRYING TO STALL, LIKE ITALY.
NO, IT'S PLAIN ANTI-FOOTBALL.
WE GET THE BALL TO JUNPEI COMING UP THE RIGHT WING,
AND SUDDENLY NUMBER 3 AND NAMEK ARE THERE TO CRUSH IT.
THEY KNOW OUR WINGERS ARE OUR STRONG POINT.
BANG
DF
IN OTHER WORDS, NAMEK IS KEEPING AN EYE ON JUNPEI.

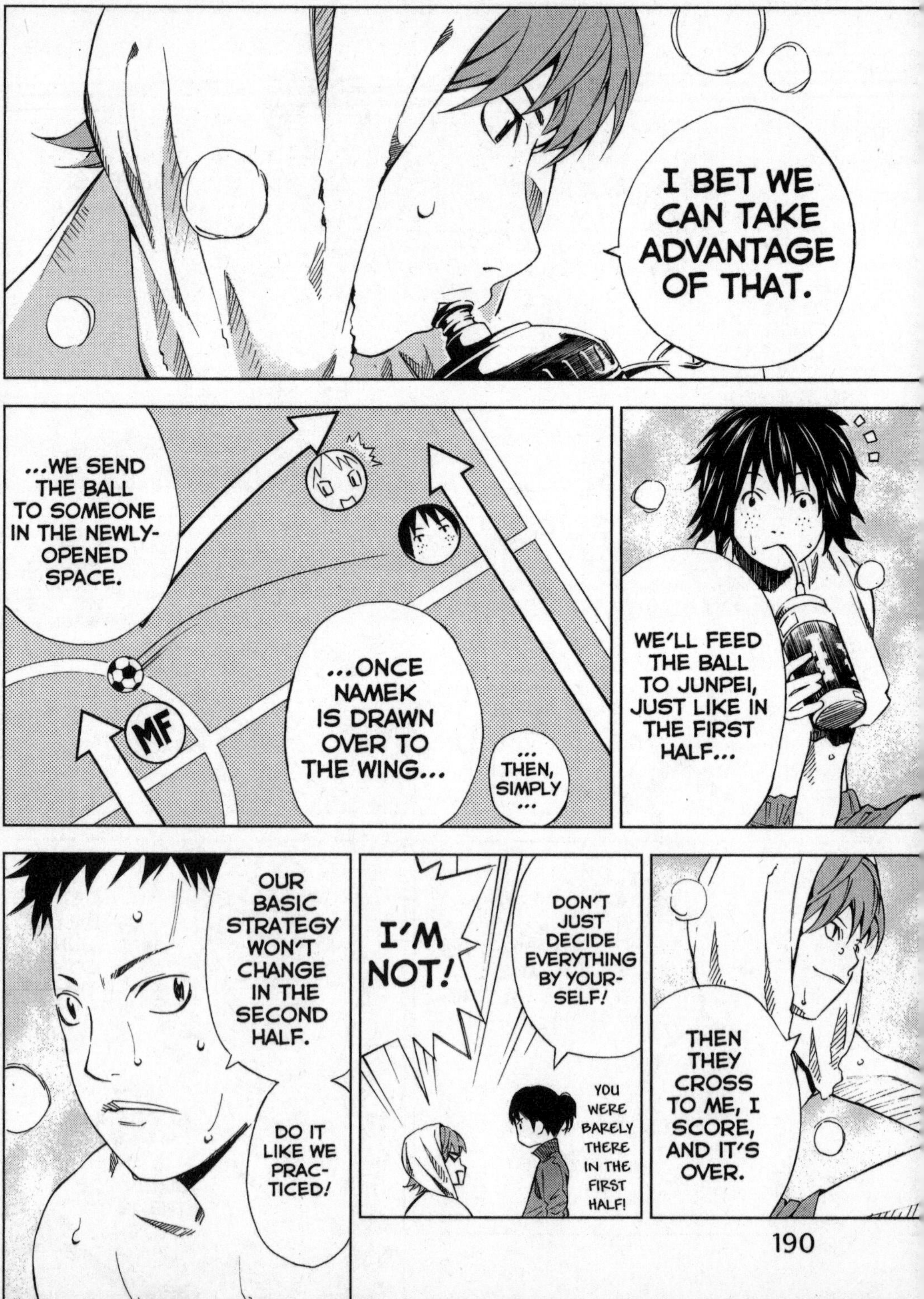
I BET WE CAN TAKE ADVANTAGE OF THAT.
WE'LL FEED THE BALL TO JUNPEI, JUST LIKE IN THE FIRST HALF...
...ONCE NAMEK IS DRAWN OVER TO THE WING...
...THEN, SIMPLY...
...WE SEND THE BALL TO SOMEONE IN THE NEWLY-OPENED SPACE.
MF
THEN THEY CROSS TO ME, I SCORE, AND IT'S OVER.
DON'T JUST DECIDE EVERYTHING BY YOUR-SELF!
I'M NOT!
YOU WERE BARELY THERE IN THE FIRST HALF!
OUR BASIC STRATEGY WON'T CHANGE IN THE SECOND HALF.
DO IT LIKE WE PRAC-TICED!

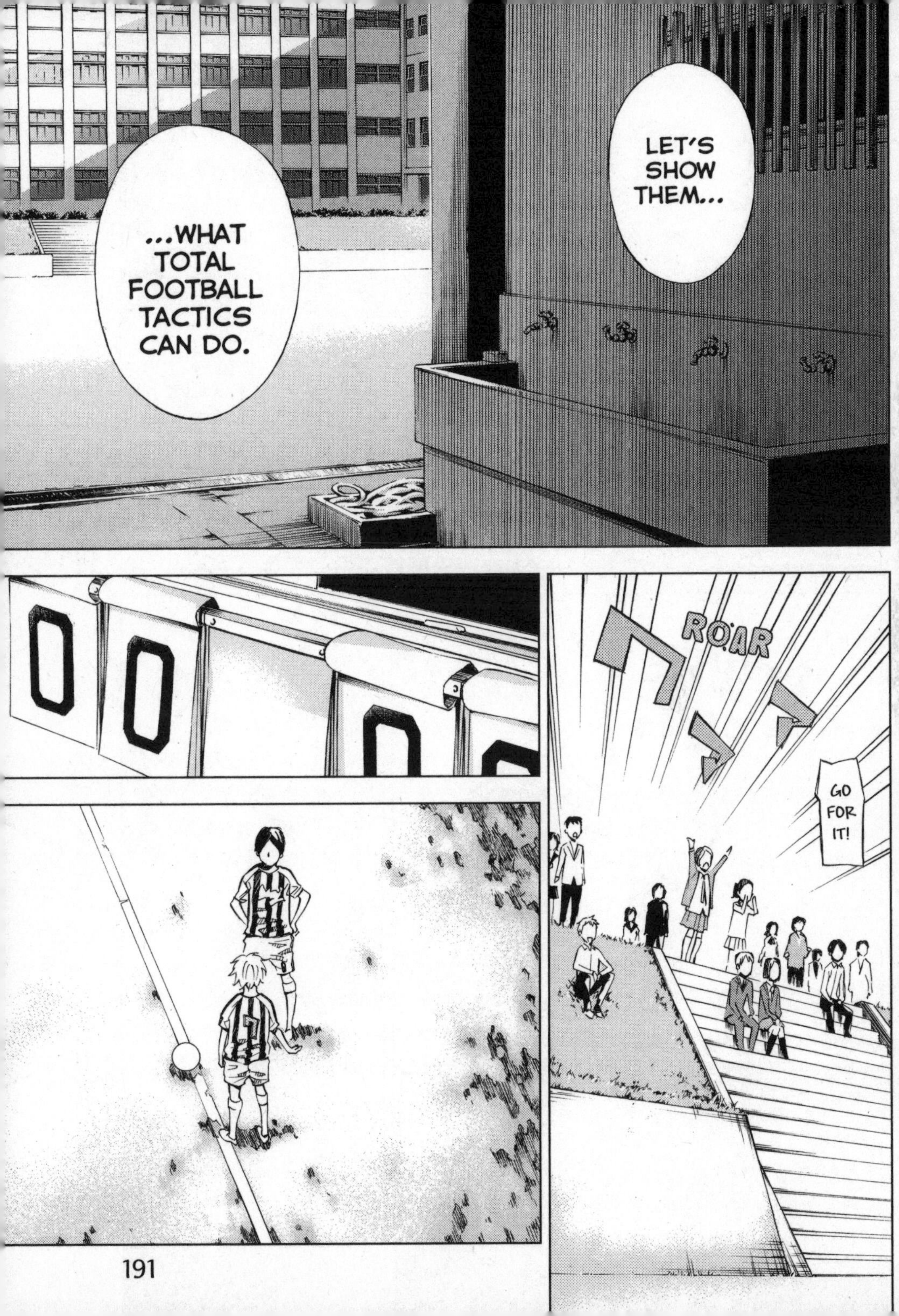
LET'S SHOW THEM...
...WHAT TOTAL FOOTBALL TACTICS CAN DO.
ROAR
GO FOR IT!

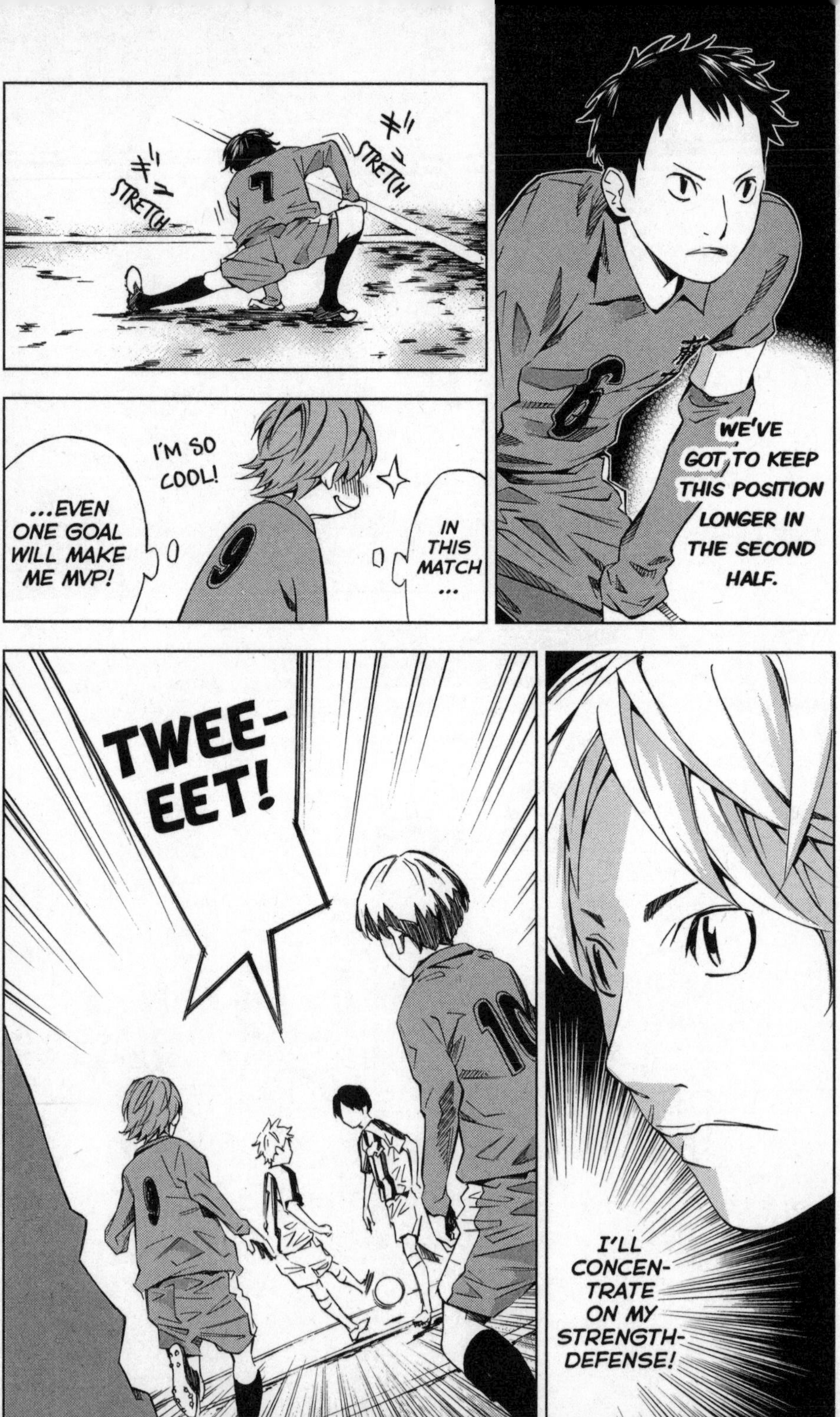
WE'VE GOT TO KEEP THIS POSITION LONGER IN THE SECOND HALF.
ギュ
STRETCH
ギュ
STRETCH
IN THIS MATCH...
I'M SO COOL!
...EVEN ONE GOAL WILL MAKE ME MVP!
I'LL CONCEN-TRATE ON MY STRENGTH-DEFENSE!
TWEE-EET!

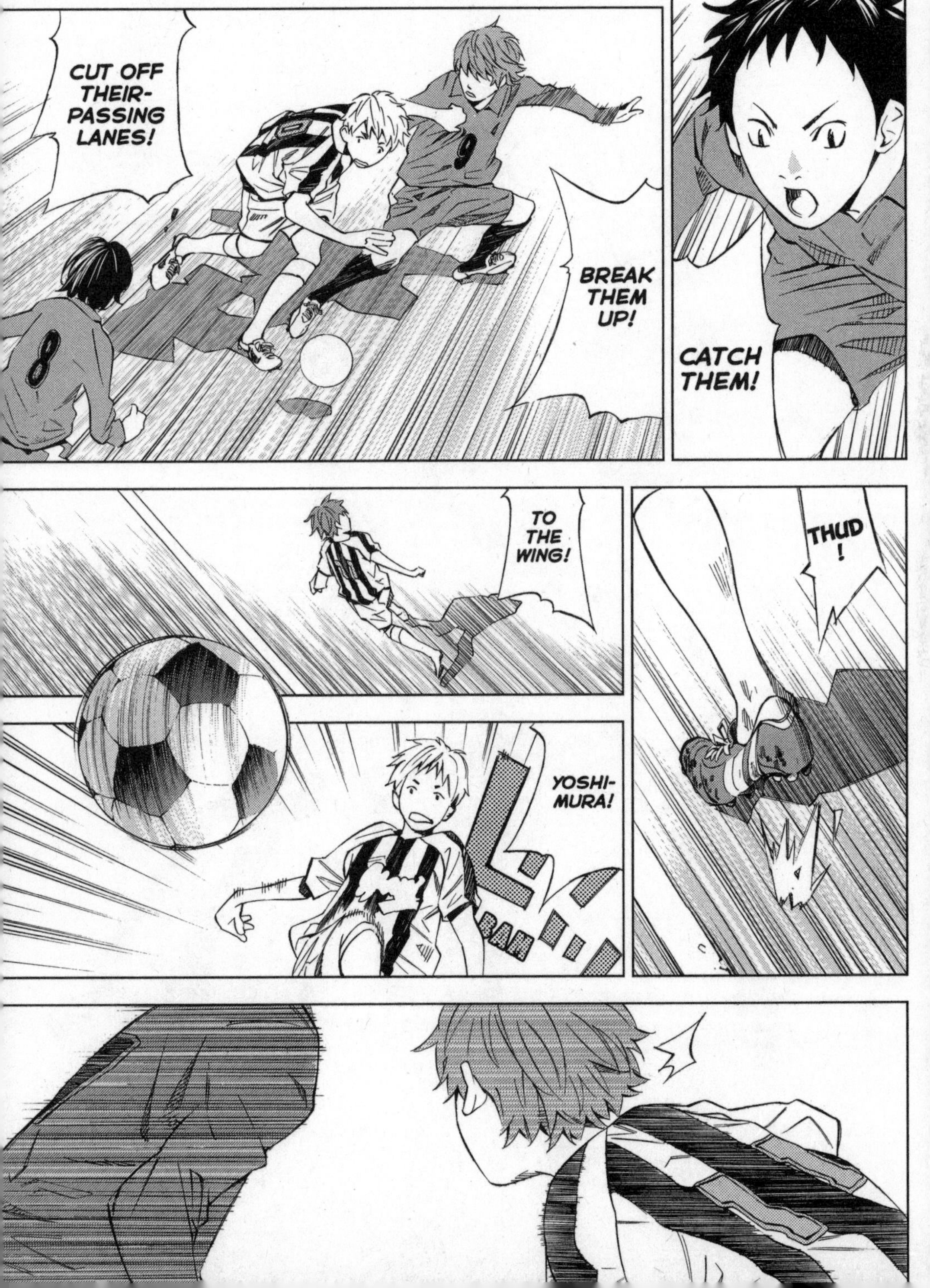
CATCH THEM!
BREAK THEM UP!
CUT OFF THEIR- PASSING LANES!
THUD!
TO THE WING!
YOSHI-MURA!
BAM

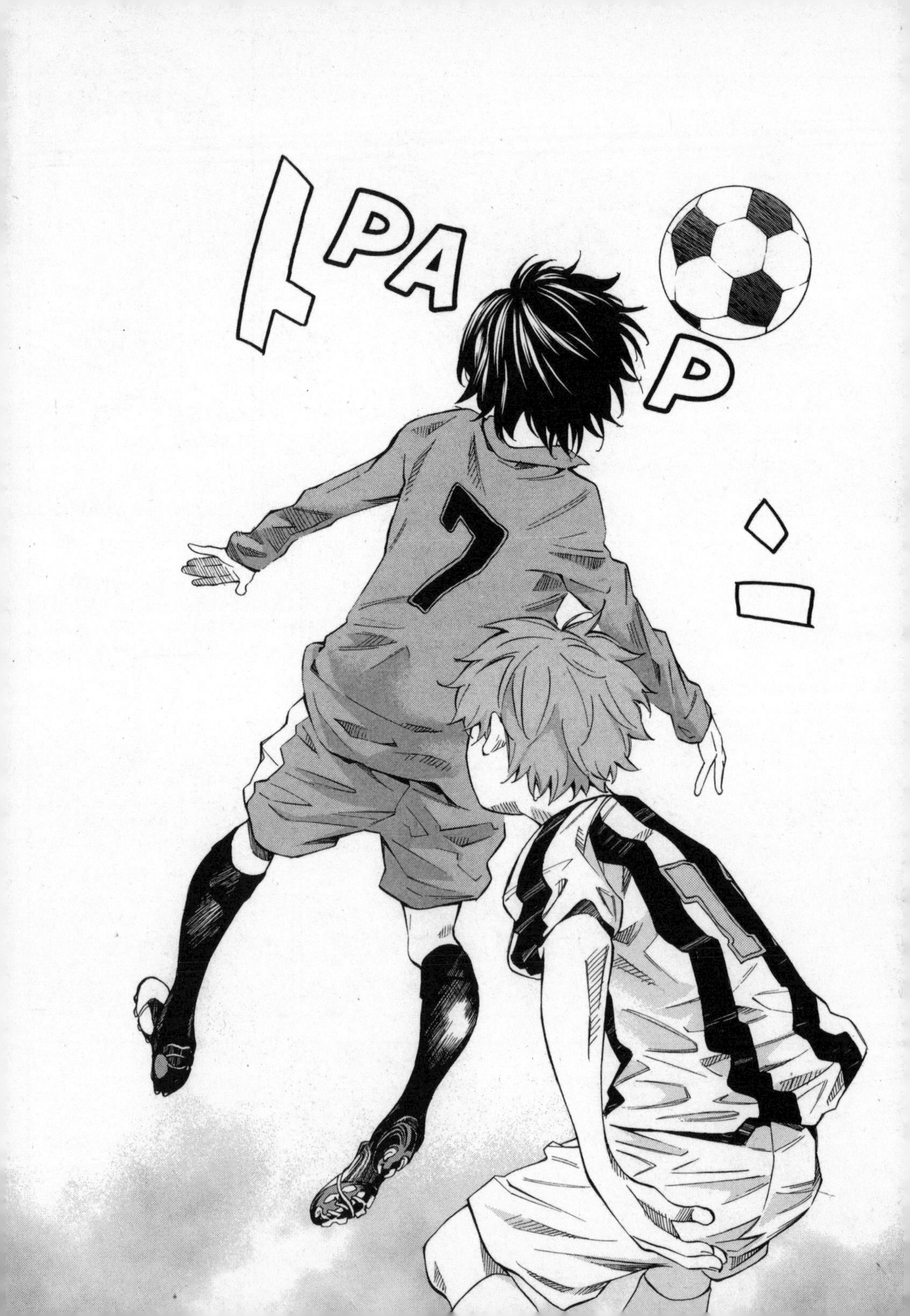
PAP

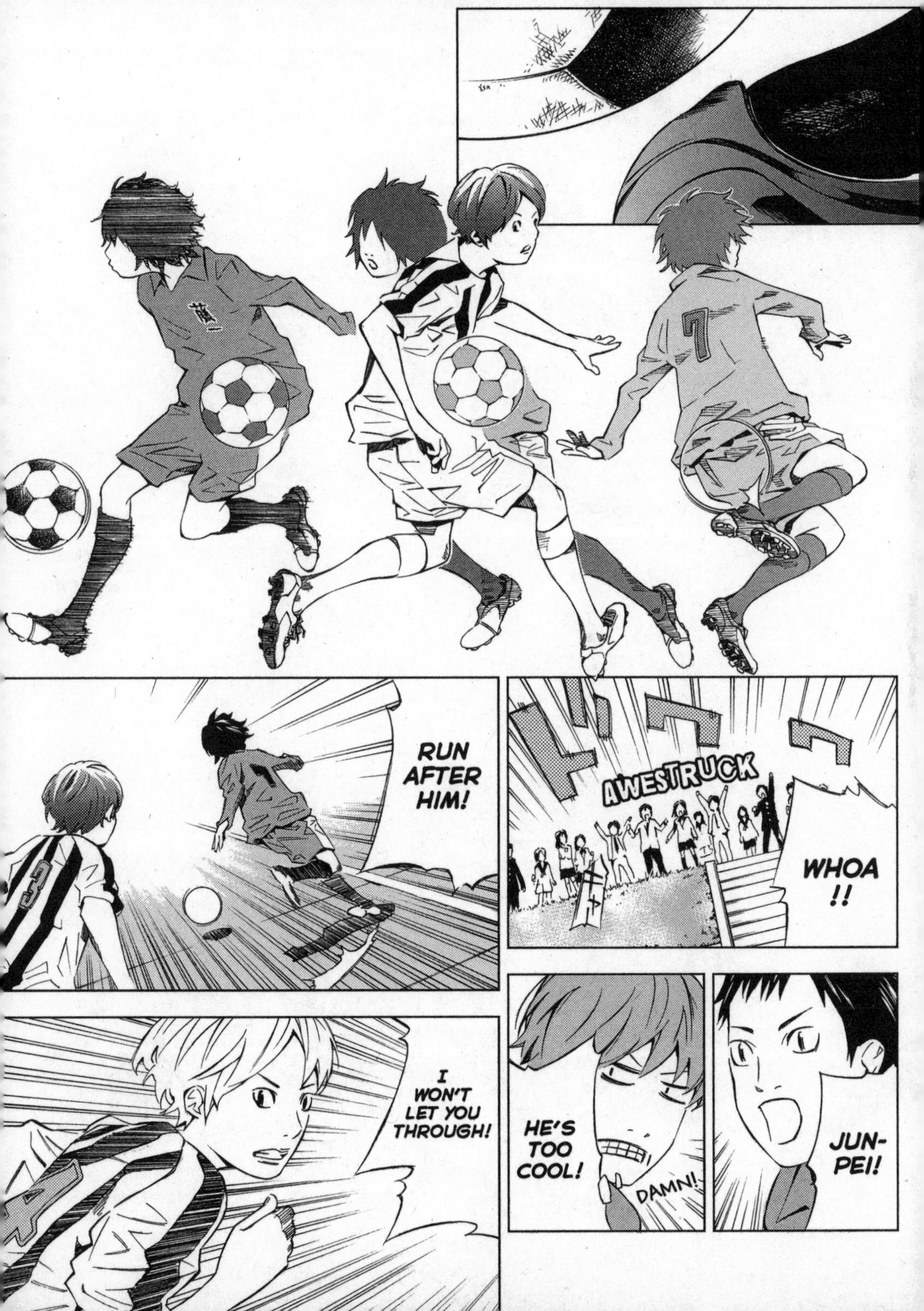
AWESTRUCK
WHOA !!
RUN AFTER HIM!
JUN-PEI!
HE'S TOO COOL!
DAMN!
I WON'T LET YOU THROUGH!

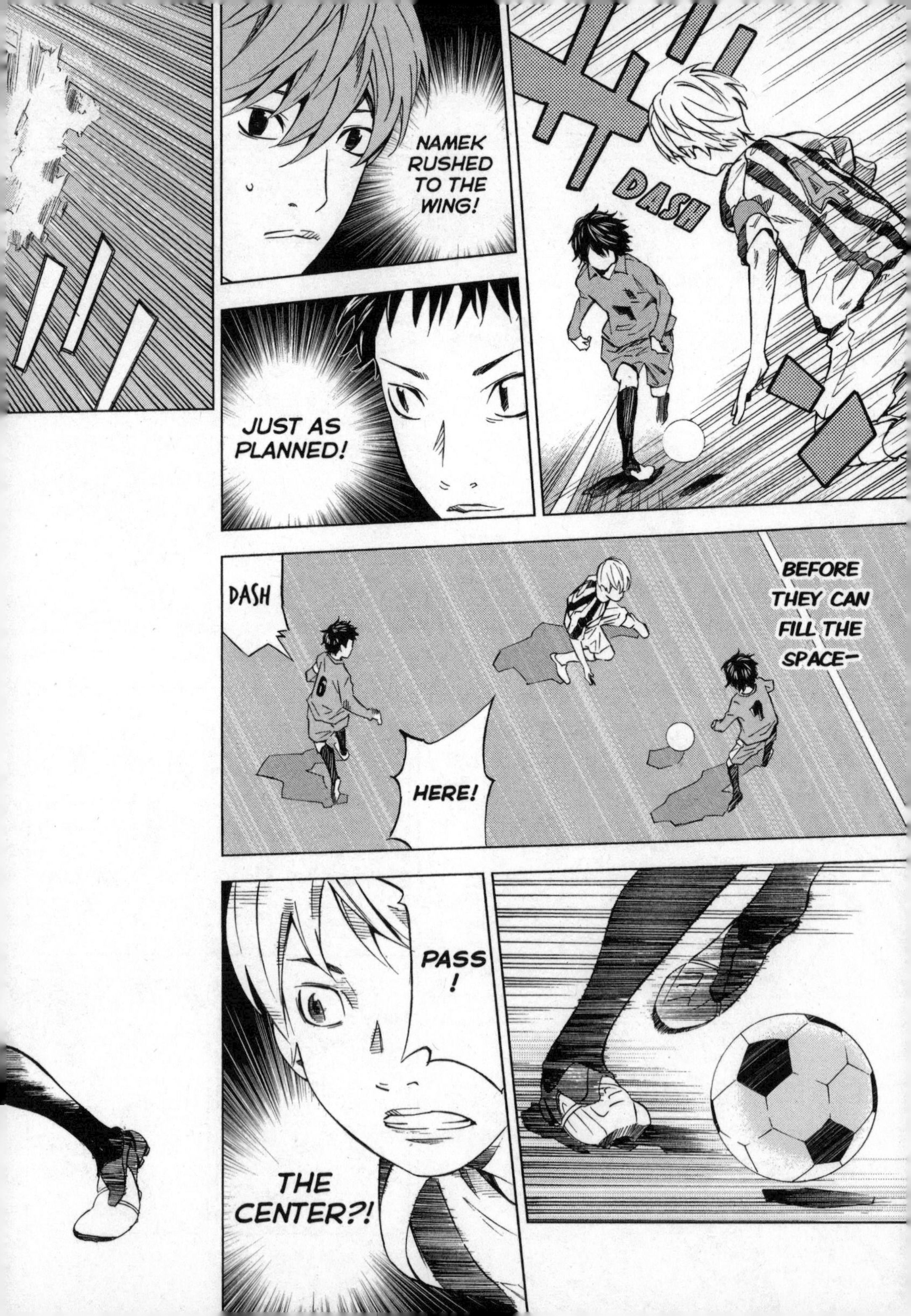
DASH
NAMEK RUSHED TO THE WING!
JUST AS PLANNED!
BEFORE THEY CAN FILL THE SPACE–
HERE!
DASH
PASS!
THE CENTER?!

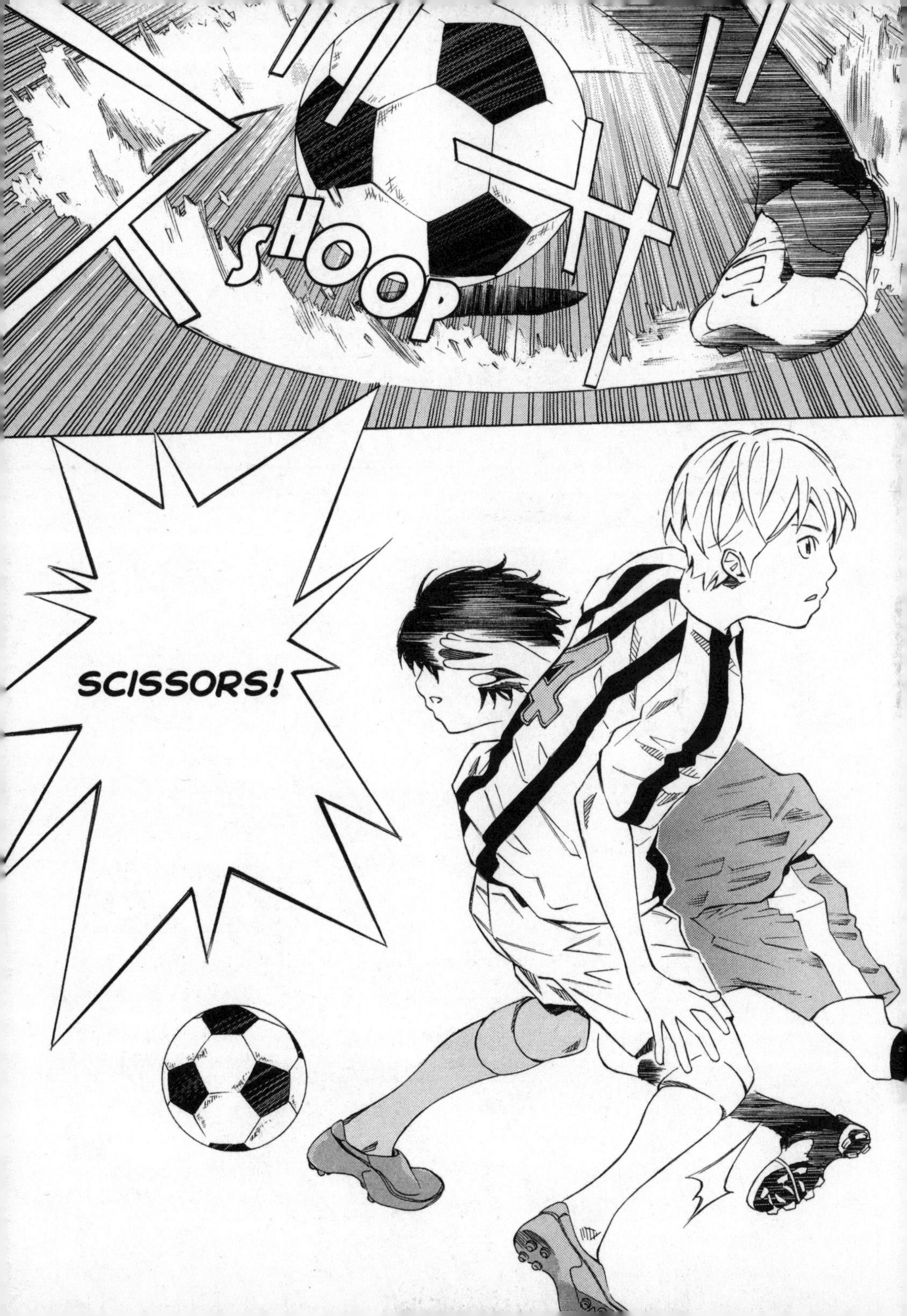
SHOOP
SCISSORS!

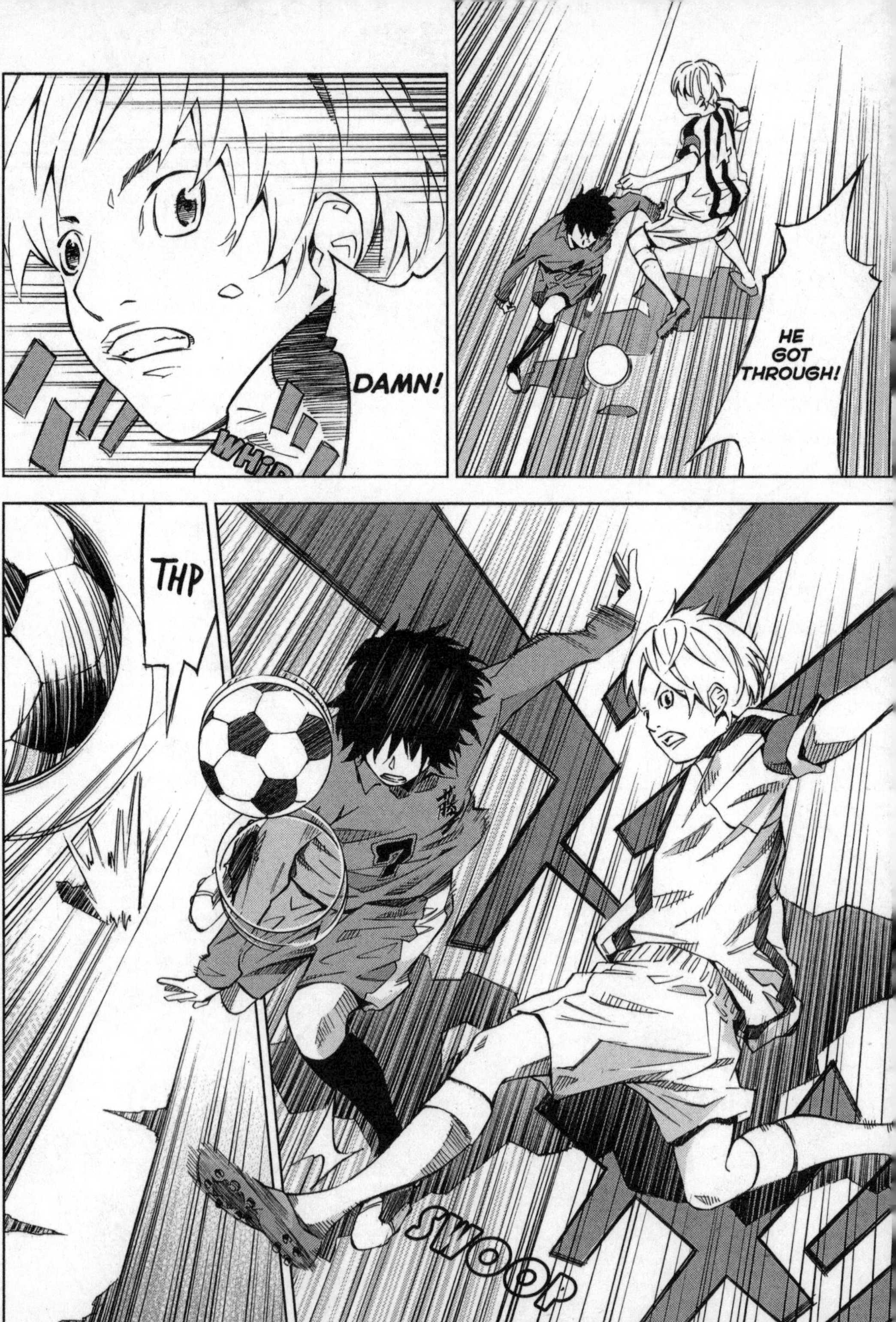
HE GOT THROUGH!
DAMN!
WHIP
THP
SWOOP

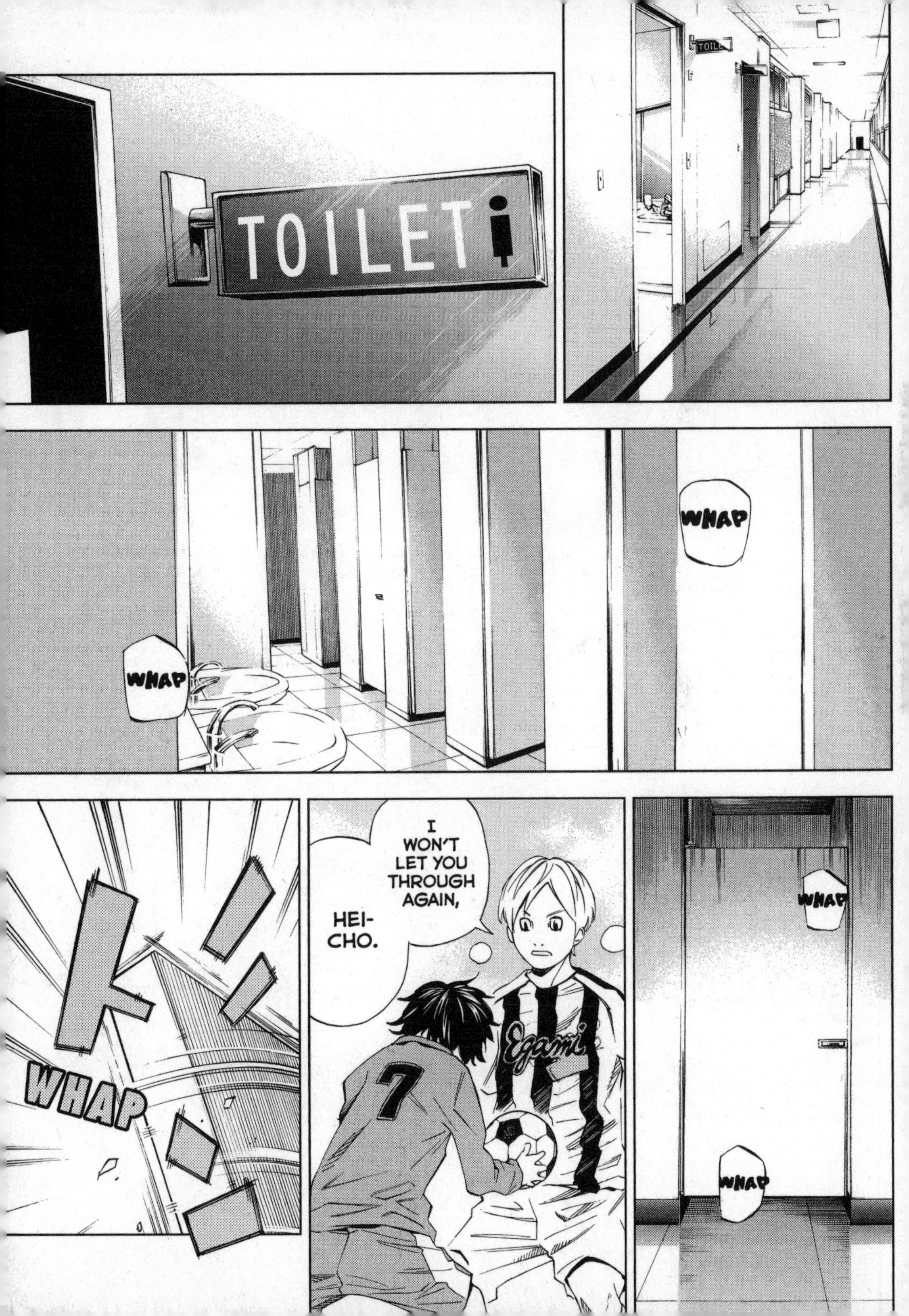
TOILE
TOILET
WHAP
WHAP
WHAP
WHAP
I WON'T LET YOU THROUGH AGAIN, HEI-CHO.
Egami
7
ド
WHAP

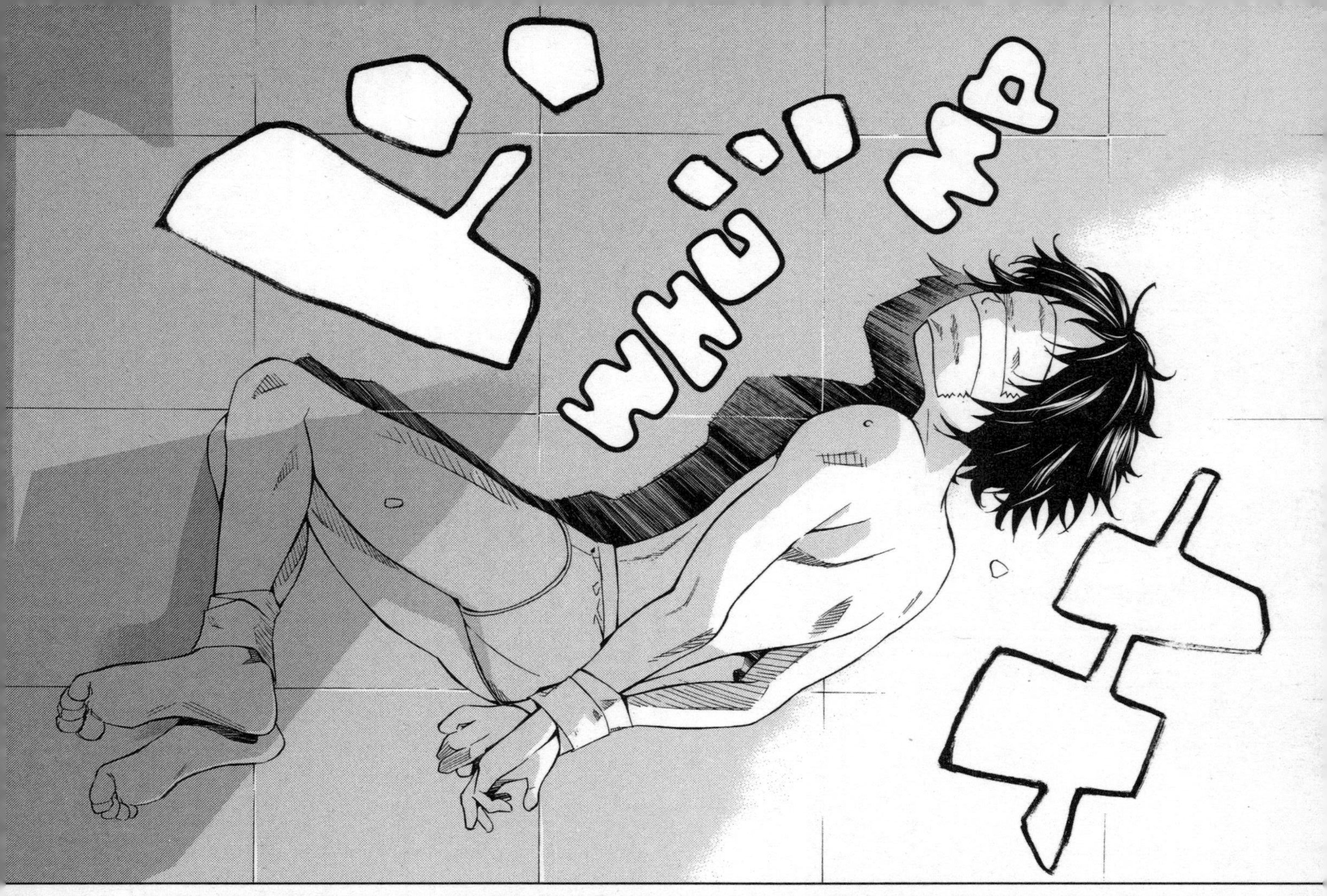
WHU...MP

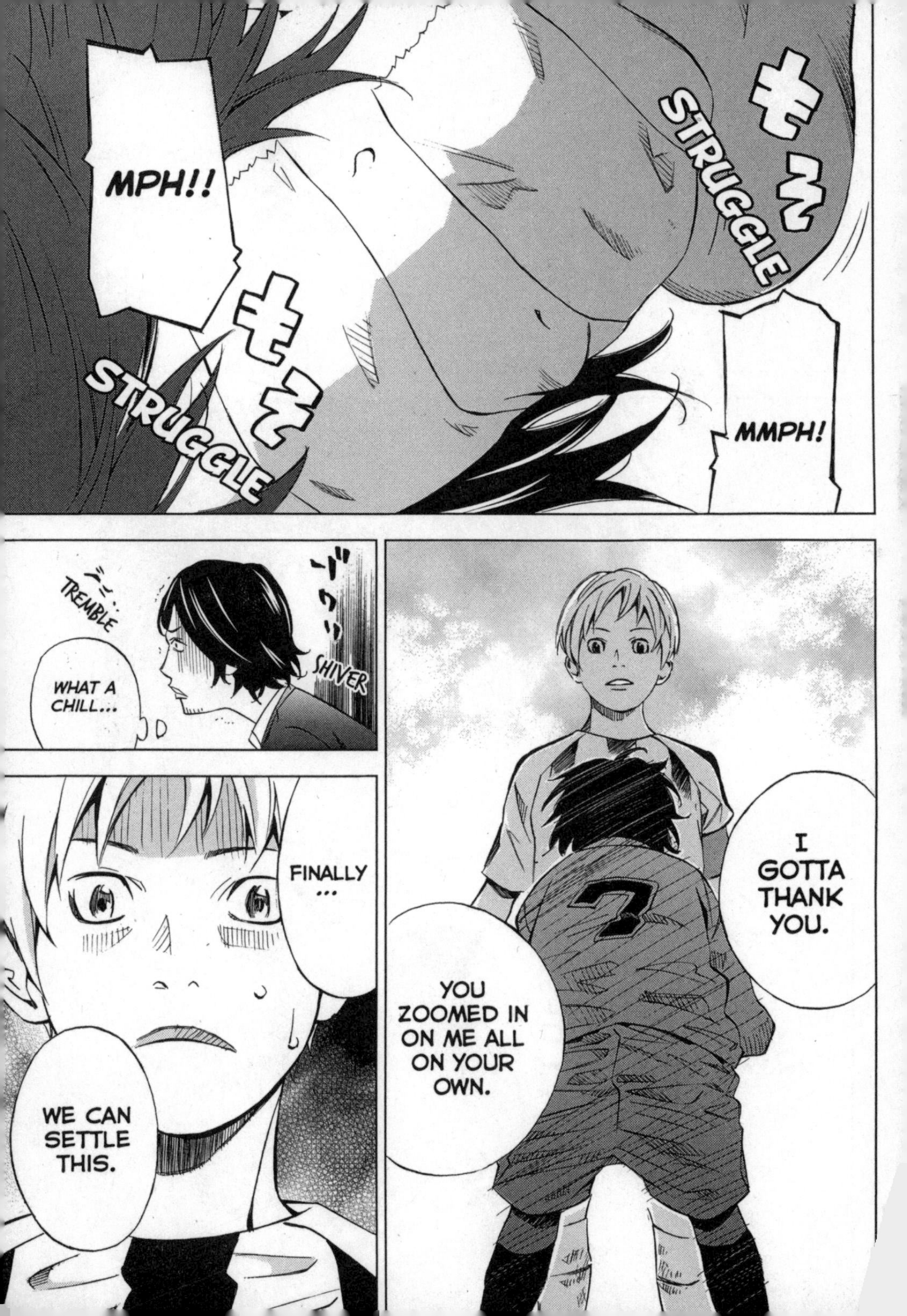
STRUGGLE
MPH!!
MMPH!
STRUGGLE
I GOTTA THANK YOU.
YOU ZOOMED IN ON ME ALL ON YOUR OWN.
SHIVER
TREMBLE
WHAT A CHILL...
FINALLY...
WE CAN SETTLE THIS.

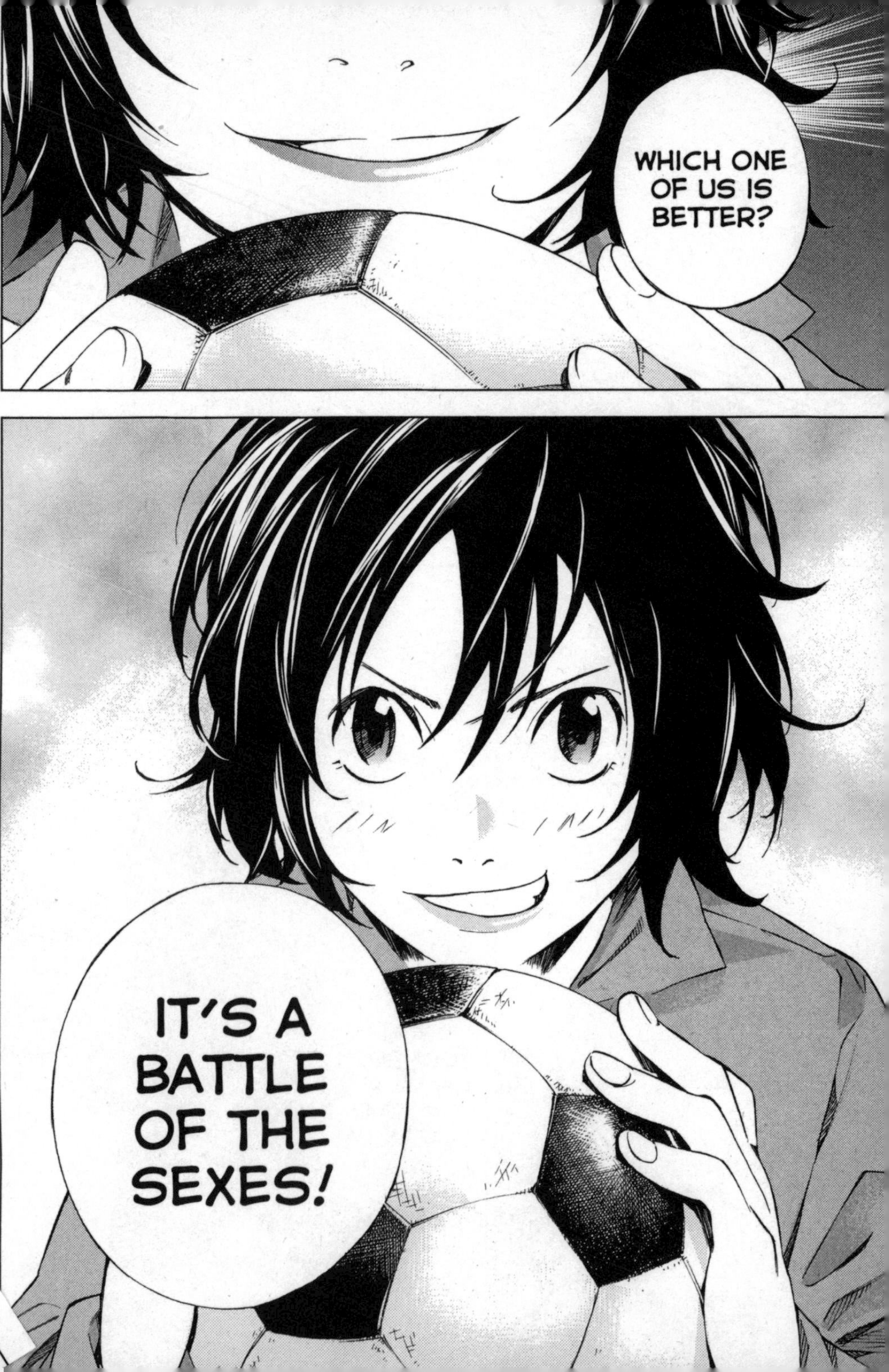
WHICH ONE OF US IS BETTER?
IT'S A BATTLE OF THE SEXES!

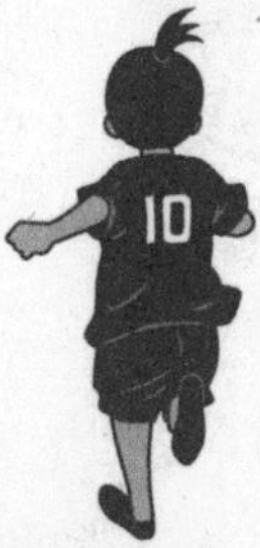
10

SAYONARA FOOTBALL

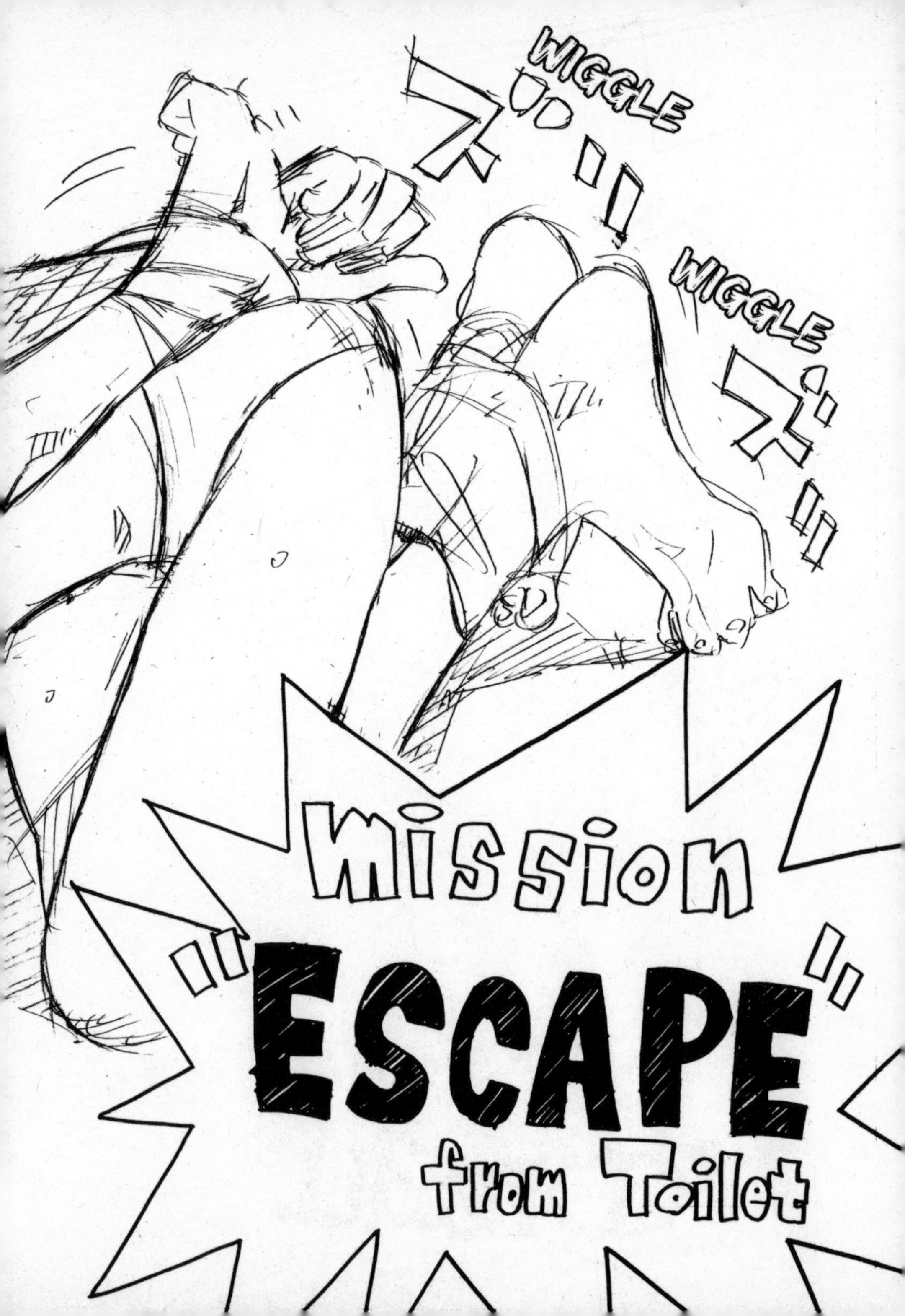
WIGGLE
WIGGLE
mission
"ESCAPE"
from Toilet

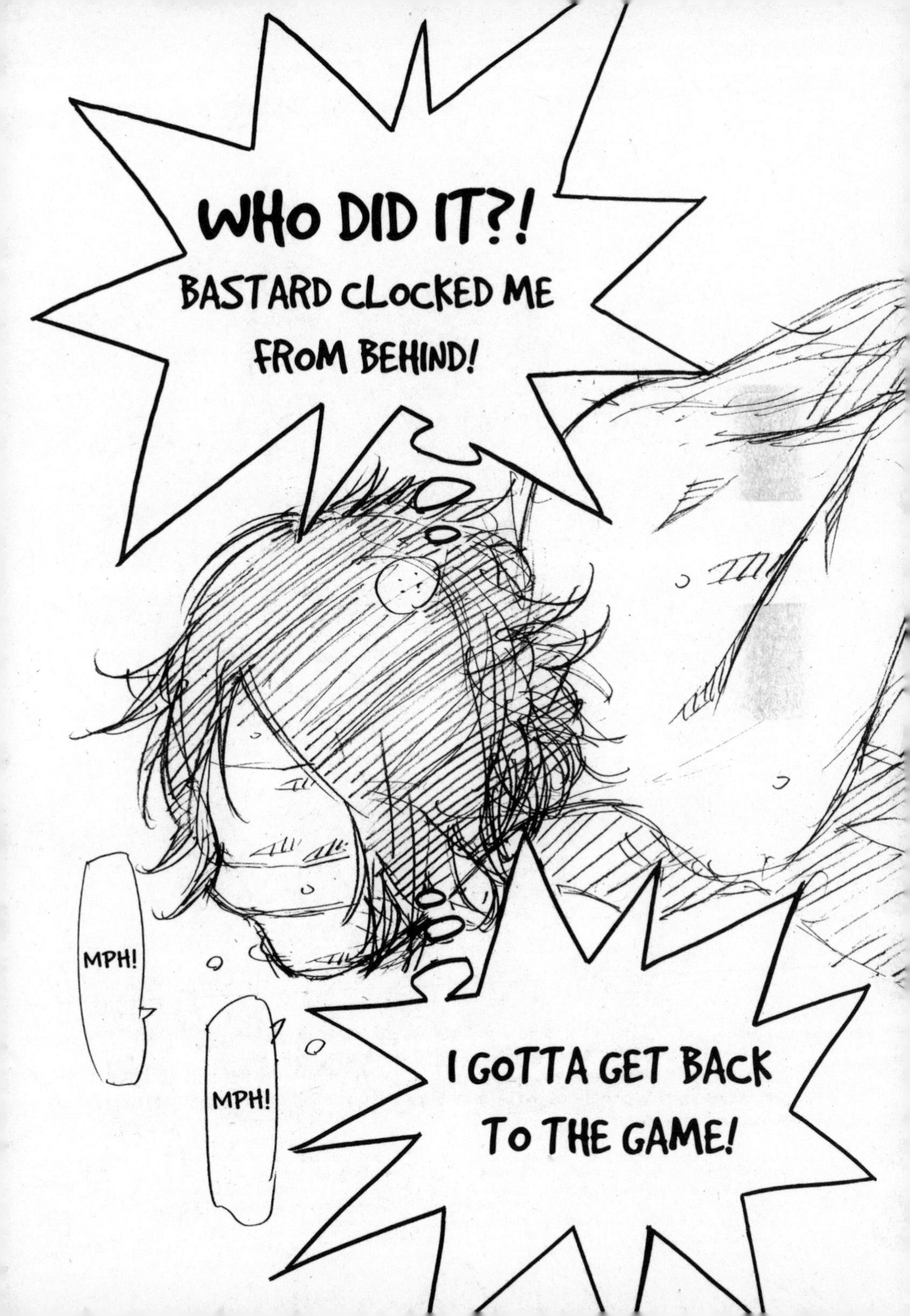
WHO DID IT?!
BASTARD CLOCKED ME FROM BEHIND!
I GOTTA GET BACK TO THE GAME!
MPH!
MPH!

PERFECT WORLD
Rie Aruga

A TOUCHING
NEW SERIES
ABOUT LOVE AND
COPING WITH
DISABILITY

An office party reunites Tsugumi with her high school crush Itsuki. He's realized his dream of becoming an architect, but along the way, he experienced a spinal injury that put him in a wheelchair. Now Tsugumi's rekindled feelings will butt up against prejudices she never considered — and Itsuki will have to decide if he's ready to let someone into his heart...

"Depicts with great delicacy and courage the difficulties some with disabilities experience getting involved in romantic relationships... Rie Aruga refuses to romanticize, pushing her heroine to face the reality of disability. She invites her readers to the same tasks of empathy, knowledge and recognition."
—Slate.fr

"An important entry [in manga romance]... The emotional core of both plot and characters indicates thoughtfulness... [Aruga's] research is readily apparent in the text and artwork, making this feel like a real story."
—Anime News Network

KC
KODANSHA
COMICS

Knight of the ICE

Yayoi Ogawa

Knights of the ice ©Yayoi Ogawa/Kodansha Ltd.

SKATING THRILLS AND ICY CHILLS WITH THIS NEW TINGLY ROMANCE SERIES!

A rom-com on ice, perfect for fans of *Princess Jellyfish* and *Wotakoi*. Kokoro is the talk of the figure-skating world, winning trophies and hearts. But little do they know... he's actually a huge nerd! From the beloved creator of *You're My Pet* (*Tramps Like Us*).

Chitose is a serious young woman, working for the health magazine *SASSO*. Or at least, she would be, if she wasn't constantly getting distracted by her childhood friend, international figure skating star Kokoro Kijinami! In the public eye and on the ice, Kokoro is a gallant, flawless knight, but behind his glittery costumes and breathtaking spins lies a secret: He's actually a hopelessly romantic otaku, who can only land his quad jumps when Chitose is on hand to recite a spell from his favorite magical girl anime!

A Kodansha Comics Trade Paperback Original
Sayonara, Football 1 copyright © 2010 Naoshi Arakawa
English translation copyright © 2020 Naoshi Arakawa

All rights reserved.

Published in the United States by Kodansha Comics, an imprint of
Kodansha USA Publishing, LLC, New York.

Publication rights for this English edition arranged through
Kodansha Ltd., Tokyo.

First published in Japan in 2010 by Kodansha Ltd., Tokyo
as *Sayonara futtobooru*, volume 1.

ISBN 978-1-63236-963-5

Printed in the United States of America.

www.kodanshacomics.com

9 8 7 6 5 4 3 2 1
Translation: Devon Corwin
Lettering: Allen Berry
Additional Layout and Lettering: Belynda Ungurath
Editing: PJ Hruschak
YKS Services LLC/SKY Japan, INC.
Kodansha Comics edition cover design by Adam Del Re

Publisher: Kiichiro Sugawara

Director of publishing services: Ben Applegate
Associate director of operations: Stephen Pakula
Publishing services managing editor: Noelle Webster
Assistant production manager: Emi Lotto, Angela Zurlo
Logo and character art ©Kodansha USA Publishing, LLC